RACE CAR
FLASHBACK

A Celebration of America's Affair With Auto Racing from 1900-1980s

Edited by John A. Gunnell

Published by

krause
publications

700 E. State Street • Iola, WI 54990-0001
Telephone: 715/445-2214

Please call or write for our free catalog of automotive publications. Our toll-free number
to place an order or obtain a free catalog is 800-258-0929 or please use our
regular business telephone 715-445-2214 for editorial comment
and further information.

Library of Congress Catalog Number: 94-77499
ISBN: 0-87341-309-1
Printed in the United States of America

Introduction

Automobile racing or motorsports is neck-and-neck with baseball as America's largest spectator sport. There are hundreds of thousands of auto racing fans. For many years, *Old Cars* magazine has published outstanding articles about the history of auto racing. Such works have been penned by numerous contributors, particularly Phil Hall, Al Krause, Robert C. Ackerson and the late Henry Austin Clark, Jr. These expertly written articles traced motorsports history from the days of the "mastodons" to the current time. Historic photos brought the words to life and added a dramatic dimension to the topics discussed.

Until the publication of *Race Car Flashback*, these articles were exposed primarily to vintage car hobbyists. They had only rarely been seen by the legions of dedicated racing fans who appreciated them the most. This book gives this wealth of racing legend and lore a wider audience. We hope it becomes the first in a series of books to reprint these great articles.

The first section of the book is entitled "Early Auto Races." It covers a variety of high-speed endeavors that took place until approximately 1920, except for "Indy 500" races. The eight stories focus largely on the cars that "Austie" Clark once described as "mastodons." These are the beasts that death-defying daredevils drove into dirt, dust and destiny.

Arrayed in the second section, called "Where the Fastest That Run, Run the Fastest," are 22 stories that trace the history of stock car racing from its "jalopy" roots to the "Aerocoupes" of the 1980s. The first 16 stories about the "stockers" detail the circuits' development from 1949 to the late 1960s. Four additional stories document the hot stock cars of the early postwar races: Oldsmobiles, Hudsons, Dodges, Chryslers and Chevys. The last two stories are salutes to a pair of great drivers, the late Alan Kulwicki and "The King" of stock car racing, Richard Petty.

Section three of *Race Car Flashback* is about "The Greatest Spectacle in Racing"... the Indy 500. From 1911 to 1994, this race-of-races has provided the magic moments of motorsports history year after year after year. We feature nine stories covering the great cars and drivers, plus the car-builders who put them in Victory Lane.

"Racing on Road-and-Track" comes next. It speeds from the days that "the giants" stalked the earth, in the Grand Prixs of the 1930s, to the days that Camaros stalked Mustangs in Trans-Am territory. Marques like Alfa, Maserati, Jaguar, Mercedes-Benz and MG share the spotlight in seven sensational stories.

Section five is called "Going Straight," and contains three somewhat longer treatments of land speed record racing with a sprinkling of drag racing history included. Sir Henry Seagrave, Malcolm Campbell and the late Mickey Thompson are some of the "motorsport monarchs" you will read about here.

Naturally, "Going in Circles" comes next, but is not as confusing as it sounds. In this case, the circle is a race track and the cars are midget racers, open-wheel roadsters and sprinters. One story tells the tale of the midget car boom after World War II. The other is about Milwaukee, Wisconsin's racing Marchese Brothers.

The book ends with "Fanfare," a story that touches on the collectibility of older race cars and the growth of the vintage racing hobby. And since we realize this book can't cover every possible racing interest, there's a directory of clubs that you can join to get involved with this skyrocketing branch of the old car field.

This book would not have been possible without the help of Phil Hall, Al Krause and Robert C. Ackerson. They not only created most of the stories, but then scoured their personal archives of racing photos to help bring their stories to life. A quick check of the credits on each photo caption will reveal the extent of their help. Works by additional selected authors are included to help you "flash back" to the glory years of motorsports.

John Gunnell
October, 1994

Contents

EARLY AUTO RACES

First man behind the checkered flag

By A-mary Abrams

Many anecdotes have survived the saga of the open road, but very little is heard about the "man behind the flag." His name was Fred J. Wagner, "dean of race starters." During his long, colorful career, he officiated at many racetracks throughout the country. His only tools were a timer, a split-second watch and a fistful of colored flags.

As a nine-year-old, the youngster sold newspapers on the streets of Louisville, Kentucky and Evansville, Indiana. When his family moved to Cincinnati, he secured a job as a copy boy with the *Enquirer* newspaper. He also ran messages for the American Union & Telegraph Company and hawked soap door-to-door.

With some money saved, he journeyed to Chicago, in 1890, to accept a job as advertising solicitor for the Chicago Cycling Club. His job that took him all over the country, canvassing programs for race meets. While performing these duties, he met N.H. van Sicklen and George Barrett, owners of *Bearings*, a cycling fan and trade publication. He was offered the position of "clerk of the course," or officiating at bicycle meets coast-to-coast. He immediately accepted. In this capacity, Wagner was thrown into contact with bicycle manufacturers. Many became involved in the fledgling automobile industry.

It was during this time that many people were experimenting with internal combustion engines. Wagner solicited the friendship of individuals such as H.H. Franklin, F.C. Chandler, J. Frank Duryea, John Willys, Alexander Winton and dozens more.

A flag man prepares to start off an early automobile race with a checkered flag. This symbol of victory was first waved by Fred J. Wagner, who was known as "the man behind the flag!" In a long, colorful career, Wagner officiated at many racetracks throughout the country. His only tools were a timer, a split-second watch and a fistful of colored flags. (Old Cars Collection)

Ten years later, in 1900, *Bearings* merged with *Cycling and Referee*, taking the name *Cycle Age*. Out of the editorial shuffle, Fred Wagner emerged as co-editor with Sam Niles, later to be known as "Big Daddy" of the National Auto Shows. It was during this period that many scorned the gasoline engine, but Niles and Wagner reserved two pages of their magazine for those horseless carriages so-powered. Meanwhile, progress was being made in the development of gasoline engines in Europe, but American progress continued to flounder. Knowing little about the newest mechanical contraption, the co-editors clipped foreign news items to fill their two pages of horseless carriage coverage.

It wasn't long before subscribers began flooding the editors' desks asking about these engines. One such letter came from a man in Detroit. He wanted Wagner to stop by his place of business the next time he passed through. It was signed "H. Ford, Engineer, Detroit Electric." It was just the letter they were waiting for from a person who could enlighten them on gasoline motors. Although the name Ford was not familiar, the address led them to believe Ford was the mechanical genius behind the Detroit Electric automobile!

In 10 days, Wagner found himself in the Detroit office inquiring for H. Ford. No one had heard of Ford. As Wagner turned to leave, it was suggested he try the boiler room engineer. He was subsequently directed to the back of the building.

Chagrined, Wagner went on down a dark stairwell leading to a huge steel door, which was locked! Inside he could hear the scraping of a shovel across the concrete floor. Wagner pounded and kicked on the door, knocking the heel from his shoe. Suddenly the huge door swung open, revealing a tall figure covered with coal dust. When asked if he was H. Ford, the man replied, "Yes, I've just banked the fires for the night."

"It's a hell of a way to welcome callers," shrieked Wagner. "I'm from the *Cycle Age*." The laborer extended his hand, "I'm Henry Ford, let me fix your shoe." The discussion that followed left Wagner in an embarrassing situation. He found that Ford's only interest was to subscribe to the publication to further his knowledge of internal combustion engines. Unable to pay the fee of $2, he gave Wagner his order "to be paid at the end of the month." Wagner played a minor role in the first sale of an American automobile, which occurred on March 23, 1898. It came about because he

Auto racing's greatest starter was Fred "Pop" Wagner. He was a bike race starter in the early 1900s, but was asked to take over starting auto races in 1905. For years, he did this job with great distinction. He was near the end of his illustrious career here. The photo was taken in 1932, when he worked in California at the Oakland Speedway. In April 1932, he was injured when a spinning car knocked down the starter's stand there. In 1933, he died of complications from his injuries. (Al Krause Collection)

Fred Wagner (standing on the right) talks to race drivers before a 1925 race on the board track at Culver City California. Many people envied Wagner's job, as it paid him $700 to $1,000 a contest. Admired by all the "knights of the road," Wagner traveled the many miles with his "gasoline galaxy." (Al Krause Collection)

was sitting in the lobby of the Hollenden Hotel in Cleveland, after spending the day with Alexander Winton in his one-room workshop.

Wagner was engaged in conversation by one Robert Allison, a mechanical engineer from Port Carbon, Pennsylvania. For three months, Allison had made the rounds of every city where a known inventor might sell a vehicle with a guarantee that it would run. He asked Wagner what he thought about Winton's invention.

The next morning, Wagner escorted Allison to the Winton factory. Following an inspection, plus a road test, Allison took delivery of a machine, complete with written guarantee. It was shipped to his home within 24 hours. The first officially recorded sale of an American auto had been made for $1,250! That afternoon, H.C. Sargeant of Westfield New Jersey, also a mechanical engineer, bought another Winton. Within 10 days, four more machines were sold. By December, 25 single-cylinder vehicles had been sold for $1,000 each;

During autumn 1899, the "dean of starters" had his "coming out party" at the old Washington Park Track in Chicago. Scheduled to meet, in a five-mile run, were four steam machines: A Mobile, a Milwaukee and two Locomobiles. As Wagner had 13 years of experience in bicycle race starting, the promoters thought him skillful enough to send off the snorting contraptions. He accepted the job lightheartedly; but before the day was over, he remembered the words of J. Frank Duryea, when he'd led Wagner to his machine shop to see Duryea's belching, flame-throwing gasoline engine. "Wag, this is going to revolutionize transportation one day," said Duryea. "Sure," commented Fred, wondering how a once-sane person could say that!

In 1900, at the old Empire City Track in New York, Wagner officially made his debut as a race starter, waving the checkered flag of victory for Barney Oldfield, a friend and recruit from the bicycle tracks.

The new racing enterprise was here to stay, but needed promotional nudging. Taking this cue was W.J. "Senator" Morgan of Newark, New Jersey. According to Wagner, the sport of "automobiling" could never pay enough tribute to this ex-racing cyclist who became a veteran writer for the Cycling Publications, which later elevated him to race promoter.

The Ormond-Daytona Beach races were one of Morgan's first promotions. Others included the famous "Climb to the Clouds" race across Florida, the "Montauk Light or Bust," and "Wilkes-Barre Hillclimb." The beach races were held every winter, for seven consecutive years, on a five-mile stretch of smooth sand. The racing surface extended from Ormond Beach to the lighthouse 10 miles below Daytona Beach.

Several weeks before the inaugural race in February 1903, S.H. Hathaway, a speed enthusiast, prepared a five-mile course. He promptly test drove a mile, at 48.39 mph, the first measured mile speed trial ever recorded on the beach. Wagner was officiating. Winton later established a new record for an American automobile, driving his eight-cylinder Bullet Number 2 over the marked mile at 69.98 mph.

Wagner also officiated at the 1904 to 1906 Vanderbilt Cup races held on Long Island, New York. Thousands of spectators cluttered the 30-mile course. They were almost impossible to control, so the event was abandoned in 1907. In 1908, the races shifted to a Savannah, Georgia track. It was a proud moment for Wagner when he started the first Vanderbilt Cup race. He also waved its final flag in 1915. The tragedy of race fatalities and the inability to safeguard spectators twice prompted Vanderbilt to withdraw the cup from competition.

The quest for another racing patron led Wagner to John Jacob Astor. Astor's response was that, should he decide to sponsor such a trophy, he would fill it with $5,000 in gold, annually. He promised Wagner a definite answer upon his return from Europe. The John Jacob Astor Cup was never translated from a dream into reality. Astor sailed for home on the ill-fated Titanic and did not survive its sinking.

Many people envied Wagner's job, as it paid him $700 to $1,000 a contest. Admired by all the "knights of the road," Wagner traveled the many miles with his "gasoline galaxy." The tragedies and confidences they shared bound them together.

Many speed records have since gone by the mileposts, but the name of Fred J. Wagner will live!

Racing great Barney Oldfield (left) served as a referee for a September 19, 1929 race at Legion Ascot Speedway, in Los Angeles, California. Posing next to him, with a green flag under his arm, is Fred "Pop" Wagner (right), who was the starter for this contest. (Al Krause Collection)

Racing helped establish auto industry

By Gerald Perschbacher

In the early years of the 20th century, it was endurance and speed competition that made the public take note of the fledgling auto industry. Among the top competitors were Wintons, Oldsmobiles, Fords and Packards. Daytona Beach, Florida, was one of the first race sites to gain notoriety.

"It all started back in 1902 at Daytona Beach, when Ransom E. Olds and Alexander Winton raced down Ormond Beach. Both of them were gentlemen and they declared the race a tie at a top speed of 57 mph," explains Ray Siracusa, who has researched the races there. A year later, in 1903; Winton won the multi-car race at a speed of 68.19 mph. He was the first person to break the one-minute-per-mile speed barrier. Little did Winton know that many more speed records were to be broken on the beach for years to follow.

Winton had been almost the dean of early motoring. Manufacture of the cars bearing his name started in 1896. Often seen as a feisty Scotsman, sometimes quick-tempered, ambitious, and competitive, Winton had come to America in 1884 and entered the bicycle business in Cleveland, Ohio. By 1897 he had organized the Winton Motor Carriage Company. He drove one of his early cars a speedy 33 mph around a horse track in Cleveland. He liked to enter cross-country endurance runs against the clock, too. Among his most historic encounters was one with James Ward Packard over the mechanical weaknesses of the 12th Winton car ever made.

Alexander Winton sits aboard his Bullet number 1, which he drove to a land speed record at Ormond Beach, Florida. He is seen here at the one-mile dirt track at Manhasset, Long Island, New York. (Al Krause Collection)

In the early days of automobile racing, Barney Oldfield was America's most popular driver. It was common to see him chomping a cigar as he sped toward another victory or record. (Old Cars Collection)

Packard bought it, but had ideas on how to improve the horseless carriage.

Winton himself, evidently, was the driver for Packard's first trip in a Winton automobile. It is believed that Winton wanted Packard's electrical company to provide wiring for the cars, hence the special treatment. Packard bought the car for $1,000 and took it back to Warren, Ohio. Within a few days, Winton's mechanic and foreman were sent the 65-mile distance from Cleveland to repair the vehicle. The Winton had not even made it to Warren, Ohio, without a breakdown. It was pulled into town by horses. That set James Ward Packard to examine how the Winton could be improved. He offered the ideas to Winton, who abrasively told Mr. Packard that if he thought he could build a better automobile, why didn't he just go out and do it. Packard did, and although he faded from the general operation of the Packard Motor Car Company shortly after the early years of the 20th century, the cars bearing his name were made through 1958.

Packard took aim at Winton on the racetracks. It was almost a vendetta, between the individuals more than between their machines. Packard was determined to prove the worth of the new make, at the expense of the Winton. Also, since a Winton was among the earliest successful race cars, it was the car to beat. Henry Ford also took aim at Winton. In 1901, he had been passed over for a job as a mechanic with Winton's company. Ford out-raced a Winton, which was extremely good publicity for a young auto mechanic with designs on making his car.

However, Winton continued to race. In January 1904, Barney Oldfield, who went on to become the first legendary race car driver in American history, took Winton's Bullet Number 2 to the remarkable speed of 83.7 mph on Daytona Beach in a one-mile run. Two horizontal, four-cylinder engines had been bolted together for a monstrous race car. It marked the first eight-cylinder engine in America. The car, however, overheated on its first run.

Winton did not restrict himself to the beaches of Daytona. He was the first American to join in a European race in 1900. He did not return to the United States with any great success in racing. However, publicity resulted and often was good. Simply to compete was a notable achievement in those early years.

11

One of the first big successes for the auto industry came from one of Winton's early trips. In 1903, he drove from San Francisco to New York City in 63 days. Although not a factory-sanctioned trip, Winton approved of it. Perhaps that was due to Winton's desire to prove the dependability of the automobile, born out of his encounters with Packard. Perhaps it was a chip left on his shoulder from 1896. One of Winton's early customers had a breakdown and hitched a team of horses to the Winton. They drew it through the streets of Cleveland with a sign reading, "This is the only way you can drive a Winton." Alexander Winton, flustered by the slam, hired a farm wagon carrying a jackass to follow behind the disappointed Winton owner. The wagon carried the sign, "This is the only animal unable to drive a Winton."

In 1903, some observers estimated the length of the trip, for the Winton to cross the continent, would be somewhere from six weeks to six months. That estimate included breakdowns, blown tires, and other disasters. The horse-and-buggy days and the accompanying speed of travel were still ingrained in the minds of the public. Taking a car across America in 63 days was viewed as being almost as difficult as landing a person on the moon. The driving team made the run, braving the elements, extreme heat, and various mechanical challenges. Crowds cheered the success. The auto industry was gaining importance as a key factor in American society.

Said the Winton Motor Carriage Company at the end of the race, "We will pay $25,000 to anyone proving that at any time on his journey across the continent conditions of transportation were other than represented by Dr. Jackson (the driver)." Some sources were critical of the race. "Dr. Jackson's great triumph with his regular Winton is a bit discomforting to some others interested in transcontinental 'stunts,' especially when it is considered that he is not a mechanic, nor was he accompanied by a factory mechanic, or met at frequent intervals en route by factory mechanics with parts and supplies of all kinds. But, the fact remains that, aside from showing himself to be a clever amateur sportsman and a good automobilist, he demonstrated beyond

Frenchman Jean Chassaene was an early holder of the world's speed record for a one-hour race. Do you think that his necktie was made of Nomax? (Old Cars Collection)

Paul Zuccarelli with the number 45 Peugeot was an entry in the 1913 Indianapolis 500-mile Race. Like the sands of Daytona Beach, the Indianapolis Motor Speedway was a well-known test bed for early cars built here and abroad. (Al Krause Collection)

Arthur Duray finished second in the 1914 Indy 500 in his number 14 Peugeot. America took keen note of the endurance, stamina, and speed of those "old-timers." (Al Krause Collection)

Ralph DePalma worked on the Packard V-12 engine in the 900 car he used to hit 149.87 mph at Daytona Beach, Florida in 1919. (Al Krause Collection)

question that the Winton Touring Car is the best automobile for long-distance touring manufactured or sold in America." Packard would beat the mark in a 1903 model called "Old Pacific," dropping the travel time for the 5,600-mile trip to 61 days.

Back on the beach at Daytona, racing was still alive. In 1905, a Mercedes driven by H.L. Bowden broke the 100-mph point with a top speed of 109.75. Barney Oldfield topped that, in 1901, in a 150-mile race at a speed of 131 mph. "The sensation of riding a rocket through space," is how Oldfield described the experience. "A speed of 131 mph is as near to the absolute limit of speed as humanity will ever travel," he claimed in 1910.

Winton's love of the races was to wane in favor of increased car production and profits. His company was successful, until 1924, when high-priced models, a post World War I depression, and weak management (often handled by Winton himself) brought an end to the company. However, the Packard Motor Car Company's interest in racing was still strong. A Packard race car called "The Gray Wolf" was driven by Charles Schmidt at the Trumbull County Fairgrounds near Warren, Ohio. In the 1903 test, it did a mile in one minute and 16 seconds. Subsequent races in Cleveland and Grosse Pointe, Michigan, brought tense moments and the promise of victory, but it did not happen. Oldfield took the Cleveland race in the Bullet Number 2; and Ford's 999 race car, driven by Tom Cooper, took the Michigan race. The Gray Wolf raced on Long Island, but crashed through a fence and required repair. It was fixed at the Packard plant in Detroit to get it ready for a 1904 race at Daytona Beach. Schmidt, in the Gray Wolf, broke Winton's record on the straight-away, Oldfield's track record in a Winton, and the 1,430-pound class world's record. It accomplished all this in a five-mile straight run.

Back in Long Island, the Gray Wolf Packard was upgraded mechanically and given a longer wheelbase (stretched from the original 92 inches to 104 inches). History records that the Gray Wolf might have won, had it not been for Charles Schmidt's popularity with the crowd. As he waved to accolades, the race was started. His late break from the line was a disadvantage. The Vanderbilt Cup was not taken by Schmidt. The car, even though it was still taking laps as the first cars roared home, performed well. It would be the last race for the car under Packard,

One early, streamlined Duesenberg race car that Tommy Milton used to establish land speed records. In 1920, at Daytona Beach, Florida, this famous race car driver set a new record of 156.04 mph. (Old Cars Collection)

Wilbur Shaw got a tow out of the Atlantic Ocean at Daytona Beach, Florida in April 1928, after trying to set a record in this Rajo Ford Special. He later came back to set a 148.4 mph mark for four-cylinder cars. (Al Krause Collection)

Unfortunately, high speeds and risk factors were catching up with racing. The first fatality at Daytona Beach came in April 1928. In this scene, an early Roamer racing car takes a dramatic leap over sand bags, during a street race. (Old Cars Collection)

Ralph DePalma, with a winning reputation in air and sea racing, took Packard's V-12 in a land contest at Daytona in 1919. He sped the length at 149.87 mph.

Daytona remained an important race site as the years progressed. It was there that Tommy Milton set a new record of 156.04 mph in 1920. Although there was a seven-year pause in beach racing, in 1927 Major H.O.D. Seagrave, an Englishman, was the first to break the 200-mph speed on the beach. He also was the first to be credited with wearing a helmet. It was made of white leather.

In 1928, Sir Malcolm Campbell and Ray Keech beat that mark with 206.96 and 207.55 mph runs, respectively. Seagrave returned to clinch the top post again in 1929. He made a 231.36 mph run, which some observers claim was faster than most airplanes of that day.

Major H.O.D. Seagrave set a new land speed record of 231.4 mph at Daytona Beach, Florida on February 3, 1929. He was driving the famous Golden Arrow streamliner seen here. (Al Krause Collection)

Unfortunately, high speeds and risk factors were catching up with racing. The first fatality at Daytona Beach came in April 1928. Frank Lockhart, in his Blackhawk race car, blew a tire. The car went airborne and Lockhart was lost.

Campbell returned to Daytona in 1935 to set the final speed record on the famed beach: He sped 276.82 mph in his Bluebird race car. He even broke the 300-mph mark on one run. The next year, high speeds and smooth surfaces were more attractive at the Bonneville Salt Flats, and beach racing at Daytona appeared to have ended. It was a transition period for the Daytona race tradition. Stock car competition was becoming popular and the first 250-mile race of that type was held at Daytona on March 8, 1936. A race course was constructed. It ran down Atlantic Avenue for 1.5 miles, made a left turn, went over dunes, and then went onto the sand. Surf and sand driving was encountered at the North Turn. The race ran a length of 3.2 miles. The first-prize purse in 1936 was a mere $5,000, but that was big money back then. Milt Marion was honored as the first winner and the City of Daytona Beach claimed it had lost $22,000 on the event.

By then, the auto world had firmly established itself. The horse-and-buggy had given way to gleaming, sleek, fast, and reliable cars. Roads were developed. Racing was becoming more scientific.

What racing did for America can be boiled down to the successes at places such as Daytona. It was on the sandy straight-aways, amid the scent of the sea and the calming splash of waves, that America's automotive pioneers met to compete. It was, at times, a cordial meeting, but always high competition. At stake were reputations and manly honor. In the balance were monetary gains derived from publicity about the rugged performance and reliability of those early cars that often looked like little more than glorified horseless buggies or boxy affairs.

America took keen note of the endurance, stamina, and speed of those "old-timers." Society itself was being caught up in the car craze. Largely, that craze began on beaches such as Daytona and Long Island, and in places such as Grosse Pointe. It was a craze that still lives in the hearts and minds of many Americans and comes to a high pitch whenever racers are told, "Gentlemen, start your engines."

America took keen note of the endurance, stamina, and speed of those ancient speed merchants as society got caught up in the car craze. It is a craze that still lives in the hearts and minds of many Americans and comes to a high pitch whenever racers are told, "Gentlemen, start your engines." (Old Cars Collection)

The ambition to own a "Mastodon"

By Henry Austin Clark, Jr.

We have a friend far away in Texas who has the ambition to own a "Mastodon." There was never a car of that name made. The name is derived from the Greek word "mastos" for beast. It was used to identify an extinct variety of elephant. In our frame of reference a Mastodon is a pre-1907, or even better a pre-1905, automobile of 50 hp or better. His desire to find and own one seems reasonable unless you try to figure just how many of these monsters there are in the world.

By this' we do not mean how many there once were, which was not many at all, but how many exist today. It is damn few indeed. Only a small percentage of all the early cars still exists. The remaining Mastodons, at least those in the United States, can be counted on any complete set of fingers. Lacking full familiarity with the European collections, we will limit this discussion not to American cars, but to those remaining examples that are here now.

There were two general categories of those huge machines. The first, and probably most numerous, would have to be those cars that were built specifically for racing. These were originally built in very small numbers, as they are today, and often never wound up in private hands. For example, only one of the giant Locomobiles built for the Gordon Bennett and Vanderbilt Cup Races was saved from demolition at the factory. A second one is said to have existed at the

This Panhard, piloted by French race driver M. Charron, was the winner of the 1901 Paris-to-Berlin contest. (National Motor Museum of Great Britain)

Due to the great interest in the history of racing, many cars, like these early Mastodons on the starting grid, have been saved in private collections or museums. (Old Cars Collection)

Pinson is seen driving his Panhard at speed in the Paris-Vienna Race in 1902. (National Motor Museum of Great Britain)

time the factory closed down, which was about 1930. Probably it went to a junk dealer in the auction.

The list is rather short of the giant early racers that remain today in Museums or private collections. We will try to enumerate those cars that we know about, but will probably miss one or two. The first one that comes to mind is a Ford, the very well known "999." This was one of two matching racing cars, the other being known as the "Arrow." Actually it *was* the Arrow that was renamed 999, after a rebuild. Driving it, Henry Ford lowered the one-mile record on January 4, 1904. Ford drove a mile in 39-2/5 seconds (91.37 mph) on the ice of Lake St. Claire, at Anchor Bay, New Baltimore, Michigan. He was the first American to hold the mile record. He lost it to none other than William K. Vanderbilt Jr., on a Mercedes on Ormond Beach. The Arrow is no longer in existence, but the first 999 was found on the Pacific Coast by William Hughson, a pioneer Ford dealer. He gave it back to Henry Ford.

Barney Oldfield did most of the racing with this car. The *Official Henry Ford Museum Color Book*, a reprint of a piece from *Automobile Quarterly*, says that Barney Oldfield lowered the "world's one-mile record with it on five different occasions." Since there is no mention of this in the AAA records, we assume that they are talking about the one-mile track record, rather than the other, which was run on straight-aways. Barney broke all world's track records, from one- to five- miles, with 999 at Indianapolis on June 20, 1903. These times were much slower than Henry Ford's time on the ice with the other car.

The existing car at the Henry Ford Museum has a bore of 7.25 inches and a stroke of 7.24 inches, giving a displacement of 1156 cubic inches. Dividing this by four, it was pointed out at the bar of the Dearborn Inn, gives a figure of 289 cubic inches per cylinder, or the equivalent of one Mustang V-8 per jug. There is no transmission and only a very crude clutch. Combined with

Arthur Lieberman was the owner of this 1904 Peerless "Green Dragon" four-cylinder Model 12 roadster. The 60-hp Peerless motor of this model is an exact duplicate of the one used in the Green Dragon racer, which Barney Oldfield used to set every track record, from one to four miles, in 1904. (Henry Austin Clark, Jr. photo)

Prominent early day speedster Joe Tracy and his riding mechanic took the Peerless Special out for a test ride in 1905. (Al Krause Collection)

handle-bar steering, and only a hand-throttle mounted on the floor, in front of the driver's seat, she must be a lot to handle.

We happily recall an occasion on the 1953 Glidden Tour, which ended at Dearborn. The powers that be got 999 out onto the old test track, on what used to be the Ford airport, for a live demonstration. A very senior race driver named Frank Davidson was assigned the handle-bars. The plan was for him to leisurely tour the oval to allow the Glidden Tourists, and other guests, to see the number one attraction of the museum in motion. After circling the track slowly for a warm-up lap, Davidson perhaps realized it might be his last time to drive a race car. He laid the throttle lever over on the floor and hung on. Like an old fire horse, the monster racer took the bit in its teeth and the two of them put on a show that had the audience cheering. Its effect was somewhat different on several rather important officials of both the museum and the Ford Motor Company, as they watched a couple of 70 mph-plus laps. Who said what to who afterwards was not recorded, but very seldom does 999 come out, to blow the cobwebs from around its open connecting rods, since that famous day.

The next famous early race cars that claim our attention are the "Bullet Number 1" and "Bullet Number 2." They were built in 1902 and 1903, respectively, by Alexander Winton. Barney Oldfield also got a crack at one or both of these unorthodox machines. Now, they are in the collection of the Smithsonian Institution. Car number one went on indefinite loan to the Frederick C. Crawford Auto-Aviation Museum in Cleveland, Ohio. Many hobbyists saw it there.

The first car has a massive four-cylinder engine that is water-cooled. It has a bore and stroke of six inches by seven inches, for a displacement of 792 cubic inches (a bit less than 999). It has automatic intake valves, operated by compressed air, an overhead cam, and cam-actuated side exhaust valves. The cylinders, like 999's, are vertical. Probably its best performance was at Daytona Beach, on March 28, 1903, when Alexander Winton drove it over the measured mile in 52.2 seconds (68.96 mph).

Bullet Number Two was unorthodox in that it had two four-cylinder engines, bolted together in line, forming a straight eight. It was placed with the cylinders and the crankshaft fore and aft in the car. The bore and stroke were 5-1/4 inches and 6 inches, respectively, for a displacement of 1029 cubic inches. This was still somewhat smaller than the four-cylinder engine in 999. Barney Oldfield drove this car over the mile at Daytona in 43 seconds. The date was January 28, 1904. At 83.7 mph, this was close to the world's record. The car had been built as America's entry in the Gordon Bennett Race, in Ireland in, 1903. Alexander Winton drove it, until forced out by a minor mechanical failure.

Neither of these cars has been run in many years, nor is likely to be in years to come.

Another famous pair of racers is both as "British as warm beer," wound up in this country. They are the 1903 Gordon Bennett and the 1904 Mark Mayhew Napier, long in the collection of Geroge H. Waterman, Jr. of Rhode Island. George almost succeeded in restarting the War of 1812 when he found the first car, in a state of neglect, in England. He bought it and spirited it out of that country, to his stable of early racing machinery near Providence. The outcry from British collectors was heard long and loud, but it was their fault for failing to act. Later on, these cars were leased to Winthrop Rockefeller. They were seen in his Museum of Automobiles, on Petit Jean Mountain in Morrilton, Arkansas, along with several other race cars.

The first car was one of several specially-built for the Irish Gordon Bennett Race of 1903. It was wrecked by its driver, Charles Jarrott, early in the race and could not continue. After it was repaired, it was entered in the 1904 race. It did well in the eliminations, but did not run. The Gordon Bennett rules called for that race to move to the country of the previous year's winner. A British Napier won, in France, in 1902, but the race was held in Ireland. This was due to a ban on road racing in England.

The 1903 race was won by Jenatzy, in a Mercedes; hence the move to Germany in 1904. Actually, this 1903 car is a bit small to call a Mastodon. It has a bore and stroke of 5-1/2 by 5 inches and a displacement of only 477 cubic inches (about the size of a large 19970s Cadillac engine). However, it will go about 65 mph, and is thought to be the oldest English racing car in existence today. It is understandable that the old guard of the Veteran Car Club of Great Britain were put off their feed when it left the British Isles.

The Mercedes "Flying Dutchman" driven by A.L. Bowden was powered by a pair of engines in 1905. (Al Krause Collection)

22

Webb Jay drove the "Whistling Billy" White steamer. Reportedly, Jay and Barney Oldfield squared off in match races many times in 1905 and 1906, with the number of wins between them being nearly equal. (Al Krause Collection)

The 1904 Napier was built for Colonel Mark Mayhew, who regularly drove on the Napier Team. It is a bit more motor car. It has a more decent bore and stroke, which is larger by an inch in each dimension for a displacement of 796 cubic inches. If you like liquid measures, it is 13 liters, which is a fair lot of beer. While built for the 1904 Gordon Bennett, it did not compete. The Colonel drove the car to the south of France. There, he covered the flying-kilometer, in the Rothschild Cup Trials, at Nice. He hit a decent 82 mph. The car did well in the 1905 Gordon Bennett eliminations, but its driver then, Clifford Earp, decided to enter a different car instead. Another driver who frequently drove the car in speed trials and short races was that daring lady, Dorothy Levitt.

Both cars were sold, by George Waterman, to Bill Harrah. They were then put on display at Harrah's Automobile Collection in Reno, Nevada, even further away from "Jolly Old England." (Some of the cars may still be part of the National Automobile Museum, in Reno, which grew out of the Harrah's Collection.)

The other general category of Mastodons is the normal touring or passenger car. These are not designed, per se, for racing, but rather for ordinary early motoring. In the pre-1907 era, the cars with 50 hp and more were rare. However, it was not until we tried to single them out as they exist today, that we realized just how rare they are. Perhaps you can think of some we have overlooked.

The first one to come to mind is the famous Gibbs Mercedes of 1903, that is now on display at the Smithsonian. Alec Ulmann wrote an in-depth article about this car that appeared, along with pages of color photos, in the *Bulb Horn* for March-April 1968. While it is impossible to be certain which car this was, there is no doubt that it is a 1903 Mercedes 60-hp model with the short racing chassis. Was it actually the winner of the 1903 Irish Gordon Bennett or could it have been one of the team cars? Could it have run, as we once heard it rumored, in the 1903 Paris-Madrid Race; the "Drive to the Death," the event was called?

With a bore and stroke of 140 by 150 mm. (We have mislaid our trusty conversion chart) that is a *big* engine. Naturally, it is a chain-drive machine. The close-coupled touring body is just

Austie Clark's famous 1906 Pungs-Finch Limited roadster. (Henry Austin Clark, Jr. photo)

Walter Christie (left) and Barney Oldfield looked at the massive Christie front-drive power unit used in the race car in 1910. (Al Krause Collection)

what some sport might have put on a former racer acquired for touring purposes. Or is it just another 60 hp Mercedes with no romantic history?

Probably, we will never know all the answers to these questions. We found the car in the garage, behind a two-family house in Astoria, New York, in the late 1940's. Like Alec Ulmann, we were unable to acquire it. Mr. Gibbs did do a fine thing when he restored it and gave it to the Smithsonian.

Another interesting giant, which we were allowed to look at in its lair of many years, is a 1903 Peerless 60 hp. It emerged from a restoration, at Hershey in 1974, under the ownership of Mr. Arthur Leiberman of Chicago. When we saw it a few years ago, it was in the corner of a hangar at Lorain, Ohio's local airport. It belonged to the owner of the airport. He, of course, insisted that it was the Peerless "Green Dragon." We of course knew better, as there were too many differences, including the fact that the Dragon was underslung and this car was not. In our opinion, it was just a regular 60-hp touring car that somebody had stripped the body off for bush league racing. Evidently, later owners agreed, because it was restored as a proper passenger car. A thing of beauty it is indeed.

Dick Teague, the designer of the Pacer and vice president of styling of American Motors, had a Fiat that easily qualifies as a Mastodon in both engine size and age. We do not know just how big the engine is, but the year is about 1904. We have seen the car, which is a beautiful, original touring that requires no restoration, to our mind. Our catalogs show no model that large, so our guess is that it is a grand prix tourer.

In 1956, we ended up at the March of Dimes' coast-to-coast "Pony Express" rally in California. We visited David Gray's home in Santa Barbara. There, he had the most fantastic Fiat we had ever seen. It was a magnificent roadster with a huge engine and beautiful flare fenders. David Gray was the son of William Gray, who was the first president of the Ford Motor Company.

Barney Oldfield bought the Christie front-wheel-drive race car in 1910. The first thing he did was to move the engine backwards, to improve handling. (Al Krause Collection)

George Wingard owned this 1913 European Mastodon. The Isota-Fraschini Type KM4 Racing Roadster has Castagna coach work and a 140-hp body. (Henery Austin Clark, Jr. photo)

The only Mastodon that remained in our collection was a 1906 Pungs-Finch Limited. It turned up in Detroit, some years ago, in the most unlikely place of all. We found it in a corner of the original factory building. The engine, at 5-3/4 inches by 6-1/4 inches, is bigger than that of a 50-hp Simplex. The cylinders are cast separately and are mounted on a long crankcase. The valves are inclined at 45 degrees in a hemispherical combustion chamber, and are actuated by an overhead camshaft.

The prototype of the Limited, which may have been our car, was tested in August 1905, by Hugh Dolnar of the *Cycle and Automobile Trade Journal.* His report was published in the September issue of that publication. *Automobile Quarterly* did a road test of our restored car in the summer of 1969. It was the only known Pungs-Finch. Don Vorderman gave the car the nickname "Iron Butterfly," because it fluttered its fenders when the engine was running. We were very fond of the car, which ran beautifully and smoothly. It was very happy at 80-plus years-old.

No discussion of Mastodons would be complete without a tribute to the greatest of them all, Peter Helck's 1906 Locomobile Cup Racer. It was nicknamed "Old 16" and participated in the 1906 and 1908 Vanderbilt Cup Races. It became the first American car to win an international competition in 1908. There is a story in this book about Old 16, so you will know all about this great car with its four copper-jacketed cylinders of 7-1/4 inches bore and stroke. It's rated variously at 90-or 120-hp. We believe the larger figure. Joe Tracy drove the car in the 1906 elimination and race. In the 1950s, he took us for a ride down Sandy Hollow Road, in back of our Long Island Automotive Museum. Moving gently through the gears, he slipped quietly into high at about 70 mph. Then, he eased the throttle up to 100 mph, before we were about to run out of road. It was a sensation we will never forget.

We have talked about America's early exotic race cars. Now we'll talk about foreign racers. The subject is special racing cars. These were made by companies whose main business was the production of passenger vehicles, rather than race cars.

France comes to mind first. The car that was my favorite was the 1907 Renault. This was known as the Vanderbilt model, because 10 were made for William K. Vanderbilt Jr. The car is shown under the name "Racing Runabout" at the front of the 1908 Renault catalog. The larger one was on the 35/45 hp chassis. It sold for $8,000.

In 1951, an elderly retired general gave up his example to be shown at our Long Island Automotive Museum. It required an enormous amount of work, but when it was finished it was a great car to drive. We had much fun with it and it is in the hands of another collector today.

In Germany, the most important car was the Mercedes. One of its greatest admirers was the same William K. Vanderbilt Jr. In our collection of early photographs, there is a good view of him in a race car carrying the number "1." This photo was taken on the sand at Ormond Beach, Florida in 1905. The photograph is marked "90 horsepower," so it had to be a very fast machine in its day.

Of course, we all know that the greatest contribution made by Vanderbilt was the organization and promotion of the Vanderbilt Cup Races. These were held on Long Island from 1904 to 1910. Books have been written about these great events. The greatest is *The Checkered Flag* by artist Peter Helck. This is illustrated with some of Peter's finest works of art. It is now out of print, but if you should ever find one in an old book store, be sure to grab it at any price.

Moving on to Italy, the obvious choice is Fiat. We found an excellent example in the 1911 Grand Prix racer owned by George F. Wingard of Eugene, Oregon. This car was not based on a passenger car chassis. It was a real Grand Prix racer. It still had the great big engine and the body that it wore when it won the 1912 United States Grand Prix, in Milwaukee, Wisconsin. George had it at the Pebble Beach Concours d'Elegance in August 1985. The day before, it had been raced at nearby Laguna Seca Raceway.

In 1903, the Gordon Bennett Race was held in Ireland, after considerable confusion. Ireland was the only part of Britain that would permit racing on public roads. One of the most powerful entries was the 80-hp Napier of Mr. Edge, of which we have a photograph. It is sad to report that this great car was disqualified for having been pushed to restart. He finished two hours after the others finished due to all sorts of other troubles.

It is fortunate that many early race cars of this period have survived the ravages of time. Many have been put into museums and private collections where they can be seen by others. We were fortunate to have at least one or two of these great cars on view at our museum when it was open. We greatly enjoy seeing those that still exist in the hands of others. Maybe some more of them will turn up and be preserved.

A half-dozen Mastodons kick up dust in an early automobile race. (Al Maticic Collection)

Old 16 from race car to artist's pride

By Robert C. Ackerson

In 1900, the Locomobile Company was just one of some 72 American auto manufacturers. They managed to produce a grand total of 4,192 cars that year. This minuscule number guaranteed that, in many parts of the nation, the appearance of an automobile would be a major news item. However, there were people of vision who saw the automobile becoming much more than a mere plaything of the moneyed class.

One such individual was George B. Selden (1846 to 1922), whose precise role in the development of the American automobile may never be fully understood. In 1899, Selden made use of a patent (No. 549,160) that had been granted to him on November 5, 1895. With it, and the assistance of William C. Whitney and his Columbia and Electric Vehicle Company, Selden took measures to force all automakers to recognize him as the dominant figure of the automobile industry.

Selden attempted to force all manufacturers to be licensed by and pay royalties to his Association of Licensed Automobile Manufacturers. This effort ended in failure. The industry was too large and robust for any person or small group to dominate. Its growth, instead of being measured in short hesitant steps, was taking giant leaps forward. At least some of this development was more imaginary than real. An example of "illusionary" expansion was the number of the firms claiming to produce automobiles. In 1901, some 38 new producers joined the 70-odd American companies manufacturing or assembling automobiles. These ranks were swelled by 47 more in 1902, and by an additional 57 in 1903. Most of these industrial dilettantes left the scene as rapidly as they arrived. In *Motor* magazine for March 1909, Charles E. Duryea concluded that some 502 companies had been created to produce automobiles from 1900 to 1908. A full 273 had dropped by the wayside and 29 had gone into some other business. Surely, the businessperson venturing into this field should have his financial wits about him.

One was John Brisban Walker, publisher of the highly successful *Cosmopolitan* magazine. In 1899, he traveled to Newton, Massachusetts to visit a company that had produced some 200 steam-powered vehicles. The firm was the Stanley Motor Carriage Company, owned by Francis E. Stanley and his twin brother Freelen Ozro Stanley. Walker's proposal to buy their business was greeted with a degree of casualness. It was not that they were totally disinterested, but their selling price of $250,000 was clearly presented as "take it or leave it." Reportedly, Walker said the company was not worth that figure. Francis Stanley's response was, "Then don't buy it." Eventually Walker and a partner, Amzi Lorenzo Barker, met the price and the company changed hands.

The Stanley Steamer was renamed the Locomobile and manufactured by the Locomobile Company of America. For obscure reasons, the partners found themselves at odds with each other. They concluded it was best that their association should end. They split up, with each retaining the rights to the Locomobile/Stanley licenses. Walker built the Mobile for a time. Barker, perhaps because he retained the Locomobile name, was more successful. He soon had three manufacturing plants in operation. Two were in Massachusetts (at Westboro and Bridgeport) and the third was on Long Island, New York.

Astute enough to sense that steam power was on the way out, Barber, in 1902, put Locomobile in a competitive position among gasoline-engine automakers. He persuaded Andrew Lawrence Riker to come to Locomobile and design its first gas motor car. Soon it was obvious that Barker had an engineer of great talent in Riker. He was a person who compared favorably with Henry Royce. Both had dedication and insisted that only top quality materials be used in automobile construction.

Riker was trained as an electrical engineer. He had been manufacturing electric-powered vehicles. They were sufficiently robust that Riker, in April 1900, won a 50-mile cross-country race in Long Island, New York. Electric, steam and gasoline-engine cars competed. Riker's winning time was two hours, three minutes, 30 seconds. Riker quickly began work on his assignment and had a new Locomobile, powered by a four-cylinder, T-head engine, ready for display at the 1902 Madison Garden Salon. This first Riker-designed Locomobile was not a particularly original creation, but was well-tested and built to exacting standards. Not surprisingly, it soon acquired a reputation for being a sturdy, reliable automobile. It lived up to its slogan; "The Locomobile Gasolene Touring Car — Easily the Best Built Car in America."

By 1904, Locomobile had a four-cylinder model and a smaller, two-cylinder, Type C. This less expensive Locomobile was produced only one year. The Type D was one of America's most expensive automobiles. The price of a Limousine was discreetly listed as "$5,000 and up." It had a four-cylinder engine rated at 16-22 horsepower. In 1905, Locomobile added the E, H, and F types, the latter being an $8,000 automobile.

By this time the value of automobile racing as a stimulant of production models and a catalyst for advancing technology, was recognized by industry leaders worldwide. The annual competition for the Gordon Bennett Trophy was probably the most widely known automobile race in the early. It dated back to late 1899 when James Gordon Bennett, the publisher of *The New York Herald* donated a trophy to the Automobile Club de France. It was to be awarded for a race under guidelines he set down for the club's officials to interpret. This race for the Gordon Bennett Cup soon became part of the chauvinistic nationalism so common then. By 1903, the race was conducted under precise regulations that were the foundation of the Grand Prix Formulas that followed the final race of 1905. One regulation required car competing to consist of parts and accessories made entirely in the country of its origin.

In America, despite opposition, desire for an equivalent racing event was intense. In the East, a contingent of wealthy enthusiasts, led by William Kissam Vanderbilt, Jr., in conjunction with the infant American Automobile Association, fought public resentment for the right to hold an American version of the Gordon Bennett Race on the public roads of Long Island. Vanderbilt

Joe Tracy brought the number 7 Locomobile across the finish line in one of the 1905 Vanderbilt Cup events. (Al Krause Collection)

and his supporters argued that such a race would encourage American automakers to produce racers equal to the great Panhards, Mercedes and Mors that were dominant in European racing. Besides technological consideration and his personal racing interests, Vanderbilt was also influenced by prevailing attitudes of the social leaders of the East. The automobile had already become part of society's "good form" and had displaced the horse-drawn carriage as the transporter of the very rich.

The Automobile magazine for, October 1899, related an early motoring event held on the grounds of August Belmont, a wealthy banker. Each auto followed a course winding between figures representing police officers, pedestrians and the outdated horse-and-buggy. The event attracted many vehicles sporting large floral arrangements. The story said the Belmont car's display of yellow field blossoms was "surmounted by an arbor of cat-o-nine tails bearing a stuffed eagle from whose beak ran blue and yellow streamers festooned to a floral pole, upon which were numerous sea gulls." Vanderbilt had something different in mind. Like Gordon-Bennett, he proposed to offer a trophy to the winner of his Vanderbilt Cup Race.

Up to the moment the first car was flagged off on the 28.4-mile course on October 8, 1904, public hostility to racing had been intense. Three days earlier, Judge Wilmot M. Smith of the New York State Supreme Court had granted a show cause order. It asked why an injunction should not be issued against the AAA and the Nassau County Board of Supervisors to prevent them from holding the race on the public roads. The plaintiff was Mr. E.M. Bennett, who acted on behalf of the People's Protective Association. The controversy involved a law, passed by the State of New York in 1903, allowing motorcycles to race on public roads. Bennett argued that the law was unconstitutional, since the Vanderbilt Cup Race would cut off a large section of country for a whole day and, "Make it a menace to life for citizens to venture upon the highways given over to the automobile." Fortunately for those who would suffer an "injury" due to the large amount of money they had expended in preparing for the race (according to Mr. A.R. Pardington, Chairman of the AAA Racing Board), the injunction was not issued.

Earlier, homeowners of the Hempstead Protective Association had actively patrolled the course with the object, "Of obtaining evidence of any violation of the speed laws" by the cars practicing for the race. Bowing to pressure, Pardington ordered all racers to carry their entry slots in 18-inch block numbers, to facilitate identification if they exceeded the legal speed limit during practice. Pardington's statement that the penalty for such an indiscretion was disqualification from the race did not satisfy the members of the Hempstead Protective Association. They warned they would report offenders to the AAA and prosecute "culprits" under the law.

Most European entrants criticized the course's condition. Fernand Gabriel, the Mohs driver who won the 1903 Paris-Madrid race (which Vanderbilt entered), complained. He said that the course was "unsuited for racing at high speeds on account of the narrowness of the roads and the frequent turns." This was a characteristic attitude.

Pre-race favorites included Gabriel's 12.8-liter DeDietrich, three 15.4-liter Panhards (which had recorded the fastest times in practice), the single entry of Bayard, and five Mercedes. From the race's early stages, it was evident that the American cars were outclassed, although Herbert Lytle's Pope-Toledo and the trim Packard "Gray Wolf" managed to finish in third and fourth places. American honor was partly salvaged by the fact that the winning Panhard was driven by American George Heath.

News reports of this first Vanderbilt Cup race were not favorable. In spite of the press's hostility, though, some admitted that the race had been a noteworthy event. *The New York Times* described the race as, "Not a great spectacle." It added, "The contest was not as exciting as a horse race. For long stretches of time, there was nothing to be seen. Then, there would be a megaphoned yell of 'car coming' and a gray, blue, or white streak would shoot by with a deafening noise, and all would be over." *The Times* quoted one observer, "It was all very fine, but the automobile will never take the place of the horse for sporting men." Nonetheless, *The Times* reporter, while calling the competing racers, "Ugly-looking mechanical demons ... stripped for action like men-of-war," conceded that the race had been an, "impressive sight."

If unsympathetic reporters were impressed, so were some American automakers. They sensed the sales boost a victory before a crowd and society's "Upper Crust" brought.

When the 1905 Gordon Bennett race was held in France, three American cars were entered. Two were entered by the Pope-Toledo Company. The third was a massive four-cylinder Riker designed Locomobile. Its seven-inch bore-and-stroke gave its engine a whooping 17.7-liter displacement.

Although Riker was a racing enthusiast, Locomobile apparently had little inclination to participate in racing. Then, Dr. H.E. Thomas, an active member of the Chicago Auto Club and a satisfied Locomobile owner, wrote and asked for a racing model that could acquit itself well in international competition. This request, as Peter Helck told this writer, "Disturbed everyone at Locomobile, except Riker, who was keen about it." Despite Riker's ardor, Locomobile management was fearful of disruptions in factory routine and reluctant to take such a step. Yet a flat "no" was hardly an appropriate reply to a valued customer. Instead, a price of $18,000, with one-third paid in advance, was quoted to Dr. Thomas. He was expected to find such terms for a competition model unacceptable. Surprisingly, Thomas agreed to the preconditions and the first racing Locomobile became reality. A sidelight to this story is experts Al Poole's view that there never was a Dr. H.E. Thomas. He believes that Thomas was invented to side-step criticism of spending a large sum of company stockholders' money on silly activity like racing.

Driven by Joe Tracy, who competed in the 1904 Vanderbilt Cup Race with a 35-hp Royal, the 1150-cubic-inch "Loco" failed to make the Gordon Bennett race's starting lineup. This was due to transmission damage sustained during practice. A Pope-Toledo fared somewhat better. It got into the race, but finished some 2-1/2 hours behind the winning French Brasier.

Despite this disappointing setback the Locomobile was later prepared for the second running of the Vanderbilt Cup Race. So many American entries were received that a preliminary elimination race was scheduled to select five cars to represent the United States. Tracy and his mechanic Al Poole placed second in this event, behind the same Pope-Toledo.

In a somewhat arrogant display of power the AAA Racing Board refused to accept the third through fifth place finishers as members of the American team. Instead, they were replaced by a White Steamer, one of Walter Christie's front-wheel-drive racers and a 90-hp PopeToledo driven by Herbert Lytle.

This attractive photograph, showing the 1906 Locomobile race car in a fall setting, appeared on the Old Cars calendar in 1976. (Henry Austin Clark, Jr. photo)

On the eve of the race, Tracy discovered a cracked cylinder. This meant an all-night garage session for the Locomobile mechanics. Apparently their efforts were not for naught, as Tracy managed to finish a respectable third. Apparently, this was the last race for the historic Locomobile. After this date, it disappeared from the public's eye. The best efforts of experts to determine its whereabouts, at the time, have been fruitless.

Joe Tracy's strong showing in the Vanderbilt Cup Race had a strong, positive impact on Locomobile in particular, and on the American auto industry in general. Riker was elated. As Locomobile sales increased, it seemed appropriate to capitalize on Tracy's strong showing with an entry in the 1906 race. Work began on two new racing models. They eventually cost $20,000 each, a tidy sum. With a bore and stroke of 7-1/2 x 6 inches, the race cars' four-cylinder overhead valve engines produced 120 horsepower. They weighed 2,204 pounds and were thoroughbred racing cars. European influence on Riker's thinking was seen in the Locomobile's cone-and-pin driven clutch, a type that had been used earlier by the French Brasier racing cars.

On September 22, 1906, a 297-mile elimination race was held to determine a five-car American team for the third Vanderbilt Cup Race. Twelve automobiles took place in this race. They included a three-car team of 10.2-liter Thomas Specials (designed by Amedee Longeron) and a like number of air-cooled, 16.2-liter Frayer-Millers. The field also included a Pope-Toledo with an enormous 18.4-liter engine for Herbert Lytle and entries from Haynes, Oldsmobile Apperson and Matheson. George Robertson, who loomed large in Locomobile history, was hospitalized after a serious crash with his Apperson race car. Walter Christie's car had collided with Lancia's race-leading Fiat in the 1905. However, he was back with what Griff Borgeson called his "clod-slinging front-drive brute. "

With Robertson not driving a top-flight racing car, the only real threat Tracy had to deal with was LeBlon's Thomas. While the Frenchman managed to give Tracy some competition early in the race, the superiority of the Locomobile was quite apparent. Tracy scored an easy victory. He also registered the race's fastest lap of 29 minutes and 29 seconds. He was clocked at 108 mph in practice. This demonstration of racing ability made the Number 9 Locomobile a serious competitor for the Europeans. One newspaper noted it was, "The only American car on the team that is actually feared by the French and the Italian drivers."

LeBlon's Thomas, was the only one of three that qualified that was subject to a protest from Rene deKnyff, the Chairman of the Sports Committee of the Automobile Club of France. Rene deKnyff argued that the Thomas was not eligible to compete since the aluminum castings of its engine were of French manufacture. The basis of this accusation came from several sources. He called particular attention to the fact that besides LeBlon, Thomas had employed a second French driver named Callois. He had previously worked as a designer for the French Brasier Company. Its automobiles had won the last two Gordon Bennett Cup Races.

The newspaper said that Thomas did not deny deKnyff's assertion that, "Certain features embodied in the Brasier cars (had) been copied in the construction of his racing machines." He also admitted that, "Certain parts of French machinery had been sent to his factory in Buffalo." However, he was adamant in asserting that his entry was completely American-built and did not violate the regulations derived from the Gordon Bennett rules. Thomas ended his defense by inviting the Technical Committee of the Vanderbilt Cup Commission to examine the car. Finally, the issue was resolved by William K. Vanderbilt who, as referee, concluded that he was satisfied with Thomas' assurances. The protest was disallowed without stronger proof from DeKnyff.

The field facing the five American cars was superb. Cars such as Fiat, Itala, Panhard, Bayard, deDietrich, Hotchkiss, Darracq and Mercedes and drivers such as Lancia, Nazzaro, Cagno, Heath, Clement, Shepard, Wagner and "Mephistopheles" Jenatzy were formidable opponents.

The race began, at 6:15 am on October 6, 1906. It soon became apparent that the vital ingredients of victory were not the skill or courage each driver possessed or speed. It was the magnificent superiority of the Michelin steel-studded tires, over the American-made Diamond "nonskids," that was the key to the third straight European victory in Vanderbilt Cup competition. Before the race, in a burst of naive enthusiasm or wishful thinking, the Diamond Tire Company had offered a prize of $2,500 to the driver of an American car winning first place.

Hopes for an American victory were initially high, as the racers were flagged off at one-minute intervals. There was no doubt Joe Tracy was the crowd's favorite. When his car moved into position at the Westbury start-finish line, he received such an enthusiastic ovation that the other contestants seemed to be departing in silence.

On his first lap, Tracy had to stop for the first of what seemed like endless of tire changes. The total number was 11, more than sufficient to dash any hope of an American victory. Each one of these tire changes was a grueling affair, since the Locomobile was not equipped with removable rims. Yet, on the fifth lap (the only one that the Locomobile had no tire failures), it set a lap record of 26 minutes, 21 seconds, or 67 mph. Although "Dare Devil Joe" did not win (he was not even credited with an official finishing position) he salvaged some honor for the American team, but the victory went to Wagner's Darracq.

After his triumph, Wagner recalled his success. He vividly described the race scene from the driver's point of view. "When you start," he told *The New York Times*, "the ground seems to be rising up in front of you, as if to hit you in the face. That is, until you get your auto eyes adjusted, but even then, there's always the thrill, and you haven't time for anything but the thrill, and the watching of the long, narrow road in front. You haven't time to see what is on one side or the other. The people — that's about all we had on the sides today — just seem to be a black and white border to the dark streak in front. Yes, you hear them shout, but by the time you realize it, you are gone. If you're used to racing, you don't think about dangers. You'd go ahead even if you know there was a precipice ahead. All you want is to go faster, faster, faster. You can't go fast enough for the man who likes to race. Never! Speed mania they call it. Ah, but it's fine, fine!"

Looming over the excitement and enthusiasm the Vanderbilt Cup Race was generating by 1906 were tremendous difficulties. The undisciplined crowds who lined the course had little concern for their personal safety. The spectators posed problems for the race officials. In both the 1904 and 1906 races, spectators were killed by cars that spun into the crowd. Even the per-

Old 16 in a corner during the 1908 Vanderbilt Cup Race. (Al Krause Collection)

sonal efforts of William K. Vanderbilt to impose some restraints upon the unruly throng had proven to be of no avail. Thus after the first five cars had crossed the finish line, the thousands of onlookers who spilled onto the course made it impossible for the remaining cars to officially finish the race.

Mr. Vanderbilt, undoubtedly heartsick at his inability to control the crowd, issued a statement after the race. In it he said, "I am deeply distressed that the contest should have been marred by any fatalities, but I am sure it was unavoidable. Every possible precaution was taken. The unfortunate and deplorable accident in which Mr. Shephard figured in (Shepard's Hotchkiss struck and killed a spectator named Kurt Gruner) is the cause of the keenest sorrow to me, and I sympathize, not only with the families of those who were the victims of the accidents but, with, Mr. Shephard and the other drivers, who could not prevent them."

Because of this situation, the American Automobile Association announced that no more races would be held on the course used in 1906. Although offers came from numerous locations throughout the country to hold the race in 1907, none were accepted. No Vanderbilt Cup Race was held that year.

After much behind-the-scenes work by Vanderbilt, a new and (hopefully) safer course was readied for 1908. It used nine miles of the new Long Island Motor Parkway, which Vanderbilt envisioned as the nucleus of a new high-speed highway. The course still had some 14 miles of public roads where the ability to control crowds was limited.

Due to several factors, the 1908 race failed to attract the quality of entrants that had made the 1906 race such a noteworthy gathering. A decision by most of the European teams to commit their cars to the International Grand Prix Race, scheduled for Savannah, Georgia the following month, had a significant negative impact. The field that assembled on October 24 consisted of a variety of old racers, private entries and modified stock models. The two Locomobiles built for the 1906 race were prepared for George Robertson and Jimmy Florida. In the weeks just before to the 1908 Vanderbilt Cup Race, Robertson had achieved victories in the Fairmont 200 and the Brighton Beach 24-hour races. In both, he was teamed, with racing mechanic Glenn Etridge, on Tracy's 1906 lap record holder. Since the Locomobile was fitted with removable rims and Michelin tires, it was Riker's hope that the fiasco of 1906 would not be repeated. For this race, Robertson himself painted the number 16 on the car's hood and radiator.

Spectator control again proved to be a problem, even before the race began. It was only after the fire department dosed the crowd with its high-pressure hoses that a semblance of order was achieved. Finally, at 6:30 am, amid fog and drizzle, Jimmy Florida's Locomobile was the first car sent on its way.

Robertson, a confident, non-conservative driver, set a torrid pace from the moment he passed over the starting line. He took Cemetery Turn, in the words of a contemporary reporter, "Without any apparent thought for the hereafter." For the first three laps, the Locomobile held the lead against Haupt's surprising supercharged Chadwick. Then, it seemed to be 1906 again, as Robertson heard one of his tires explode. The time Robertson and Ethridge lost due to an unwelcome tire change dropped them back to fourth place behind the Chadwick, a 14.4-liter Mercedes and a 50-horsepower Isotta (driven with great skill by Herbert Lytle). Undaunted by the setback, Robertson fought back into second-place, behind the Chadwick. When it suffered magneto failure, at the 140-mile mark, he moved into the lead again. From this point, the Robertson's primary opposition came from Lytle's red Isotta. Lytle's challenge was very strong. Peter Helck once said he had to risk "neck, car and tires" to maintain his lead, plus engage in all sorts of sensational cornering techniques.

With 18 miles to go on the 11th and final lap, Robertson's Locomobile was in the midst of negotiating the Plainville Turn. Then, in spectacular fashion, it threw a tire. With only one spare remaining and a four-minute lead dissolving as the seconds ticked by, the two set about their tasks with determination. Since Lytle started the race 10 minutes before Robertson, his Isotta crossed the finish line first. If Number 16 reached the race's end within that span of time, it would become the first American winner of the Vanderbilt Cup.

This Peter Helck painting shows Old 16 leading H.J. Kilpatrick's Hotchkiss around a turn on the 23.46-mile course, during the 1908 Vanderbilt Cup Race. (Henry Austin Clark, Jr. photo of a painting from the collection of Lew Gotthainer)

The suspense was magnificent. A relatively primitive telephone network kept the huge crowd advised of events on the course. It soon advised that, "Robertson had just passed Westbury." That meant he was seven miles away. Someone in the crowd made a rapid calculation. Two minutes had passed since Lytle had crossed the finish line. The Locomobile should be able to travel seven miles in six minutes. Robertson could still win! A second report crackled out of the telephone receiver. "Number 16 has gone by Meadow Brook," it said That left three miles to go. Before the crowd had a chance to digest that news, the cry of "Here he comes! He wins!" was heard. However, in a classic case of blind excitement, it wasn't Robertson's Locomobile bearing down on the finish line. It was one of the "also-rans," a Knox, that was some two laps behind the leaders.

When it seemed that just about all was lost, suddenly the sound of another car was heard. When it crested the fill leading to the race's end, there was no mistaking its identity this time. The Locomobile, with Robertson at the wheel, appeared. After a momentary delay, the announcement came loud and clear. The Locomobile had crossed the finish line at 11:45:48 am. It was the winner by a margin of one minute, 48 seconds!

This victory could have easily ended in tragedy. Both sides of Jericho Turnpike were lined with exuberant spectators. They crowded onto the road with little apparent concern for their safety. "Robertson forever after wondered," Peter Helck recalled later, "How he had not 'mowed 'em down.'"

The second Locomobile was in contention for third-place honors at this point. However, since the remaining cars were flagged off on their 10th lap, due to the uncontrollable crowd, any chance Florida had to etch a place in history for it was lost.

The following day, newspapers carried the glorious headline, "America Wins Big Auto Race" in triumph. *The New York Times* described the Locomobile as a, "Little square thing that looked like a cigarette box. It duly proclaimed, on its front page, "George Robertson, an American boy in an American racing automobile, has given America, for the first time since it became a prize to be struggled for, the W.K. Vanderbilt Jr. Cup."

Although Vanderbilt Cup Races continued through 1916, this race was the last of the great Long Island-based series. The following year it was limited to production cars with engines ranging in displacement from 301 to 600 cubic inches. After 1910 the Vanderbilt Cup races were transferred to Savannah. A not insignificant feature of the 1908 race was the last racing appearance of Robertson's Locomobile which, as the years passed, became known as "Old 16."

For a time, Locomobile capitalized on the great publicity the Vanderbilt Cup victory had generated. Old 16 was displayed various auto shows and dealerships around the country. Its victory was relived, countless times, by young boys who climbed on board. With a close of their eyes and what they imagined was the sound of a Locomobile at speed emanating from their mouths, they imagined themselves to be George Robertson. Gradually, the aura of glamour and excitement faded from Old 16. It took up residence in a barn located on Andrew Riker's farm. In 1914, Joseph Sessions, whose firm had done a good deal of casting work for Locomobile, purchased the old racer. He kept it at his Bristol, Connecticut farm, where he had a garage especially constructed for its storage. During the 1920s and 1930s, it was Sessions' pleasure to take Old 16 out for drives once or twice a year. In the process, he often got a speeding ticket.

The George Vanderbilt Cup Race was revived in 1936. The first revival took place at the new Roosevelt, Raceway in Westbury, Long Island. George Robertson was reunited with Old 16. He made what the *The New York Times* reported was, "A leisurely tour of the course in the ancient crate with which he had triumphed in 1908."

Robertson was not the only individual present who recalled that glorious day. Also on hand was William K. Vanderbilt, Jr. After completing his tour of the track, Robertson remarked that he, "Wondered how the hell he had managed to handle such a tough car for almost 250 miles in the

For the Vanderbilt Cup Race, George Robertson himself painted the number 16 on the car's hood and radiator. (Henry Austin Clark, Jr. photo)

(Vanderbilt Cup) Race." For the record, the length of the 1908 race had been 250.06 miles, although the Vanderbilt Cup engravement reads 258.6 miles.

Upon Mr. Sessions' death in 1941, automotive artist Peter Helck acquired Old 16, through his friend Joe Tracy. Thus it was that, at 3 am, one bitter cold morning in January 1942, Joe Tracy and the Helck handyman Ernest Roberts arrived at Helck's home in Boston Corners, New York. They had the old Locomobile in tow. During the 1940s, Helck often gave Joe Tracy and George Robertson opportunities to drive Old 16. One such occasion was the first modern Glidden Tour, held during 1946, in which Tracy participated. In 1944, a car meet was held at Fairfield, Connecticut to benefit the China Relief Fund. There, Joe Tracy joined Peter Helck and Helck's son Jerry in displaying Old 16. With darkness fast approaching, the trio set out for the 80-mile trip back to Boston Corners. Since the only lights on the car were a pair from a Model T Ford, which Sessions had installed, Mr. Helck felt a certain amount of apprehension. "I'll never forget that ride," he recalled later in *Old Cars*. "Joe chose a different route to save time (on) back roads, and with his foot heavy on the throttle. Then one of the lights failed. We pounded along just the same. The only reassuring thing was Joe's big strong hands gripping the wheel. On the other hand, there was the thought that Joe could conceivably want to terminate his long life in one grand final bust-up, which would make the front page! As we neared Lakeville, on good roads now, I yelled, 'Stop sign ahead!' Joe may not have heard me, but on his seeing the sign, he braked hard and the Loco swung completely around! When we got to our driveway, he cut it wide and butchered the left front tire on hitting the stonewall. Though it had been a couple of hours of torture for me, 14-year old Jerry, tucked in behind the dash, loved every minute of it. (The) next morning I looked at the speedometer. Somewhere along the line he had hit 78 mph!"

Years later, Helck gave Chuck Yeager (the first person to break the sound barrier) a ride in Old 16. "We were looping up a grade at a good clip," Helck recalled. "Just ahead were two static cars blocking the road, their occupants engaged in a leisurely talk fest. I braked and managed

Lou Disbrow stripped down a Pope-Hartford and built it into the Pope Hummer Special for the 1911 Vanderbilt Cup race. (Al Krause Collection)

37

Pioneer auto racer Frank Lescault helps artist-owner Peter Helck prepare the Old 16 Locomobile Vanderbilt Cup Racer for an exhibition run in 1954. (Al Krause Collection)

to stay on the road, but it was a close one." According to Helck, Yeager's reaction was, "Boy, it beats flying!"

When the 50th anniversary of the first Vanderbilt Cup Race was commemorated in 1954, Old 16 was given the number one spot in a line-up of some 50 cars touring what remained of the original circuit. George Robertson was at the wheel with Glenn Ethridge seated next to him. Peter Helck had to manage as best he could, on the Loco's floor, with his son Jerry. Just before the start, a committee member advised the participants to hold their speeds down to 40 mph. Robertson's response, as Peter Helck remembers, was "That's out. We'll overheat at that crawl." An exchange of unpleasantries followed. Eventually, Robertson was informed that, if he persisted in complaining, he would be invited to leave. With this preliminary issue supposedly resolved, the tour began. When the signal to start was given, the two police motorcycles that were alongside Old 16 took off in a flash. Robertson yelled, "This is okay, swell, let's go." Unknown (maybe) to Robertson, the motorcycles had sped ahead to control traffic at the next traffic intersection and had not intended the old Locomobile to keep up with them. By Hicksville, Robertson had been running along at a 70 mph clip. He was pulled over by one of the motorcycle officers and held there until every car in the parade had passed by. With both tempers and Old 16's engine red hot, the policeman told the three men; "Okay you guys ... you're now on your own." With normal highway traffic now swarming around them, and with numerous red lights adding to their plight, Robertson, Ethridge and Helck were forced to abandon their attempt to circle the course. However, they were able to attend the main celebration held at the Garden City Hotel.

It's entirely appropriate that Peter Helck's favorite painting of Old 16 was entitled "The Old Champ." Now nearly 90 years old, the car is in some ways an anachronism ... a living dinosaur from another age. However, in the things that really count, it is a pure joy. Seemingly oblivious to the passage of time, its place in history as the first American Champion is well-deserved.

Postscript:

What happened to Old 16's mate?

For many years, the fate of the second Locomobile racer built in 1906 has been an unknown element in history. Joseph Sessions believed its engine had been removed for use in a motor-boat. Beyond this rather slim lead nothing else had surfaced concerning its ultimate destiny. In 1976, the late-Peter Helck, who had attempted unsuccessfully to solve the mystery, received a telephone call from Elmer McFarland. He said that he wanted to present Peter Helck with a piston and connecting rod from the phantom Locomobile. McFarland also sought to share knowledge the car's fate. Later, this gentleman visited Boston Corners to deliver the artifacts. He told Helck he had worked at the Locomobile Plant, in Bristol, Connecticut, before 1920. One day he, along and several other employees were assigned to clean out an old shed. It was found to contain several old Locomobile steamers and the remains of the Locomobile racer driven by Jimmy Florida in the 1908 Vanderbilt Cup Race. Without appreciating the significance of his action, the young man pulled a piston and connecting rod from the old car's remains and put them to one side. Then, he and his co-workers finished their assignment. They pushed the ancient steamers and the forsaken old racer into the waters of Long Island Sound.

Winner of the Peking-to-Paris Rally

By A. Stanley Kramer

Examining its mechanical specifications today, it is hard to believe a 1907 Itala motor car was once the most famous automobile in the world. As crude as it was, the Itala was in the forefront of automobile design in 1907. Then, the most popular car in this country was the "Merry Olds-mobile," a tiny, curved-dash, buggy-like one-cylinder runabout of seven horsepower.

Manufactured by Fabbrica Automobili Itala in Turin, Italy, the Itala weighed 2,700 pounds and had a 7433-cc four-cylinder, side-valve, T-head engine that developed 45 hp at 1,250 rpm. It had four forward speeds and shaft-drive, rather than the chain-drive favored by many of its con-temporaries. In almost every respect, it was a standard production roadster. Extra equipment was added for the Peking-to-Paris Rally. The special features included four gasoline tanks hold-ing a total of 84 gallons, a 12-gallon oil tank and another 12-gallon tank for water. It managed eight mpg.

The Itala also had specially-made Pirelli tires capable of lasting as much as 2,500 miles. There was four spare tires and heavy detachable straight steel fenders (abandoned en route because they were too heavy) designed to help the car pull out of mud and ford shallow streams.

What the Itala did not have is much more impressive, considering what it accomplished. It had no windshield, top, or side curtains; no doors; no shock absorbers; no heater; no rear light; and no odometer. Because they did not come along until five years later, it had no starter or other electrical system of any kind.

In this primitive buggy, an Italian Prince, Scipio Borghese, his chauffeur and mechanic Ettore Guzzardi and a journalist and photographer named Luigi Barzini, undertook a 10,000-mile race from Peking-to-Paris, against astronomical odds.

The exact mileage can only be "guesstimated" as there were no route maps and practically no roads. Innumerable detours had to be taken to avoid impassable mountains, lakes, and riv-ers, as well as the aforementioned lack of any mileage recorder.

Incredibly, they completed their nightmare journey in two months, arriving in Paris 21 days ahead of their competitors.

The June 9, 1907, *New York Times* headlined the start of the race: "Peking to Paris by Auto Car. Prince Scipio Borghese and His Companions Leave The Chinese Capital Tomorrow." The *Times* said further, in part: "A caravan of automobiles will start on its journey westward, with the prodigious idea of reaching Paris ... the following well-known automobilists will be ready to start: Prince Scipio Borghese in an Itala, M. Pons on a three-wheeled Contal, M. Cormier on a De Dion-Bouton, M. Collignon, also on a De Dion-Bouton, Baron Duquesene on a Panhard, and M. Godard on a Dutch Spyker.

Just five months ago *Le Matin* of Paris published a short article and called attention to the claims made by the manufacturers of certain automobiles how their machines could go any-where and everywhere. Is there one who will undertake this summer to go from Paris to Peking by automobile?

That evening *Le Matin's* challenge was telegraphed all over Europe. The next morning brought the following communique from the Marquis de Dion of the De Dion-Bouton Company; 'If it is possible for an automobile to go through, a De Dion-Bouton, will accomplish the feat. '"

The 1907 Itala is still a symbol of automotive integrity and strength. The car is seen here, in the mid-1980s, at an auto show in Cologne, Germany, organized by Prosper DuBois-Reymond for the Roth-Handle Company. (Roth-Handle Raritaten)

The Times article further explained that other letters had arrived accepting the challenge. Quoting Prince Khilkoff of St. Petersburg, the former Russian Minister of Ways and Communications, it explained that he was personally familiar with all the country between the Pacific coast and the Urals (having laid out the Trans-Siberian Railway) and that the obstacles to be encountered on the Desert of Gobi were not insurmountable.

Moreover, said Khiikoff, "By taking a southern route the automobiles could at easy stages avail themselves of the oil wells and an unbroken line with them could be maintained with the point of departure if supplies were sent out in advance from Peking and placed at various points."

Among themselves, the contestants agreed to assist each other in case of accidents. They would also disqualify anyone who took advantage of a railway, although transportation could be accepted across streams were there were no bridges, and particularly across Lake Baikal.

For most of the Itala's trip, there were no roads, paved or otherwise. Yet, the rugged automobile went from China over the Gobi Desert, through Siberia to Moscow, St. Petersburg, Berlin, Amsterdam, Brussels and on to Paris.

There was brutal heat and cold, endless downpours, mud without end, rivers, lakes, quicksand, swamps, narrow, gullies, deserts, cliffs and mountains. The performance of the car was a major miracle; the simple fact that it held together. Three times it caught fire due to over-heated brakes. It broke both rear springs. Repairs were improvised in tiny villages. In one instance, a Siberian blacksmith who had never seen an automobile had to replace a collapsed rear wheel. He used wood from a pine stump for spokes. His principal tool was an ax and a red hot poker for making necessary bolt holes.

Endless successive teams of oxen, horses, men, and mules had to pull the Itala through mud, streams, and quagmires, as well as haul its dismantled pieces straight up cliffs and mountains.

In *Peking-to-Paris*, written shortly after the journey, Luigi Barzini wrote, "After the Nankow Gorge, a narrow slit between two crags, and beyond the Great Wall of China, the road became a river bed full of broken stones, boulders, and pools; and from here on over the mountain range the machine had to be manhandled by mules and coolies through points where a pick-ax was sometimes necessary to clear sufficient room for the car to pass. The Mongolian prairies followed and, then, 500 torrid miles across the parched monotony of the Gobi Desert, marked only by whitening bones. "

Of another instance, Barzini wrote, "The soil under our feet was heaving. It was as if we were walking over floating cork. We realized that the mass of mud would swallow up our car if we did not succeed in saving it at once. To make matters worse, a trekking burial tribe appeared on the scene, but after one look at the sinking car, refused to do anything to help. It was no use, they said.

Providentially enough, however, some Mongolian horsemen also rode up and they set to work. Yet, even by putting planks under the wheels and getting oxen to pull, they failed to drag the car out of the mud. Finally, someone had a brain wave and started the engine. At the sudden noise, the four terrified beasts pulled desperately and suddenly the car came out of its furrow with one bound.

Finally we reached the river Iro, where again the help of local oxen was necessary to ford the car through waist-high water, after the magneto had been removed and the engine covered with grease. Here, in a sandstorm, we took our leave of the Celestial Empire ... faces literally black with dust, and over our clothes, a thick crust of the different kinds of mud with which we had come in intimate contact all along our way ... the black mud of the bogs, the yellow mud of the Char-gol, the white mud of the Iro."

Mud and water were not the only threats. Barzini detailed another. "Halfway across an old wooden bridge over a small torrent, there was a frightful crash as the planks gave way. The car slowly turned a somersault and plunged into the abyss, carrying its passengers down in a debris of splintered woodwork. Miraculously, a single beam saved them from catastrophe and the car's fall was, to some extent, cushioned by the four spare tires strapped on the rear. No less miraculous, the sturdy machine, once it had been hauled inch-by-inch back on the road by the neighboring population, proved (as the Siberians put it) to be 'still alive.'"

Gasoline, oil, tires, and water were stored in dumps along the route. Supplies were brought there by mules and camels and placed so the travelers could find them. Often, natives kindly directed them to the caches.

Other than the one big tent they all slept under, there was seldom shelter for the riders. En route there was no top or windshield. Pre-electricity carbide lamps illuminated the way when they could manage to light them in the wind.

(If we sometimes find our cars hard to start on winter mornings, imagine how it must have been cranking the Itala during a desert sandstorm!)

The Itala produced a steady touring speed of 40 mph, ground surface permitting, and a top speed (under seldom-encountered conditions) of 60 mph.

Henry Ford is reputed to have said when asked where the shock absorbers were on his Model T: "The passengers are the shock absorbers." So it was with the Itala. Yet it ran over the ties of the Trans-Siberian Railroad for well over 1,000 miles! It was surely a bone-shaking, excruciating experience. That tires, frame, springs, axles, wheels and transmission survived was a true miracle, not to mention the men.

The civilized world was informed of the Itala's progress by sporadic telegraph dispatches from Luigi Barzini. He sent reports to the *New York Times, Corriere Della Sera*, and the *London Daily Telegraph*. He later wrote his world bestseller, *Peking-to-Paris*, illustrated by on-the-spot photographs taken with his cumbersome, but miraculously intact, photographic equipment. Written in Italian, the book was speedily translated into English and a half dozen other languages.

The Itala had a romantic history even after it proudly chugged into Paris 21 days ahead of its competitors. After its great performance, it was incredibly abandoned in an unused warehouse by its makers. It was accidentally discovered in 1923. Carlo Biscaretti, then Itala's director of publicity, supervised its superb restoration.

On March 24, 1989, the completely rebuilt Itala again set out from the Chinese capitol (now re-named Beijing) at the head of a caravan of modern automobiles. Included were a Fiat, Lancia, and Alfa-Romeo. After three months (by an extended route) the Itala reached Paris on June 24 in perfect condition. The caravan also celebrated an important anniversary: 90 years from Fiat's beginning.

Today the Itala is on display in factory-fresh condition in the Turin Automotive Museum.

Four gas tanks were added to the car to hold 84 gallons of fuel for its long journey. One of the large tanks, lettered "Pechino," can clearly be seen in this profile view. (Roth-Handle Raritaten)

Dust, death and ... DePalma

By Al Krause

Race car drivers come en masse from the Indianapolis 500-mile race to Wisconsin State Fair Speedway. Many auto racing fans think that this practice began with promoter Tom Marchese and the 100 miler in 1947. We're sorry, but that honor belongs to the Milwaukee Auto Dealers Association (MADA). It began when MADA staged a two-day speed carnival on Tuesday and Wednesday, June 20 to 21, 1911.

The auto dealers had originally received the dates, Friday and Saturday, June 16 to 17, but heavy rains forced a postponement into the following week. In those days, the fair park management would not schedule auto racing on Sunday, to head off any complaints from nearby churches of excessive noise.

Recognizing the importance of the races, the contest board of the sanctioning body, the American Automobile Association, sent three of its best officials to help. They included legendary starter Fred Wagner, referee A.F. Pardington, and board member George A. West. Since there would be no time, trials, Wagner and Pardington served as handicappers, doing an excellent job of setting the starting lineups. West helped the race organizers with the nuts-and-bolts paperwork.

The start of an early heat race at Milwaukee. It took place during the Milwaukee Auto Dealers Association two-day race event at Wisconsin State Fair Park Speedway. The date is June 20 or June 21, 1911. (Al Krause Collection)

The wreckage of the Cino driven by Walter Donnelly. The driver was fatally injured in the accident, which occurred in the second to last race, at Milwaukee, on June 21, 1911. (Al Krause Collection)

Ralph DePalma and Hughie Hughes were sixth and 12th place finishers, respectively, in the first Indy 500 some three weeks earlier. They were among the list of 10 nationally-rated drivers entered to compete at Milwaukee. Others signed to race at the fair park included Bob Burman, Teddy Tetzlaff, Eddie Hearne, Louie Strang, Joe Jaegersberger (who had moved to Racine, Wisconsin after his tie-up with the J.I. Case team earlier), Bill Jones — another member of the Case team — Billy Knipper, and Frank Fox. The irrepressible DePalma had his 90-hp Simplex "Zip" finely tuned and was the star. He won both the 20- and 50-mile races held each day.

Ralph DePalma, in the number 2 Simplex, in the pits at Indianapolis during the first 500 mile race in 1911. DePalma and Hughie Hughes were sixth and 12th place finishers, respectively, in the first Indy 500 some three weeks before the Milwaukee event. They were among the list of 10 nationally-rated drivers entered to compete at Milwaukee. (Al Krause Collection)

Bob Burman in the Blitzen Benz set a new one-mile dirt mark of 50.15 seconds at Milwaukee. He came back to set a three-mile mark and took a couple of five-mile races. The old one-mile record, of 51 seconds, was set by Barney Oldfield in the same car. (Al Krause Collection)

The 95-plus degree heat, generated by bright sunshine both days, drew the moisture from the track, leaving it hard and dry despite many lengthy waterings. When race chairman Bart Ruddle asked that the track be given a coat of oil to lay the dust, the fair park management demurred. It said the oil would leave a noxious odor in the air and might hurt the hoofs of the horses that would be in trotting races on the track later that summer. There was some justification for the decision, as owners claimed that oil-soaked clumps of dirt would lodge between a horse's hoof and shoe, resulting in a possible infection.

The decision not to allow the track to be oiled was not a good one. The billowing dust clouds took their toll. In the next to last race, on the second day, Walter Donnelly lost his way entering the north turn. His stripped-down Cino pleasure car hit the outer fence and turned over, resulting in fatal head injuries to the Chicago speedster. In addition, the abrasive track surface ground the rubber tread off the tires resulting in a bumper crop of blowouts for contestants.

DePalma nearly lost the first 50-miler while enjoying a sizable lead, when a tire let go on the 23rd mile. Three laps down after the tire change, DePalma set a furious pace and "unlapped" himself twice. He was about a half-mile behind race leader Eddie Hearne and his Fiat. A tire on Hearne's, car let go at around the 45-mile mark. DePalma then took the lead and came home an easy winner. Hearne's crew replaced the blown tire, allowing him to finish second. Hughes, who also had tire trouble early on, finished third.

DePalma's strategy for the second day of racing was to set a fast pace and conserve his tires. His plan worked, as he won both the 20- and 50-mile races.

There were a number of "names" with cars entered. Five were entered by auto race impresario Ernest Moross. These included Burman in the 120-hp Mercedes dubbed the "Blitzen Benz" and Knipper in the "Baby" Benz, rated at 110 hp. Still another Benz appeared. It had been driven in 1909 by former land speed record holder Camille Jenatzy of Belgium. There was also a pair of Marquette-Buicks, with Burman and Erwin Fahr listed as drivers. Burman won five-mile races in the Jenatzy Benz in each of the two days, while Fahr won a 10-miler in the Buick the first day.

Knipper failed in his attempt for a three-mile record in the "little" Benz the first day, but Burman did better. He guided the Blitzen Benz to a new one-mile mark of 50.15 seconds. That broke the old mark of 51 seconds, which was set a year earlier, in the same car at the fair park, by Barney Oldfield. He had sold the car to Burman late in 1910. Burman came back again to set a new three-mile mark for the final event in the first day.

Oldfield had signed in at Milwaukee as a "newspaper reporter" even though he was under a one-year suspension for running in an unsanctioned event in 1910. That was for his appearance in the match race fiasco in October of that year, at Sheepshead Bay, New York against black heavyweight boxing champion Jack Johnson. At the fair park, Oldfield was spotted by Pardington, who ordered him out of the paddock area. Oldfield then watched the races from the infield in the car of his longtime friend, Milwaukee auto dealer George W. Brown.

There were two other accidents besides the one that took Donnelly's life. In the early laps of the first 50-miler, John Schillo in the Mercer team car of Hughes, lost his way in the blinding dust. When he veered sharply to miss the outer fence, his mechanic; Fred Weston, was dumped onto the track. Weston escaped with a sprained ankle. Otto Boursch, in a Warren-Detroit, tangled with Hughes early in the second day's 50-miler, but there were no injuries reported. Tetzlaff, Strang, and Fox all had mechanical problems or minor accidents and were not factors in either day of racing.

Anticipating a car shortage for the second day's 50-miler, race officials decided to run all three classes simultaneously. DePalma was the overall winner in Class C, comprised of cars rated 301- to 600-cubic-inches. Frank Kulick was best in the Class B, for cars rated 161- to 300-cubic-inches, in his Ford. Bill Jones of Chicago was the winner of Class C, for non-stock cars rated 231- to 300-cubic-inches. He was driving a Case.

The two-day speed jamboree was reportedly witnessed by more than 8,000 spectators the first day. No crowd numbers were announced for the second day. DePalma took home the big end of a purse reported at more than $5,000.

Ruddle pronounced the two days of racing a complete success. The caliber of the field and handling of the events by the MADA committees were excellent. They were certainly a big factor in the selection of the Milwaukee auto dealers to host the American Grand Prix and Vanderbilt Cup races. They were held on a course laid out on the streets of Wauwatosa, in the fall of 1912.

The caliber of the field and handling of the events by the MADA committees were excellent. They were certainly a big factor in the selection of the Milwaukee auto dealers to host the American Grand Prix and Vanderbilt Cup races. This 1911 Fiat Model 574 Grand Prix Racer was the ultimate winner of the 1912 United States Grand Prix held in Milwaukee. Caleb Bragg was the winning driver. The car was photographed when George F. Wingard exhibited it at the 1985 Pebble Beach Concours d' Elegance. The day before, it had competed in the Monterey Historic Races at Laguna Seca racecourse. (Henry Austin Clark, Jr. photo)

Case swept Milwaukee's first big-car race

By Al Krause

The first 100-mile big-car race held on Milwaukee, Wisconsin State Fair Park's one-mile dirt speedway was on Sunday, June 13, 1915. It was won by Louis Disbrow of Philadelphia, Pennsylvania, in the Jay-Eye-See Special. This car was entered by J.I. Case Company, the farm machinery manufacturer in Racine, Wisconsin whose cars swept the first three positions before an estimated crowd of 12,000.

The race's promoter was Frank Mulkern, a prominent local boxing matchmaker. He, apparently, had been impressed by the large crowds earlier motor car races had attracted, including a series of road races held at Milwaukee in 1912.

Promotional piece highlighting the Jay-Eye-See Special sponsored by the J.I. Case Manufacturing Co. of Racine, Wisconsin. This art was taken from an old letterhead owned by driver Caleb Olson. It depicts Louis Disbrow at the wheel of the then-new 290-hp 1912 race car. Disbrow was the winner of the 100-miler at Milwaukee. Held on June 13, 1915, it was the first race for big cars at the Milwaukee State Fair Park dirt oval. The letterhead read, "World's Greatest Racing Organization." It carried the names of manager J. Alex Sloan and assistant manager Frank Lowry. (Al Krause Collection)

The six-cylinder Case Special Tornado, here at the 1913 Indy 500 with "Wild" Bill Endicott (right) and riding mechanic C.R. Newhouse in the cockpit. This car was driven by "Texas" George Clark in the June 1915 race at Milwaukee's State Fair Park. Endicott also participated in the 100-miler, behind the wheel of a Maxwell that was a featured attraction of the event. (Al Krause Collection)

Case's thrust into auto racing started with three cars in the first Indianapolis 500 in 1911. Case drivers included Louie Strang, William Jones and Joe Jaegersberger. The latter was from Racine. He would gain prominence, later, as designer and builder of the famed "Rajo" racing cylinder head. Case had manufactured and marketed pleasure cars from 1910 to 1927, so fielding a racing team seemed to be an excellent advertising and publicity medium.

Strang was hired to build the Jay-Eye-See. Plans were to use the 290-cubic-inch engine from the Fiat "Red Devil" that Strang had campaigned, successfully, two years earlier. The chassis was reportedly from the famed Simplex Zip race car that had been driven to many victories by Ralph DePalma and Disbrow, and which Disbrow had a major role in rebuilding.

The project stalled when Strang incurred fatal head injuries, on July 20, 1911, at Blue River, Wisconsin. The car he was driving, in a reliability run, slid off the road and overturned as he attempted to pass a slow moving hay wagon. Ironically, three other passengers escaped with minor injuries.

Disbrow, whose racing career began around 1905, was then hired to finish the car and drive it as well. The tough, wiry 140-pounder completed the vehicle and drove it to victories at tracks nationwide over the next four years. This generated much publicity for the Case "Eagle" marque with the motoring public.

Case entered four cars for the 100-miler at Milwaukee. These included Disbrow in the Jay-Eye-See "show" car; "Texas" George Clark in the Tornado; John Rainey in the lightweight "Comet" and Eddie Hearne in a Case Special.

The diversity of the field was considerable both as to body styles and engines used. The body on the Jay-Eye-See was most pronounced. It looked as if a canoe had been set upside down on the chassis, with part of it scalloped out for the driver's compartment.

Practice and time trials were held on Saturday, June 12. Hearne, a truly gifted driver, was fastest qualifier at 53.20 seconds (65.46 mph). Other qualifiers, in order, were Disbrow and "Farmer" Bill Endicott (Maxwell), both at 54 seconds flat; Frank Jennings (Keeton) and Clark, each at 55.04 seconds; Captain Kennedy (Edwards), 56.00 seconds; Art Klein (King), 57.00 seconds; Billy Tidmarsh (Great Western), 60.20 seconds; Rainey and George Brown (Chalmers), each at 60.40 seconds; and Harry Milton (Mercer) and Ben Gotoff (National) each at 62.80 seconds. Several other cars did not take time trials but were added to fill out the field.

Endicott was in one of three Maxwell team cars. Two others, usually driven by Eddie Rickenbacker and Billy Carlson, did not appear. Harry Milton, in reality, may have been Tommy Milton, who would go on to win the 1921 and 1923 Indy 500s and score many wins before his retirement in the late 1920s. One of the more prominent non-qualifiers was Louie LeCoque, of France, in the Ford 999, which had been built and driven by the great Bob Burman. Milwaukee entries included Tidmarsh and Brown, both in stripped-down stock cars.

The only excitement on Saturday occurred off-track when Tidmarsh, who had taken the engine muffler off his car before coming to the track, was stopped by a policeman who said the car was noisy. An irate Tidmarsh later told a reporter, "This machine is one of the noisy kinds and, if I expect to get any money out (of the meet), I'll have to run the car without the muffler." There was no mention that Tidmarsh received a ticket from the officer. Endicott won the first race on Sunday. It was a five-mile free-for-all for those involved. Milton, Gotoff, LeCoque and Kennedy followed Endicott across the finish line in order.

Two events featured "show" cars in special trials against the clock. Despite an excellent track surface compacted by a Saturday night rain, Hearne (who had moved into Barney Oldfield's famed Blitzen Benz), could only manage a time of 53.80 seconds. Disbrow did somewhat better in the Jay-Eye-See at 52.80 seconds.

The "Ohio 999," here with constructor Bob Burman behind the wheel, was a well-known race car. Burman hailed from Imlay City, Michigan. The car had a four-cylinder 40-hp motor and a nine-foot seven-inch wheelbase. Frenchman Louie LeCoque drove it in the 100-miler at Milwaukee on June 13, 1915. (Al Krause Collection)

In the 100-miler, Hearne was the early leader but was passed by Disbrow around the 30-mile mark. Disbrow was passed by the fast-moving Rainey who sped through traffic after starting well back in the field. Just past the halfway mark, Disbrow again took the lead, which he held to the finish. His time was one hour, 36 minutes, 00.60 seconds (62.99 mph).

Since the lead was exchanged among the three Case entries, there's every indication the Case drivers may have decided to pass the honors around among themselves. The official finish was Disbrow, Hearne, Rainey, Endicott and Gotoff in the first five places. Victory was worth $2,500 to Disbrow out of the announced $5,000 purse.

After the 100-miler, a five-mile state championship race for stock cars was won by John Pierce of West Allis, Wisconsin in a Marmon. He was followed by Jim Pauling in a Ford. Other finishers in order included Art Martin (Benz); Bill Yockey (Packard); Jack Butler (Pope); Tom Klein (Stout); Charlie Bach (Stearns); Harry Nelson (Mercer); and Bill Burke (Petral).

At the conclusion of the races, Mulkern pronounced the weekend of speed a complete success.

Eddie Hearne in the streamlined 1912 Case Comet. It appeared at the inaugural big-car race at Milwaukee's State Fair Park on June 13, 1915. Driver John Rainey placed third in the 100-mile race. (Al Krause Collection)

1917 Oldfield-DePalma match races

By Al Krause

When auto racing fans at the Wisconsin State Fair Park Speedway saw the celebrated match races between Barney Oldfield and Ralph DePalma on June 25, 1917, they also got a brief glimpse of the shape of things to come for the American race car.

Oldfield drove a new car designed and built by Harry A. Miller, a native of Menomonie, Wisconsin. It was called the "Golden Submarine," because of its torpedo-shaped body. It completely enclosed the driver, leaving only narrow slits covered with wire mesh for the driver to peer through. Miller would later design and build several racing cars which would alter the record books of American automobile racing,

Miller made liberal use of aluminum, in both engine and body components, to save weight. He also used an all-electrically-welded steel chassis, a first for an American race car. The four-cylinder, single-overhead cam Miller engine put out 130 hp from 290 cubic inches of piston displacement. Its dry weight was only 410 pounds.

Compare that to DePalma's considerably heavier, more conventional two-man racer. This car was powered by a 12-cylinder Packard aircraft engine. It developed more than 300 hp from about 400 cubic inches. The motor was built and mounted in the car at the Packard engine plant, located near Chicago, Illinois.

For nearly 10 years, Oldfield and DePalma competed against each other in many races, but never head-to-head. The 1917 Indianapolis 500 was scrubbed by America's entry into World War I. Auto racing was cut back as part of the wartime rationing of fuel and rubber. Of course, few objected to just two cars competing in shorter races. It was agreed that a series of six such events would be held at tracks across the country.

Oldfield, whose racing career began in 1902 in Henry Ford's famed "999," found it difficult to stay within the guidelines set by the American Automobile Association's auto racing board. He had "tweaked" their regulatory noses many times by running in races not sanctioned by the board. He was suspended twice for these infractions, but he did not care. He appeared in special races against all comers or against the clock. He wound up making more money than most of the established AAA stars.

DePalma was an organization man all the way. He moved as easily among the titled and wealthy, as he did on the race track. DePalma personified class and personal dignity and was noted for his high degree of sportsmanship. The high point of his career was victory in the 1915 Indianapolis 500.

Oldfield was regarded by many as a mountebank. It could not be disputed that many of his early wins had been orchestrated. However, he did not lack courage or skill. On occasion, he could drive with the best of them. When Peugeots and Delages from France ran away with the 1914 Indy 500, Oldfield's fifth-place finish made him the first American driver in an American car over the finish line. He also won the great Los Angeles-Phoenix road race that year. Two years later, he turned the first 100-mph lap at the Indianapolis Motor Speedway, in the awesome free-formula Christie front-wheel-drive car.

DePalma's career began in a road race at Briarcliffe, New York, in 1908. By the time of the wartime match races, he had won about a dozen national championship races. One was the 1912 Vanderbilt Cup, a 299-mile race on a road course laid out in Wauwatosa, Wisconsin.

Both drivers had large followings among Milwaukee fans. Oldfield had competed with great success and set many records at Milwaukee. One was set in 1905 in the Peerless Green Dragon; another in the famed Blitzen Benz in 1910. DePalma had logged an easy win in a 50-mile feature in 1911 driving a Simplex.

Barney Oldfield drove the "Golden Submarine." It was built by Harry Miller, in 1917, for $15,000. (John Gunnell Collection)

On June 17, 1917, the pair competed, as part of the AAA champ car race series, at the six-mile board speedway at Maywood, Illinois. Oldfield qualified the "Submarine" at 107-plus mph, while DePalma was three miles per hour faster. The Golden Submarine failed to finish the race and was referred to by some as the "Golden Lemon" or "Golden Egg," even though it was the first time the car had appeared in-competition.

Oldfield brought two cars to Milwaukee, the Submarine and his Delage Devil. Both were housed at the Overland Auto Sales Agency owned by former driver George W. Browne. Oldfield and his wife were the guests in the Browne home in Waukesha.

DePalma supervised the final tune-up of the Packard at the Chicago plant. He then stayed at Milwaukee's Plankinton Hotel. While he was there, he renewed his friendship with many of the doctors and nurses who had treated him for his near fatal injuries suffered in the 1912 United States Grand Prix race. The match races were his first at Milwaukee since his grave accident.

The races were originally set for Saturday, June 24, but heavy rains forced a one-day post-ponement. That suited both drivers, as it gave their publicity men a chance to drum up more interest in the race. A few days earlier, the AAA officials barred the Golden Submarine from running in the Maywood champ car race, citing safety factors. Oldfield, who was furious, then switched to his Delage and finished third in the race on the boards. On June 15, the AAA board announced it would sanction the races in Milwaukee to keep out "barnstormers." In other words, these were invitational events.

The drumfire of publicity continued. Then on June 21, DePalma won the right to have calcium chloride applied to the track surface to lay the dust. As it turned out, it was a verbal exercise, as heavy rains more than solved the problem. Oldfield countered that dust was, "part and parcel of dirt track racing." He was later quoted: "I have been waiting a long time to get DePalma on a dirt track. I'll show him what racing is all about."

DePalma countered, "Modesty is a word Greek to Oldfield and he probably has been telling everybody how he is going to make me eat his dust." Actually, both drivers had great respect for each other's abilities, but went along with the publicity buildup.

Following the rains on the night of June 23, both drivers walked around the course with starter Fred Wagner and fair secretary Oliver Remey on Saturday afternoon. All pronounced the course to be in excellent condition, thanks to its superb drainage system.

The races were anticlimactic, as the estimated crowd of 15,000 discovered. Oldfield easily won all three heats. His lighter car handled better in the turns, more than making up for DePalma's superior speed on the straightaways. Using the outer groove all the way, Oldfield won the opening 15-miler by a quarter-mile. He covered the distance in 13 minutes and 15 seconds, averaging 67.8 mph. In the second heat, a 25-miler, Oldfield won by a half-minute. His time was 22 minutes and 42 seconds, for 66.07 mph.

In the third race, a 10-miler, Oldfield won in nine minutes and 2.18 seconds. This came out to 66.41 mph. However, he gave it a different finish, as the *Milwaukee Sentinel* reported: "In the final event, Oldfield's well-known love of the spectacular made a close finish for what was otherwise a one-sided race. He simply slowed up on the final mile, until DePalma was almost abreast of him. At that point, Oldfield put his foot on it. He beat Ralph down the stretch and across the finish line by a foot or two. It was a sensational finish and gave the crowd a thrill."

The *Milwaukee Sentinel* also reported that some of the fans got an even bigger post-race thrill. A switching engine was pulling a string of freight cars from a rail spur just north of the racetrack. Several hundred race fans had been sitting on the tops of these cars. The less nimble among them got a free ride down to rail yards in the Menomonee Valley, some four miles away.

As far as the series went, Oldfield won at Milwaukee, Wisconsin; St. Louis, Missouri; Naragansett, Rhode Island; New Hampshire; and the Indianapolis Fairgrounds. DePalma won at Detroit and Atlanta. In the latter race, Oldfield's car went through the inner rail and turned over, landing in a lagoon. He escaped injury by kicking open the door. Not long after, the Golden Submarine was trimmed to a bobtail style. The entire skin and tail of the car were removed. The driver then sat in a bucket seat.

The Milwaukee event marked Oldfield's final auto racing appearances at Wisconsin State Fair Park. However, during fair week in 1934, he made a driving exhibition there in an Allis-Chalmers tractor. DePalma's last Milwaukee-area race was at a sprint car show in 1931. He spun out in a heat race. His last Milwaukee driving appearance was in 1933, when he drove a new Ford convertible on the mile track, at the invitation of the Greater Milwaukee Ford Dealers Association. His time for one lap was 50.18 seconds.

Both of these legendary drivers survived many close calls and accidents throughout their careers. Oldfield died of a heart attack in his sleep on October 9, 1946, less than four months after serving as honorary referee at the International Motor Contest Association races at Milwaukee.

DePalma died at his home after a long illness on March 31, 1956. Both were living in California at the time.

At the start of one of the three match races, DePalma leads the Golden Submarine that Oldfield is driving. (Al Krause Collection)

WHERE THE FASTEST
THAT RUN,
RUN THE FASTEST

'Where the fastest that run, run the fastest'

By Phil Hall

It lasted less than two years. It operated out of a gas station. Most of its "national champion-ship" events were packed into a small region of the country. Its name is all but forgotten today. However, the National Championship Stock Car Circuit (NCSCC) probably exerted more influence on motorsports in this country, than all but a few auto race sanctioning bodies. When you connect the name of William ("Big Bill") H.G. France, Sr., to NCSCC, people start to listen. Fit it in just after World War II, before the National Association for Stock Car Auto Racing (NASCAR) was formed, and people really pay attention.

Fonty Flock (with helmet) was handed his point fund check by Bill France, Sr., after winning the 1947 National Championship Stock Car Circuit title in the series finale at North Wilkesboro, North Carolina. Other drivers and officials gathered after what turned out to be the last NCSCC event ever held. (Phil Hall Collection)

France lived in the Washington, D.C. area and became an auto racing fan. He borrowed his father's Model T Ford, took it to the board track at Laurel, Maryland, and raced it, unbeknown to his dad. He later tried his hand at both motorcycle and auto racing on the East Coast.

In 1934, Bill France moved with his wife Anne and year-old son Bill, Jr., to Daytona Beach, Florida. He operated a gas station there and continued to race his Riley-modified Ford. While he lived there, a race for strictly stock cars was run on the beach and adjacent road by the local government. The date was March 8, 1936. Despite several big name drivers coming in, France finished fifth in a Ford. The City of Daytona Beach claimed it lost money on the event. For 1937, the Daytona Elks Club was persuaded to run a Labor Day stock car race. That, too, lost money.

Starting in 1938, France and local club owner Charlie Reese took over the Daytona Beach race promotion. It was a combination of Reese's money and France's work. Work France did, making the races a success. He also continued to participate in them and other events in the region. After 1941, World War II stopped all racing at Daytona.

Following World War II, it would be different. Reese died in 1945, leaving France to run Daytona. If that was not enough work, France's skill at attracting crowds drew him to promote events at other tracks. In fact, his 1946 promotion of an event on the old Charlotte, North Carolina Fairgrounds ran him into trouble with a local sports editor.

"I wanted to run a 100-mile national championship race at the fairgrounds, but Wilton Garrison said I couldn't call it a national championship race," France recalled in a 1976 interview.

"You might call it a North Carolina championship race, but you have got to have some kind of a national organization to call it a national championship race," Garrison lectured France.

"I asked what I had to do to start such an organization," France explained. "He (Garrison) said I had to develop some kind of point standings and give out more than just a trophy at the end of the year and run races in more than one state."

With that, France went on to form the National Championship Stock Car Circuit during the 1946 season. He withheld a small part of the purse for the point fund, kept standings, tried to have uniform rules, and made sure the drivers were paid the money they had coming. He used his gas station as headquarters. All that (except the gas station) is the norm for sanctioning bodies today. However, back in 1946, it was unheard of for the stock car gang to follow rules. Most of the cars were prewar Fords back then. More than a few drivers gained experience on the back roads, evading government agents with their loads of illegal homemade spirits.

The NCSCC sanctioned tracks at Daytona and Charlotte, as well as at other Southeastern United States locations. They included Greenville, South Carolina; Greensboro, North Carolina; Birmingham, Alabama; Richmond, Virginia; Spartanburg, South Carolina; and Orlando, Florida, among others. They also did events at Trenton, New Jersey; Langhorne, Pennsylvania; and other Northern tracks. Ed Samples of Atlanta, Georgia, took the 1946 NCSCC championship. Many drivers were joining NCSCC, but it lost one during the 1946 season. Bill France announced he was retiring ... to concentrate on the administrative side of the growing organization. Stock car racing was booming in the Southeast and elsewhere in the country and NCSCC was in on the ground floor. New tracks were being built and there was a steady stream of track owners that wanted to be on the NCSCC schedule.

The 1947 season kicked off, on January 26, with a 160-mile event on the Daytona beach-road course. Red Byron drove a 1939 Ford to victory. As the season progressed, France's NCSCC boasted more than a dozen tracks, a guaranteed purse of $2,000 for each event and the slogan, "Where the fastest that run, run the fastest."

A new racing magazine, *Speed Age*, debuted in May of 1947. It was heavily open wheel racing biased. That was until the June issue, when France bought an ad on the outside back cover for NCSCC and himself. In the first ad was a photo of himself and his name in big red letters. NCSCC was in much smaller type near the bottom. From that time on that year, *Speed Age* covered France and NCSCC in great detail.

The 1947 NCSCC season ended on November 9 at the North Wilkesboro, North Carolina Speedway, which had just opened that year. Red Byron scored the win on the half-mile dirt oval. Fonty Flock finished second and clinched the championship. He received a large trophy and $1,000 share of the point standings. Samples, unable to repeat his 1946 title, finished second in points. He was followed by Red Byron, Buddy Shuman and Bob Flock (Fonty's brother), who had to sit out part of the season with a broken back.

France called for an annual meeting of NCSCC for December 14, 1947. It was held at the Streamline Hotel, in Daytona Beach. He proposed major changes, involving insurance for drivers, rules, leadership and publicity. He wanted to take what he had learned with NCSCC to a new level of professionalism. Not only did a new organization emerge from that meeting, but also a new name. The National Association for Stock Car Auto Racing (NASCAR) was created. The Grand National Circuit, for newer model cars, would not come for a year and a half. However, starting in 1948, stock car racing had a major sanctioning body.

The fate of the sport is interesting to speculate if France and his National Championship Stock Car Circuit had not been a success. France died in 1992 at the age of 82, but his NASCAR has long been the most successful stock car racing sanctioning body in the country.

Bill France, Sr. in a 1976 photo. France died in 1992 at the age of 82, but his NASCAR has long been the most successful stock car racing sanctioning body in the country. (Phil Hall Collection)

Richard Petty (right) became known as "The King" of NASCAR Grand National stock car racing. He is seen here discussing the hemi V-8 in his 1964 Plymouth with Chrysler racing boss Ronnie Householder. This car took the checkered flag at the Daytona 500 that year. (Phil Hall Collection)

Race car flashback

By Phil Hall

In 1993, the 40th anniversary of this writer's first attendance at an auto race passed. It was Sunday, Sept. 20, 1953 at the Wisconsin State Fair Park Speedway, where the American Automobile Association (AAA) Contest Board sanctioned a 200-mile stock car race. It turned out to be the last race on dirt at the mile oval in the Milwaukee suburb of West Allis. The track was paved before the 1954 season.

While much of the pre-race publicity belonged to the "Fabulous Hudson Hornets," the day belonged to Don O'Dell and the 1951 Packard he drove to victory.

The dusty afternoon in the south turn bleachers didn't immediately convert one young Milwaukee Braves baseball fan to an immediate auto racing enthusiast. However, a combination of the team's declining fortunes later in the decade and the boy's exposure to more forms of auto racing created another convert to motorsports.

While 40 years hardly qualifies one for old-timer status as a race fan, it does put perspective beyond the "Golly, I can remember clear back to the early '90s" syndrome of many of today's younger fans.

Obviously there have been many changes in the sport over the past 40 years, some for the better, some not. Speeds have increased significantly, but what is more important, so has driver safety.

Back in 1953, the hot topics in late-model stock car racing revolved around what factory equipment was legal. The cars were supposed to be stock vehicles that were equipped only with parts available over the parts counter at your local dealer.

A typical stock car racing scene shows two Hudson Hornets battling on a dirt racetrack. Marshall Teague in car number 1 and Jack McGrath in car number 2 raced at Wisconsin State Fair Park. (Phil Hall Collection)

By 1966 the sport of stock car racing was sophisticated with plenty of factory support, at least from Ford and Chrysler. Here a pack of 1966 Fords laps Daytona International Speedway. In the group are Cale Yarborough's number 27, Curtis Turner's number 41 and Fred Lorenzen's number 28. (Phil Hall Collection)

In 1969, two of USAC's newest chargers were Butch Hartman (car number 75) and Verlin Baker (car number 40). The two drove hemi-powered Dodge Chargers in the late-model opener, on April 20, at the half-mile dirt oval in Cincinnati, Ohio. (Phil Hall Collection)

The traffic got a little thick during the only caution flag in the 200-mile stock car race at the Wisconsin State Fair as Roger McCluskey (car number 2), Frank Freda (car number 9), Sal Tovella (car number 14) and Bobby Unser (car number 15) bunched up in the northwest turn. Al Unser blew his engine on his 1969 Dodge Charger to bring out the yellow flag. (Phil Hall Collection)

Engine modifications, drivelines and suspensions all were stronger than stock, but listed in the various manufacturers' parts catalogs.

Hudson was famous for its swiftness at getting "export" parts listed. Its cars carried Twin-H power, a 7-X engine and export suspensions.

Oldsmobile was a few steps behind, but had an extensive list of racing parts cataloged. Dodge, with its first V-8 in 1953, was rapidly following the others.

Of course there was cheating occurring, as the teams fielding cars did their best to become competitive by using aftermarket or homemade parts.

As the sport grew in popularity and more was at stake, the tendency to open up the rules increased. The appearance of super speedways in NASCAR, from 1959 on, brought higher speeds and the need to run equipment stronger than what was offered by the factories.

The result was a gradual taking of the 'stock' from stock car racing. Today most so-called late-model stocks you see are silhouette cars. They look like production cars on the outside, but are anything but under their exteriors.

Some forms of late-model stock car racing have rules that permit every part except the engine block to come from racing equipment manufacturers instead of automobile manufacturers.

The car may look like it is a Pontiac Firebird or Oldsmobile Cutlass, but in some cases what you see is a fiberglass body made to look like cars on the street. What you don't see are components that are made to produce the needed speeds, stand up to the strain of competition and protect the driver from injury, in case of an accident.

Starting in 1986, NASCAR Winston Cup bodies no longer had to even be for rear wheel drive cars, even though the race cars remained of that configuration.

While the purist may be upset at the path stock car racing has taken, a little glance at history proves there was little choice if the sport was to continue to progress.

The horsepower race of the 1950s produced faster cars nearly every year, until the Automobile Manufacturers Association banned performance activity in 1957. This progression started again in the 1960s. The manufacturers again increased performance (and later aerodynamics) in each year of the muscle car era.

However, when the relative performance of the cars took a nose dive with the regulated 1970s, stock cars didn't slow down accordingly. By then the rules permitted using the latest in specified speed equipment. This assured continued competitiveness.

Even though there is a resurgence of performance activity on the part of the new car manufacturers, it in a way parallels the level of performance on the racetracks, which by now is nearly totally dependent on aftermarket racing parts.

The short oval tracks, dragstrips and many classes of sports cars also followed the parade away from production cars and parts.

While a short track racer of 1953 scouted the area junkyards (before they were "automotive recycling centers") for parts for his 1939 Ford coupe, today many classes see most of the parts bought new from racing shops. Stock components are often as hard to find as they are in national and regional event cars. Usually it is only in the "low buck" beginners' classes where production cars are actually raced using most of their original parts.

We older racing fans may lament the way the "kids" are spending money for specially manufactured components for their cars today, but times have changed. Serious injury is no longer common as it was in the true stock car days, and there certainly is no shortage of good competitive racing today.

Still, from this corner, nothing can quite replace memories from that golden afternoon, 40 years ago. When the dust settled, a Packard was the center of attention after 200 miles of hard competition against Hudsons, Oldsmobiles, Dodges, Chryslers, Fords and Chevrolets. Real ones!

In the 1970s, when new car performance was declining, stock car racing speeds on the nation's superspeedways were increasing, thanks to greater reliance on aftermarket parts that were specially manufactured for racing. This 1978 NASCAR Winston Cup scene shows David Pearson in his 1976 Mercury Cougar, car number 21, and Cale Yarborough in his 1977 Oldsmobile, car number 11. (Phil Hall Collection)

Jalopies blazed trail for modern stockers

By Phil Hall

Late-model stock car racing has become one of the most popular forms of automobile racing in this country, and national championship competition of late-models is a major sport in itself.

The idea of two or more self-propelled vehicles competing is nearly as old as the automobile itself, with the Paris-Rouen race in France being recorded in 1894.

The sport of stock cars got its big boost after World War II. Since that time, the development of the domestic automobile and automobile racing have gone hand in hand, with varying degrees of involvement.

When World War II ended, the major domestic automobile manufacturers were concerned with getting back into production and meeting the demands of the car-hungry public. Engineering departments were involved in getting their all-new postwar designs ready for production. The thought of building cars for racing, if it existed at all, was well below the surface.

On the auto racing side of the fence, the country seemed as hungry for races as it was for cars. Open cockpit cars were kings, as they were before the war. Midgets (scaled down Indianapolis-type cars) ran before packed houses on short tracks from coast to coast.

With passenger cars still scarce, the thought of stripping one down to race was less than popular. The new cars being sold were anything but candidates for race cars, anyway, with their high, narrow bodies and lackluster power plants.

A trio of Oldsmobile Rocket 88s, kings of stock car racing in 1949, lead a lone Nash around the mile oval at the Wisconsin State Fair Speedway. (Phil Hall Collection)

Cadillacs, Lincolns and Oldsmobiles predominated the starting lineup for the August 25, 1949, late-model stock car race at the Wisconsin State Fair Speedway. On the pole is Paul Russo's winning Lincoln. (Phil Hall Collection)

Prewar coupes (mostly Fords) were popular after World War II, although they were being challenged by the new cars. This late-1940s action took place at Lakewood Park near Atlanta, Georgia. June Cleveland is shown flying off the track, while Gober Sosebee motors by. Cleveland was not hurt. (Phil Hall Collection)

Things began to change around 1948 as a number of prewar cars that had been worn out by their owners during the war began glutting used car lots and junkyards. Inflation and their rise in popularity had made setting up a midget racer a costly proposition. When the midget racing crowds began to wane, the search for a cheaper form of racing was on.

It didn't take long to realize one could set up a junker for a lot fewer dollars. They would also have a seemingly endless supply of cheap, though somewhat tired, spare parts. "Jalopy" racing was on its way to becoming a success. Soon, the jalopies began to replace the midgets at some tracks. They also became the basis upon which new tracks were started. The majority of the jalopy race cars were prewar Fords with flathead V-8s behind their battered noses.

Though the races were capturing the imagination of many a potential race driver and mechanic, things were not going all that well. The majority of the fans came to see crashing, rather than racing. It was not uncommon for the promoter of the race to leave the track, with the money, before the checkered flag fell. Driver safety was almost directly proportional to good luck.

Respectability officially entered the picture on December 14, 1947, when a meeting was held at the Streamline Hotel in Daytona Beach, Florida. A number of men with the common interest of bettering stock car racing held the first of several meetings which spanned four days. The result was the formation of the National Association for Stock Car Racing (NASCAR). Named president was a tall promoter of racing events on the beach. His name was Bill France.

The first NASCAR event was held February 14, 1948. That was a week before the organization was officially incorporated. It was for modified stock cars (mostly prewar Fords) and took place on a 3.2-mile beach road course at Daytona Beach. Half was on the beach and half was on a narrow old road, which ran parallel to the beach. This locale was to be the scene of important competition for the next decade. Red Byron won the 150-mile event in a Ford coupe, finishing 15 seconds ahead of Marshall Teague. Byron won $1,000.

The idea of strictly stock car racing, with current models invited to compete, got a shot in the arm on August 22, 1948, a Thursday. Despite the midweek date, 23,259 fans turned out at the Wisconsin State Fair to watch stock cars take to the one-mile dirt oval. There were a few postwar models in the field, and the usual high percentage of prewar Fords. Stunt driver Paul Bjork, of Minneapolis, Minnesota, was declared the winner. He raced a 1948 Kaiser. The fans loved the show, and promoter Tom Marchese announced the stocks would be back the following year.

Early postwar late-model races were a combination of the new and the old. At Milwaukee, Wisconsin, on July 11, 1949, Jim Rathmann (number 37) kept his 1940 Ford coupe ahead of a pack of 1949 models, including Carl Hunter's number 21 Mercury, Ray Knepper's number 9 Oldsmobile and Paul Russo's number 6 Oldsmobile. (Phil Hall Collection)

The hot Olds 88 was chosen as pace car for the 1949 Indianapolis 500-mile race. The special convertible model was driven by race driver and speedway manager Wilbur Shaw. Large moldings, shaped like rocket ships, were added to the pace car's front fenders. (Old Cars Collection)

One of the 1949 Olds 88 "Official Pace Cars" is seen here in Gasoline Alley at Indianapolis Motor Speedway. The early postwar years were kind to Oldsmobile on the ovals and in other forms of racing. The most publicized portions of the Speed Weeks events at Daytona Beach, Florida, were the top-speed runs, where the Olds proved to be fastest again. (IMSC Official Photo)

Socony Vacuum Oil Company converted a "Blue Streak" coaster wagon into a fuel delivery vehicle. It was used to gas up the 1949 Oldsmobile Indy pace car. One of the "Rocket 88" Oldsmobile's biggest threats in stock car racing came from the greater fuel and tire efficiency of the small Plymouths driven by aces like Lee Petty and Johnny Mantz. (IMSC photo)

The next year, 1949, turned out to be an important one for late-model stock car racing. Bill France decided that product identification would add interest to the sport. If fans saw a racing car like the one they drove to the track (or the one they hoped to afford someday), their interest could be intensified. In addition, the new postwar bodies were out for all makes. Most had lower and wider styling more suited for safe racing.

Perhaps the most important 1949 model for stock car racers was the Oldsmobile 88. Although General Motors did not have racing in mind, the "Olds 88" was a natural. It had a powerful, 135-horsepower V-8 in the small body shared with Chevrolet and Pontiac. Consider that the more powerful cars (Cadillac, Lincoln, Buick) were also heavies and you begin to see some logic here. Then realize that the Fords and Mercs didn't have great horsepower, and you can see why the stampede to Oldsmobiles was on.

On June 19, 1949, when a 150-mile race was held at the Charlotte Speedway, NASCAR initiated its Grand National division to late-model, strictly stock automobiles. A crowd of 13,000 fans was on hand, at the 3/4-mile dirt track, to witness Jim Roper's victory in a big Lincoln.

There were nine Grand Nationals that year. The rules called for strictly stock components and the tracks soon became littered with broken parts of suspensions, loose wheels, and the like. Though the fans loved the racing, it was apparent that the cars were not up to the pounding they were taking.

Oldsmobiles ruled the Grand Nationals, with Byron taking two of six Olds victories in his 88. This was good enough for the championship. Lincoln was credited with a pair of wins. The remaining flag went to a little Plymouth, driven by Lee Petty. Petty chose to run his Plymouth, in a sea of Oldsmobiles, because he felt it would be easier on tires and fuel. He was right. Though he did not have the speed of the Olds contingent, his 97-horsepower, flathead six was still motoring on late in the race. He was often well up in the standings, while competitors were busy replacing burned off tires and fueling their thirsty mounts. Petty (the father of Richard) finished second in points, ahead of such Olds driving stars as Bob Flock, Bill Blair, Fonty Flock and Curtis Turner.

Meanwhile, back in Milwaukee, the stock cars had a couple of races in 1949. On July 10, of that year, 31,898 fans turned out to see their new favorites run. Myron Fohr took the victory in a less-than-strictly-stock 1949 Chevrolet. Without a formal organization like NASCAR to keep everyone honest, he slipped by with a GMC truck six under the hood. There was a variety of cars in the field, with postwar models outnumbering prewar entries. Ed Rostan was second in a Cadillac. Indy driver Paul Russo notched third in a 1949 Oldsmobile.

Russo came back, on August 25, 1949, to win the second stock car race held at Milwaukee. Word had it that he used his girlfriend's car in the event. The first she heard of it was when she saw it racing on the track, while she was seated in the stands. Despite his win, she was not overjoyed about the whole thing.

The success at Milwaukee did not go unnoticed. The American Automobile Association (AAA), which sanctioned open cockpit racing (including the Indianapolis 500) took notice. It scheduled five events in 1950, including two at Milwaukee. AAA rules demanded that the cars be current or one-year-old models and have only the equipment with which they were originally equipped.

Fohr started the season with a win at Milwaukee in an AAA-approved 1949 Lincoln. Other events were run at Milwaukee, Atlanta, DuQuoin and Springfield, Illinois. The series drew 115,548 fans and paid $61,033 to drivers. Late-models had hit the big time. Jay Frank was crowned the AAA champion and Norm Nelson was runner-up, giving Olds the top two spots.

In NASCAR, 1950 was a banner year for Oldsmobile. With 19 events on the schedule, the 88s batted better than .500, with 10 wins. The pesky Plymouths were still around and took four victories. Ford, Lincoln and Mercury divided the rest. Despite the domination of the powerful Olds contingent, the prize plum was picked off by Plymouth.

The Southern 500, held on Labor Day, was the first stock car event scheduled on a super-speedway. The Darlington (South Carolina) Raceway was a 1-1/4-mile banked-and-paved oval that was a natural for the powerful Oldsmobiles. Driver Johnny Mantz wrecked his 88 in an earlier race and needed a car. With the new pavement, he thought tire wear would be more a factor than power. He chose Plymouth, which had established a reputation (mainly through Lee Petty) for conserving rubber. Mantz's 1950 Plymouth was fitted with Firestone sports car treads. The idea worked. Mantz pitted only three times, for right-side rubber. He didn't blow a tire, but the Oldsmobiles that tried to keep up with him did.

Not only was 1950 kind to Oldsmobile on the ovals. In addition, a couple of related events also found the Rockets in the limelight. The most publicized portions of the Speed Weeks events at Daytona Beach, Florida, were the top-speed runs. Joe Littlejohn got in his nearly-new Olds 88 fastback and turned a two-way average of 100.28 mph. This was the fastest speed for any American production car. It shattered the old mark, set in 1936 by a Hudson. The new mark would stand until 1953.

The manufacturers remained aloof to racing, but were beginning to notice that the car that won on Sunday would show a boost in sales on Monday. Despite this, no efforts to provide special parts or publicize the victories were apparent. You still could buy a car that was close, mechanically, to those that raced.

In May 1950, the first Pan American Road Race was held in Mexico. When the 2,178-mile trip through the countryside was finished, Hershel McGriff and Ray Elliott were the drivers of the fastest of the domestic cars. Naturally, they were in an 88.

With this combined record of wins, the question became: Can anyone stop the 88s? The answer was not long in coming. When the 1951 models were introduced, two were included that could do just that. The Chrysler New Yorker had a new FirePower V-8, and the Hudson Hornet had a huge inline six.

IMCA racing 1949 to 1976

By Phil Hall

Although probably best known for its sprint car races, the International Motor Contest Association (IMCA) had a stock car division for 28 years. It operated from 1949 to 1976. For 18 of those years, the stock car champion came from the southeastern Iowa river city of Keokuk. For a dozen seasons, the champion was a small, quiet man with a pencil thin mustache named Ernie Derr.

IMCA started sanctioning races in 1915. It put its label on sprint car races that packed 'em in. They ran mainly on dirt fairgrounds ovals throughout middle America. The legendary battles between the likes of Gus Schrader, Emory Collins and Sig Haugdahl were part of the attraction. Some of these battles were real; some were show business.

IMCA more or less disbanded after the 1976 season, but the rights to the name were purchased by a racing newspaper publisher, the late Keith Knaack. He revived the name in the 1980s as a sanctioning body for grass roots type modifieds. So today, IMCA, which bills itself as America's oldest sanctioning body, is booming, not only with modifieds, but with other types of stock cars as well.

After World War II, racing for new-model stock cars became popular in many areas of the country. NASCAR's Grand National circuit started in 1949, the same year that the IMCA stock-

Ernie Derr drove this 1957 Pontiac Chieftain two-door sedan to the IMCA championship in 1959. He scored 30 feature wins that season. Due to the discontinuation of factory support, Derr raced the same car during part of the 1960 season. (Phil Hall Collection)

Championship caliber in race car drivers and in cars is an enduring quality reflected by the 1956 (top) and 1966 (bottom) Dodges in these photos. Ernie Derr, of Keokuk, Iowa (left) was a six-time IMCA late-model stock car champion in 1966. He was also tops in the standings that season with 233 points on that circuit. His brother-in-law Don White (right) captured IMCA crowns in 1954, 1955 and 1958, before moving to USAC. His 1966 Charger won eight consecutive major victories and was runner up for the year's USAC stock car racing title at the time this photo was issued. (Phil Hall Collection)

ers started rolling. Record keeping in 1949 wasn't the science it is today and many IMCA records were lost in a fire, but Eddie Anderson from Grinnell, Iowa, is listed as the champion. He drove a 1949 Mercury to the title.

Shreveport, Louisiana Nash driver Herschel Buchanan took back-to-back titles in 1950 and 1951. Dominic Perlick of Minneapolis, Minnesota was the 1952 champion aboard a 1952 Oldsmobile.

Derr, at age 31, collected his first IMCA crown in 1953 in a new Oldsmobile. His brother-in-law, Don White, also of Keokuk, used current-model Oldsmobiles to win the 1954 and 1955 stock titles. Johnnie Beauchamp of Harlan, Iowa, broke the Keokuk string at three, with 1956 and 1957 championships, the first two for Chevrolet. For 1958, Derr drove the same 1957 Pontiac he used the year before and battled 1958 Ford-mounted White down to the last race of the season. Derr lost to White 3,185 to 3,128 in the point standings. White scored 22 wins and Derr 13.

White moved to United States Auto Club (USAC) stock car competition for the 1959 season. Derr, still in the 1957 Pontiac, hit his stride. He entered 47 of the 55 feature races held that year and scored 30 wins in his black number 1 two-door sedan. He was fastest qualifier a dozen times. Derr finished the season with 3,368 points to 2,095 for rookie standout Dick Hutcherson, another Keokuk resident.

Derr's winning of the championship in a two-year old car was a first in IMCA. The only other champion not listed in a current-model car was Buchanan, who took the 1951 title aboard a 1950 Nash Ambassador. However, in 1959, it was not unusual for many of the nation's late-model stock car drivers to be in one- or two-year-old equipment. The domestic factories had stopped their open backing of stock car racing in 1957. Also many 1959 models were just plain huge compared to the older models. This was especially true of the "Wide Track" Pontiac of that year. IMCA was mainly short track racing and the bulk of the new cars was seen by the racers as a disadvantage.

For 1960, Derr started the season in the same 1957 Pontiac, but this time his number 1 decal was earned, instead of borrowed from his brother-in-law. Derr started that season by winning

Ernie Derr drove his 1965 Dodge Coronet two-door sedan to the International Motor Contest Association (IMCA) stock car racing title in 1965. It was the first time in three years that the Iowa driver took the championship. (Phil Hall Collection)

72

the first three events on the schedule. He rolled up five wins in the first seven events. However, a new 1960 Pontiac Catalina two-door hardtop had been delivered to Derr's shop. In June, he reluctantly shifted to the current model. It took a while to work the bugs out of it. Meanwhile the old 1957 Pontiac was being raced by Jerry McCredie, although it was still owned and prepped by Derr.

Derr went on to score 22 wins in the 1960 season, taking the title over Ramo Stott. Hutcherson finished third. Derr and Stott would do battle for much of the remaining decade, but Stott, also from Keokuk, would never take a title. Stott moved on to ARCA and USAC racing, and later returned to ARCA.

Factory help was the main reason that Derr raced the 1960 Pontiac. He got new cars in 1961, 1962 and 1963, just before General Motors got out of racing. Derr drove Pontiacs to titles all years, except the last, when factory help dried up.

In 1963 and 1964, Hutcherson, backed by Ford, drove current-model cars to the titles, stopping Derr's streak at four. However, being from Keokuk, he ran that string to seven. He moved to NASCAR after the 1964 season.

While Hutcherson was showing the way, Derr locked up a lucrative deal with Dodge. He built and drove Dodges to seven consecutive IMCA stock car championships between 1965 and 1971. Stories abound of his domination of the division. Many times he did his own work on the car during pit stops, buckled back in, and re-entered the race.

After the 1971 season, Derr had won 12 titles. He won seven in a row. Keokuk drivers had accounted for 17 championships in 22 years, 14 of them in a row. When Irv Janey, of Cedar Rapids, Iowa, was crowned after the 1972 season, it broke the string, but there was one more Keokuk based champion. Gordon Blankenship took the title in 1973.

Derr became disenchanted with IMCA and ran his final nationally sanctioned events with USAC. He was part of Chrysler's factory supported Kit Car program in 1976.

IMCA came upon rough times as the 1970s progressed. In 1970, factory support for the stock cars dried up. Other organizations were stealing the spotlight, for both the sprints and stockers. The 1976 season was the last of the era. Today, the chances of a dozen-time champion in any regional or national organization are small. The chances of 18 title-winning performances coming from one town are just about nil.

By 1968, Ernie Derr was credited with more wins and more national championships than any other driver in United States stock car racing. He was driving the number 1 Dodge that season in his campaign for an unprecedented ninth title. (Phil Hall Collection)

1951: Hornet's buzz meant the end of "queen bee" Rocket's reign

By Phil Hall

In February 1951, pioneer automotive scribe Tom McCahill was test driving a 1951 Chrysler New Yorker in Florida, for *Mechanix Illustrated*. He stopped by Daytona Beach to look over the NASCAR speed trials about to be run there. McCahill, not unfamiliar with rapid motoring, was challenged by NASCAR president Bill France to run the big FirePower V-8 in the trials. Accepting the challenge, McCahill had the big sedan tuned at a local dealer. On February 8, 1951, he turned in a two-way average of 100.13 mph over a less than ideal beach. McCahill was declared the winner in the strictly stock passenger car class.

Three days later, the 160-mile Grand National event on the beach-road oval course found a newcomer car in the winner's circle. It was a 1951 Hudson Hornet driven by former hot rodder Marshall Teague. He was then a Daytona Beach garage owner.

Within three days, the once invincible Oldsmobile 88 had been shot out of the winner's box by a pair of makes that were not ever considered challengers the year before. Looking at the

Norm Nelson drove his Olds 88 to victory on August 23, 1951, in the AAA race at Milwaukee, Wisconsin. Later, he was disqualified for having illegal equipment. Rodger Ward was declared winner. (Phil Hall Collection)

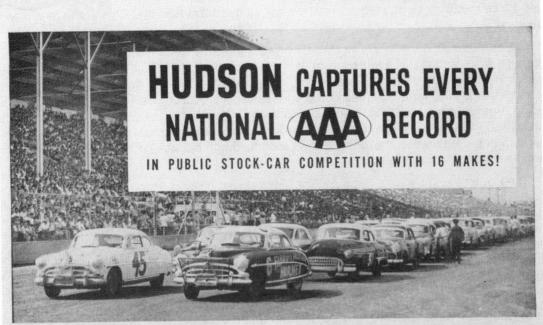

HUDSON CAPTURES EVERY NATIONAL AAA RECORD

IN PUBLIC STOCK-CAR COMPETITION WITH 16 MAKES!

THESE TRIALS REVEAL THE RELATIVE ROADABILITY, STAMINA AND SAFETY, AS WELL AS SPEED, OF THE COMPETING CARS.

Here's dramatic proof⁺ of Hudson's superior
PERFORMANCE, DURABILITY, SAFETY
to help you choose your family car

Now it is easy to choose your family car —just compare the records of *all* cars in stock-car competition!

These grueling trials are impartial tests of practically every make of car (just like those you can buy from your dealers) for performance, durability, safety—the very qualities that are so vital in your family car.

Of the 13 stock-car races held by the American Automobile Association this year, Hudson won 12.

In these same 13 races, Hudson also finished 2nd, 3rd, 4th or 5th a total of 20 times! In these races, Hudson set new records over every distance, from one-half mile to 200 miles! Hudson now holds every national AAA competition stock-car record in the books!

This proves Hudson's exclusive "step-down" design, with America's lowest center of gravity, results in a better-performing, more durable, safer car for you and your family. Try Hudson today!

HUDSON MOTOR CAR COMPANY

⁺OFFICIAL RESULTS AAA STOCK-CAR RACES

[All American makes competing, except one!]

Make of Car	1st PLACE	2nd PLACE	3rd PLACE	4th PLACE	5th PLACE	TOTAL
HUDSON	12	6	7	5	2	32
Other Makes*						
Make B	1	3	1	1	3	9
Make C	0	0	2	1	1	4
Make D	0	0	0	1	2	3
Make E	0	1	2	1	0	4
Make F	0	1	0	1	1	3
Make G	0	1	0	1	1	3
Make H	0	0	1	2	1	4
Make I	0	0	0	0	0	0
Make J	0	0	0	0	0	0
Make K	0	0	0	0	0	0
Make L	0	1	0	0	0	1
Make M	0	0	0	1	0	1
Make N	0	0	0	0	1	1
Make O	0	0	0	0	0	0
Make P	0	0	0	0	0	0
Make Q	0	0	0	0	0	0

*Your nearby Hudson dealer will supply the names of all cars shown in the above record.

HUDSON OFFERS you sleek styling and luxurious interiors in addition to its unsurpassed performance, durability and safety. Visit your Hudson dealer, or phone and a new Hudson will be brought to your door.

TWIN H-POWER, Hudson's sensational new engine development, is available on the Hudson Hornet and the Hudson Wasp at slight extra cost. New Dual-Range Hydra-Matic Drive, Solex Safety Glass (tinted, anti-glare) and Overdrive optional at extra cost on all Hudsons. Standard trim, other specifications, accessories subject to change without notice.

59

"Hudson Captures Every National AAA Record," said this advertisement highlighting the company's stock car racing wins. Of the 13 stock car races held by the American Automobile Association this year, Hudson won 12. In these same 13 races, Hudson also finished in second to fifth place a total of 20 times. (Old Cars Collection)

cars themselves, the two brash newcomers for 1951 each offered something that the Olds did not. Since strictly stock was the name of the game, there was little that Oldsmobile fans could do about it.

Chrysler offered raw power. The chassis was still the basic 1949 model and known more for strength than handling. The transmission was the rather inefficient Fluid-Matic. Yet, the engine was something else. The 331.1-cubic-inch, hemispherical head V-8 was advertised with 180 horsepower at 4000 rpm. That made it the most powerful production car in the country, at a time when Americans were starting to notice such things. The potential of the power plant seemed unlimited. The early model had big valves, but a low compression ratio and a restrictive two-barrel carburetor. Meanwhile, the 1951 Olds 88 continued with the same 135-hp, 303.7-cubic-inch engine it started with in 1949.

The Hornet's long suit was handling. The "Step-Down" chassis, introduced on 1948 models, had always made for a good handling car. Contributing to this was the wide tread, low center of gravity, center point steering and the combination of front and rear anti-roll bars. Hudson, however, was not popular among stock car entrants because of a lack of power. That was remedied with the introduction of the 1951 Hornet. It featured a bored and stroked version of the 262-cubic-inch Super Six. The new 308-cubic-inch flathead six turned out an honest 145 hp, 10 more than the Olds.

McCahill's run was 100.13 mph. It did not break the 100.28 mph record Joe Littlejohn had set in a 1950 Olds. Beach conditions were responsible for the drop. They become more apparent when it is considered that the fastest Olds in 1951, driven by Bill Trent, turned in a time of 93.95 mph.

In the beach-road event, Tim Flock finished second in a 1950 Lincoln. The first Olds was driven by brother Fonty, who took third. However, Oldsmobile did not roll over and die in 1951. After Daytona, it returned to its traditional "king of the hill" role. However, in NASCAR racing, the monarch had a very potent challenger named the Hornet. Marshall Teague took a second in the

Teague's number 6 "Teague-mobile" eases through the north turn in his first appearance at the Wisconsin State Fair Speedway. He is about to pass the 1951 Chrysler driven by Aaron Woodard, who finished 21st. An unidentified Packard follows. (Phil Hall Collection)

112-mile Grand National race at Charlotte, North Carolina. It then won the event on the half-mile at Gardena, California. It was time for a visit to the Hudson factory in Detroit.

The combination of his two victories and a history of Hudson hot rodding made Teague a welcome visitor to a company that was looking for a new way to promote sales. Hudson had an extensive background in the world of speed, so the idea of helping stock car racing was a bit more palatable to them than to the other manufacturers.

At Daytona, Teague used the heavy-duty or export suspension right out of the Hudson catalog. He also used another cataloged item, the 3.58:1 ratio rear axle. His talks with Hudson enlightened them on the advantage of an extensive chassis and engine parts option list for race car builders. The rapport Teague established with the factory was the harbinger of a new necessity in auto racing. Factory backing of race cars, both overt and covert, would continue for the next four decades.

After his return from the Hudson factory, Teague set a second Hornet up for NASCAR racing. He persuaded Herb Thomas to drive it. Thomas had already started the season in a Plymouth and switched to an Olds 88. Then, he joined Teague and raced Hudsons.

One of the most important events on the 1951 NASCAR Grand National schedule was the 250-mile race at Detroit, Michigan. The track was nothing to be excited about, unless you were a thrill seeker and liked to see cars bounce around. More important was that the auto company bigwigs would be there to see what stock car racing was all about.

Packard supplied the pace car. Hudson and Olds backers were sure their favorite car would show who was boss. However, a Chrysler won the contest. The victory was the only one of the season for Chrysler, but it could not have come at a more opportune moment. After the event, Chrysler engineers filled the pit of winner Tommy Thompson. They offered to rebuild the car for him, at least acknowledging that the sport existed.

Thompson's early example of "factory support" was not especially beneficial, however. When it was delivered, a day before the race at Langhorne, Pennsylvania, it looked nice enough. However, the engineers had replaced the export springs and special reinforced parts with stock ones. As a result, Thompson was unable to race it.

Executives of the other companies were amazed to see their creations dumping broken parts all over the track, especially wheels. This did not look good to a crowd of potential buyers. Other than Chrysler's token involvement and Hudson's cooperation with Teague, little evolved from the Detroit show on the surface.

A 1-1/4-mile, banked and paved oval at Darlington, South Carolina, was the only superspeedway existing in 1951. Hudson's first race car "engineered" by Teague was ready for its premiere. It sported a new Twin-H carburetion system. Instead of standard two-barrel carburetors, the Teague and Thomas Hornets sported two one-barrel carburetors. They were spaced to give better fuel distribution to the big six-cylinder motor. Yes, the Twin-H setup *was* in a parts bulletin Hudson issued before the race. With it, Teague set the fastest time of the day and Thomas won the race.

"Although my qualifying time at Darlington was the fastest, it was not the maximum speed of the car, as was later proved in the race," Teague said in a letter to *Speed Age*. "After running the track enough to learn the groove, I was able to obtain a top speed of over 110 mph at the end of the straightaway. Even with all these tremendous speeds, I never once ran at maximum speed, as tires are the governing factor at Darlington. Hudsons are able to run at greater speeds, for longer periods, with less tire wear, due to their superior roadability, aided by their low center of gravity," Teague noted. In addition to being a good driver and builder, Teague was also a good public relations man for Hudson.

Plymouth continued to pester the more powerful makes on the short tracks. Lee Petty notched a couple of victories in his venerable 1949 business coupe. Still, the remaining 39 checkered flags went to other makes. Oldsmobile, again, accounted for the majority of Grand National victories, with 20. Hudson was next, with 12. Studebaker was good for three. Mercury had two. Nash joined Chrysler in the one-shot category.

Olds clinched the manufacturer's championship in NASCAR with 163 points to 98 for Plymouth and 92 for Hudson. Part of the reason for Hudson's poor showing was a lack of Hudson race cars. There were many 88s and Plymouths around from the previous season, and relatively few of the new Hudsons. This was changing fast, however.

When the drivers' points were tallied, Thomas was declared the champion, which was a gold star for Hudson. Meanwhile, up North, the American Automobile Association (AAA) contest board stock car racing circuit was in trouble. Only three events were held in 1951. All were in Milwaukee on the one-mile dirt oval. The rules were very prohibitive, both in requirements for the racetracks and requirements for the cars. Only strictly stock passenger cars were allowed, with no reinforcement for safety and no options. Rodger Ward won the first event, on July 8, driving an Olds 88. On August 23, Norm Nelson finished first in an 88. However, he was dis-

At 222 pounds, Marshall Teague hardly had the lean, hard, race driver image that many people cherished. In this 1954 photo, he is interviewed after a win by Ed "20 Grand" Steinbock. (Phil Hall Collection)

qualified for having non-stock equipment. The runner-up, Rodger Ward, got the win. The next day featured a race for cars with 120 hp or less. Nelson got the win honestly in a Mercury. Ward, needless to say, was the 1951 AAA champ and Olds was the top car. After this embarrassing season, AAA voted to open up the rules to permit safety modifications to wheels, hubs, and steering. It also decided to let the cars compete on shorter tracks.

Chrysler had the initial and final glory of the 1951 racing season. Tony Bettenhausen drove a 1951 Saratoga coupe to third overall spot (first for American cars) in the Carrera PanAmericana, or Mexican Road Race, as it was known. His red number 7 Chrysler was prepared by the Kiekhaefer Corporation, builders of Mercury outboard motors. The car was fully set up for the 1,933-mile run through the Mexican countryside, from Tuxtla Gutierrez to Cuidad Juarez. It was reportedly producing 30 percent more power than a stock Saratoga and the record 114.33 mph average speed would seem to verify that something had been done. It broke the old mark, set by an Oldsmobile, by 13.9 mph. The Kiekhaefer-Chrysler combination would be heard from again in the racing world.

Looking over the 1951 season, Chrysler won two major non-oval speed events: The Daytona Speed trials and the Mexican Road Race. Oldsmobile took the most wins and the manufacturer's championship in NASCAR. Oldsmobile also had the best record in the limited AAA competition. However, it was Hudson, that made the most of its accomplishments in stock car racing. In June 1951, Hudson issued a folder entitled *Meet The Winner, The Fabulous Hudson Hornet*. It touted Hudson victories at Dayton; Ohio; Gardena, California; Canfield, Ohio; and Phoenix, Arizona. More important, the brochure tied in the wins with the car itself. "The superiority of Hudson's new and better way to build passenger cars proved in overall competition," it noted over a photo of Teague leading the pack at Daytona. Teague also gave some biased testimonial, saying "My Hudson Hornet is strictly standard!" There was nary an official mention of racing accomplishments from Chrysler and Oldsmobile in their promotions or advertising.

The statement, "Hudson rules the road and America knows it" was adopted by the company as part of a plan to psyche out its racing competition. Unfortunately, Hudson's competition promotions did not seem to help the company in marketing more cars. Its 1951 sales dropped from 143,586 to 92,859. Yet, despite this lack of performance in the showroom, the stage was set for Hudson's takeover in stock car racing.

Taking stock of 1953

By Phil Hall

Things were getting out of control. Cars were being illegally modified as the pressure for makes to win races took precedent over the rules. The rules called for stock production passenger cars and components thereof to be used. The sanctioning body stepped in and set strict rules so that the cars raced got back to being stock.

Sound familiar? It should, since it's happened countless times over the long and sometimes rocky history of the automobile and organizations that tried to govern the speed competition between two or more vehicles.

In this case, the calendar read 1910 and the group trying to get things back to stock was the American Automobile Association (AAA) Contest Board. It tried to bring order to the sport of racing starting the year before. At the time, most racing was based on production cars, though the term "stock car racing" was not yet a familiar one. AAA's efforts to get things under control

Marshall Teague sought to repeat his 1952 AAA stock car driving championship in his "Fabulous Hudson Hornet." He had all kinds of problems, scored only three wins and finished fourth in points in the 1953 battle. (Phil Hall Collection)

Hudsons dominated AAA stock car racing in 1953, taking 13 out of 16 events that counted for the title. One of two wins scored by big-car driver Sam Hanks came on August 23. Hanks drove the number 71 backup Hornet of Frank "Rebel" Mundy to victory in the 100-miler at Milwaukee. Second-place Marshall Teague, driving number 1, parked next to Hanks after the event as the victor was greeted by officials and the press. (Phil Hall Collection)

Jack McGrath, the fastest qualifier for the August 23, 1953, race of 100 laps at Milwaukee, hit a car on the 43rd lap and flipped several times. That season, AAA required all stock cars to have roll bars. McGrath credited the device with keeping the roof up and saving his life. He was not seriously injured. (Phil Hall Collection)

Jack McGrath checks the tire pressure on the 1953 Hudson Hornet he drove in AAA competition, at Milwaukee, in 1953. Note the stock chrome trim and license plates. The car was later demolished. (Phil Hall Collection)

resulted in a demand that 50 or more examples of the car being raced had to be produced. Later, that was modified to 50 copies had to be produced or sold in the 12 months before its racing appearance.

Despite the serious attempts at such regulations, cars raced at the Indianapolis Motor Speedway, and elsewhere, had gotten away from the production category. Racing fragmented into several branches, including the big-cars (Indy), sprint cars, midget cars, sports cars and modified cars. There were also several local variations that fell between the established categories.

In the decade before World War II, interest in stock car racing featuring recent and current models was gaining popularity in local areas around the country. It was happening on the sand at Daytona Beach, Florida, on the tracks of Pennsylvania and on the desert in Southern California. The sport picked up steam after the war. Bill France's National Association for Stock Car Auto Racing (NASCAR) attempted to bring order in the Southeast.

Milwaukee, Wisconsin was drawing large crowds for the stocks startng in 1948, but there were other events that were less than successful. Accusations of cheating and illegal modifications grew as fast as the cars did. Again, some 40 years after its first similar attempt, the AAA Contest Board was asked to bring order. In 1950, the AAA stock car circuit was announced. AAA again had its hands full and with each new season, as it tried new ways to make sure the cars raced were stock, yet safe for race car drivers.

The 1953 season, which we will look at this time, saw Detroit in the formative stages of the "horsepower race" that would gather steam for a good part of the decade. The big players in the stocks at the time were Hudson and Oldsmobile. Oldsmobile featured modern, overhead valve

V-8 power in its lowest-priced model, the 88. It had been a factor in the stock car wars since this setup was introduced in 1949.

Independent Hudson countered with its fine-handling "Step-Down" unitized chassis and big 308-cubic-inch flathead six. This motor was optioned with dual carburetion called Twin-H Power. A long list of heavy-duty (export) suspension parts were available, too.

NASCAR standout Marshall Teague wanted to pursue a big-car career and run the AAA-sanctioned Indianapolis 500. He came north to race AAA stocks for the 1952 season, bringing along his factory-backed "Fabulous Hudson Hornets" as he called and painted them.

Teague led a Hudson domination of the AAA stock car circuit in 1952. He won seven of the 14 events on the schedule and captured the championship by 1,000 points. Teague had 1,980 points to Frank Luptow's 980. Luptow was killed during the 1952 season. In all, Hudsons won

Frank "The Rebel" Mundy scored a win for Hudson in the July 12, 1953 AAA stock car race at Milwaukee. Presenting the trophy, topped by a model Hudson, was welterweight boxer Kid Gavalan. (Phil Hall Collection)

The winner and fastest qualifier at the August 23, 1953 AAA stock car contest at Milwaukee posed with their trophies. Sam Hanks (left) won the 100-miler and Jack McGrath was the top timer. Note the Hudsons on the trophies. Both drove Hornets. McGrath's wrist wrap was his only injury after his car was destroyed in a crash. (Phil Hall Collection)

13 events in 1952, leaving one checkered flag for Oldsmobile. For 1953, Teague got his wish and started his first Indy 500, placing 18th. However, the AAA circuit, which featured Indy drivers in stock cars, was a lot tougher this time around.

Teague started the season, on February 22, at the Carrell Speedway in Gardena, California. He became one of six victims of serious accidents, by flipping his Hornet twice. He was not hurt. One of the victims, Harold Morse, died of his injuries. Frank "Rebel" Mundy, of Atlanta, Georgia, won the race in a Hudson.

AAA issued new safety rules. They required roll bars in all cars, as well as heavy-duty axles. With the safety equipment in place, Teague, Mundy and Jack McGrath put on a Hornet show on the Phoenix, Arizona fairground's dirt mile oval. Teague took the win, but another AAA rule hit him. His carburetor setup was declared non-stock. It was not on the Hudson parts list as required. McGrath then got the win.

Mundy, with the rebel flag painted on his doors, ran up a pair of short track wins. One was at Gardena on April 26 and the other was at Toledo, Ohio, on May 10. This was notice of Mundy's intent to unseat Teague as AAA champion. McGrath flipped at Toledo, but was unhurt. He came back, on June 14, to win at Williams Grove, Pennsylvania. Teague was in hot pursuit.

Mundy came back with wins at Heidelberg, Pennsylvania, on July 4, and on the dirt mile at Milwaukee, on July 12. In the latter, Frank Burany and Jim Rathmann made serious challenges to the Hudsons' domination of stock car racing. Burany took second, ahead of Teague, who hit the wall during the event. Another racer, Don O'Dell, made his presence felt at the Illiana Motor

Speedway in Schererville, Indiana on July 25. He challenged winner McGrath. Mundy had a day to forget when his steering wheel fell off and he ended up outside the track, thanks to a trip through the fence.

Hudson's 1953 string of eight straight wins ended on the high banks of the Sharon, Pennsylvania oval. Clarence LaRue finished the 200 laps with fellow Olds 88 driver Cal Niday right behind. Finally, Teague flashed his winning Hudson form, taking a pair of Indiana short track events. These were at Winchester, on August 9, and Salem, on August 16. Hudson also mounted big-car driver Sam Hanks, who took the 100 lapper at Milwaukee on August 23. Teague and Mundy were right behind him. However, it was a different story four days later, when O'Dell won a 150-miler on the same track. His green four-door 1951 Packard, was followed by Bob Christie, in a Nash Ambassador, and Norm Nelson in an Olds 88. The dirt mile on the fairgrounds, in Syracuse, New York, gave Hanks his second win of the season. Mundy placed second, but clinched the 1953 AAA stock car title.

With the pressure off, Teague won on September 13 at Ft. Wayne, Indiana. He was followed by Hanks and Mundy. The 1953 season ended a week later, at Milwaukee. The 200-lapper was the last event on the dirt mile and in a record-setting finish. O'Dell added another win for Packard, which was not active in the building or selling of high-performance or racing components.

By the end of the 1953 campaign, Hudsons had won 13 of the races that counted for the championship, compared to two for Packard and one for Oldsmobile. Mundy took the driving title with 2,080 points. O'Dell, who only started 11 events, took second with 1,405 points. He was followed by Christie, Teague and McGrath.

AAA continued to sanction stock car and other types of racing through the 1955 season. After that, it got out of the business for good. This was due, in part, to the serious World Championship accident in Europe in 1955. The AAA's duties were taken over, for 1956 and beyond, by the United States Auto Club (USAC).

As for the task of keeping stock cars "stock," many organizations have tried. Some attempted to "police" racing before the AAA in 1910. Countless numbers tried thereafter.

The "Fabulous Hudson Hornet" stock car of Herb Thomas (number 92) races over a track towards the finish line. The 1953 coupe featured the 308-cubic-inch inline six with "Twin H" power. (Jack Miller Collection)

Stockers get factory backing in 1953

By Phil Hall

The year 1953 represented the dawn for the entrance of the "Big Three" automakers into the sport of national championship late-model stock car racing. Oldsmobiles, Cadillacs, Fords, Lincolns, Plymouths and Chryslers had been racing since the start of late-model racing in 1948. However, their competitiveness was based mainly on the skill of mechanics and the courage of drivers. Then, something happened that sparked the interest of General Motors, Ford and Chrysler. The thing that happened was that the Hudson Hornet started winning and got direct race backing from the Hudson factory.

Late-model stock car racing grew in popularity by leaps and bounds. The outsider, Hudson, was taking all the gravy. The big automakers would have to do something. They had to stop Hudson from getting all the glory from involvement in racing.

On paper, the Hudson Hornet should not have been dominating the sport. It was a big, heavy car. It was powered by an outdated, flathead six. However, a combination of excellent handling, full cooperation with the factory's parts division, and a large number of top drivers in Hornets,

Hudsons and Oldsmobiles hogged the up-front starting spots in this August 23, 1953, AAA 100-mile stock car race at Milwaukee. The Hornets got the front row, with Jack McGrath's unnumbered car on the pole and Marshall Teague's number 1 on the outside. In the second row were Clarence LaRue's number 57 Oldsmobile and Johnny Mantz in the number 45 Hudson. Holding down row three were Norm Nelson, in the number 4 Olds, and Sam Hanks in the number 71 Hudson. Hanks took the win. (Phil Hall Collection)

Oldsmobiles and Hudsons fought for supremacy in stock car racing in 1953. Going at it in an AAA race at Milwaukee are Norm Nelson's number 4 Olds 88 and Marshall Teague's "Fabulous Hudson Hornet." (Phil Hall Collection)

made Hudson the king of stock car racing. Proof was the 1952 record of 40 wins in 48 events in National Association for Stock Car Auto Racing (NASCAR) and American Automobile Association (AAA) Contest Board events.

Hudson's challengers for 1952 were Oldsmobile, Chrysler, Plymouth, Nash, and Ford. Oldsmobile had a modern design V-8. However, despite twin suspension stabilizers, its handling was inferior to Hudson's. The Chrysler, with its very powerful hemi V-8, also had an outdated chassis. The Chrysler-built Plymouth had a 97-hp, six-cylinder engine that would not go as fast as the big cars. However, that little motor would seemingly run forever. In addition, Plymouths were easy on fuel and tires. The Nash had soft springs, but the optional twin SU carburetors on

Packards enjoyed some success in AAA stock car racing in 1953. Here, Cecil Hays, in the number 87 car, uses straight eight Packard power to chase home Hanks in a six-cylinder Hudson Hornet. (Phil Hall Collection)

Stock cars were just that in 1953. They had chrome trim and all production car features. The rules were fairly strict regarding optional equipment. This Hudson Hornet is set up for dirt track racing, with a screen in front of its grille. Johnny Mantz drove it in AAA events. (Phil Hall Collection)

its Ambassador six could provide power. Ford drivers had a choice of the outdated flathead V-8 or an OHV six that was almost as powerful.

Hudson was really in for a rough time in 1953. Potent new challengers from Dodge and Lincoln were announced. Also introduced was a new, lightweight Buick Roadmaster V-8. This engine would be very potent the next year, when used in the lighter Century.

Dodge for 1953 was built on a smaller chassis, with reductions in length, wheelbase and weight (It was 200 pounds lighter). Under its hood was the Red Ram V-8, a scaled down "semi-hemi" displacing 241.2 cubic inches and putting out 140 hp when breathing through the stock two-barrel carburetor.

Lincoln unleashed a four-barrel carburetor and some performance-oriented options. They included solid valve lifters. The unoptioned 317.5-cubic-inch V-8 produced an advertised 205 hp. Lincoln premiered its 1953 models in the PanAmericana Road Race late in 1952. With a bit of tweaking, they took the first four positions in their class.

Hudson, on the other hand, did relatively little to its 1953 Hornet. The standard 308-cubic-inch six with a two-barrel carburetor put out an advertised 145 hp. That was the same rating it had when introduced in 1951 models. The "police" or "7-X " engine, with two one-barrel carburetors (called the "Twin-H" option) produced more power than the standard version. However, its horsepower rating was never advertised. Many guesses put the figure over the 200 mark. In 1952, Hudson driver Marshall Teague figured that Twin-H was good for 10 extra horsepower throughout the range. So, other than cosmetic changes, the 1953 Hornet was altered little from the 1952 model.

Though late-model stock car racing is usually contested on ovals, the first events of the 1953 season were the Speed Trials over the sands of Daytona Beach in February. Supervised by NASCAR, these events included the flying-mile and standing-start acceleration tests in a mile.

The modern Speed Trials started in 1950, as contests between individuals to see who had the fastest car. They developed into a contest between manufacturers to see who had the fastest automobiles.

Proof of more than casual interest from Big Three manufacturers was the Oldsmobile contingent at the 1953 Daytona Speed Trials (Speed Weeks). Six cars were entered. Four ran in the Grand National race on the beach-road course. Two were used specifically for the Speed Trials. Some of the Oldsmobiles did double duty. All were equipped with "packages" of optional equipment listed by Oldsmobile. The packages (there were six in all) covered modifications to the engine, differential, axle shaft, radiator, suspension and fuel tank. They carried Oldsmobile parts numbers. They were considered legal by NASCAR, as long as they were made available to the public, which Oldsmobile had promised would be the case.

Somewhat controversial was the statement that these packages were authorized for installation on all 1951 and 1952 Oldsmobiles, which happened to be the model-years that were legal for NASCAR and AAA racing. Shades of Hudson! ... The bulletin covering the packages listed five items not manufactured by Olds or listed on Olds parts lists. However, they were supposedly "authorized" for installation on Oldsmobiles. These items included: A heavier steering linkage, Air-Lift spring boosters, reinforced wheels, harder rear engine mounts, and straight-through dual exhaust pipes.

Tom McCahill complained about racing modifications in *Mechanix Illustrated*. "This sounds to me like saying, 'pick your own speed shop, it's okay with us,'" McCahill wrote. "Now, I maintain that this is hardly 'factory available optional equipment.' If it is, all George Mason of Nash has to do is 'authorize' any Rambler owner to install a 270-Offenhauser in his little gem and stock car records would be blown sky-high overnight," McCahill added.

The Olds packages did their thing. As a result, Oldsmobiles took all three events they entered. Bob Pronger of Blue Island, Illinois, drove his 88 two-door sedan to a two-way flying-mile average of 113.38 mph. That was well above the old mark of 100.28 mph, which was set

Driver safety in 1953 greatly depended on car construction. This Hudson Hornet protected driver Jack McGrath very well during his crash in Milwaukee. (Phil Hall Collection)

by Joe Littlejohn in 1950 in an Olds. In the acceleration trials, Pronger also swept honors, with a 74.41 mph average through the traps.

In the Grand National stock car race, Pronger rolled his car over on its roof. However, Bill Blair skipped a pit stop and snapped Hudson's win streak in the event, at two. Marshall Teague took both Hudson victories, perhaps proving the driver had a lot to do with setting records. Fonty Flock, in another factory Olds, took second. That gave the "package" cars a one-two sweep. Tommy Thompson was third in a 1953 Lincoln and Herb Thomas brought the first Hornet across the finish line in fourth place.

Things got even more uncomfortable for Hudson in NASCAR country after another change. Its long-time nemesis, Lee Petty, switched from his 97-hp Plymouth to a Dodge Red Ram V-8 for short tracks. He continued to use Chryslers on the larger tracks. Chrysler stayed with its two-barrel carburetor and 180 advertised horsepower for 1953, despite getting a new body.

Though not as direct as Oldsmobile's version, Dodge issued a parts bulletin, "In response to occasional requests from Dodge dealers and car owners for a maximum output package for their cars when under certain types of special service." The term "special service" undoubtedly referred to stock car racing. The "maximum output package" contained some MoPar parts and some "authorized" parts. Included were special cylinder heads, manifolds, valve springs, suspension parts and differential gears, plus heavy-duty wheel and hubs and dual exhausts. These were not for the Dodge flathead sixes by any stretch of the imagination. They were to give more thrust to the "crimson ram" hemi V-8.

The packages helped both Oldsmobile's and Dodge's fortunes in NASCAR in 1953. Olds tripled its victory total from the previous year, scoring nine wins. They included Daytona and Buck Baker's big win in the Southern 500 at Darlington. Dodge, thanks to Petty, took six wins. That was not bad, considering that a Grand National stock car race had never been won by a Dodge before.

With 37 events on the 1953 schedule, that left 22 to the competition. Hudson took all 22 flags, making the Hornet the undisputed king again. Herb Thomas won the title, repeating his performance of 1951. Petty finished second. Hudson driver Jim Rathmann took third. Baker, the leading Olds driver in the standings, was fourth.

Up north, in AAA racing, Hudson was as tough as ever. It took 13 wins in 16 starts. Frank (Francisco Edwardo Menendez) Mundy, of Atlanta, Georgia won five events. The former stunt car driver also took the championship. Other Hudsonites taking victories were Marshall Teague (three wins), Jack McGrath (also three wins) and Sam Hanks (two victories). Clarence LaRue of Akron, Ohio, scored Oldsmobile's lone AAA win. The surprise was a 1951 Packard, driven by Don O'Dell of Blue Island, Illinois. With absolutely no factory help, O'Dell finished second in the point standings. He even picked up a pair of wins on the Milwaukee Mile, where the biggest purses were paid. O'Dell's final win there came in the September 20 race. It was a 200-mile contest and the last race of the season.

Though it will never be recorded in the win column, a Hudson victory ... of sorts ... came at Milwaukee on August 23, 1953. Don Dunfee's 1953 Dodge had stalled just off the south turn. Dunfee got out of the car, but left it on the track. Jack McGrath did not see the car, until it was too late. He crashed into it going full bore in his Hornet. The Hornet was demolished, but a roll bar structure around McGrath held up. He escaped with a cut on his wrist. This was truly amazing after viewing the wreck and the car.

Lincoln repeated its winning ways in the Carrera PanAmericana. This was no surprise. The nameplate received an unprecedented degree of factory backing from Ford Motor Company. This event would become the playground of the "Road Race Lincolns" one more year.

The "paper threat" at the beginning of 1953 did little to change Hudson's winning ways, but the Big Three factories did not intend to hang it up so soon. The year 1954 would find a lot more potent ammunition to shoot down the Hornet.

NEW LOW PRICE

FOR THE NATIONAL CHAMPION

Winner of more stock-car events than all other makes combined!

"Family cars like those you buy from dealers, compete in stock-car events throughout the U. S. Records show which is safest, most roadable, durable. These records show it's Hudson—with no other make even close," says Frank Mundy, AAA champion, shown in his winning Hornet.

Hudson Hornet Special Club Coupe. Also available in Four-Door Sedan and Club Sedan.

New HUDSON HORNET SPECIAL

Now! You can own the fabulous champion of the U. S. stock-car tracks . . . at a new low price. It's the Hudson Hornet Special. It has a Hornet engine, full Hornet size, gives you full championship performance.

It gives you a silk-smooth, rock-solid, safe ride due to its low center of gravity . . . the result of Hudson's exclusive "step-down" design. It's the safest car built; and one of the most comfortable.

The Hornet Special gives you Flight-Line Styling, luxury far beyond its low price. Nothing, save the Hornet itself, can equal it. Your Hudson dealer will gladly let you drive the new Hornet Special. Call him soon.

THE **HORNETS**
THE **WASPS**
THE **JETS**

HUDSON DIVISION OF AMERICAN MOTORS

Standard trim and other specifications and accessories subject to change without notice.

"New low price for the National Champion," proclaimed a Hudson advertisement promoting its 1954 Hornet. "Winner of more stock-car events than all other makes combined," pointed out the selling copy. Shown in the ad was Frank "The Rebel" Mundy's number 7 Hudson Hornet, complete with a Confederate flag on its door. (Old Cars Collection)

1954 saw Hudson fade away as the "Big Three" heated up their stockers

By Phil Hall

The first lap of the NASCAR Grand National beach road race at Daytona Beach, Florida started on February 21, 1954. The fans in the north turn of the 4.1-mile oval waited anxiously to see what the first car would be ... a Hudson or an Olds. To their surprise, it was a Chrysler driven by Lee Petty. To their further surprise it was going too fast for the turn. The big New Yorker missed the turn, crashed through a wooden barrier and went down a small embankment.

Not discouraged, with his car not seriously damaged, Petty returned to the fray, only to have his brakes go out 19 laps later. Using large amounts of courage and downshifting, Petty motored on. Late in the race, while in contention for the lead, Petty had to stop for fuel. He forgot he had no brakes and overshot his pit by a wide margin. He had to put the car in reverse to get back to the race. This cost him nearly a minute of precious time. Tim Flock took the checkered flag in an Oldsmobile. Petty settled for second, which was not bad considering his experiences of that day. The next morning, Petty and his family were eating breakfast in a local restaurant. Then he spotted headlines in the paper indicating Flock's car had been found illegal. He was the winner at Daytona.

That Flock's car was found illegal was not a complete surprise, in view of a recent ruling by NASCAR declaring that stock car racers had to be strictly stock. At the beginning of the 1954

Hudson had all kinds of V-8-powered challengers in 1954. In this September 12, 1954 AAA 200-mile stock car race at Milwaukee, Marshall Teague (number 6) was on the pole in his trusty six-cylinder Hornet, while Jim Rathmann (number 21) was next to him in an Olds 88. Behind Rathmann was Chuck Stevenson, in a Chrysler New Yorker. He was followed by Don Miller, in another Chrysler. Teague beat them all and won the race. (Phil Hall Collection)

Marshall Teague was the center of attention after winning the September 12, 1954, AAA stock car race at Milwaukee with his Hudson Hornet. (Phil Hall Collection)

Despite more powerful challengers, Marshall Teague was able to keep the "Fabulous Hudson Hornet" ahead of the pack for one more season. (Phil Hall Collection)

The Chrysler New Yorker Deluxe boasted 235 hp from its hemi V-8. Here, Chuck Stevenson's example of this MoPar product is getting the attention of his crew, before a 1954 AAA race at Milwaukee. (Phil Hall Collection)

season, NASCAR issued the following rules: "No extra cost parts or optional equipment, which would boost the basic horsepower rating of standard off-the-line models, will be permitted. This does not apply to spark plugs or piston rings. Any automobile manufacturer's optional parts or equipment must be approved by the National Stock Car Racing Commission, before being eligible for use in Grand National Circuit competition."

In 1953, the factories had gotten carried away with optional equipment. Not only did they offer extra-cost parts to be added to their machines, but they also started listing "authorized modifications" to the cars. Dodge, Chrysler, Lincoln and Oldsmobile authorized parts made by other manufacturers, that did not carry their parts numbers, to be put on their cars. In some cases, they were blanket authorizations, like the Oldsmobile bulletin authorizing straight-through dual exhausts of any manufacture.

Although vague in many respects, the NASCAR ruling meant increased horsepower would have to come off the production line and be available to the general public. With the horsepower race in a healthy trot, the ruling "spurred it on" to a full gallop. Since the 1954 models were already on the showroom floors, little could be done. However, the edict was to have a direct effect on the 1955 models, which were in the final planning stages.

Buck Baker won the 1953 Southern 500 at Darlington International Raceway, in South Carolina. He said in an interview in *Car Life*, "I drove an Olds last season because I believed it was a better all-around car after the 'factory kit' had souped it up some. Without this kit, the Hudson will take the Olds on torque alone. That's why I predict you'll see Hudson winning more than ever in 1954, now that NASCAR has outlawed the factory modifications."

With cars reduced to their production line merits, it was indeed another Hudson year. However, it brought the stiffest competition the Hornet faced since 1951, when it wrested the crown from Oldsmobile. Though in serious financial trouble, Hudson wanted an OHV V-8 for the Hornet. It knew the days of the dated flathead six outdoing V-8s were numbered. Still, the basically 1948 chassis retained a handling edge over its more modern competitors. With help from the

NASCAR ruling and some key engine modifications, Hudson again came up with enough to keep it a step ahead.

The body on the big Hornet got a facelift, complete with a functional hood scoop. Under the hood was where the changes in the cars counted most, however. The 308-cubic-inch Hornet "Big Six" mill now had a longer duration camshaft, redesigned combustion chambers and higher compression heads. All these parts were labeled "Instant Action with Super Induction" by the advertising department. The changes were enough to produce the first increase in advertised horsepower since the Hornet's' introduction in 1951. The all-important torque curve was upped and flattened a bit. The two-barrel "308" was now rated at 160 hp, compared to 145 hp in previous seasons. The "Twin-H" version was now rated for the first time, with a 170-hp figure on the books.

Fully into the racing thing, Hudson freely advertised the Hornet as "America's Stock Car Champion" and usually had one of its drivers, Marshall Teague, Herb Thomas or Frank Mundy, on the cover of the sales brochure. Twin-H versions of the Super Wasp and compact Jet also were offered, demonstrating a direct relationship between race cars and Hudson's passenger models. Unfortunately, the public was not buying it (literally), but more on that later.

Chrysler also chose 1954 as the year to make its first production line modifications since 1951. Its 331.1-cubic-inch hemi V-8, with two-barrel carburetion, had been rated at 180 hp since its introduction. It was common knowledge that there were all kinds of "ponies" hiding in this engine. The versions in Chrysler's experimental K-310 and in the Chrysler-powered Cunningham sports-racing cars were churning over 300 hp from the mill.

The 1954 New Yorker, still on the same basic body as the 1953 model, picked up a four-barrel carburetor and other modifications. They brought the advertised horsepower to 235. This was not spectacular, but it was five more than Cadillac offered.

Marshall Teague used handling, knowledge and driving skills to beat all comers in AAA racing. Here he battles the Chrysler of Chuck Stevenson at Milwaukee, on September 12, 1954. Teague was the victor that day. (Phil Hall Collection)

Oldsmobiles got longer, wider and lower. They came complete with a "Panoramic" windshield. On the plus side, they gained 21 cubic inches (to 324.3) and 20 hp in Super 88 format. The Super 88 was now rated at 185 hp.

Buick stuffed its top-line 322 V-8 into the all-new Special-based body and revived the old Century name. The lightweight power plant produced 200 hp, when equipped with Dynaflow. It gave anyone interested in using a Buick as a late-model stock car something to work with.

Dodge found 10 more horses in its mini (241.2-cubic-inch) hemi, despite sticking with a two-barrel carburetor. Lee Petty liked to use a Dodge on the short tracks. Basically unchanged from 1953, the Dodge could be had with 114- (on the hardtop) or 119-inch (on the two-door sedan) wheelbases.

Lincoln, its game being the Carrera PanAmericana or Mexican Road Race, was still rated at 205 hp. This really did not make much difference, as the Bill Stroppe/Clay Smith-prepped machines probably could have won with 105 hp, considering all the other preparation that went into the annual fall project.

Ford and Mercury introduced new OHV V-8s. However, with 239- and 256-cubic-inches, respectively, and two-barrel carburetors, they were a mite too small. FoMoCo would have to wait another year to go stock car racing with any authority.

Plymouth and Nash stuck to six-cylinder engines exclusively. That hurt any chances to pull off upsets. The 140-hp, twin-carburetor "LeMans" version of the Nash Ambassador six was still available, but had few takers in the racing world.

The hotbed of AAA activity, the Wisconsin State Fair Speedway, was paved in 1954. It was felt that the new surface would take away much of the Hudsons' advantage in handling. Marshall Teague dispelled this notion by putting his Hornet on the pole for the last three of the four races held there. He also scored a solid win in the 200-miler that ended the season there on September 12.

Meanwhile, Herb Thomas was trying to win his third NASCAR title with his Smokey Yunick-prepped Hornet. Thomas did win the big Southern 500 at Darlington, which he also took in 1951. Thomas broke records on the way to his September 26 victory in the 250 at Langhorne, Pennsylvania. However, when the counting was over, Petty had 8,649 points for the season and Thomas had 8,366. Oldsmobile's Baker had 6,893 and "Hudsonite" Jim Rathmann notched fourth place with 6,760.

Although Hudsons were still winning, the sun had already set for the Hornet. On May 1, 1954, the Hudson Motor Car Company and the Nash-Kelvinator Corporation merged to form American Motors Corporation. The effect was not immediate, as both entities functioned separately, but it was announced that the 1955 models would all be made in Nash's facilities and that the "Step-Down" Hudsons would be discontinued. Nash was known for many things, such as room, comfort and size. Handling was not among its attributes. Although the Hornet six was to survive two more model years, the sting of the beast was gone.

On the tracks, it was another year for the "Fabulous Hudson Hornet." In NASCAR competition, 36 races were held on the Grand National circuit with 17 won by Hudsons. Up north, in AAA Contest Board competition, there were 16 stock car events and half went to Hudsons. Batting .500 or less, it was the worst year for Hudson since 1951. Oldsmobile scored 11 NASCAR wins for its best performance since 1951. Chrysler accounted for seven and Dodge had one. Splitting up eight other AAA wins were Chrysler with three, Packard (yes Packard) with three and Oldsmobile and Nash with one each.

Although still the winningest cars on the circuit, there were signs of erosion in Hudson's domination. Petty's win in the Daytona race previewed his season's performance, as he went on to win the Grand National Championship for the first time, after five years of coming close. It was the first time a non-Hudson driver took the crown since 1950.

Hudson factory driver Frank Mundy, the 1953 AAA stock car champion, had trouble getting a 1954 model from the factory. After running half the season in a Hornet, he switched to Chrysler. Mundy took the August 22 race, a 100-miler at Milwaukee, in a Hornet, before switching to a Kiekhaefer Chrysler for the Thursday 200-miler. He won the longer contest.

All was not gloom for Hudson drivers, as Teague won five AAA events and reclaimed the championship he won in 1952. Hudson racing people kept their hopes alive as long as possible. In a letter, dated October 13, 1954, Tom Rhoades, Hudson director of public relations and the driving force behind the factory's involvement in racing, consoled Thomas on his loss of the title. He said, "You can rest assured that you will be in next year's picture ... as far as we are concerned; so until we find out where we stand, sit quiet for the moment." However, the Nash-Hornet was later tested and found to be non-competitive, even with the Packard V-8 power plant that American Motors Corporation bought to get in the V-8 game.

As was tradition, Lincoln carried off the Carrera PanAmericana for the third straight year. Dodge, not having much luck on the racetracks, garnered some publicity with speed runs at Bonneville, Utah in its 1954 models.

The year 1954 was the last for the Hornet and the last before the horsepower race and the factory invasion exploded wide open in 1955.

Tim Flock (in light-colored car on inside) got a new Hudson Hornet coupe to race in 1954. Jim Rathman, on the other hand, had to make do with his 1953 model (dark-colored car on the outside). This was understandable, as Hudson was having financial problems and poised to merge with Nash to form American Motors Corporation. (Jack Miller Collection)

GM and Chrysler led factory stocks in 1955 NASCAR racing season

By Phil Hall

The 1955 National Association for Stock Car Auto Racing (NASCAR) Grand National season opened on February 6 of that year at the West Palm Beach, Florida speedway.

Late in 1954, two-time Grand National champion Herb Thomas had been promised continued factory support and a new Hudson, but they never came. The result was that Thomas, and other Hudson stalwarts, stayed with the 1954 models. Dick Rathmann won the pole in his Hornet and Thomas came back to take the win, leading three other drivers who were on the same lap. Jack Choquette was second in a Hornet. Buck Baker took third in an Oldsmobile and Rathmann settled for fourth. That was a sweep of three of the top four positions for Hudson. There

This is the front row of the 1955 Southern 500 at Darlington. On the pole is Glenn "Fireball" Roberts in the 1955 Buick Century that he won at Daytona with, only to be disqualified. Buck Baker is in the middle with his 1955 Century, while "Speedy" Thompson is on the outside with the 1954 Oldsmobile Baker used much of the season. Baker fared the best of the trio with a sixth-place finish. Thompson was sidelined with vapor lock and placed 45th. Roberts was involved in an accident and was credited with 66th place in the 69-car field (Phil Hall Collection)

were only three 1955 models in the field, two Oldsmobiles and a Chrysler.

The win was the 79th Grand National triumph for Hudson and the last in a fabulous string that started in 1951. Though Hudsons still raced in national championship events throughout the 1955 season (most of them were 1953 and 1954 models), their reign as the "king" of stock car racing ended on February 6, 1955. No longer could their handling make up for the lack of horses under the hood.

Starting In 1954, NASCAR mandated that increased horsepower would have to come off the production line and not off the options list. That is exactly what happened in 1955, with increased power being advertised for all makes that had even a remote chance of becoming a race car. The horsepower race was at full gallop.

The biggest surprise out of Detroit was the Chrysler 300, with an unheard of 300 hp unleashed from a hardtop model that looked like a cross between a New Yorker and an Imperial. When the Chrysler hemi was introduced, in 1951, it took little time to realize that there were stables for a lot more than the 180 advertised horses in the bores of the big brute. Briggs Cunningham chose Chrysler power for his Cunninghams. They easily churned out more than 300 hp from the 331 cubes. An experimental Chrysler K-310 was said to produce that many horses. The Chrysler hemi got a two-barrel "annex" to its initial two-barrel carburetor. The new four-barrel unit produced an advertised 235 hp in the 1954 model. The 300 produced its advertised 300 hp at 5200 rpm. The compression ratio went up a point from 7.5 to 8.5 to 1 and other alterations took advantage of the hemi's breathing capabilities. Built on the 126-inch wheelbase New Yorker chassis, the 300 was no small car. It covered 218.8 inches end to end, with a width of 79.1 inches. It weighed over 4,400 pounds.

Another notable addition to the horsepower race was the new Chevrolet "Turbofire" V-8. Checking in at 265 cubes and 162 hp, it was no immediate threat to the stock car racing world, until the "Plus-Power" package was added. That option produced an advertised 180 hp. A four-barrel carburetor and dual exhausts helped account for the added gusto. Also, Chevrolet introduced an all-new body that lowered the center of gravity by several inches.

Frank "Rebel" Mundy keeps his number 30 Chrysler 300 ahead of Marshall Teague's number 6 Chevy, Jim Murray's number 46 Buick and Les Snow's number 45 Buick in the August 21, 1955 AAA 100-mile stock car race at Milwaukee. Teague won. (Phil Hall Collection)

Tim Flock's Chrysler 300 (number 16), was NASCAR Grand National champ in 1955. Here he is on his way to third place in the 1955 Southern 500 at Darlington. Following is Junior Johnson in the 1955 Olds (number 55). They are both about to pass Larry Flynn's 1955 Ford (number 96). Johnson finished 36th and Flynn brought his FoMoCo in fifth. (Phil Hall Collection)

Also unveiling V-8s for the first time were Plymouth and Pontiac. While neither shook up the checkered flag set in 1955, both had potential that would be used for their entrance to racing in the next year or so. Plymouth, like Chevrolet, also received an all-new body in 1955. Its engineers seemed preoccupied with making it the longest, widest and lowest car in the low-price field. Under the hood was the "Hy-Fire" V-8, of 277 cubic inches. It featured polyspherical cylinder heads rather than hemispherical heads used on the Dodge, DeSoto and Chrysler V-8s produced up to that time. The Hy-Fire engine fired out 167 hp (advertised) in its initial version. Pontiac got a longer version of the all-new Chevrolet body for 1955, plus a new "Strato Streak" V-8. (Detroit was never at a loss for dramatic engine names.) The Pontiac's power plant, which was considerably heavier than the Chevrolet mill, pumped 180 hp from 287.2 cubic inches.

Makes that had been used in late-model competition in previous seasons were not left out when added power was being passed out. Oldsmobile, Buick and Dodge all picked up hefty horsepower increases. The 324.3-cubic-inch Super 88 Olds power plant was rated at 202 hp for 1955. It was up 17 from the top 1954 figure. The top 1954 rating for Buick was 200 hp from its vertical-valve 322-cubic-inch V-8. For 1955 the rating climbed to 236 hp and the compression ratio went from 8.5: 1 up to 9.0:1. Dodge got Plymouth's larger body for 1955 and its 241.2-cubic-inch mini-hemi was inflated to 270 cubic inches. A midyear version, with a four-barrel carburetor, dual exhaust and special manifolding, was rated at 193 hp. It was available on all models.

Ford and Mercury also got more power, but, like Plymouth and Pontiac, didn't come in to their own in racing until after 1955. The Thunderbird created reams of publicity for Ford and the top version of its 292-cubic-inch engine put out 198 hp. Later, high-performance packages would boost this considerably. The Mercury also used the "292" in 1955.

The first true indication of the new models' performances came at the 1955 Speed Weeks at Daytona Beach in February. The crowds were way up from previous years, as were the number of factory personnel. Perennial winner Joe Littlejohn drove a 1955 Cadillac to another victory, this time in the standing-start mile. His average speed of 80.428 mph was over two mph faster than the second-place car. However, the second-place car was the surprise of the day. It was a 1955 Chevy with the power pack. It was driven by Sheriff Jack Trapscott. Another Chevy was third, a Buick Century was fourth and the first Chrysler 300 came in fifth. That was the last event a 300 entered that it did not win. Warren Koeschling, an Eastern Airlines pilot, averaged 127.580 mph in the flying-mile. Brewster Shaw was second at 126.542 mph. The third place car, a Cadillac, just got above the 120 mph mark.

The big contest was the 160-mile NASCAR Grand National on the 4.1-mile beach-road course. Glenn "Fireball" Roberts ran away with the race in his number M-1 1955 Buick Century. He had up to a 30-second lead at times. In a post race tear down the Buick was found to have shortened push rods. The victory was awarded to Tim Flock, in a 300. Ironically, Flock finished first in the 1954 version of the race, only to be disqualified for illegal equipment.

Lee Petty finished second making a one, two sweep for Chrysler. Ray Duhigg took third in a Buick, followed by three 1955 Oldsmobiles.

Taking a page from Hudson, Chrysler was quick to advertise its Daytona victories. Ads saying "The car that swept Daytona" appeared everywhere. Chrysler had clearly taken the upper hand for the 1955 season. It let the world and its competitors know it. Noteworthy in the finish of the Daytona race was that the first Hudson to cross the line was Choquette's 12th place 1954 Hornet. Rathmann was in a 1955 Olds and Thomas in a 1955 Packard. In other early NASCAR Grand National races Chrysler kept up its dominance, but not all with the 300. Petty drove his 1954 model to three victories in the first 10 races and 300s took that many. Olds took a pair and Chevy got its first Grand National flag.

Herb Thomas was looking for a suitable replacement for the Hornet and settled on the Buick Century. On May 6, at Charlotte, North Carolina, he was battling for the lead. His car hit a rut and flipped four times, ejecting Thomas in the process. He received a broken leg and bruises, which took him out of competition for a while. He was also out of the point race. The accident set the stage for one of the more dramatic races of the year.

Some of the big names and their cars in NASCAR were Junior Johnson (Oldsmobile), Tim Flock (Chrysler), Jim Paschal (Oldsmobile), Buck Baker (Oldsmobile), Petty (Chrysler); and Bob Welborn (Chevrolet). Thomas returned to action on August 7 in the 100-miler at Winston-

Salem, North Carolina. He was back at the wheel of his old Hudson. Though he qualified well, a bad clutch gave him 21st place in the 22-car field. He drove a Chevrolet in the 100-miler at Memphis, Tennessee the next week. He finished an uncompetitive 14th. Back in a Buick; he won the 100-miler at Raleigh, North Carolina on August 20, but the big one was ahead at the Southern 500 in Darlington, South Carolina. He had two victories in the first five races on the 1.5-mile superspeedway and said he wanted a third.

For five hours, 25 minutes and 25 seconds, Thomas wheeled his power pack Chevy around the track on that hot, sticky day. When it was over, he got his wish. He finished better than a lap up on Jim Reed, who was also in a Chevrolet. Tim Flock ran third in a 300, interrupting a Chevrolet sweep of the top four positions.

It was Chevrolet's finest four performances to date in NASCAR, but only a hint of things to come. When it was over, 1955 went down as a Chrysler year in NASCAR. Tim Flock won the championship over Baker, Petty, Welborn, and Thomas. In the victory tally, Chrysler took 27 wins in 45 events. Oldsmobile accounted for 10 wins. Ford, Chevrolet and Buick took two wins each. Hudson and Dodge each scored one victory.

Up north in America Automobile Association Contest Board (AAA) stock car racing, the story was much the same. Chrysler 300s won 10 of 13 events on the schedule. Chevrolet took a pair. Mercury won the season finale with Jack McGrath at the wheel. Jim Rathmann scored one of the Chevrolet victories. Marshall Teague, the 1954 champion and the most involved person in Hudson's racing program, put his number six on a Chevrolet. Teague won a 100-miler at Milwaukee. Frank Mundy won the first five races on the schedule and seven of the first eight in his Chrysler 300. His string was broken by Norm Nelson in another 300. In all, Mundy took eight wins on his way to a runaway victory in the point standings. Mundy also won the 1953 AAA title.

The rash of Chrysler 300 victories in 1955 were no accident. Carl Kiekhaefer, whose Kiekhaefer Corporation made Mercury outboard motors, entered three cars in both NASCAR and AAA competition. They accounted for most of the wins. Tim and Fonty Flock and Speedy Thompson handled the NASCAR chores, while Mundy, Nelson and Tony Bettenhausen were the AAA entrants.

Carl Kiekhaefer had been building race cars for several years, starting with entrants in the Carrera PanAmericana. He knew how to set up a car. The 300s were set up to race in his Wisconsin factory and came to the track ready to race. "Our two national championships won during 1955 were not gained by accident or luck," Kiekhaefer said in an article in *Speed Age*. "Our cars quickly established a reputation of being properly set up for competition." By set up, he meant prepared, not illegally hopped-up. His cars were inspected more than any on the stock car racing circuits. They were never found to be in violation of the rules.

Though the factories were involved, most of the entries in 1955 were by independents. They built the cars themselves, using all the technology available from the factory. However, on October 9, 1955, Thompson drove a Ford to victory at Memphis. It was the brand's first win since 1950. It was no ordinary Ford, but a 1956 model with a Thunderbird engine. Marvin Panch was second in another 1956 Ford. They were both part of the Ford factory team, which was by no means independent. Their appearance was only the beginning of the factory era, which covered the 1956 season and the first half of the 1957 season.

Jack McGrath, in a 1955 model (number 24) gave Mercury its sole win in national stock car racing. It came at Milwaukee in the 200-mile AAA race on September 18. Battling side-by-side are Wait Faulkner in a 1955 Merc (number 25) and Marshall Teague in a 1955 Chevy (number 6). (Phil Hall Collection)

Wisconsin State Fair 1955 AAA race attracted stellar lineup

By Al Krause

The drawing power of the late-model stock cars on the one-mile paved track at Wisconsin State Fair Park was underscored, on Sunday, August 21, 1955, as Marshall Teague of Daytona Beach, Florida, guided his 1955 Chevrolet to victory in the 100-mile national championship test. It was the first of three races held during the 1955 annual state fair.

A total of 10 Indianapolis 500 drivers were among the 40 starters in 11 different makes of American cars. Future Indy winners included Pat Flaherty (1956), Jimmy Bryan (1958), and Jim Rathmann (1960). Other "500" favorites in the race included Teague, Jack McGrath, Walt Faulkner, Jimmy Davies, Jimmy Reece, and George Lynch.

The good mix of "factory iron," with cars entered by auto dealers and private citizens with nominal factory backing, pleased Promotor Tom Marchese mightily. Surprisingly, Buick led the

Tony Bettenhausen in a 1955 Chrysler 300 (number 99) makes a run for the lead at the start of the August 21, 1955, one-hundred-mile AAA stock car race at Wisconsin State Fair Park. He is passing his 1955 Chrysler 300 teammates, Frank Mundy (the fastest qualifier) and Norm Nelson. Just behind Nelson is Jack McGrath's 1955 Mercury (number 25) stock car. (Al Krause collection).

Action in the north turn in the 100-mile AAA stock car race at State Fair Park involves Frank Burany's 1955 Chevy (number 5) and Jim RathMann's 1955 Chevy (number 9). Behind Rathmann is Jim Reece in another 1955 Chevy (number 8). (Al Krause Collection)

Glenn Barnhart, of Detroit (1953 Hudson) blows a tire. He finished 31st and earned $20.

Jack McGrath, of Pasadena, California, and his 1955 Mercury Monterey, prior to the 100-mile AAA stock car race at State Fair Park in Milwaukee. This car was entered by the Milwaukee Mercury Dealers Association. McGrath was forced out of the July 17 contest, after his car tangled with several others in a minor crash. McGrath had vast racing experience, having driven big cars at Indianapolis. He had been a consistent scorer in AAA championships for several years. He was the first driver to exceed 140 mph at Indianapolis Motor Speedway and held numerous track records there. (Al Krause Collection)

Marshall Teague made the switch from a Hudson to a 1955 Chevrolet 150 two-door sedan for the 1955 AAA stock car season. It paid off with a win at the 100-miler on August 21, 1955 at Milwaukee State Fair Park. Teague's race car was finished in pale blue, with a white top. Chuck Johnson, a sports writer for The Milwaukee Journal, can be seen with dark sunglasses and his arms folded, in front of a Ford pickup truck. Hank Sayrs, a sports writer for The Milwaukee Sentinel, is at the extreme left. (Al Krause Collection)

Tony Bettenhausen (left) and Mauri Rose talk racing at State Fair Park.

way with nine cars in the race, followed by Chevrolet with seven, and Oldsmobile with five. There were four each for Chrysler, Mercury, and Hudson; three for Packard; and one each for Nash, Plymouth, Dodge, and Kaiser.

Teague's victory was the first for the new Chevrolet V-8 engine here. It would be the fourth and final win for the pudgy Floridian at Milwaukee. (The race was also the last 100-miler at Milwaukee, until July 7, 1985, when Bobby Schacht won the 100-miler sanctioned by Sal Tovella's International Racing Association.) The 1955 race would also be among the last carrying the sanction of the American Automobile Association's Contest Board, which earlier had voted to end its ties with all racing events. The board's decision was undoubtedly influenced by the two-car crash that resulted in the death of 83 spectators in the sports car road race at Le Mans, France.

Frank Mundy of Atlanta, Georgia, driving one of three Chrysler 300s entered by Outboard Marine's Carl Kiekhaefer, led the field of 46 cars in time trials. It posted a new one-mile qualifying mark of 43.169 seconds (83.393 mph). Teague kept the streak alive by winning the race in one hour, 18 minutes, .048 seconds, averaging a record 76.23 mph. Keep in mind that these were stock cars, complete with body trim, bumpers, and all the other "goodies" most cars had right off the showroom floor.

Six lead changes in the race were divided equally among Mundy, McGrath, and, of course, Teague. Mundy's tenure was from laps one through three and from 45 to 49 miles. Then he pitted for two right side tires. McGrath led from the fourth through the 44th mile and again from the 87th through 96th mile. Teague led from the 49th mile. He had built up a 12-second lead by the 86th mile. At the unfurling of the last of three yellow flags, caused by Bill Rexford's car losing a wheel at

Marshall Teague, of Daytona Beach, Florida, and his "hardware" for winning the August 21, 1955, AAA 100-mile stock car race.

81 miles, the field slowed to allow the cleanup crew to police the track. At this point, Teague's mount began to slow imperceptibly, allowing McGrath to take the lead at 87 miles. The malfunction in Teague's engine, termed by some as "vapor lock," cleared up shortly after the green flag came out again. Teague again took the lead at 96 miles. He held onto it until the end. His margin of victory was less than four seconds.

Teague and McGrath were the only starters who did not have to stop for tire changes. They were running on tires specially built for the annual 12-hour Sebring (Florida) endurance test some five months earlier. Some of the tires, made of the newer, more wear-resistant compounds, were also used in the 24-hour run at LeMans. Since the special tires did not fit the conventional wheels, Teague and Mercury boss Bill Stroppe built their own wheels, using standard measurements. When Mercury Outboard boss Kiekhaefer heard about the tires, he wanted some for his cars. But none were available. After threatening to pull his cars out of the race, he thought about it and let them start.

A hot Hudson Hornet had paced an AAA race at Milwaukee in 1954, but the four Hudsons entered in the August 21, 1955 contest were not as successful in stock car racing as the earlier Hornets. (Phil Hall Collection)

105

Horsepower race revved up in 1956 as factories hit tracks full-bore

By Phil Hall

Since it was formally organized in 1948, late-model stock car racing had been trying to attract the attention of Detroit. What could be better for the sport than to have the factories openly testing their products against one another on the race tracks of America?

The answer to that question was found in 1956, and the first half of 1957, because factory teams dominated National Association for Stock Car Auto Racing (NASCAR) and United States Auto Club (USAC) stock events. When the factories left the sport in mid-1957, there were few unhappy people, except those who were on the factory payrolls. The competition had gotten too serious. Horsepower and skill no longer determined the winners. The biggest bankroll did. There were problems even determining winners. Advertisements and press releases from many factories claimed their cars were winners in various events. This left the general public believing that no one lost any major events.

The days of the "factory wars" were not without benefit to the sport of national championship stock car racing. The crowds at the races increased dramatically, thanks to greatly increased publicity. Stock car drivers were also elevated in public esteem. In some areas, they were more famous than drivers who raced at Indy.

With the Chrysler 300s gone, the newly formed USAC circuit was an open game for 1956. Battling at the start of this July 15, 1956 race at Milwaukee, Wisconsin are Marshall Teague's Chevrolet (number 6) and Johnny Mantz's Ford (number 8). Behind them is eventual winner Troy Ruttman, in the number 16 Mercury. (Phil Hall Collection)

In June 1957, the Automobile Manufacturers Association issued a proclamation banning all factory participation in the sport. However, the kingdom of stock car racing did not fall. The crowds did not fade away and the drivers did not revert to the image of maniacs wearing helmets. Stock car racing remained a "big league" sport, as it does to this very day.

Let's get back to just before those two furious years of 1956 and 1957, to begin our story. In 1955, all the automakers whose cars were used in racing announced hefty horsepower increases. Still, they were knocked off their collective feet when Chrysler introduced its 300 with 300 hp. That output was unheard of up to that time in a production automobile. Naturally, the Chrysler 300s dominated both NASCAR and American Automobile Association contest board (AAA) events in 1955. Chrysler 300 driver Tim Flock took the NASCAR title and Frank Mundy did the same in AAA.

Four marques have at it in a September 16, 1956, USAC race. They include Les Snow's number 2 Chevy, Jim Reece's number 28 Ford, Whitey Johnson's number 75 Packard and Sam Hanks' number 15 Mercury. (Phil Hall Collection)

Both Flock and Mundy drove cars prepared by Wisconsin industrialist and sportsman Carl Kiekhaefer, whose company produced Mercury outboard motors. The Kiekhaefer Chryslers became the class of the sport and their meticulous preparation by the "Kiekhaefer Krew," (in a factory) was a new dimension in the sport. Until this time, independent car owners built their machines in garages (if they were lucky) or sometimes in old barns and sheds. Things were about to change, however.

In mid-1955 Chevrolet entered a 1956 Chevrolet in the Pikes Peak hill climb. In late 1955, Ford entered a factory team, headed by former Indy winner Pete DePaolo, in a few Grand National races. The Fords came away with two victories. Mercury arranged with California builder Bill Stroppe to prepare its race cars for the 1956 season. Chevrolet obtained the services of Indy winner Mauri Rose to head its racing program. Later in 1956, Plymouth and Dodge signed former midget great Ronnie Householder as their top racing man. Pontiac Division chief Semon "Bunky" Knudsen saw racing as a way to improve Pontiac's image and inked a contract with Indiana car builder Ray Nichols, to make Pontiac race cars.

Late-model stock car builders looked over the specifications when the new models came out each fall, to see which cars had the best possibilities for racing conversions. With the factories building the cars and hiring drivers, the specs suddenly lost significance. No matter how much potential a model had, without factory help there was little chance of it being a winner. The factories enjoyed an added benefit from racing. In the past, the racers took models that had potential, like the Olds 88 or Hudson Hornet, and made race cars out of them. Now the factories were making racers, then making a model of it to sell. For example, Chrysler followed its 1955 C300 with the 1956 Chrysler 300B. The company then added similar special models to its Plymouth, Dodge and DeSoto lines. The 1956 version of the Chrysler 300 boasted 340 hp. The hemi engine also got its first displacement boost since its introduction. It went from 331 to 354 cubic inches.

Plymouth's midyear special was the Fury. It was essentially a Belvedere two-door hardtop with special trim that included a gold anodized side spear. A 303-cubic-inch V-8, the largest in the line, churned out 240 hp. Dodge offered the D-500 high-performance option on Custom Royal two-door hardtops, convertibles and lowly Coronet two-door sedans. Other than a pair of crossed flags and the 500 symbol on the exterior, the differences were all under the hood. From 315 cubic inches came 260 hp. Though not destined for racetracks (except to pace the Indianapolis 500 that year), DeSoto offered its Adventurer as a midyear 1956 offering. The displacement went from 330.4 to 341.4 cubic inches and the advertised horsepower was 320. Note that all the horsepower ratings and engine sizes in the Chrysler Corporation lineup followed a strict pecking order. Plymouth had the smallest and Chrysler the largest. Except for the Dodge D-500 Coronet sedan, all special models were additions to top-of-the-line models.

One other change the 1956 season established was the trend to low-price sedans as the best race cars. Since 1949, medium-price cars were the predominant force in race cars. Oldsmobiles, Hudsons, Chryslers, Buicks and even Packards, were the choices of winners. Oval track racing takes more than power to win. The faster you go, the more important handling is. The balanced combination of a powerful (but not overly-powerful) engine in a light chassis could be a winner, as Chevrolet proved in 1955.

In 1956 and 1957, low- and low-medium price sedans took over as the big winners in racing. Dropouts for 1956 included Oldsmobile and Buick. Chrysler would last out the season, before it disappeared from competition. Ford and Mercury did not introduce special performance models for 1956, but did increase the size of their top engines. Ford used the 312-cubic-inch Thunderbird "Y-8" with a rating of 225 hp. Mercury started the year with the same engine, but a midyear M-260 engine, with dual four-barrel carburetors, produced 260 advertised horses. Ford also got a copy of this motor. Chevrolet went the dual four-barrel route and got 225 hp from its "small-block" 265-cubic-inch V-8. Pontiac did the same. It aroused 285 hp from its 316.6-cubic-inch V-8, which had grown in just its second year of existence.

One model that was thought to have great late-model potential was the Studebaker Hawk. The first major facelift on the Lowey-designed coupes had a Packard 352-cubic-inch V-8 with 275 hp stuffed under the hood. (Packard had startled the industry in 1956 with a 10.0:1 compression ratio in the Caribbean. It came with two four-barrel carburetors and was rated at 310 hp from a hefty 374-cubic-inch block.) The Studebaker-Packard engines looked good on paper, but turned out to be something else on the test track. The Packard engine made the Golden Hawk nose-heavy and anything but a race car. Of course, the company was having all kinds of financial difficulties. The last thing it wanted do was invest hundreds of thousands of dollars to back a stock car team.

Going into the 1956 season, NASCAR faced a problem. The demand for its Grand National races exceeded the number they could reasonably supply. With a schedule that covered the country from coast to coast, only a certain number of tracks could be accommodated in a season, with only one or two races available per track. Before the season began, NASCAR and the Society of Auto Sports, Fellowship and Education (SAFE) completed a merger where the latter would become part of the former. SAFE officers would be worked into the NASCAR structure. The Midwest-based SAFE sanctioning body combined its stars and tracks with those of NASCAR. One direct result of this merger was formation of a National Convertible Championship Division. The cars were to be late-models, like those in Grand National racing, but with their tops open so the fans could see drivers at work. The idea was supposed to combine the popularity of late-model stock cars with the successful elements of open cockpit racing.

Another move by NASCAR, at roughly the same time, was designed to keep the factories in line. While NASCAR President Bill France welcomed the factories, he wanted to establish early in the season who was boss. On December 11, 1955, a 1956 Grand National race was held. Ford driver Joe Weatherly finished first, Jim Reed placed second, and Herb Thomas ran third. Weatherly celebrated the victory. Two days later, both he and Reed were disqualified for illegal modifications to their engines. Thomas was declared the winner.

Furthermore, NASCAR listed maximum displacements for the various makes of cars, based on their new model announcement figures. If a more powerful version came along, it would have to be announced 90 days before its first use in competition. Also, it had to be advertised at least 30 days before its first race. This rule created a rash of midyear announcements of new performance-oriented models and engines. This practice then continued, every year, through the 1960s.

The 1956 season for the Grand National stockers began in late 1955 with little change. The Kiekhaefer Chryslers, still 1955 models, remained the "class act" of the field, despite the fact there were several other brands of 1956 cars entered. Defending champion Tim Flock won the opener, on November 13, 1955, at Hickory, North Carolina. He was driving a 1955 Chrysler 300.

His brother, Fonty, came back to best him in the second race, at Charlotte, North Carolina, on November 20. He was also in a 1955 Chrysler 300.

With the factories' all-out involvement in racing, Daytona Speed Weeks took on new importance. The annual two week February assault on the sands was a good chance for automakers to score a victory they could advertise in time for the start of the spring selling season. Attendance records, both from the fans and factories, were set in the 1956 edition of Speed Weeks, but the rough beach did not smooth out until the very end of the schedule. As a result, two weeks worth of activities were crammed into two days.

Tim Flock drove a brand new Chrysler 300-B to a new flying-mile mark of 139.373 mph. Danny Eames (part of the Dodge team that set a group of records at the Bonneville Salt Flats in Utah) blasted his Dodge D-500 to acceleration honors, averaging 81.762 for the standing-start mile. Thunderbirds and Corvettes put on their show, but that's a different story that's out of the realm of this section on stock racing cars.

In the 160-mile beach-road Grand National, Tim Flock came back with his 300-B to take the win over Billy Myers' Mercury. Curtis Turner won the first of the new convertible races. He drove a Ford to victory over the Ford of "Fireball" Roberts and the Chevy of Herb Thomas. With questions as to the success of the new USAC stock circuit (USAC replaced AAA as a sanctioning body), Carl Kiekhaefer decided to concentrate his Chrysler attack on NASCAR Grand National racing in 1956. He also entered the new convertible division. Defending AAA champ Frank Mundy was selected to drive in that circuit. A small fleet of Kiekhaefer-backed Dodge convertibles was built for that purpose.

Tim Flock left Kiekhaefer after a disagreement over policies. After a short period of inactivity, Flock joined up with Bill Stroppe and Mercury. Not hurting for good drivers, Buck Baker joined Speedy Thompson on the "Kiekhaefer Krew" and the combo helped account for an unbelievable string of 16 straight Grand National wins. Also bordering on the unbelievable was that Curtis Turner went on to score 22 wins in the 1956 convertible series. However, he missed on the title, which was taken by Chevy driver Bob Welborn.

Baker won the Grand National title in 1956. Thomas finished second, despite being injured in a late-season crash. The Kiekhaefer Chryslers won 22 of 56 Grand Nationals to easily top the list. Ford's factory efforts netted 14 flags. Dodges accounted for 11 victories. Mercury had five wins, Chevrolet had three and Oldsmobile had one. Turner won the big NASCAR race of the year, the Southern 500 at Darlington, South Carolina, driving a Ford.

Chevrolets were more successful in the new USAC circuit. In 19 events, Chevys took 11, including the first six events on the schedule. Marshall Teague and Les Snow divided Chevy honors for wins, with three each. Troy Ruttman was the other three-race winner, taking one each in a Ford, a Chevy and a Mercury. Ford drivers captured four events, as did Mercury pilots. Driver Johnny Mantz entered nine USAC events. He won just two of them, but his consistently high finishes gave him the driver championship with 1,838 points to 1,662 for Marshall Teague. Les Snow finished third. The Mercury team seemed to do best at Milwaukee, where three of its four victories came. Big Car drivers Ruttman, Sam Hanks and Jimmy Bryan knew the Milwaukee Mile well and used their experience to each score a win there for Bill Stroppe's Mercury team. For USAC's initial year, things did not go as badly as some predicted, but it had a long way to go to match NASCAR.

At Soldier Field, Bill Poor managed to keep his relatively clean 1956 Chevrolet (number 711) ahead of an unidentified Dodge ragtop driver. Curtis Turner won this 500-lap race in a Ford Sunliner. (Phil Hall Collection)

Factory stockers tamed down by NASCAR's ruling hand

By Phil Hall

By the time 1957 model-year announcements started, it was an open secret that the hot models would be held back from introduction. The idea was not to tip off competitors, who might introduce a better car before NASCAR's 90-day limit. About the only early-year surprise was Chevrolet's fuel-injection. It was available for both the Corvette and Chevrolet. With its enlarged 283-cubic-inch engine, the fuel-injected Chevy V-8 produced a heavily advertised 283 hp. That was one horsepower per cubic inch.

The midyear parade began and Chrysler was back at it with the Plymouth Fury, Dodge D-500, Dodge D-500-1, DeSoto Adventurer, and Chrysler 300-C. All were under all-new, finned bodies. All were longer, wider and lower and had more power under the hood. The Fury was good for 290 hp from 318 cubic inches (thanks to dual four-barrel carburetors). This option, called the V-800, was also available on other models. Dodge's D-500 and D-500-1 equipment remained optional and available on all models. From 325 cubic inches came 285 hp on the

Pontiacs had some surprises to offer at the 1957 Daytona Speed Weeks. Cotton Owens wheeled this Tri-Power job to victory in the 150-mile Grand National beach-road race. (Phil Hall Collection)

Troy Ruttman, number 98, and Ralph Moody, number 22, cruise in the hot ex-factory NASCAR team racers at USAC's Milwaukee track. Ford won two of six USAC races in 1957, with Mercury claiming the other four. (Phil Hall Collection)

D-500 (with a single four-barrel) and 310 hp on the D-500-1 (with dual four-barrels). There also was the super-rare D-501 with the Chrysler hemi 354 at 340 hp installed in a few cars. DeSoto's top-line Adventurer had dual four-barrels and 345 hp from 345 cubic inches. The shocker was the 300-C. It was up to 392 cubic inches and the powerful hemi emitted 375 hp. An optional version was good for 390 hp. That was quite a lot of "ponies" for 1957.

Ford and Mercury again chose to stay away from exterior gingerbread, but offered the goodies under the hood. Both cars had all-new bodies. The Ford "312" sprouted a supercharger that prompted 300 hp, while an unblown version was good for 285 hp. Mercurys got 368 cubes and extracted 335 hp from them with a pair of four-throat carburetors. Pontiac went a different route. The Tri-Power option on its "347" V-8 was good for 317 advertised horses. For those not in the know, Tri-Power meant triple two-barrel carburetors. Oldsmobile, not happy at being frozen (or burned) out of a game it helped invent, came back in 1957 with its J-2 option. J-2 also stood for triple-two barrels and up to 312 horses. Even though they were not racing, American Motors and Studebaker-Packard also came up with a couple of interesting high performance models of their own. They were designed just to compete in the horsepower sales race. From AMC came the Rambler Rebel, a silver four-door hardtop. It had a gold spear down the side and other goodies. The 327-cube Nash-Hudson engine was installed. Rambler also introduced its own 250-cubic-inch V-8 at the beginning of the model year. In stock form, the Rebel produced 255 hp. This made this compact car quite fast. A fuel-injected version was promised and rated at 288 hp, but apparently never made it to volume production. With Packard V-8 engine production suspended, Studebaker had to look for a new way to make its Hawks sensational. The company went to a supercharger to keep the advertised rating at 275 hp, the same as when the Golden Hawk used the 352-cubic-inch Packard mill in 1956.

Despite all his success, Carl Kiekhaefer quit fielding race teams before the end of the 1956 season. He cited the increased competition from the factory teams, rules problems, and the expenses of fielding cars in both the Grand National and convertible circuits. This left the door

Fireball Roberts pushes a 300 hp supercharged 1957 Ford through a turn. After the supercharged "312s" were run out of NASCAR by midyear rule changes, they were shipped to USAC. Ralph Moody used this Ford to win three USAC races at Milwaukee that year. (Courtesy NASCAR photo via Phil Hall Collection)

Paul Goldsmith drove Smokey Yunick's fuel-injected 1957 Chevrolet 210 two-door hardtop in the February 17, 1957, NASCAR 160-mile Grand National race on the Daytona beach-road course. Goldsmith was leading with a 25-second advantage and had eight laps to go when his engine expired. He placed 24th. (Phil Hall Collection)

open for Chrysler's factory-backed efforts to get into gear. A team of factory-backed Plymouths was ready for 1957.

Lee Petty, who drove Chrysler products from the first year of NASCAR racing on, was more or less left out in the cold by the Chrysler move, but not for long. Oldsmobile enticed him with their J-2 setup. Petty agreed to campaign Oldsmobiles in 1957. This seemed ironic. It was Petty and his pesky Plymouth sixes that were a thorn in the side of Oldsmobile in the early 1950s.

Everything pointed to Daytona. The 1957 Speed Weeks at Daytona Beach would be the speed trials to end all speed trials. The factory cars were fully in command and swept all the major events. The publicity personnel were there to echo every glowing detail for their respective makes ... and to overlook every defeat. Six factory teams were entered: Ford, Mercury, Chevrolet, Pontiac, Oldsmobile and Plymouth. Missing were the big white cars of Carl Kiekhaefer.

The teams took over garages in the area and came with armies of personnel to make sure they had everything possible going for them. There was a little something for almost everyone, as long as they were connected with a factory team. The independents were completely shut out of contention. Chevrolet garnered the most points in all events. Tim Flock drove a Mercury to victory in the 150-mile convertible race. Cotton Owens surprised many with his win for Pontiac in the Grand National 150-miler. After a Pontiac was disqualified, a Chrysler 300-C took the flying-mile competition, but another Pontiac was close behind. A second Chrysler 300-C grabbed acceleration honors.

Things were not all glory for the factories, however. General Motors told its divisions to cut back on the performance advertising for 1957. This hurt Chevrolet, which was promoted as "The Hot One" in previous seasons. Pontiac, which had a story to tell of newly-found muscles, was also impacted by the decision.

After a dismal Daytona performance, Plymouth ordered its forces cut. A Dodge team never materialized. Promoters were complaining that the lack of the big Chryslers left their races looking like "cheap used car lots." Stock car racing was boiling down to Chevy versus Ford battles. Furthermore, Chevy's fuel-injection and Ford superchargers were hard to come by (and even harder to set up) without factory help. The race car fields were dwindling and independents fell by the wayside. Drivers and teams began to fight. Before too long, dollar competition set into the sport. Drivers hopped to the teams offering the biggest bucks. This was a change that the corporate accountants did not plan for or care for. The beginning of the end came on April 23, 1957, when a NASCAR technical bulletin was issued prompting additional factory pullouts from NASCAR.

USAC stock car racing was somewhat less affected by the factory pullouts. Ford was king in the USAC competition. Ford driver Ralph Moody won all three high-points races held in Milwaukee, Wisconsin. However, Jerry Unser, of Pikes Peak fame, took the 1957 USAC title.

The sport of stock car racing had come of age. NASCAR's ruling hand tamed the abuses of the factory teams and drivers. If the factories had gotten into the sport it in its infancy, the factory pullout might have killed it. However, this was not the case. National championship stock car racing did some regrouping in 1957, but it was to come back stronger than ever. A new era was ahead, that of the superspeedway. The sport would be ready for it. Stock car racing had a definite influence on production line cars and it still has today. The romance between Detroit and stock car racing has been hot, cold and at times, secret, but it has never died. It was the years of 1948 through 1957 that established the sport. Come what may, stock car racing is here to stay.

Fords, Chevrolets, Mercurys and Pontiacs spiced the field for the start of the August 22, 1957, USAC stock car race at the Wisconsin State Fair Speedway. Ralph Moody, in the number 22 Ford, started on the pole. He won the event, just as he won two other races held on the same one-mile oval that year. (Phil Hall Collection)

Stamina-testing 600-mile races are a tradition that began in 1960

By Phil Hall

Short tracker Joe Lee Johnson drove Frank Strickland's 1960 Chevrolet to his lone NASCAR Grand National victory in the 1960 World 600 at the new Charlotte Motor Speedway in North Carolina. In doing so, he began a tradition that is gaining on the Indy 500 as the most important Memorial Day weekend race for motorsports fans. The World 600 (Coca-Cola 600 since 1986) is NASCAR's longest race and has proved to be a test of man, machine and fan stamina that gets bigger every year.

Back in 1960, fans were getting used to 500-mile races for stock cars on superspeedways such as Darlington International Raceway in South Carolina (in operation since 1950) and the 2.5-mile Daytona International Speedway (which opened in 1959). There were two new super-speedways in 1960: The 1.5-mile tri-oval in the Charlotte suburb of Harrisburg, and the new Atlanta International Raceway, another mile-and-a-half circuit in Hampton, Georgia.

To extend the horizon, as well as to stand out a bit, the 600-mile distance was tried at Charlotte. Joe Lee Johnson averaged 107.735 mph. The race was approaching the six-hour-long time span at its finish.

Nelson Stacy scored the first World 600 victory for Ford and car owners Holman & Moody in 1962. (Phil Hall Collection)

Jim Pascal won both the 1964 and 1967 World 600s. This is the winning 1967 Plymouth that was owned by Friedkin Enterprises. (Phil Hall Collection)

The 600-mile distance would turn out to be the longest for regular Grand National (later Winston Cup) competition. A 600-miler was scheduled on August 17, 1969, at the new Michigan International Speedway in Brooklyn, Michigan. This was a two-mile superspeedway. Rain and darkness cut the contest to 330 miles. Thus, no further 600s were planned at that track. There was less rain in North Carolina. Only in 1968 did the World 600 have to be shortened. That was when precipitation stopped the counter at 357 miles.

Jim Pascal's 1967 Plymouth Belvedere two-door hardtop (number 14) featured the 426-cubic-inch MoPar hemi under its hood. It flew the Friedkin Enterprise colors. (Phil Hall Collection)

LeeRoy Yarbrough won the 1969 World 600 aboard Junior Johnson's 1969 Ford Torino Talladega. It was the first of three wins for a 1969 Ford in the event. (Phil Hall Collection)

In addition to the 1969 Torino he campaigned in 1970, LeeRoy Yarbrough also drove this 1970 model. Both had the same number (98), but the 1970 carried "Cobra" identification. (Phil Hall Collection)

The World 600 was a key player in making NASCAR into a major sanctioning body and marketer of the product. As other superspeedways were built, Grand National grew to its present status as America's most important racing series. Over the years, the Charlotte area has become the hub of the NASCAR racing teams. Many race shops are located nearby: The track itself has seen extensive improvements in recent years, under the direction of current chairman of the board O. Bruton Smith and president and general manager H.A. "Humpy" Wheeler. Charlotte Motor Speedway can now brag of condominiums, a new private club, and new seating. On race weekends, the crowds exceed a quarter of a million fans.

The history of the World 600 is an interesting one, with a number of famous drivers and several makes of cars accounting for the 35 wins in the record books. Newcomer David Pearson was hot in 1961 and took that year's 600 in a Ray Fox-prepared 1961 Pontiac Catalina. Nelson Stacy came back in 1962 driving a notchback 1962 Ford Galaxie owned by Holman & Moody. Fred Lorenzen drove a Holman & Moody 1963-1/2 Galaxie fastback to win the next year. Smooth driving Jim Paschal guided one of Petty Engineering's famous hemi-powered 1964 Plymouths to the win that season. In 1965, Chrysler was boycotting the NASCAR Grand National series over a rules dispute. Fords dominated stock car racing. Fred Lorenzen became the first driver to repeat a World 600 win and Holman & Moody had their third checkered flag in four consecutive outings.

Marvin Panch, driving a year-old Plymouth Belevdere for Petty Engineering, took the 1966 edition of the race. Paschal became a two-time victor in 1967. That year, he was aboard Tom Friedkin's 1967 Plymouth Belvedere. Buddy Baker, the son of the legendary Buck Baker, flourished by winning the shortened 1968 World 600 Race. He was aboard a Ray Fox-prepared 1968 Dodge Charger. It was Fox's second winning car. The late LeeRoy Yarbrough was red hot in 1969. He brought Junior Johnson's 1969 Ford Torino Talledaga home first at the long one in Charlotte. This marked Ford's fifth win, well ahead of Plymouth's three.

For 1974, David Pearson won the World 600 with a 1973 Mercury Montego fastback. It was his second of three triumphs in the long race. It was also the first of four wins for the Wood Brothers. (Phil Hall Collection)

The new decade began with Donnie Allison scoring his lone World 600 triumph in the 1970 running. However, he was aboard a 1969 Ford Talledaga. The car was owned by Banjo Matthews. Donnie's younger brother, Bobby, took the 1971 World 600 Race in a Holman & Moody 1969 Mercury Cyclone. That marked three straight years of the event being won by the same year of car. It also marked the fourth and last win for Holman & Moody.

Buddy Baker hit his stride and won both the 1972 and 1973 World 600s. He became the first three-time winner and the first to record back-to-back victories. He drove a 1972 Dodge Charger for Petty Engineering in 1972 and a 1973 Charger for Nord Krauskopf the following year. David Pearson revisited the Charlotte winner's circle, while driving a 1973 Mercury Montego for the Wood Brothers in 1974. It was 13 years since his original win! Although his company's cars had scored three previous wins, Richard Petty did not take a World 600 until 1975. He did it driving a 1974 Dodge Charger.

David Pearson joined Buddy Baker as a three-time winner by taking the 1976 race in a Wood Brothers 1976 Montego. Richard Petty made it two wins for himself and five for Petty Engineering with his 1977 victory in the 1974 Charger. The tally for the company was more than any other car owner. One of the hottest drivers of the late 1970s, Darrell Waltrip, took consecutive wins in 1978 and 1979. He drove DiGard 1975 Chevrolet Monte Carlos. The 1978 triumph was the first for Chevrolet since the inaugural World 600 in 1960.

Benny Parsons made it three straight for Chevrolet with his 1980 win in M.C. Anderson's 1977 Monte Carlo. The year 1980 was the last one before the Grand National series required down-sized cars. Most racers competing were in older models. The smaller cars ran in 1981 and Bobby Allison made it two career wins in the 600 in the Ranier Racing 1981 Buick Regal. Allison's protégé, Neil Bonnett, won both the 1982 and 1983 World 600s. The first came in a Wood Brothers 1982 Ford Thunderbird. The second came in the Rahmoc 1983 Chevrolet Monte Carlo SS, the first year for that model. Allison scored his third World 600 win in 1984 in a new DiGard Buick Regal.

Darrell Waltrip became the fourth three-timer in 1985. He drove a 1985 Monte Carlo SS entered by Junior Johnson. Waltrip returned to score back-to-back wins, again, in 1988 and 1989. He was also driving Chevrolets in both those years, as he had in his 1977 and 1978 victories. New sponsorship from Coca-Cola led to dropping the "World" part of the name from the race's title in 1986. Dale Earnhardt won that year's Coca-Cola 600 in the Richard Childress Monte Carlo SS. It was the seventh win for the bow tie brand. (Earnhardt returned with consecutive victories, driving Chevrolet Luminas, in 1992 and 1993.) Ford drivers wasted little time tying the total, in 1987, when Kyle Petty (Richard's son) won the year's Coca-Cola 600 in a Wood Brothers 1987 Thunderbird. It was the fourth win for the brothers' team, one short of the record held by Petty Engineering.

Rusty Wallace put a Pontiac Grand Prix in the victory circle in 1990. The late Davey Allison scored Ford's last win, so far, the following season. In 1994, Jeff Gordon took his first career Winston Cup win in the Coca-Cola 600. He was aboard a Chevrolet Lumina.

"King Richard" Petty didn't win his first World 600 until 1975. He scored his second two years later. Petty drove 1974 Dodge Chargers on both occasions. (Phil Hall Collection)

Three decades of hemi history

By Phil Hall

As this is being written, the winner of the 1994 NASCAR Winston Cup is not known yet. However, it is safe to say that the age of the engine design on the winning car can be measured in decades. All cars in this year's battle are powered by either a Chevrolet small-block V-8, which was first introduced in the 1955 models, or a Ford small-block V-8, which first was fitted to the 1962 Fairlanes. New engine designs are forthcoming from the domestic manufacturers. However, it will be a few years before they are developed enough to power the sleek machines in NASCAR Winston Cup events on superspeedways.

This year's Daytona 500 marked the 30th anniversary of the introduction of an engine that won races right out of the box. It was the famous Chrysler hemi. Teams racing Plymouths and Dodges were issued new hemi V-8s for the February 1964 event, even though the power plant was not available as a production option that model-year. It could be bought over the parts counter. That was good enough for NASCAR, which had approved the Chevrolet Mark IV big-block V-8, in similar fashion, the previous season.

It should be clarified that the hemi V-8 was not a purely new design for 1964. It used the Chrysler 426-cubic-inch big-block as a base and added hemispherical cylinder heads. The B-block first appeared in 1958 MoPars. The hemispherical head design was first used by Chrysler on its FirePower V-8, which was used in the 1951 through 1958 model passenger cars.

Driver Paul Goldsmith was among the successful Plymouth campaigners in 1964. Here he pits during a race at Atlanta International Raceway. (Phil Hall Collection)

Still, the combination of the block and heads was new. It produced massive horsepower compared to the 1964 Ford 427-cubic-inch conventional wedge head engine.

The hemi caught the troops by surprise. When the MoPars began practicing at five miles in an hour faster than the Fords and Mercurys, the howls of protest from the Ford camp were almost as loud as the hemi's distinct growl. When Richard Petty and Paul Goldsmith easily won the two qualifying races in hemi-powered Plymouths, the critics conceded their speed superiority. However, they also guessed that the new engine would not hold up for 500 miles of racing. Richard Petty proved them wrong.

Petty scored his first career victory in the Daytona 500. To back it up, Jimmy Pardue and Paul Goldsmith ran second and third, respectively, in Plymouths. Marvin Panch brought the first Ford across the finish line, more than two laps in arrears. Jim Paschal was fifth in a hemi-powered Dodge. Petty went on to win his first career championship in 1964.

Ford tried to counter the hemi with a "high rev" kit for its 427-cubic-inch V-8. It also started a series of political maneuvers that culminated in the MoPar drivers boycotting part of the 1965 season and the Ford drivers boycotting part of the 1966 season. The issue they battled over was rule changes, or the lack thereof.

The "street hemi" made its production debut in 1966 models. Today, a genuine hemi-powered production car commands unbelievable prices in the collector's market. The "race hemi" continued to be a factor in NASCAR racing well into the 1970s, even after hemi-powered production cars stopped coming off the assembly lines.

Eventually, small-blocks replaced big-blocks. Not long after that change, Chrysler products fell by the wayside in racing. They have not been competitively campaigned in top-division NASCAR racing in nearly two decades. Chrysler products are not legal in Winston Cup races today and the factory has little interest in reviving its once proud competition image. Anyway, it's three decades since the history of the second-generation hemi began.

Chrysler's hemi V-8 provided many victories for MoPar-mounted NASCAR race drivers. Here Cotton Owens works at setting up a hemi motor in 1970. (Phil Hall Collection)

The fastbacks were faster

By Phil Hall

Looking back to the start of the 1988 NASCAR Winston Cup late-model stock car racing season, the speculation surrounded which make of car would be fastest. To keep the guessing game going, test speeds were leaked out from the various teams before the season opener at the Daytona 500. The race took place on February 14, at Daytona International Speedway in Daytona Beach, Florida.

With no new V-8 engine designs, plus strict power plant regulation, aerodynamics seemed the key to top speeds on the NASCAR superspeedways. The domestic manufacturers were deeply engaged in a battle of sleekness for cars that were legal to race. For 1988 that meant an all-new Pontiac Grand Prix, Oldsmobile Cutlass Supreme and Buick Regal. Ford was then on the second year of a reworked Thunderbird. An all-new, smoother 1989 version was waiting in the wings. Chevrolet, the winningest make, had still another half-season to go with its boxy looking Monte Carlo SS Aerocoupe.

Wind tunnel testing of new designs became the rule by the 1980s, as computers and engineers worked to find the ultimate in vehicular aerodynamics and incorporate it into a production car. Turning the calendar back a quarter-century or so, one can find an early example of aerodynamics being successfully applied to stock car racing in the 1968 Ford Torino SportsRoof hardtop. This fastback model put Ford at the top of the win list for Grand National (later to become Winston Cup) stocks in 1968. It carried David Pearson to a NASCAR driving champi-

This 1966 to 1967 Dodge Charger was aimed at racetrack competition. This example was raced in NASCAR by the late singer Marty Robbins. (Phil Hall Collection)

Torino WINS Rebel 400

1968

Torino—

Success Car '68

The record speaks for itself

- May 11, 1968—Torino takes Rebel 400 at Darlington, S.C. —widens its lead in the NASCAR Manufacturer's Championship race.
- May 5, 1968—Torino double-header—wins Yankee 250 at Indianapolis and the Fireball 300 at Weaverville, N.C.
- April 21, 1968—Torino wins Gwyn Staley Memorial 250 at Wilkesboro, N.C.

- March 24, 1968—Torino takes the Richmond 250.
- March 17, 1968—Torino wins Southeastern 500 at Bristol, Tenn.
- February 2, 1968—Torino named Official Pace Car for the Indianapolis 500.
- January 21, 1968—Torino starts the season, taking the first 5 places in the Riverside 500.

Is it any wonder that Fairlane/Torino is the best selling car in its class! Out there on the big banked tracks of the NASCAR circuit it's flat out go—no favors asked, none given. All the Grand National brutes (Torinos, Road Runners, Chargers and all the others) are specially prepared and modified and driven by the world's best professionals. So what it all grinds down to is the fact that the car that took the checkered flag packed an extra lot of something the others couldn't come up with. And the fact is that Torino has won 6 out of 9 major NASCAR races held so far this year.

One further fact: The Ford engineers who create the winners on Sunday have built into the Torinos you drive on Monday the kind of ruggedness and reliability you need.

Torino hardtops, fastbacks and sedans have a full 116-inch wheelbase (longer than 38 competing models) for a smoother ride, more room, and up to 20% more trunk space. There's a whole range of Six and V-8 engines and a total of 14 models to choose from.

So get in a Torino and know what it's like to drive THE LEADER!

See the Light.
The switch is on to Ford.

FORD

Ford has a better idea

Big Savings now at your Ford Dealer's SEE-THE-LIGHT Sale!

Ford's advertising department did not miss the opportunity to play off racing successes, such as the 1968 Torino fastbacks' seven early-in-the-year NASCAR victories. They included the first five places at the January 21 Riverside 500; first-place in the March 17 Southern 500 at Bristol, Tennessee; first-place in the Richmond 250 on March 24; first-place in the Gywn Stanley Memorial 250, at Wilkesboro, North Carolina, on April 21; double-header wins, on May 5, in the Yankee 250 at Indianapolis and the Fireball 300 at Weaverville, North Carolina; and a victory at the Rebel 400, in Darlington, South Carolina, on May 11. "One further fact," said the ad copy. "The Ford engineers who create the winners on Sunday have built into the Torinos you drive on Monday the kind of ruggedness and reliability you need." (Old Cars Collection)

onship. In addition it was also used by A.J. Foyt, the United States Auto Club (USAC) stock car champion, and Benny Parsons, the Automobile Racing Club of America (ARCA) champion.

Before 1968, engines were considered the most important factor in stock car racing. In the 1950s and early 1960s, the horsepower race brought almost yearly engine displacement changes. New designs for engines also came at a rapid pace. The turbulent '60s also brought several disputes between the factories, which resulted in withdrawals from racing, or rules changes that helped or hurt one manufacturer or another. When engines passed the 400-cubic-inch mark in the early 1960s, the famous "406," "409," "413," and "421" V-8s evolved. There were rumors of test engines with up to 500-cubic-inches being developed.

After 1969, engine rules became stricter. The racing powers got together and slapped a seven-liter displacement limit (with tolerances around 430-cubic-inches) on the fastest classes. It was designed to keep things from getting out of hand. When the maximum engine size was capped, the increases in cubic inches stopped, but engine development work continued. Domestic manufacturers turned towards designs that gave maximum power from a given displacement. Chrysler introduced hemispherical heads for its 426 in 1964. Chevrolet had a "semi-hemi" V-8, which made a brief appearance in 1963. Ford tried to legalize overhead camshafts for its "427," then later came out with an all-new big-block racing engine. One version of it had hemi heads. However, with emission and safety standards on the horizon the development budgets of the manufacturers began to dry up.

The changes left aerodynamics as the next battleground. It was cheaper to put some swift tin on a body than to design a whole new engine. Therefore, the way a car's body went through the air became more of a consideration for those models selected to compete in superspeedway racing.

It is not that aerodynamic considerations were unknown before 1968. In 1960, Ford came out with a neat two-door hardtop called the Starliner. The racers loved this car with its slanted rear pillars. It returned for 1961, but then disappeared for 1962. The formal T-Bird look was in by that time. Racers complained that the 1962 notch backs were not as fast on the big tracks. If they wanted to run the new 406 V-8, they had to use a 1962 body. Ford answered with the Starlift option for the 1962 Ford convertible. It was basically a Starliner-type hardtop that gave the

Dodge redesigned the 1968 Charger with superspeedway stock car racing in mind, but it still took some work to get it right. This example, shown with Bobby Issac, had a recessed grille and rear window, which caused the racers problems. (Phil Hall Collection)

Cobra strikes again!

1969 Cobra SportsRoof with
428 CID Cobra Jet Ram-Air V-8

Torino Cobra wins Daytona 500

Three races—three wins. Right on top of a 1-2-3 finish in the Riverside 500 and victory in the ARCA 300, Ford's Torino Cobras take three of the top four places in the Daytona 500, with Lee Roy Yarbrough piloting the winning car. All of the 50 cars that started were specially modified for racing. Only 28 finished. Proof that Torino Cobra can take it.

You get a lot of this same kind of winner-take-all action in the Cobras at your Ford Dealer's Performance Corner. Cobra comes with a standard 4-barrel 428 CID V-8, rated at 335 horsepower. There's a Cobra Jet Ram-Air version available. Transmission is a trigger-quick, fully synchronized 4-speed box. There's a chassis to match, with competition suspension, staggered rear shocks, 6-inch wheel rims, belted wide-tread F70 x 14 white sidewall tires, hood lock pins—the works. Two-Door Sports-Roof or Hardtop models. Try some Cobra action for yourself at your Ford Dealer's Performance Corner. See why Going Ford is the Going Thing!

Ford has a Corner on Performance

February 1—Riverside 500*. Torino Cobras sweep 1st, 2nd and 3rd—Richard Petty sets new record in his first race in a Ford.

February 16—ARCA 300*. Torino Cobra wins with ARCA champion Benny Parsons at the wheel.

February 23—Daytona 500*. Torino Cobras win, taking three of the first four places. Lee Roy Yarbrough drove the winner.

*All cars entered were specially modified for racing.

COBRA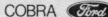

61

By the end of February 1969, the midsize Ford fastbacks had three races and three wins to their credit. "The Cobra strikes again" read the bold headline on an ad for the 1969 Torino Cobra SportsRoof with the 428-cubic-inch Cobra Jet Ram-Air V-8. Torino Cobras swept first, second and third places at the Riverside 500 on February 1, with Ford driver Richard Petty setting a new track record. Fifteen days later, at the ARCA 300, a Torino Cobra with Benny Parsons behind the wheel crossed the finish line first. A week after that, the Torino Cobras took three of the top four places at the Daytona 500, with Lee Roy Yarbrough piloting the winning car. All the 50 cars that started the Daytona 500 were specially modified for racing and 28 finished. (Old Cars Collection)

same reduced drag as the earlier models. After a period of controversy, NASCAR disallowed the Starlift and Ford drivers went back to the notch backs. For 1963, Ford introduced a midyear hardtop with a fast back roof line in its Ford and Mercury lines. From that point on, the cars Ford raced had sleeker lines. They also had a new 427-cubic-inch V-8.

Chrysler Corporation was Ford's main NASCAR adversary in the mid- and late-1960s, as General Motors forbade its divisions to get involved in racing. Chrysler tried to get into the aerodyamic olympics with the 1966 Dodge Charger, which was a fastback version of the Coronet body. It took Dodge racers awhile to get the Charger to work. Its rear end tended to lift at speed, which is just the opposite of what racers want. For 1968, Dodge reskinned the Charger. Visually, the changes looked progressive, with a Coke bottle shape, recessed grille and rear window. However, visual and racetrack aerodynamics are not always the same. It was found that the grille and rear window hurt, rather than helped, the racers.

Ford reskinned its intermediate Fairlane. One version was the fastback two-door hardtop. Mercury had a similar model in its Cyclone line. Both were to be the NASCAR racers. The initial reaction was that it looked a lot like the 1966 to 1967 Chargers. However that changed when the Ford fastbacks were seen on the track. With the backs jacked up and fronts dropped, the fastback was now nearly parallel to the ground. To be brief, the Fairlanes and Cyclones were the fastest cars on the big tracks. Cale Yarborough drove the Wood Brothers' Cyclone to four superspeedway wins, including the Daytona 500. He took a record $136,786 in winnings. David Pearson wheeled Holman & Moody's Fords to 16 wins and the driving championship. When the counting was over, Ford had 20 wins out of 49 races and Mercury added seven more. Ford scored the most wins for the first time since 1965, when Chrysler had withdrawn for a good part of the season.

It obviously takes more than a fastback roof to win races, but it was enough of a factor that the race car builders were not willing to neglect it. For 1969 Dodge returned with the Charger 500. It later added the winged Charger Daytona. Ford added the Torino Talledega and Mercury the Cyclone Spoiler II. For 1970 there was the Plymouth Road Runner SuperBird.

Only the backing away of the factories from racing kept this increased development from continuing. However, by the late 1980s, the factories went to it again, with each new season bringing new aerodynamic efforts. The latest versions always seem sleeker and slipperier than what came before. Although they may not look all that sleek today, 20 years ago the fastbacks from Ford changed the shape of superspeedway stock car racing forever.

Racing was a major consideration in the design of the 1968 Dodge Charger, but it needed some reworking to be competitive. Buddy Baker is at the wheel here.

Ford wins Virginia 500!

Torino Talladegas finish 1-2

The 1969 winning streak rolls on. The Ford victory at Martinsville makes it six big wins for Torino over all the other specially modified stock cars.

DATE	EVENT	DRIVER
February 1	Riverside 500	Richard Petty
February 16	ARCA 300	Benny Parsons
February 23	Daytona 500	Lee Roy Yarbrough
March 9	Carolina 500	David Pearson
April 13	Richmond 250	David Pearson
April 27	Virginia 500	Richard Petty

With a roaring start like this the Torinos are well on their way to a repeat of last season's Grand Slam when Torino took the NASCAR, USAC and ARCA championships.

1969 Torino GT SportsRoof

TORINO GT corners performance for you!

Torino GT SportsRoof, Hardtop and Convertible have the same kind of muscle car personality as the roaring Talladegas. The difference is we've cooled them down just a bit and added enough style and comfort to make them America's plushest performance cars. You get a lively 302 CID V-8, GT handling suspension, belted wide-tread tires, hood scoop and more—all standard. Want more? Then option the mighty 428 4V Cobra Jet, 335 hp with Ram-Air, 4-speed fully synchronized floor shift, Ford pioneered front power disc brakes, buckets, Traction-Lok differential, and 6,000 rpm ta-chometer. Join Ford's winning streak yourself; check out one of these new Torino GT's. You'll find them in your Ford Dealer's Performance Corner.

TORINO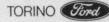

67

"Ford wins Virginia 500!" was the headline on a mid-1969 ad for the Ford Torino GT SportsRoof. By that time, three victories had been added to the company's three February 1969 wins. David Pearson took checkered flags at the Carolina 500 on March 9 and the Richmond 250 on April 13. In addition, Richard Petty was first in the April 27 Virginia 500 at Martinsville Speedway. "With a roaring start like this, the Torinos are well on their way to a repeat of last season's Grand Slam when Torino took the NASCAR, USAC and ARCA championships," the ad copywriters boasted. "Join Ford's winning streak yourself; check out one of these new Torino GTs. You'll find them in your Ford Dealer's Performance Corner." (Old Cars Collection)

The USAC Fords of A.J. Foyt

By Phil Hall

The legendary A.J. Foyt has done much and won much in auto racing. Often, individual segments of his long career seem to blend together in all the acclaim for his Indy car, open wheel, and NASCAR accomplishments. Something that becomes lost is his many years of United States Auto Club (USAC) stock car racing. He collected three championships in this venue. Foyt ran up 41 career victories, which turned out to be second-best on the all-time list for this now disbanded form of competition.

Foyt's accomplishments are even more impressive when it is taken into account that he had to run limited schedules each year. This was due to his commitments in the more lucrative National Championship races, which included both Indy cars and Championship Dirt cars.

USAC took over the sanctioning of many forms of auto racing after the American Automobile Association (AAA) got out of racing after the 1955 season. Open wheel racing was the most important product of both AAA and USAC, but the races for late-model stock cars were always good drawing cards. Fans liked seeing the heroes of Indianapolis racing new-model passenger cars. The automobile factories were involved in stock car racing in the mid-1950s and again in the 1960s. Therefore, having top-flight representation in USAC was just as important as it was in NASCAR Grand National competition.

A.J. wasn't always a FoMoCo driver. In fact, here he is seen here chasing Parnelli Jones' Mercury Marauder (number 15) with his hemi-powered Dodge (number 47) in a USAC stock car race at Milwaukee on September 20, 1964. (Phil Hall Collection)

A.J. Foyt's first ride in a Jack Bowsher Torino was during the USAC stock car season at the Yankee 500 on May 5, 1968. He started last at the Indianapolis Raceway Park event, and finished first with the point lead. (Phil Hall Collection)

A.J. Foyt wheeled Jack Bowsher's 1968 Ford Torino to the 1968 USAC stock car championship. It was Foyt's first title in the division and the last for a Ford driver. (Phil Hall Collection)

A.J. Foyt rapidly became a master at the open wheel cars. After racing a midget near his Houston, Texas hometown in 1953, he showed his abilities with the modifieds, sprints, and the so-called "Big Cars" that ran at Indianapolis and other tracks. He first started his racing in USAC. He took his first two championships in 1960, when he was Eastern Sprint Car Champion and National (Big Car) Driving Champion. Foyt won the Indianapolis 500 in 1961 and repeated as National Driving Champion.

Foyt's first serious season of stock car racing was 1962 when he got a ride in the factory-backed Pontiacs of Ray Nichols. He scored two wins and finished fifth in points. Since then, Foyt has been a front runner in all the events he tried. He even expanded his exploits to NASCAR Grand National competition, where he also won his share of victories.

In USAC, Foyt got some of the best stock car rides. He drove Norm Nelson's Plymouths in 1963, Ray Nichols' Dodges in 1964, and Holman & Moody Fords in 1965 and 1967. Ford was interested in turning back the Mopar hemis in USAC in the mid- and late-1960s, but lacked a competitor who could make all the events on the schedule. They ranged from races at short dirt ovals and events on the road course at Indianapolis Raceway Park to competition on the paved mile at Milwaukee, Wisconsin. Ford finally found its warrior in 1966. That's when Springfield, Ohio's Jack Bowsher came to USAC to run Ford products. Bowsher had dominated events sanctioned by the Automobile Racing Club of America (ARCA). After a season of learning the tracks and wrestling the full-size Galaxies around in 1966, Bowsher proved he could win in 1967. He was the top driver in four events that season. However, stock car specialists like Don White and Norm Nelson were in the Mopar camp and each of them had multiple titles. Ford still needed a "top-gun."

This need was attended to in the 1968 season, when Foyt was teamed with Bowsher. They both campaigned 1968 Torinos on the stock car circuit, with Foyt making as many events as he could. The point system was top heavy. Drivers could do well in the bigger events, while missing some small ones, and still make a run for the points title. Bowsher had provided cars for Foyt to run in a couple of USAC races in 1966. Foyt placed in the top five both times. Although both racers had temperamental personalities, there was no question that Bowsher could set up a car just right for the variety of USAC tracks and that Foyt could drive them all. Bowsher had strong Ford backing at the time. By the start of the 1968 season, Foyt had five National Driving Championships and three Indy 500 firsts. Based on his record, he was also solidly connected with the "big blue oval" at that time.

Launching the 1968 season was a 250-mile contest on a road course at Phoenix, Arizona. Don White won the race in a Dodge. Roger McCluskey was second in a Norm Nelson Plymouth. NASCAR star David Pearson took third in a Ford. Foyt placed fourth in a Holman & Moody-prepared 1968 Torino.

The next contest was not until May 5, 1968, on the road course at Indianapolis Raceway Park. Foyt started last in the field in a Bowsher Torino. He flew around the 2.5-mile circuit, took the lead, blew a tire, regained the lead, and ran away with the race. Foyt also took the point lead immediately. He kept it for the rest of the season and never lost first place. Bowsher's machinery was based on the 1968 Torino fastback two-door hardtop. The racing chassis was similar to the full-sized Ford chassis, but had rear leaf springs from the 1967 Fairlane, which had the same wheelbase. Power was supplied by the trusty 427-cubic-inch Ford V-8 with a single four-barrel carburetor. For most of the season, Bowsher cars were white with dark blue trim. Bowsher retained his familiar number 21 markings and Foyt used number 31.

Three more victories came Foyt's way in the 1968 season. They included the first-ever Miller 200 at Milwaukee, Wisconsin, on July 14, 1968; a 100-mile dirt race on the one-mile track at the Indiana State Fairgrounds on August 23, 1968; and a 50-mile contest on a half-mile dirt oval near Cincinnati, Ohio, on September 13, 1968. Those wins gave checkered flags on a road course, paved mile, dirt mile and dirt half mile. USAC definitely had a variety of race tracks and venues. However, winning in different races did not get Foyt the title. His consistency was more important. He entered 15 of the 18 races on the schedule and placed in the top five a dozen times. He also took three pole positions. Bowsher finished fifth in points. He scored three wins, giving Ford seven firsts. That total was second to Dodge's eight wins.

Foyt continued to drive for Bowsher into the 1971 season. He finished second in points in 1969, third in 1970, and fifth in an abbreviated 1971 season. After a layoff, he returned to race in the division on a regular basis late in the 1970s. He took his second and third division championships in 1978 and 1979. They and the 1979 Gold Crown Indy car championship were his last career season championships. Foyt's 1968 crown was Ford's last in USAC stock car com-

Dirt tracks were common on the USAC stock car schedule in 1968. At DuQuoin, Illinois, A.J. Foyt (number 31) started fourth next to Butch Hartman (number 75) in the second row. Don White (number 1) is on the pole in a Dodge Charger for the September 1 contest. White won and Foyt finished second. (Phil Hall Collection)

petition by one of its drivers. Earlier in USAC's history, Ford was the dominant make. Dearborn equipped drivers took the 1956, 1957, 1958, 1959, 1960, and 1963 titles. Parnelli Jones even won one for Mercury in 1964. Ford's factory backing in USAC dried up after the 1970 season. However, Mopar pilots found things more friendly. This was especially true, starting in 1976, with Chrysler's "Kit Car Program."

The USAC stock car division died in the 1980s, but the exact year of its demise is a subject to debate. A.J. Foyt, despite his announced retirement, still raced occasionally in 1993. In fact, he was even seen in NASCAR stock cars that year, although without success, and he raced in the Indy Brickyard 400, August 6, 1994.

A versatile race driver, A.J. Foyt drove the handsome Sheraton-Thompson roadster at the Indy 500. (John Gunnell photo)

Teammates Jack Bowsher (number 21) and A.J. Foyt (number 31) steer clear of a spinning car at Milwaukee on August 15, 1968. Foyt drove Bowsher Torinos to the USAC stock car title that year. (Phil Hall Collection)

Not your father's "Rocket 88"

By Phil Hall

Oldsmobile Division of General Motors once had a sales campaign with the theme, "This Is Not Your Father's Oldsmobile." It was not especially successful, turning off a number of the older buyers of the make. Sales nosedived and the theme was quietly put to rest.

About the same time this theme was used, Oldsmobile was actively involved in motorsports on several levels. Its involvement included cars in NASCAR, Winston Cup and Busch Grand National stock car racing; SCCA and IMSA road racing; and several forms of drag racing. Success came to the division, particularly in drag racing. It captured the National Hot Rod Association Manufacturer's Cup six consecutive times and the Pro Stock Cup.

In the Grand National stock car class, which was by then dominated by V-6 power, Oldsmobiles won seven of 29 events, with young Rob Moroso earning four victories and the 1989 championship. In the Winston Cup series, Harry Gant's win in the April TransSouth 500, at Darlington, South Carolina, was a victory for an Oldsmobile that year.

The Cutlass Supreme coupe used by Gant, and all others on the Winston Cup tour, truly was not "your father's Oldsmobile." It was as different from the production version as you can get. It had a Chevrolet-made "corporate" small-block V-8, rear-wheel-drive, and a special racing chas-

Among the popular Oldsmobile drivers early in Grand National history were brothers Tim Flock (left) and Fonty Flock. They are shown with their mechanic "Buckshot" Morris (center). Fonty used a coupe at the time, while Tim was wheeling a four-door sedan. (Phil Hall Collection)

Bill Rexford won the 1950 NASCAR Grand National championship driving an Oldsmobile 88 coupe. The masking tape on the front of the car and around the windshield was there to prevent paint chips, so the vehicle could later be sold as a used car. (Phil Hall Collection)

Tim Flock, in car number 91, used his Oldsmobile 88 four-door sedan to battle a pair of Ford coupes and a Plymouth in this scene from an early NASCAR Grand National race. The dirt track is not identified on the photograph. (Phil Hall Collection)

sis similar to that used by most other competitors. Only the body was made to resemble the assembly line version, which is front-wheel-drive and Quad Four or V-6 powered.

Back when NASCAR started to sanction races for new cars in 1949, the Oldsmobiles and other makes being raced were not *like* production cars ... they *were* production cars. The sport of "new-model" stock car racing was growing rapidly in popularity immediately after World War II. Oldsmobile was the right place, at the right time, with the right engine. It was called the Rocket V-8.

After satisfying the demand for cars with warmed-over prewar models, the domestic manufacturers gradually brought their new designs to market as the 1940s waned. Priority went to all-new body and chassis designs. Drive train advances were to follow. General Motors (GM) brought all-new vehicles to market starting with the 1948 Oldsmobile 98 and Cadillac (except for limousines). For 1949, the all-new styling bowed on Chevrolets, Pontiacs, smaller Oldsmobiles and all Buicks.

Sharing top billing for 1949 were the new overhead valve V-8 designs that debuted in Cadillacs and some Oldsmobiles. Corporate engines were not the ticket within GM then. Cadillacs and Oldsmobiles got different power plants. However, they were similar in concept.

The interesting aspect was that Oldsmobile chose to stick its Rocket V-8s into its small 76 models, as well as its big 98s. The Olds 76 shared its basic bodies with Pontiac and Chevy. The result was the big-engine-in-small-car 88 series, which was an instant hit with the hot rodders of the time. The Ford L-head V-8 had been their favorite engine up to that time. Until the "Rocket 88" came along, nothing could challenge the Ford engine as a low-cost source of horsepower.

New-model stock car races were held by NASCAR in its Grand National (now Winston Cup) division. Other groups and race promoters followed the trend. However, there was no such thing as factory backing. If you wanted to race, you bought or borrowed the fastest car you could afford and went racing. Those that could afford an Oldsmobile got a winner. The 303-cubic-inch V-8 produced 135 hp in stock tune and had the potential for many more with its free-breathing cylinder heads.

After it was out of production, the 1977 Oldsmobile Cutlass 4-4-2 became a popular race car in NASCAR Winston Cup competition. It had a sloped nose and could use Chevrolet power plants. This example was driven by Darrell Waltrip in 1978. (Phil Hall Collection)

The combination of a sleek nose and Chevy small-block V-8 made the 1977 Oldsmobile Cutlass 4-4-2 popular in Winston Cup racing from 1978 to 1980. Cale Yarborough drove this one for Junior Johnson in 1979. (Phil Hall Collection)

In 1949, eight NASCAR Grand National events were held in the Southeast. Oldsmobiles captured five of them. For 1950, the race tally jumped to 19 and the Olds tally went to 10. Also in 1950, the first Carrera PanAmericana (Mexican Road Race) was held. The stock portion win went to Hershell McGriff and Ray Elliott in an Oldsmobile.

For 1951, Oldsmobile 88 used a slightly larger GM corporate B-body. That was not the only problem for the "Rocketmen," as Chrysler introduced a new V-8 with a hemispherical head design. This FirePower V-8 was bigger and more powerful than the Olds V-8. It had more potential for hop-ups, too.

Luckily for Olds, the Chrysler FirePower V-8 came only in large, not especially good handling Chryslers. Unluckily for Olds in the stock car wars, Hudson added a 308-cubic-inch version of its flathead six in the Hornet. The company was already producing a car with a low center of gravity that was known as a good handler. At midyear, it added multiple carburetion to its option list. The high torque of the 308-cubic-inch six was just what was needed coming off a corner in a stock car race.

Racers were still buying or borrowing their "mounts" at the time. Some of them chose Hudsons. There were 41 NASCAR Grand National races in 1951. Chrysler took only one. Hudson snared a dozen. Olds was the still king, with 20 checkered flags.

Oldsmobiles got four-barrel carburetion for 1952. By that time, however, Hudson racers were getting help from the factory. They got engine options, plus much needed heavy-duty chassis parts. When the dust cleared after the 1952 season, Hornets stung the competition 27 times in 34 events. Old's victory count was a minute three.

By this time, Olds engineers began to realize that winning major races was important. Several heavy-duty "export" parts were made available to those who wished to put them in cars with numbers on their sides. Hudson countered with a hot 7-X version of its six for 1953. Dodge got a down-sized chassis and a new mini-hemi V-8. The so-called "horsepower race" was started. When the 1953 Grand National checkered flag count was in, the Olds' total was up to nine. Dodge, which had never won before, took seven. All other 22 races on the schedule went to Hudson.

All-new styling greeted Oldsmobile buyers for the 1954 model-year. It came with a "Panoramic" wraparound windshield. There was also a power plant size boost to 324 cubic inches. However, the competition was advancing as well. NASCAR rules called for stricter control of options for 1954, which turned out to help the aging Hudsons, even though they were in their last year with the Step-Down chassis. The results saw Olds drivers taking 11 wins in 36 events. Chryslers, which boasted 235 hp engines, claimed seven victories. Dodge scored only one checkered flag. Hudson, in its last blaze of glory, again got the most with 17 wins.

Hudson faded from the scene in 1955, but there was a new monster. The 300-hp Chrysler 300, under the direction of Carl Kiekhaefer, claimed 27 of 45 events. Olds was next at 10.

Low-priced makes like Ford, Chevrolet and Plymouth launched a major assault on performance by using smaller, lighter packages in 1956. Sales and performance of mid-size cars suffered in comparison. The big 1956 Chrysler 300-B was stronger than ever, though. On the other hand, Olds had just one NASCAR Grand National win in 1956. That compared to 14 for Ford and 22 for Chrysler. The makes that wanted to win no longer got by with offering hot options. To win the manufacturers had to buy and back racing teams that used their products. This "tie-in fever" hit epidemic stages by the start of the 1957 racing campaign. Production options like fuel-injection, supercharging and multiple carburetion were announced by the major automakers.

Oldsmobile chose the latter. It offered triple two-barrel carburetors in its J-2 Rocket option. It also hired Lee Petty to race its cars for the 1957 season. With heat from the safety lobby and Washington, the manufacturers agreed to get out of racing by June of 1957. NASCAR banned exotic engine options. As a result, most racers were allowed to buy their cars and parts at little to no cost. That left the Petty stable with a stockpile of 1957 Oldsmobile stuff, which Lee raced in the 1957 and 1958 seasons. In fact, son Richard drove his first race in a 1957 Olds convertible in 1958. The Olds victory tally climbed, with Petty's assistance. It included five events in 1957 and seven in 1958.

Using the leftover Oldsmobile mechanicals and a new 1959 Olds 88 two-door hardtop, Lee Petty won the first-ever Daytona 500, in February of 1959, in a photo-finish with Johnny Beauchamp. There was a total of four Olds' wins that season, but the Pettys switched to Plymouths in midyear.

While other automakers returned to racing in the 1960s, Oldsmobile did not. When the factories got out again in the early 1970s, Oldsmobile was still a non-entity. It was not until the 1978 season, when Chevrolet engines were discovered in production Oldsmobiles, that GM crossbreeding was allowed. The 1977 Oldsmobile Cutlass, with the 4-4-2 front end, was already out of production when racers discovered it was a sleek body to put a Chevy engine into. That year, Chevy-powered Oldsmobiles won 11 races, more than Chevy's 10 and far from everyone else's totals. However, it was a hollow victory for Rocket V-8 fans. The watering down of the "stock" in stock car racing was already well underway.

Those who remember when true Rocket 88s raced across America can only give a knowing nod when someone says that his new front-driver with a meek V-6 power plant is, "Not your father's Olds."

The last Oldsmobile (so far) to compete in NASCAR Winston Cup racing was the Cutlass Supreme. This 1989 version was driven by Harry Gant. Olds withdrew from NASCAR Winston Cup competition after the 1992 season. (Phil Hall Collection)

Dodge's stockers started in 1953

By Phil Hall

Don't look for any Dodges in NASCAR Winston Cup competition these days, since they're illegal. Despite the fact that Dodge is fourth on the all-time win list in major league stock car racing, no models built today meet the rules. And, despite Chrysler Corporation's interest in motorsports, it chooses to ignore the highly popular Winston Cup circuit, concentrating its efforts on the International Race of Champions (IROC) events, drag racing, smaller engine sports car events and off-road competition.

Also not legal in stock car racing are Plymouths and Chryslers. Plymouth is third on the all-time win list with 190 victories. Dodge has 162 victories and Chrysler has 59. That's a total of 411 victories for the MoPars since the NASCAR Grand National (later Winston Cup) racing series started in 1949.

Getting back to Dodge, the last time one took a stock car race was 1977. The first time was 1953, the first year of the small hemi V-8. The best year for Dodge was 1969 when 22 wins were recorded. That is second only to Ford's 26.

"Ah ha!" you muscle car historians say, "That was the year of the wild 'winged thing,' the Charger Daytona. Sure, the competition must have had a hard time beating those on the super-speedways."

Well, that's not quite right. The all-time hero in the Dodge camp in 1969 was another Charger. The Charger 500 accounted for 20 of those 22 wins. Today the Daytona is a valued collector's car while the 500 is all but forgotten.

For events that led up to Dodge's best year in 1969, a bit of historical perspective is needed. Dodges scored seven wins in 1953, with the short wheelbase and small V-8 a potent combina-

In 1954, Dodge promoted a racing tie-in by providing the Official Pace Car for the year's Indianapolis 500-Mile Race held on May 31. (IMSC Official Photos)

Taking the checkered flag on the beach race course at Daytona Beach, Florida is a 1956 Dodge D-500 two-door sedan (car number 500) that competed under Mercury Outboards sponsorship. These hot Dodges captured 11 wins in stock car racing during that season.

A 1956 Dodge D-500 (car number 502) from Carl Kiekhaefer's Mercury Outboard Racing Team gets a load of fuel during a stock car race.

tion on the short tracks, which dominated the NASCAR Grand National schedule at the time. Single wins were added in 1954 and 1955, but the hot D-500 option for 1956 was recognized by several teams and 11 wins went in the books.

With no factory help, NASCAR Dodges were few from 1957 on. A lone 1960 win bridged the gap to the return of the Dodges, with factory backing and a potent 426-cubic inch wedge engine, in 1963.

However, Dodge was again winless and it wasn't until the injection of second generation hemi power for 1964 that Dodges again carried checkered flags in Grand Nationals. Dodge then had its best year with 14 wins. But a boycott by Chrysler, for part of the 1965 NASCAR season (over a rules dispute) cut the total to two.

The fastback Charger replaced the Coronet as the Dodge standard bearer for 1966. Improved aerodynamics were the goal, if not the result. David Pearson won the 1966 title in a Dodge and a new high of 18 wins were recorded. A Ford boycott over another rules problem helped that total.

Ford returned with a strong Fairlane program for 1967, but Richard Petty scored a record 27 wins for Plymouth. Dodge's total fell to five.

Aerodynamics was again the key to an all-new Dodge Charger for 1968. Ford had a similar redesign with the fastback Ford Torino and Mercury Cyclone and the battle of the shapes was on.

In racing on the superspeedways (tracks at least a mile long) the FoMoCo products were faster. Fords got 20 wins and Mercury joined in with seven. Even Plymouths were first 16 times, leaving Dodge at five again. The Charger, bulged rear fenders and all, looked sleek. However, factory-backed teams racing them were not happy. The recessed grille hurt airflow and cooling and the sail-panel-flanked rear window furthered the problem.

Dodge had the answer for 1969. Just after the start of the model year, Dodge introduced the Charger 500. It featured a flush grille with fixed headlights and a flush rear window. A "street" version was made to legalize the model. It was shown in the November 1968 Detroit Auto

With increased horsepower, the 1957 Dodge D-501 was found suitable for various types of motorsports. Very few of these cars are believed to survive. (Ron Kowalke photo)

Dodge flexed its new hemi muscles in NASCAR Grand National competition with Bobby Issac's win in a qualifying race at Daytona International Speedway in February 1964. It was a sign of things to come. (Phil Hall Collection)

Show. Driver Pete Hamilton was on hand and said, "It's been five to seven miles an hour faster than this year's car in tire tests."

Dodge farmed out manufacturing of the production Charger 500s and made the required 500 units. The cars came with a choice of the 426 hemi engine, with dual four-barrel carbs, or the 440 Magnum engine, with a single four-barrel. A choice of TorqueFlite automatic or four-speed manual transmissions was available.

As it turned out, Dodge showed its hand a bit too early. Just in time for Daytona, Ford introduced its long-nosed Torino Talladega and Mercury anounced its Cyclone Spoiler II. The "droop-snoots" did for the front of the two FoMoCo cars what fastback styling did for their rears. If that wasn't enough, Ford announced a new engine. This was the Boss 429 or "Shot-gun" V-8. It replaced the aged "427 wedge" with a hemispherical head design.

The 429 had problems getting legalized. It didn't appear until the Atlanta 500 in late March 1969. The 1969 Grand National season came in phases. Two late-1968 races were held on short tracks to start the points chase. The first event of calendar 1969 was the rain-delayed, Motor Trend 500 at Riverside (California) International Raceway on February 1. Ford convert

Richard Petty won in a conventional 1969 Torino. The best Dodge showing was a fourth by USAC driver Al Unser in a new Charger 500.

Ford saved the Talladegas for the February 23 Daytona 500 and its preliminary events. The NASCAR Dodge teams also had their Charger 500s ready for the big shootout. Back then, the two 125-mile qualifying races counted as Grand National events. In the second of those contests Bobby Isaac, in the K&K Insurance Charger 500, led a Dodge sweep of the first three places. In the 500-mile race itself, Charlie Glotzbach, in Ray Fox's Charger 500, lost the lead to Lee Roy Yarbrough's Talledega on the final lap. Dodge's next win didn't come until the March 23 Southeastern 500 on the half-mile, track at Bristol, Tennessee, thanks, to Bobby Allison piloting a Mario Rossi Charger 500.

Isaac was a master of the short tracks, and proved it by winning three straight events over a six day period. This was in April, when he won at Columbia, South Carolina and Hickory, North Carolina and Greenville, South Carolina. While today the Winston Cup Circuit runs a schedule of 29 or so big events per year, back then there were 54 dates on the schedule, with several in a week on the short tracks.

Allison returned to victory in the April 20 Gwyn Staley Memo rial 400 at the North Wilkesboro, North Carolina Speedway. Then it was Isaac, driving the Nord Krauskopf-owned, Harry Hyde-wrenched Charger 500s to a series of short track wins. He scored two in May and three in June.

While the wins looked fine in the record books, the publicity value of a short track win was nil compared to the prestige of a superspeedway victory in front of tens of thousands of people and major press coverage.

Here there was no question, the Fords and Mercs ruled. Led by Yarbrough, the fastbacks were taking all the big ones. The combination of good aerodynamics and the "429" working well right out of the box, made the Dodges look bad. To answer the problem, Dodge announced the Charger Daytona in May. It featured the famous pointed nose and high rear wing, It looked awesome and, somehow, NASCAR approved it.

Putting in appearances at many 1964 stock car races were the Jake Kochman "Hell Drivers" who did their stunt driving behind the wheels of powerful Dodge models. This 1964 convertible soared through the air in a spectacular 70-foot ramp-to-ramp jump at the New York World's Fair Auto Thrill Show. (Old Cars photo)

However, the time between approval and the production numbers being met was measured in months. For most of the summer of 1969, the Charger 500 was the best the Dodge boys had. Isaac continued his winning ways, taking two more short track flags in August and one in early September. Ford was very concerned that it might lose the manufactuer's championship to Dodge. It ordered its Mercury mounted teams to switch to Ford Talladegas for the rest of the season.

The Charger 500 was announced as a new model in the Dodge line up with this Dodge News Photo issued for release on or after Sunday, September 1, 1968. (Old Cars photo)

Bobby Allison scored Dodge's 15th win of the season September 7 at Richmond, Va. The 16th win would be a history maker. The first race at the newly-built Alabama International Motor Speedway was the September 14 Talladega 500, It was to be the debut of the Charger Daytona. A driver walkout over track conditions forced a patched together show made up of various types of cars. Grand National regular Richard Brickhouse broke ranks and drove the Ray Nichols Charger Daytona to victory. That made the Ford Talladega's first race a win at Daytona and the Dodge Daytona's first race a win at Talladega.Though the winged cars were entered in superspeedway events for the rest of the season, the Charger 500s were still standard battle issue for the short tracks.

Isaac returned to his winning ways by taking a short track victory at Columbia, South Carolina four days after Talladega, a pair of Georgia flags in October, and a 100-miler at the Jefco Speedway (in Jefferson, Georgia) on November 22. A week later, Allison gave Dodge it's 21st win at Macon, Georgia.

The season ended up with a rain-battered inaugural, for the two-mile paved oval at Texas International Speedway, in Bryan, Texas, on December 7. Both Dodge and Isaac shook their superspeedway jinxes with a win in the Texas 500. The win came in a Charger Daytona, making only the second one for the winged warrior and the first with a full field of competitive drivers. Isaac's 17 wins were the most for any driver on the circuit and he was voted the most popular driver that year. However the bulk of the publicity went to champion David Pearson (his third) and Yarborough, who won a record seven superspeedway events and earned $188,605 in winnings.

High style in a family-size sports car was the sales pitch used to promote production versions of the Dodge Charger 500 model. The manufacturing of a limited number of these cars was farmed out so that Dodge could qualify the Charger 500 as a stock racing car. (Old Cars photo)

Buddy Baker was just one of many 1969 racers who chose the Charger 500 for NASCAR competition. His car number 6 flew the colors of Poole-Gable Dodge of Gainesville, Florida. (Old Cars photo)

A detail of the Charger 500 front end shows the flush-mounted front end, which was designed to provide better aerodynamics. (Old Cars photo)

The production Charger 500 could be had with "bumble bee" striping. A "500" badge decorated the rear flanks on the widest stripe. (Old Cars photo)

Although many race fans think of the Dodge Charger Daytona when they think of 1969, this droop-nosed, high-winged model took only two of the company's 22 wins in big league stock car racing that season. (Old Cars photo)

Late in 1969, the racing world was agog over the new Plymouth Roadrunner SuperBird winged machine for 1970 and the re-signing of Richard Petty. Lost in the shuffle was Dodge's all-time best total of 22 wins, 20 of which went to the unheralded Charger 500.

Dodge won 17 events in 1970. Then, it enjoyed a resurgence by Richard Petty driving 1974 Chargers in the mid-1970s. However, it faded from the scene gradually, after the Dodge Magnum was introduced as a 1978 model. Since that point, Dodge has not had much of an impact on stock car racing.

Bobby Allison accounted for four of Dodge's NASCAR Grand National wins in 1969 while driving Dodge Charger 500s. This example (car number 22) was owned by Mario Rossi and raced for Stan Dobbs Dodge of Fort Meyers, Florida. Under its hood was the 426-cubic-inch hemi V-8. (Phil Hall Collection)

Dodge announced the Charger Daytona to improve the aerodynamics of its racing machines. The car bowed at midyear in May 1969. It looked awesome and won the approval of NASCAR. (Old Cars photo)

Kiekhaefer's big, white cars were big winners in the 1950s

By Robert C. Ackerson

Bill France once described Carl Kiekhaefer as, "The most competitive man I've ever known." He was, without a doubt, one of the most controversial and colorful figures of the American racing scene of the middle 1950s. A sensitive, proud person who was quick to reprove writers who referred to him as a multi-millionaire sportsman, Kiekhaefer was the dominant force in American stock car racing during the 1955 and 1956 seasons .

Kiekhaefer was despised by some who saw him as determined to achieve victory at any cost. He was admired just as fervently for his ability to field a team of cars capable of outrunning their factory-entered counterparts. Whatever one's bias, few would deny that Elmer Carl Kiekhaefer was the living embodiment of the American success story.

In his youth, Kiekhaefer, found little to hold his interest on the family's Wisconsin dairy farm. He later noted, "I wanted nothing to do with a cow unless it could give 30 SAE." At age 19, he

The domination of the powerful Kiekhaefer Chrysler 300s can be seen at the start of the August 21, 1955, AAA stock car race at Milwaukee. Up front, in Chrysler 300s, are (from left) Norm Nelson, Frank "Rebel" Mundy and Tony Bettenhausen. (Phil Hall Collection)

Tony Bettenhausen waits to qualify for the August 25, 1955, AAA stock car race at Milwaukee. He's sitting in the number 99 Chrysler 300. Even while waiting, two technicians stand by his side, in case there are last minute problems. (Phil Hall Collection)

enrolled at the Milwaukee School of Engineering. After one year of study, Kiekhaefer worked as a draftsman at Nash Motors. He stayed there for several years. In 1928, he moved to the Stearns Magnetic Company of Milwaukee. There, he accepted an engineering position.

Kiekhaefer worked on diverse projects. They included a magnetic brake for industrial elevators and a sensitive magnetic separator that could detect a single grain of salt with an iron rust stain. His native engineering talent held him in good stead. However, he was far from satisfied. Despite a salary of $300 per month and a number of patents to his credit, after 11 years at Stearns, Kiekhaefer saw himself as heading nowhere.

It was his desire to strike out on his own that led Kiekhaefer, in 1939, to buy the bankrupt Thor Outboard Company factory in Cedarburg, Wisconsin. To many industry insiders, this was an act of complete folly. Thor's assets, for which Kiekhaefer paid $25,000, were seen good only for scrap metal. A quick look at what Kiekhaefer acquired for this amount seemed to confirm that the industrial soothsayers were correct. The factory was a dismal sight. Broken windows allowed both light and the elements to fall upon some 700 outboard motors inside. They were so poorly designed that Montgomery-Ward, for whom they were intended, had rejected them as totally inadequate.

Undeterred by the prophets of doom and the apparent hopelessness of his situation, Kiekhaefer set to work making a few basic but vital changes in the construction of the Thor motors. He installed a new crankshaft, water pump and a flutter value of his design (eventually adopted by the outboard industry). Next, he persuaded Montgomery-Ward to take a look at the product. The result was a group of extremely impressed purchasing officials. They not only accepted the 700 already built motors, but placed an order for an additional 2,300. This breakthrough was followed by an order from Western Auto for 3,000 motors and Kiekhaefer was off and running.

The first outboards with the Mercury name were the sensation of the 1940 boating season. Some 16,000 orders resulted from the Kiekhaefer display at the 1940 Motorboat Show. Before World War II, Mercury Outboard sales were at 35,000 units per year. This success was matched by an equally impressive record in outboard motor racing. It included the world's outboard motor speed record of 76 mph.

This rather wild and woolly age of outboard racing was ended with a decree from the American Powerboat Association. Kiekhaefer regarded it unfair for a manufacturer to compete with its customers in racing. So, he was not at all unhappy with this development, particularly since he was becoming interested in another type of competition.

As a boy, Carl Kiekhaefer had often looked forward with youthful exuberance to the stock car races held at the Wisconsin State Fair Grounds. In 1950, he read of the first Carrera PanAmericana or Mexican Road Race. The idea of a Kiekhaefer entry in the 1951 race was quite a natural development.

For his first foray into the world of international motorsports competition, Kiekhaefer selected two 1951 Chryslers with the then new 331-cubic-inch hemi V-8 engine. With just three weeks existing between the announcement that a Kiekhaefer team would participate in the race, preparation took place at a fast and serious pace. From its onset however it followed Kiekhaefer's formula for facing success: "Eliminate luck, pick the best cars, the best mechanics, most competitive drivers, and then work like hell!" On all four counts, Kiekhaefer practiced what he preached. Ed Metzler, a mechanic experienced in the preparation in Indianapolis cars, was selected to head up a team of mechanics recruited from the Kiekhaefer factory. For drivers, Kiekhaefer tapped current AAA champion Tony Bettenhausen and John Fitch, an ex-World War II fighter pilot. Young Fitch was just embarking on a racing career of great distinction.

Both Chrysler V-8s were fitted with twin, dual-throat Zenith carburetors, Mallory ignition systems and spark plugs designed by Kiekhaefer for use in his Mercury outboard engines. The engine of Bettenhausen's car retained the stock bore and stroke. Fitch's engine was bored out to four inches. When the two engines were put on the Kiekhaefer dynamometers at Fond Du Lac, Wisconsin, they proved capable of transmitting about 30 percent more power to the rear wheels than in their original form. Suspension changes included: Stiffer front and rear springs, dual telescopic shock absorbers at each wheel, and heavier sway bars fore and aft. While front disc brakes from the Chrysler Imperial might have been more logical, the Kiekhaefer approach to upgrading the Chrysler's braking capability was novel. In each car a tank of liquefied carbon dioxide was installed with tubes leading to each set of brake drums. Thus, when the mechanic opened a valve on the tank, dry ice was brought into contact with the brake drums, hopefully cooling them to a more efficient temperature when the need arose.

For a fuel tank, a 54-gallon steel drum was carried in the trunks of the two Chryslers. The drums' carrying capacity was boosted to 64 gallons by filling them with water until their ends bulged. Afterwards, of course, they were drained and thoroughly dried.

Frank "Rebel" Mundy wheels a Kiekhaefer Chrysler 300 around the Milwaukee Mile in a September 15, 1955, AAA stock car race. (Phil Hall Collection)

146

As it set out for Mexico, the Kiekhaefer team was an impressive sight. Besides the two race cars, there were two stock Chryslers, and a large GMC truck laden with supplies and tools. Kiekhaefer's twin-engined Beechcraft airplane also flew to Mexico for the second Carrera Pan-Americana.

When the two Chryslers appeared at the Tuxtla, Mexico starting line, they attracted considerable attention from the other race entries. Especially inquisitive was Piero Taruffi, whose Ferrari was to emerge the eventual winner. However, neither Kiekhaefer car had a good start in auto racing. Bettenhausen spun his car while traveling at over 100 mph. He badly damaged all his tires and lost valuable time while they were changed. Adding to Bettenhausen's woes were the mountainous stretches and curves of the first leg, which made quick work of the Chrysler's pepped up, but woefully inadequate, brakes.

When Bettenhausen approached the town of Oaxaca, at the end of the first day's racing, he no longer had brakes. With his supply of carbon dioxide exhausted, he had to resort to scrubbing and bumping his left front tire, against the curb of Oaxaca's public square, as a means of slowing his car. Finally, members of his pit crew manhandled the big Chrysler to a stop. For his efforts Bettenhausen was credited with 66th position. This was not exactly a stellar performance, but teammate John Fitch, driving the second Chrysler, never even got to Oaxaca. Starting from 32nd position (starting positions had been arranged by lot), Fitch had literally blasted past all the cars ahead of him, except for the much-modified 1948 Mercury of Troy Ruttman and Clay Smith. Then, just four miles from Oaxaca, the oil pressure relief valve on his engine stuck open, preventing lubrication of the main bearings. This burned up the engine.

On the second day of racing, Bettenhausen advanced to 49th position. The following day, he moved into 45th place on the strength of posting the day's fourth fastest time. The types of roads Bettenhausen now met were more to his liking and the Chrysler's capability. Increasingly, as the course moved north, long fast straight sections became the norm. This allowed the big Chrysler to make the most of its powerful engine. Bettenhausen's averages for the last two legs were 112.5 mph and 114.33 mph. Both were faster than the averages posted by the two leading Ferraris of Taruffi and Ascari (although neither Italian driver was over-extending his car, with the race well in hand). Nevertheless, at one point, the Kiekhaefer Beechcraft clocked Bettenhausen's Chrysler at 130 mph on the Chihuahua-Juarez straight. On this section, Bettenhausen's mechanic used their tachometer to calculate that they touched 142 mph. Despite a miserable start and having little experience in setting up an American sedan for this type of racing, Bettenhausen crossed the Cuidad Juarez finish line with a respectable sixteenth-place finish. Underscoring its stamina, the Chrysler made the 2,500-mile trek back to Fond du Lac, Wisconsin under its own power, and without any mechanical malfunctions.

The 1952 Carrera began the Lincoln's domination of the American stock car class. It was also the setting for the first skirmish in Carl Kiekhaefer's long battle with the Detroit motoring dynasty over what equipment was eligible for use in racing. Kiekhaefer's team consisted of the faithful 1951 Chrysler from the previous year's race, driven by Roger McFee, and a new 1953 Lincoln for driver Robert Korf. From the start of the race, ill-feelings existed between the Lincoln factory team and Carl Kiekhaefer. The dispute revolved around the fact that race officials had denied Kiekhaefer's request to block off the heat riser passage to the carburetor of Korf's Lincoln. This small change would have reduced the air temperature at the carburetor intake, thus providing a slight boost in power. The explanation given to Kiekhaefer for this ruling maintained that only the components listed in Lincoln's optional "special maximum duty kit" would be allowed. This kit included a Ford truck camshaft and mechanical valve lifters, plus a number of suspension changes. The factory kit created racing machines with handling that was even more impressive than their additional top-end power. Not surprisingly, factory Lincolns dominated the stock American class, finishing in the top three positions. Trailing the Lincolns in fourth- and fifth-places were Kiekhaefer's Lincoln and Chrysler.

White-coated technicians prepare Norm Nelson's 1955 Chrysler 300 for racing at Milwaukee that year. Nothing was left to chance by the Kiekhaefer team. (Phil Hall Collection)

The fireworks began when the top 10 finishers were inspected to verify compliance with the race regulations. When the factory Lincolns were inspected, each was found to have its heat riser passage blocked by a special gasket. This was not the only revelation that was to irritate Carl Kiekhaefer. Each factory-sponsored Lincoln was also equipped with intake manifolds and ports that had been ground and matched for better airflow and power. When contacted to explain these modifications, which had been available to all Lincoln entries, except Kiekhaefer's, the factory claimed that the engines supplied to both Kiekhaefer and to the Clay Smith-prepared factory cars were stock. Lincoln "explained" that when 1953 cars were sold to the public, the heat riser passage gasket and the matched manifolds and ports would be available.

This position failed to satisfy Kiekhaefer. He noted that his 1951 Chrysler (without a four-barrel carburetor, solid valve lifters or additional controversial Lincoln features) had averaged only 1.8 mph less than the winning Lincoln. He hinted that the race outcome might have been quite different, if he had been allowed the same degree of latitude in preparing entries. The validity of Kiekhaefer's argument was underscored by the ability of his fourth-place Lincoln to maintain an average speed only 0.6 mph slower than Chuck Stevenson's race winner.

The issue of the heat riser manifold gasket and port modifications was furthered by Clay Smith, who masterminded the preparation of the Lincolns in both 1952 and 1953. He reported, "The factory issued a service bulletin, 30 days before the race to all dealers, approving corrections on mismatching intake manifolds and gaskets on 1953 models." However, Lincoln's telegram response to the race committee's questions about these modifications stated that the necessary information would be issued as an official service bulletin.

At one point in this morass, Kiekhaefer decided to withdraw his Lincoln from the list of prizewinners and "forget the whole thing." However, after a session with race officials in Mexico City resulted in more stringent rules for 1953, Kiekhaefer canceled his request that the Lincoln be removed from the list.

Unlike his two previous forays, Kiekhaefer's participation in the 1953 Mexican Road Race, (with four Chryslers), was a dismal failure. The Chryslers for McFee and Fitch were equipped with Chrysler's "heavy-duty" engine and suspension option. This consisted of a higher compression ratio, roller tappets, a high-lift camshaft, dual four-barrel carburetors, Air-Lift suspension stiffeners, front and rear stabilizer bars, and disc brakes from the Imperial. As a result, they were required to run in the sports car class. Without this impressive list of exotic equipment, the Robert Korf and Frank Mundy cars competed in the stock section. Mundy's Chrysler was the last Kiekhaefer entry to retire. It got as far as Chihuahua, some 358 miles from the finish, before its engine gave up the ghost.

Passing up the 1954 Carrera, Kiekhaefer instead entered one of his Chryslers in a late-season AAA stock car race in Milwaukee. Bettenhausen drove the car to a win. His victory was sufficient to encourage Kiekhaefer to take a closer look at American stock car racing.

While these events were transpiring, Chrysler Corporation was about to introduce its C-300. This car was the first of a new breed of American high-performance automobiles. Briggs Cunningham contributed to the C-300's development through experience, at LeMans, with Chrysler engines. Carl Kiekhaefer deserves recognition for applying the maxim "racing improves the breed" to Chrysler's marvelous masterpiece.

Under NASCAR rules, the 1955 Grand National season began at High Point, North Carolina. However, Daytona Speed Weeks really started a year of intense competition. It saw the end of one racing age, in which the Hudson Hornet and the Oldsmobile 88 were the dominators. Replacing these two cars were Kiekhaefer's Chrysler 300s. They began what was to be one of the most impressive and memorable eras in the history of American stock car racing.

The Kiekhaefer entourage had arrived at Daytona with a single 300. Neither Buck Baker or Herb Thomas were interested in offers to drive the Chrysler in Speed Week's climactic event, the Grand National Race. Later in the 1956 season, they would feel differently. However, in February, the Kiekhaefer team was an unknown quality. Driver Tim Flock did not share the same view. He was not inclined to be particularly choosy at that point in his career. Writing in the January 1956 issue of *Speed Age*, Flock recalled that when he first saw the Kiekhaefer Chrysler he told himself, "If I had that Chrysler, I'd win the Daytona Beach Road Race. And I was right." Flock was convinced. He called the Orlando, Florida dealer for Mercury outboards and said, "I'm Tim Flock and if you don't have a driver for the Sunday race, I'd like to drive for you. I think I can win it."

Kiekhaefer accepted Flock's offer, although he later noted, probably correctly, that Flock wouldn't have signed on if he could have gotten another car for the race. Flock had been out of racing for 18 months, due to a freak, nearly fatal accident in which a truck had run over his head. Adding to Flock's woes had been a dispute between himself and NASCAR. It resulted in his disqualification at the 1954 Speed Weeks. Despite these setbacks, Flock was a driver of proven ability and just what Kiekhaefer needed.

Crawling on the dirt of the quarter-mile track in the infield of the paved mile at Milwaukee, Kiekhaefer technicians went over the big 1955 Chrysler 300s thoroughly before each race. Getting the treatment here is Frank "Rebel" Mundy's ride. (Phil Hall Collection)

This pair of 300s was sponsored by Carl Kiekhaefer and flew his Mercury Outboard colors. The big white Chryslers were the "class act" of AAA stock car racing in 1955. The photo shows Frank Mundy (car number 30) and Norm Nelson (car number 55), passing Marshall Teague in the number 6 Chevrolet. (Phil Hall Collection)

Flock came from an interesting family. His brothers Bob, Carl and Fonty raced cars or boats. He had nine sisters. One sister, named Ethyl by her automotive-minded parents, made 37 parachute jumps. Another sister, named Red raced modified stock cars. Flock grew up immersed in an interest in speed. His two-way flying mile run in the Chrysler 300 at an average speed of 130.293 mph entitled him to the pole position at Daytona's 160-mile Grand National race. In addition, his 93.158 mph run for the standing-start mile earned him a new record for this event. In the race itself, Flock could not match the shear speed of "Fireball" Robert's stick-shifted 1955 Buick Century, which virtually led the race from beginning to end. However, sometimes victory does not go to the swiftest. After the race, Robert's Buick, along with the C-300s of Tim Flock and Lee Petty (who finished second and third) was impounded to be inspected. It was discovered that its push rods were not stock. Roberts was disqualified and Flock and Petty were advanced respectively to first- and second-place slots.

After this pleasant turn of events, Kiekhaefer offered Flock a contract the driver described as, "Such a good deal, I couldn't believe it." Carl Kiekhaefer was about to make believers out of many people. When the NASCAR season ended months later, Tim Flock was the champion with 29 Grand National victories to his credit. In AAA competition, Frank Mundy's eight victories earned the Kiekhaefer team a second championship. Out of 13 starts in triple A competition, Kiekhaefer's Chryslers won 10 races. Norm Nelson and Tony Bettenhausen each added single victories to Mundy's total.

The factors behind Kiekhaefer's success were similar to those Alfred Neubauer used in the operation of the great Mercedes-Benz teams. Kiekhaefer, who owned a 300SL coupe, was a great admirer of Neubauer. The similarity between the two men's approach to the fielding of a winning team of racing cars was predictable. Kiekhaefer started with the best car on the track, which was the C-300 Chrysler. He then paid very close attention to details. This included the compilation of copious records of each race. This logical, business like approach paid handsome dividends.

Kiekhaefer was modest in his description of preparation of his cars. At one point he commented, "We do almost nothing to the engine except put it in peak tune". Yet, this one procedure, applied to three engines, consumed some 500 man-hours. While Kiekhaefer denied any direct relationship with Chrysler Corporation, he did benefit from contact with Chrysler's top management. However, he was the source of a tremendous amount of practical racing experience, which proved of great value to Chrysler. He did not get the type of corporate aid that

Chaparral got from Chevrolet in the late 1960s. Nonetheless, his special rapport with Chrysler did ensure him of getting the best pieces and parts that the corporation could provide.

Kiekhaefer's working relationship with Chrysler dated back to his Mexican Road Race adventures. In those days, members of the Chrylser engineering staff, like Bob Rodgers, would often receive personal phone calls from Kiekhaefer. He would exhort them to make specific changes in the company's products that would improve their racing prowess. Such production-model changes as stronger universal joints and valve springs can be directly attributed to Carl Kiekhaefer. Kiekhaefer harshly criticized the corporate brass about weak links in the C-300's competition armor. However, he held the big Chrysler in high regard. He considered its chassis "rugged," its handling "exceptional" and its engine already competitive as it came from the factory.

One frustration experienced by the Kiekhaefer team (which Fonty Flock joined soon after his brother) was having the cars lead easily in the early stages of a race, but lose their speed later. This made them drop out of contention. Eventually, Kiekhaefer traced the problem to the oil-bath air filter on the C-300. They collected large amounts of dirt, which was eventually drawn into the engine. This often resulted in the destruction of oil rings and rod and bearing failures. Kiekhaefer's solution was to resort to a dry paper filter of a design based on those used on Mercury outboards.

Kiekhaefer's domination of the 1955 season (which saw his cars win 22 of the first 29 Grand National race's) included victories in 16 consecutive races. When that streak was broken at Memphis, by Jim Paschal, Kiekhaefer walked over to his pit and congratulated him and his team on their achievement. Chrysler's happiness with Kiekhaefer's racing successes was evidenced by their use of his victories in their advertising. However, his triumphs made his vanquished competition unhappy and determined to make the 1956 season follow a different script.

For the Darlington 500, on September 15, 1955, Ford, entered two 1955 models with considerably more potent 1956 engines. This was a harbinger of things to come. Three weeks later, at Memphis, Tennessee, the 1956 models made their first full-fledged appearance. The best that Tim Flock could manage was a fourth-place finish. The 1956 Fords of "Speedy" Thompson and Marvin Panch finished one-two. However, the trusty Chrysler 300s were not yet ready for the scrap heap. They won the first two Grand Nationals of the 1956 season.

With the participation of factory-backed teams in NASCAR, its president, Bill France, took measures to update his racing format to accommodate this momentous change. During the middle of November 1955, France spent a week in Detroit attempting to resolve the details of rules changes for the 1956 season. Before this time, he had allowed racing equipment to be used in competition 45 days after its approval by NASCAR. For 1956, this rule was tightened. The new rule permitted use of an engine larger than original specifications only if public announcement of its availability was made 90 days before its use. In addition the engine had to be nationally advertised at least 30 days before its first NASCAR race. Penalties dealing with rules infractions were strengthened. In the case of disqualification, the driver/owner now lost all points previously earned in 1956, as well as the old loss of prize money and points from the race in which the offense was committed. In addition, a second offense now brought a $200 fine and a 15-day suspension.

None of Kiekhaefer's cars were ever disqualified, even though they were probably subjected to more scrutiny than any other cars on the NASCAR circuit. Underlying this tribute to Kiekhaefer's integrity was Bill France's 1957 statement, "With all the races that Kiekhaefer won in 1956, we were never able to find a Kiekhaefer car that was illegal, and brother did we try."

At the outset of the 1956 season, all indicators seemed to point towards a repeat of the Kiekhaefer triumphs of 1955. At the Daytona Speed Weeks, Tim Flock's 300B (which Kiekhaefer called "The Beautiful Brute") vanquished its competition in the Flying Mile event with a 139.373 mph run. The Kiekhaefer 300B was beaten in the standing-start mile by a Dodge D-500. It won by a razor-thin margin of 0.02 mph (81.78 mph to 81.76 mph). Flock had little difficulty in winning his second consecutive Daytona Grand National. He lead Billy Myer's 1956 Mercury across the finish line by over 50 seconds. Out of the first 29 Grand Nationals of the 1956 season, Kiekhaefer cars won 22. At one point they racked up 16 consecutive victories. Competing in both Grand National and convertible races with Chrysler 300Bs, Dodge D-500s, Fords and Chevrolets, the Kiekhaefer scuderia consisted of 10 cars, six vans, four drivers and 30 crew men at its peak. Rumors of a "stop Kiekhaefer or get out" move among the factory teams and the switch of Tim Flock from Kiekhaefer to Chevrolet proved of little consequence in altering the pattern of the 1956 season.

On May 27, the Kiekhaefer cars even managed to win two major events at Charlotte, North Carolina and Portland, Oregon. Then just three days later, dual victories came at Syracuse, New York and Eureka, California. Unfortunately, the victories were changing the public's image of Carl Kiekhaefer from underdog to Goliath. This shift in public sentiment, while totally unwarranted, was to have severe ramifications. When his drivers were jeered and his victories booed, Kiekhaefer felt as if he had been personally betrayed by the fans. "What have I done wrong?" He asked. "This is a sport in which I'm not competing with my own customers, as we sometimes did in outboard racing. I'm fighting against General Motors and Ford Motor Company. I'm peanuts compared to the factory teams. Yet, the fans almost riot when they see our cars. I guess they want me to quit."

Ironically, at this low ebb in Kiekhaefer's popularity, his cars began to suffer a long string of winless efforts. From June 22 (when Herb Thomas' 300B crossed the finish in 11th place at Portland, Oregon) to September 9, the best Kiekhaefer showing was Speedy Thompson's second-place finish at Raleigh, South Carolina in a 1956 Dodge. By mid-July, Kiekhaefer publicly admitted he had considered dropping out of racing. He hung on in the face of an intensive racing effort by the Ford, Mercury and Chevrolet factory teams. Over the entire season, Kiekhaefer entered 51 of the 56 NASCAR Grand National races held and came away with 30 victories. That record was more than sufficient to give Buck Baker the Grand National Championship.

The season was marked by the full-scale invasion of the factory teams and a shift, in Kiekhaefer's racing image. There was also an intense three-way debating contest between Kiekhaefer, NASCAR and the factory teams over rules, their interpretation and enforcement. In Bill France's mind, the controversy was essentially of Kiekhaefer's making. "Carl is a dynamic, energetic man (and) one who needs to have problems to overcome," he said. "And when problems don't exist, he'll make them."

To Kiekhaefer, the issue was simple. He believed NASCAR was favoring the factory teams. He used the 250-mile Grand National race at Martinsville, Virginia as a case in point. At that event, a ruling that no power tools were to be used during pit stops was waived by NASCAR Commissioner "Cannonball" Baker. Kiekhaefer's view of this decision was that Chevrolet had

The last appearance of the Chrysler 300s at Milwaukee came in the September 18, 1955, AAA stock car race. Starting in the front row are Tony Bettenhausen (left) and Norm Nelson. Kiekhaefer efforts were restricted to NASCAR in 1956. (Phil Hall Collection)

Wisconsin industrialist and sportsman Carl Kiekhaefer posed for a photograph with two of his C-300 race cars. It was used in a 1955 Champion Spark Plug Company advertisement. Chrysler also featured racing achievements in its auto ads, even though the Mercury Outboard cars did not get direct factory sponsorship. (Old Cars Collection)

originally planned to run the race without a tire change, thus eliminating the need for power tools, but tire changes were needed in practice and NASCAR bowed to Chevrolet pressure to allow power tools. Neither Chevrolet or NASCAR accepted Kiekhaefer's interpretation of this situation. In an interesting twist of fate, Kiekhaefer cars finished first and second in this event and NASCAR officials rejected a protest that they were shod with illegal tires.

As the 1957 season approached, no one except Carl Kiekhaefer knew if the big white cars would be competing in the NASCAR circuit. At one point in the off-season, he intimated that he would race if NASCAR would make some fairly radical rules modifications. Kiekhaefer had three basic changes in mind: A reduction in the number of Grand National races; The freezing of specifications from January 1 to July 1; The division of Grand National cars into two classes, one for factory teams, the second exclusively for independents. These proposals were not heeded. Kiekhaefer said this allowed the factory teams to, "Simply overwhelm everybody in the stock car game." His mind was made up. On the eve of the 1957 Daytona Speed Weeks, Kiekhaefer announced that he was withdrawing from automobile racing competition.

After initially refusing to elaborate on this decision, Kiekhaefer issued a short, terse statement expressing the opinion that, "That particular phase of our activity that caused us to race, which incidentally resulted in three successive championships, has passed. With due credit to President Coolidge, we did not choose to run this year. As always, our number one activity is building Mercury outboard motors." Ironically, within months of this statement, the Automobile Manufacturers Association issued its June 1957 decree prohibiting participation in competitive events by its members.

Perhaps it was Kiekhaefer himself who best summed up his experiences of the two years his cars competed in Grand National competition. Speaking to *Speed Age* magazine's stock car reporter, Sandy Gracy, he reflected, "I have had a lot of pleasure in racing and met many fine people, but I've been lucky in not having a driver scratched or hurting anybody else." Bill France, recalling those days, once remembered Carl Kiekhaefer as, "A man of his word, a great American and a great sportsman, with only one goal in mind ... to win."

AAA Champion Bob Sweikert—won at Indianapolis and placed in six other "big car" races

Biggest winners in AAA and NASCAR races prove Champions best for <u>your</u> car!

Bob Sweikert and Tim Flock used 5-rib Champion Spark Plugs in every one of 43 races!

Here's solid proof of what Champion Spark Plugs can do for *your* car:

Not only in racing cars, but in NASCAR races with all makes of standard cars—regular passenger sedans just like the one you drive—98% of the winners were powered by *Champions.*

Bob Sweikert, 1955's AAA champion—who finished first in the Indianapolis "500"—powered his racing car with Champions.

Tim Flock, the year's top NASCAR winner, drove his Chrysler "300" with Champions. In fact, virtually every racing driver in America

insists on Champion Spark Plugs—*regardless of the make or model of car he's driving.*

These men really know cars and know engines. What stronger evidence could there be that Champions are best for your car, too!

No matter what make of car you drive, new Champion Spark Plugs will give you quicker starts, fuller power, more miles per gallon.

Remember—even the best spark plugs become inefficient after about 10,000 miles. So have yours checked today. If you need new plugs, get the best—5-rib Champions.

CHAMPION

LOOK FOR THE 5 RIBS

NASCAR Champion Tim Flock—Champions powered his Chrysler "300" to 18 wins, 15 placings

NASCAR champion Tim Flock poses next to his number 300 Mercury-Outboard stock car racer. Flock was one of many racing pilots who turned up in a series of Champion Spark Plug ads. This put the young Southerner in heady company, as drivers such as Bob Sweikert, 1955's Indy 500 winner, also appeared in these promotions. (Old Cars Collection)

1957 version of the Nascar winner for the past 3 years — The Mighty Chrysler 300-C boasts 375 horsepower. Now available in both hardtop and convertible models.

Announcing

THE MIGHTY CHRYSLER

300⚡C

America's Most Powerful Car!

Here are the thrills of sports car motoring without the limitations. Enjoy the stirring surge of 375 horsepower putting bite to the wheels, the feel of sure-footed cornering. The kind of control that make a car and its master almost one.

Sounds like a sports car, and it is, in terms of sheer driving pleasure. But here's the difference. No bundling to the ears to go around the block. No tears and red faces from the merciless wind. No acrobatics to get in and out.

For the Mighty Chrysler 300-C has the same spacious interior as any new Chrysler model, magnificently finished in rich sports-car leather. If this seems like your kind of car, your Chrysler dealer will give you all the details.

SPECIFICATIONS—375 horsepower engine, 9.25 to 1 compression ratio, 2 four-barrel carburetors. Special high output camshaft. Ball joint, anti-dip, rubber isolated, torsion bar front suspension. 14-inch wheels. High spring rate – low deflection. Total Contact Brake System. Over-all length: 219.2 inches. Height 54.7 inches. Special racing-type nylon tubeless tires.

As late as 1957, Chrysler advertisements alluded to the Chrysler letter car as the "NASCAR winner for the past three years."

Racing Chevrolet's small-block V-8 powered stock cars from 1955 to 1986

By Phil Hall

During the 1986 NASCAR Winston Cup (formerly Grand National) Series, Chevrolets won 18 of the 29 events on the schedule. That was not particularly unique. It marked the fourth straight season that cars carrying the blue bow tie finished first in wins (Ford tied for the lead in 1985). It marked the 12th time that Chevy held the distinction since it seriously entered competition with its new small-block V-8-powered 1955 models.

Grand National racing started in 1949. By 1986, Ford had the most wins, with 335 through the 1986 season. Chevrolet was gaining fast, with 308 to its credit. Chevrolet did very well between 1983, when the Monte Carlo SS was introduced, and 1986. During that time span, Chevrolets won 68 events to Ford's 27. Chevrolet and Ford models were far from the dominant forces they were in 1986, when they were first entered stock car racing. Their respective facto-

One of the 13 Chevrolet NASCAR Grand National wins for 1960 came in the second annual Daytona 500. Junior Johnson, in car number 27, drove his year-old Biscayne sedan to victory. He is shown battling with Curtis Turner's car number 26 Ford Starliner, a 1960 model. (Phil Hall Collection)

Chevrolets didn't have many big moments in NASCAR in the mid-1960s, but one of them was when Curtis Turner put Smokey Yunick's 1966 Chevelle on the pole for the 1967 Daytona 500. (Phil Hall Collection)

ries ventured into Grand National racing in 1955. Then, the more powerful medium- and upper-medium-priced cars, with their larger power plants, dominated racing. Chevy scored only two wins in 1955, but one of them was the most important race on the circuit.

That race, the Labor Day Southern 500 at Darlington, South Carolina (back then the circuit's only superspeedway) was won by Herb Thomas. Ford only got a pair of wins that year in its first serious campaign. Meanwhile, the mighty Chrysler 300 invasion of Carl Kiekhaefer netted 27 victories. The 1956 season wasn't much better for Chevrolet, as only three flags came its way. In comparison, Chryslers racked up 22 of them. The factories introduced exotic equipment for 1957. Chevrolet got fuel-injection. Early in the year NASCAR backed off and disallowed most of the trick setups. The factories were out by June, leaving independents to continue.

This change was to the advantage of Chevrolet. It was very competitive with its new 283-cubic-inch version of the small-block V-8. While Fords took 27 wins, Chevrolets were second with 18. Buck Baker became the first Grand national champion to drive Chevrolets. For 1958, Chevy had its one-year car with a new X-frame and a 348-cubic-inch big-block engine. Racers mostly stuck with the older cars, which were proven in competition. Despite a total lack of factory support, it was Chevy's first year at the top. Twenty-three races went in its favor. Ford, which also had a new "352" big-block was second with 16 victories.

Another new Chevrolet design bowed for 1959. It had huge fins and the same basic chassis setup as the 1958 models. Racers were still split, running 1957, 1958 and 1959 models that year. When all the wins were totaled, Chevy was on top again. It had 14 wins if you believe NASCAR records, but there was a catch. For some reason NASCAR counted standard Ford and Thunderbird wins separately that year. If you added 10 Ford wins and six for the T-Bird, Ford got the edge with 16. Consequently, Chevy's "most wins" honor for 1959 will have to have an asterisk.

Ford returned to backing racing for 1960 and collected 15 wins, to 13 for Chevrolet. This began a long and unproductive decade for Chevy fans and drivers. However, Chevy driver Rex White won the championship. For 1961, Chevrolet got a new 409-cubic-inch version of the big-block to accompany a new, down-sized body. When the final count was made, Chevrolet came up with 11 wins to its credit. It was enough to beat Ford's seven, but no match for Pontiac's 30. Ned Jarrett did win the title, making the second straight for a Chevy pilot. Chevy pilots in 1962 used the semi-fastback Bel Air two-door hardtop, avoiding the formal roof Impala, but the 14 wins were still second to Pontiac's 22.

For 1963, Chevrolets scored only eight wins. It was the marque's worst output since 1956, but that was no indication of the importance of the victories. Before the season was much underway, Chevrolet and Pontiac were ordered to quit backing cars in racing. Just before they left, Chevy came out with a new Mark IV big-block design with radical canted valves. Chevy drivers, notably Junior Johnson, raced them until they ran out of parts and thrilled the fans. They ran against the factory-backed Ford, Mercury, Plymouth and Dodge entries.

That was the last of the glory for Chevrolets for a while, as the Fords and MoPars romped. The Chevelle came out for 1964. This intermediate-size Chevrolet underwent some development by Bobby Allison, Smokey Yunick and others. The Chevrolet Mark IV engine eventually made production status in 1965 and got into race cars thereafter. Chevelles became the choice of the independents racing Chevys through the 1960s. However, for the rest of the decade, Chevrolets were seldom in victory lane. There was one Chevrolet win in 1964, none in 1965, three each in 1966 and 1967 and one for 1968. They dropped back to zero in 1969 and again in 1970. Ford, meanwhile, was building an impressive win total. Its biggest year was 1965 when the MoPar contingent boycotted most of the season and Fords took 48 wins.

For 1970, a stretched Chevelle was aimed at luxury buyers. It was named the Monte Carlo. That year Ford got out of backing stock cars and Chrysler cut back to only two racing cars after the season ended. The time was right to put competitive Chevrolets on the track. Promoter

Chevrolets became a dominant make in NASCAR Grand National competition in the 1970s. Cale Yarborough drove Junior Johnson Chevrolets to consecutive titles in 1976, 1977 and 1978. His 1977 ride was this 1976 Chevelle Laguna S-3 with the sloped nose. The design was manufactured for the 1975 and 1976 model-years and banned by NASCAR after 1977. (Phil Hall Collection)

Although they were no longer current models, 1977 Chevrolet Monte Carlos became the winningest nameplate near the end of the 1970s. They were raced through the first event of the 1981 season. Dale Earnhardt won the 1980 driving championship behind the wheel of Rod Osterlund's old Monte Carlo. (Phil Hall Collection)

Richard Howard financed the Chevrolet return and encouraged others to start racing Monte Carlos.

Chevrolets did win three races in 1971, but that was only the beginning, as the Bobby Allison/Junior Johnson combo took 10 wins for the shorter 1972 season. Again Chevrolet was back on top in the win department. With a plentiful supply of relatively cheap Chevrolet racing parts available, the cars were popular. As the supply of old factory-issued Ford and MoPar racing parts dried up, racers started making a wholesale switch back to Chevy.

159

Chevelle and Monte Carlo were both redesigned for 1973, and Benny Parsons became the fourth Chevrolet driver to take the national championship. However, by the end of the season, only seven races went Chevrolet's way. The Wood Brothers' 1971 Mercury, with David Pearson driving, went on a rampage that year and took 11 wins. For 1974, Chevrolets knocked off a dozen wins to again finish first, but it was close. Dodge had 10 checkered flags.

A sloped-nose Chevelle called the Laguna S-3, came out for 1975, but only a half-dozen Chevy wins went in the books. Richard Petty was red hot in his 1974 Dodge Charger, and that make's 14-flag count was tops. The 1976 bicentennial season saw Chevy back on top, with Cale Yarborough winning the championship. He was driving a Chevy for Junior Johnson. That year, 13 Chevrolet wins went in the books. For 1977 it was much the same with Cale Yarborough taking two titles in a row. Chevrolet's 21 wins were easily the best.

It probably would have continued for 1978, but a rule change hurt Chevrolet's total for those and future years. In 1977, the scandal of discovering Chevrolet V-8s in new Oldsmobiles hit the country. The racing sanctioning bodies had to let Chevrolet engines be used in Pontiac, Oldsmobile and Buick race cars. With the V-8s of those makes long out of the racing development stage, the use of Chevy engines breathed new life into their racing status. Teams then chose the most aerodynamic body. The sloped-nosed, base-level Olds Cutlass was the sleek setup. To make matters worse, the Chevrolet Laguna S-3 nose was banned.

General Motors down-sized its intermediate-size cars for 1978 and they were too small to fit the stock car racing rules. NASCAR teams stuck with the 1977s, something they would continue to do through 1980. While Cale Yarborough made it three titles in a row in 1978, he split his driving between Chevy and Olds bodies. When the year was over, it was Oldsmobile in first with 11 wins and Chevrolet in second with 10.

For 1979, the 1977 Monte Carlo became the standard of NASCAR. Chevrolets took 18 wins out of 31 events. For 1980, Chevy was even more dominant, with 22 of 28 races going in its favor. Dale Earnhardt won the title. He was Chevy-mounted of course.

Chevrolet used a wind tunnel to help design a new nose for its Monte Carlo in midyear 1983. It came up with the Monte Carlo SS, which was a winner right out of the box. This 1983 example was driven by Ricky Rudd. (Phil Hall Collection)

NASCAR changed the rules and allowed only the down-sized cars to compete after the first race of the season. A 1977 Chevrolet Monte Carlo won it. Since the current model Monte Carlos were as aerodynamic as bricks at the time, a shift was on to the other General Motors intermediates. Buick's Regal was the sleekest setup. For 1981, a total of 22 events went to Regals. For 1982 it was even more of a Buick year with 25 wins out of 30 races.

With the factories getting back into racing at the time, Chevrolet engineers were less than thrilled with the fact that their engines were taking most of the wins, but cars with their nameplates were not. For 1982, three races were won by Chevy, but Chevy power was victorious in 28 events. The situation was handled by putting the Monte Carlo into a wind tunnel, designing a new nose aimed at the superspeedway, then putting it on the 1983 Monte Carlo SS at midyear. The SS was faster than anything the other GM intermediates had and the result was immediate. For 1983, 15 races went to Chevrolets and it was back on top. For 1984, the story was more impressive. More teams went to Chevys. That year 21 wins went to Chevy and Terry Labonte took the title in SS equipment. For 1985, Bill Elliott put it all together and set many records in a Ford Thunderbird. However, Darrell Waltrip won the title in a Junior Johnson Monte Carlo SS. Chevy and Ford tied with 14 wins each.

The superior performance of the Ford T-Bird on superspeedways in 1985 was not lost on Chevy, which added the Aerocoupe rear window to its Monte Carlo SS. Pontiac also tricked up its Grand Prix with a similar 2+2 option. When 1986 was over, it was another Chevrolet year with 18 wins out of 29 events. Elliott had an off year, and so did Ford with only five flags. Earnhardt took the title for the second time in the strong-running Richard Childress Monte Carlo SS.

The 1986 Chevy stock car racers seemed very different from their 1955 counterparts in many ways. However, one basic thing had not changed. The Chevy engine used in NASCAR racing in 1986 was a direct descendent of the 265-cubic-inch V-8 introduced in 1955. Although it had grown in capacity to 355-cubic-inches, it was still the standard of the NASCAR scene.

During the 1986 season, Chevrolet Monte Carlo SS Aerocoupes scored 18 wins in the NASCAR Winston Cup circuit. Examples here are driven by Dale Earnhardt (car number 3), Darrell Waltrip (car number 11) and Ernie Bierschwale (car number 17). Earnhardt went on to win the championship and Waltrip finished second in points. (Phil Hall Collection)

A champion from Milwaukee

By Phil Hall

Temperatures were cool and rain was threatening, but it looked as if the 1973 season of late-model and sportsmen's stock car racing would get underway. It was Saturday night, May 12 at the Hales Corners Speedway, a quarter-mile clay bullring in the Milwaukee suburb of Franklin, Wisconsin. There were the usual amounts of new cars and drivers, but less than the usual amount of fans for a season opener. Only 3,625 spectators were on hand that night.

A blue and white 1969 Camaro with the number 73 on the side was there. The Camaro's driver was only 18 years old. This was the first year 18-year-olds could legally race in Wisconsin. Instead of starting in the lower-dollar sportsmen's class, the youthful driver chose to go right into the late-models. This decision made the officials scratch their heads.

That night, the young driver of the Camaro, which was in its second year of short track racing, placed fifth in the 15-lap semi-feature. He took home $27. Few noticed his appearance. The next week he came back to race again. He took a third in one heat and eighth in the semi-final. He upped his earnings to $39.60. His third week of racing showed that he was a fast learner. He won the semi-feature and $66 that evening. He also started a career of winning that carried him to the top NASCAR Winston Cup stock car drivers in the country.

His name was Alan Kulwicki. In the next 20 years, he would forge one of the brightest careers in modern stock car racing history. It would be a career that ended all too suddenly, when he died on April 1, 1993, in a plane crash in Blountville, Tennessee.

Even though Alan was an unknown quantity behind the wheel of a race car in 1973, his name was familiar to racers. His father, Jerry Kulwicki, was a top-rated engine builder for United States Auto Club stock car racer Norm Nelson. Among the drivers who had been successful in Norm Nelson's Plymouths at that time were A.J. Foyt, Jim Hurtubise, Lloyd Ruby and two-time

In his rookie year at the Hales Corners Speedway, Alan Kulwicki (number 73) battled it out with John Reiser (number 2) in a late-model feature race, late in the season. (Midwest Racing News)

By 1977, Alan Kulwicki was an accomplished late-model dirt track racer. He is shown in car number 32, winning a feature at the Hales Corners Speedway on July 17. He beat Aaron Solsrud, in car number 4, who was a master of dirt racing. (Midwest Racing News)

USAC champ Roger McCluskey. Nelson had won three titles, the first in a Ford and the last two Plymouths. All had used engines prepared by Jerry Kulwicki.

Showing an independence that was generated not entirely by choice, young Alan started in a 1969 Camaro originally built for the 1972 season. It had a stock steel body, reinforced frame and small-block Chevrolet V-8. That type of car was the hot setup in short track late-model racing at the time. Alan picked up the second-hand racer, helped set it up himself and went about the process of learning to be a dirt track racer.

Jerry Kulwicki was not thrilled with his son's new hobby and did not help him with the mechanical chores. Only after Alan demonstrated that he could be successful on his own, did his father gradually become a fan. Still later, he became a limited helper.

Alan went through the summer of 1973 racing at Hales Corners and at Cedarburg Speedway, a quarter-mile dirt oval north of his West Allis home. He raced as much as he could. However, when money was not available for repairs, there were nights he had to sit out the races. As the season progressed, he began to erase the doubts of his fellow competitors and fans. He gradually made the feature races, which were for the fastest 18 cars.

On 1973's final night of racing at Hales Corners, on September 22, Kulwicki qualified 12th fastest. He won his heat and he led the feature for a while. He also scored his best feature finish, placing fifth in the Farewell 50. His $129.90 paycheck was the best of his rookie season. That year, a total of 89 late-model drivers earned points at the two tracks, which together were known as the PRO-STAR circuit. Alan Kulwicki finished 15th in the final point standings.

On a cold Saturday night, November 10, 1973, the top drivers were honored at the annual PRO-STAR awards party. Alan Kulwicki, still more than a month away from his 19th birthday on December 14, was chosen late-model "rookie of the year." It was a seemingly impossible feat, considering a strong field of veteran competitors. The seeds of a great racing career were clearly sown with most of the ingredients Alan possessed right up until his untimely death.

When Alan received his rookie award, he already had his sights set beyond Hales Corners and Cedarburg. He was enrolled at the University of Wisconsin-Milwaukee. There, he pursued a college degree in engineering. This was a rarity for short track racers.

The next season was one of limited competition, on the dirt, for Kulwicki. The Hales Corners and Cedarburg ovals were enlarged to third-mile configurations for 1974. However, another change took place in the Milwaukee area. It was one that would have an important affect on Kulwicki's racing career. For 1974, the Slinger Speedway, once a short, dirt quarter-mile, was rebuilt into a high-banked paved oval. At the start of the season, modifieds were running there. However, Slinger switched to late-models late in the year.

Kulwicki tried the pavement and his abilities, as a driver and a mechanic, took on new horizons. He quickly became known as the "Boy Wonder" of the area's paved short tracks.

Ironically, it was Kulwicki's love of pavement racing that led to his biggest success on dirt. The promoter at Slinger Speedway did not want local racers to be "blown away" by professional asphalt racers who ruled Wisconsin motorsports. He mandated that a driver had to race one night a week on a dirt track to qualify for the competition at Slinger. This mandate brought Alan Kulwicki back to Hales and Cedarburg. In 1976 he made a few of the dirt shows. The 1977 and 1978 seasons were his best by far. He placed fourth in PRO-STAR standings for both years.

Alan Kulwicki had several fast-time honors in 1977. On July 13, he won his first dirt feature at Cedarburg. He came back on July 16 and won again at Hales Corners. Alan capped his drive the next night by winning the Slinger main event on pavement. He became the first Milwaukee area driver to take three straight at the three different tracks. Alan won again at Cedarburg, two weeks later, and added a third career win at the same track in 1978.

Kulwicki could have been one of the top late-model drivers on the dirt tracks. However, he liked the pavement and concentrated on it, exclusively, starting with the 1979 season. Not only did he master the short tracks, but he also ran the USAC circuit for experience. Later, he raced on the American Speed Association (ASA) circuit, before making his move to the NASCAR

One week in 1977, Alan Kulwicki won three Milwaukee area feature racing events, two on dirt and one on pavement. He is on the right, receiving one of his trophies at Hales Corners during the 1977 season. (Midwest Racing News)

Not only did Alan Kulwicki learn how to win on the dirt, he learned what it was like to crash and have to repair his own car. This was the remains of his car after a late-1977 crash at the Hales Corners Speedway. (Midwest Racing News)

Winston Cup circuit in 1985. Along the way to racing success, he earned an engineering degree.

Kulwicki was talented in engineering and held the promise of a successful career behind a computer and drawing board. However, he never gave up his spirit of independence. He ran his own ASA team, instead of driving for others. He ran five Winston Cup events in 1985, driving for others. Alan failed to crack into the top 10 and tallied $10,290 for all his hard work. Convinced that he could make it on the toughest national championship circuit of them all, he loaded his possessions into his vehicle and moved south to set up his own shop for the 1986 season.

Shades of 1973! In 1986, at 31 years of age, Alan Kulwicki started his own race team, since no one would give him a good ride. The season was legendary. With one car and hardly any money compared to the big teams, he was voted the circuit's "rookie of the year." He earned the honor against all odds, just as he had 13 seasons before. He finished 21st in points.

Major sponsorship from Zerex came along in 1987. Then he won his first Winston Cup event at Phoenix, Arizona in the fall of 1988. Alan Kulwicki went on to win the 1992 Winston Cup Championship. He never got to enjoy a full season as the defending champion, however, as he perished in his fateful air crash in the spring of 1993. Alan became a champion the hard way, by being both a driver and car owner. By the start of the 1990s, his annual winnings were in the $450,000 range and his sponsorship was reported to be worth upwards of $1 million. However, through it all, Alan Kulwicki still acted like that 19-year-old Camaro driver whose enthusiasm and independence once paid off with $27 in prize money.

Good-bye Richard Petty: "The King" of stock car racing retires

By Phil Hall

A list of Richard Petty's accomplishments in stock car racing is nearly as long as the list of items and promotions that were part of his "Fan Appreciation Tour" of 1992. Petty has been a seven-time NASCAR champion and a 200-race winning driver. He recorded the most consecutive victories, the most wins in a season, seven Daytona 500 wins and much more.

Petty's 35th season of NASCAR racing was announced as his last as a driver. To commemorate the event, a season-long celebration of the career of "The King" took place along the NASCAR-Winston Cup schedule and in a variety of places. A seemingly endless supply of Petty souvenirs was hawked. He even made a guest appearance on a home shopping cable television channel to sell souvenirs.

Petty turned 55 years old on July 22, 1992. In that time span, he became the unquestioned all-time leader in many statistical categories of NASCAR competition. Playing an even bigger role in his popularity, and his farewell extravaganza, was his attitude toward his fans and the public. Perhaps no other national racing hero has taken as much time to talk with, sign autographs for, and appreciate his fans.

An example of Petty's power is that his retirement sparked Pontiac Division of General Motors to issue a 1992 Richard Petty Edition Grand Prix SE coupe. The car featured decals of the lanky driver's famous signature and other special trim to commemorate Pontiac's most famous race car driver.

For most of his racing years, Petty was strongly associated with the cars he raced, with direct factory backing, for many seasons. Pontiac was the seventh make of car he campaigned on a regular basis. The 11 years from 1982 to 1992 was the longest number of consecutive years that Petty stayed with one marque. His father, a tough, three-time NASCAR Grand National

Richard Petty's father, Lee Petty, poses with his winning Dodge at an April 1953 race at Richmond, Virginia. Lee Petty took 54 career wins. (Phil Hall Collection)

Richard Petty emerges victorious from his famous 1964 Plymouth wearing number 43 on its door. (Phil Hall Collection)

His T-shirt clearly identified his favorite racing car, when Petty posed for this shot in 1964. (Phil Hall Collection)

For 1966, Ford drivers sat out the season, leaving the Mopars to rack up checkered flags. Richard Petty responded early by winning the Daytona 500 pole position. Then, he took his second 500 in a row. He was driving a 1966 Plymouth Belvedere, number 43, like the one seen here in action at the 1966 Southern 500. (Phil Hall Collection)

Richard "The King" Petty poses with some of his prettier fans in a 1966 publicity shot. That season he was driving a 1966 Plymouth Belvedere and went on to score eight wins and claim third in points. (Phil Hall Collection)

Petty (left) and his Plymouth Belvedere are seen on the starting line at the Southern 500 on September 5, 1966, next to Darel Dieringer and his Bud Moore Mercury Comet. (Phil Hall Collection)

Champion, gave Richard his first experience with factory racing support. Lee Petty had campaigned Plymouths, Dodges and Chryslers early in NASCAR history, before becoming an Oldsmobile factory driver. His Lee Petty Engineering signed a factory deal with Oldsmobile in 1957. It was inked shortly before the auto manufacturers withdrew from racing in June of that year.

The racers got to keep the cars and parts the factories had provided. Lee kept and used his 1957 Oldsmobiles. Richard Petty's first season of racing was 1958. During that year, and a good part of the next one, he wheeled those somewhat battered 1957 Oldsmobiles for his dad. Richard's first race came shortly after his 21st birthday. It was in NASCAR's convertible division. The race took place July 12, 1958, on the half-mile dirt track at Columbia, South Carolina. He finished sixth. His first Grand National (now Winston Cup) start was six days later, on the one-third-mile paved oval at the Canadian National Exposition in Toronto, Ontario, Canada. Petty remembers the latter race well. "Cotton Owens was leading and daddy was second," he recalls. "They came up on me and I moved over to let them pass. Cotton went on, but daddy bumped me in the rear and my car went right into the wall." Richard finished 17th out of 19 cars.

Lee Petty used his remaining. Oldsmobile parts to put together a 1959 Oldsmobile. With it, he won the first Daytona 500-mile race in 1959. Richard finished 57th out of 59 cars. He drove a 1957 Oldsmobile convertible. As its Oldsmobile parts supply dwindled, Petty Engineering selected the 1959 Plymouth as its car of choice for the 1959 season. Lee Petty had enjoyed great success racing six-cylinder Plymouths in NASCAR in the early 1950s. Overt factory support was nonexistent then.

It was in the transition period between racing Oldsmobiles and racing Plymouths that Richard Petty scored his first win ... or thought he did. In the 150-mile Grand National race, at Lakewood, Georgia, on June 14, 1959, Richard finished first in an Oldsmobile convertible. Lee was second in a Plymouth hardtop. Lee protested his son's win. The protest was upheld. Lee got the win with Richard falling to second. Though Richard did not win a Grand National event in 1959, he did claim his first NASCAR win in a 200-lap convertible contest at Columbia, South Carolina on July 18. He was driving a 1959 Plymouth. Petty finished fourth in convertible points in 1959, the last year for a full-season schedule including the topless cars.

Petty had reason to smile after winning the Southern 500 at Darlington on September 7, 1967. (Phil Hall Collection)

The 1960 season would be significant for Petty Engineering. Lee Petty won back-to-back Grand National titles to accompany his 1954 crown. He and his son ran in Plymouths the whole season. It would be their last year of racing together. A 1961 crash would end Lee Petty's racing career. His son scored his first

168

Petty's 27 victories in 1967 made him America's winningest stock car driver. He's on the right of this photo taken at the Darlington 500, with Buddy Baker next to him. (Phil Hall Collection)

Richard poses with Karol Kelly, of Zephyrhills, Florida, before a 1960s Weaverville race. Kelly, the reigning Miss Dixie, appeared at the Western North Carolina 500 and Petty held the track qualifying record. (Phil Hall Collection)

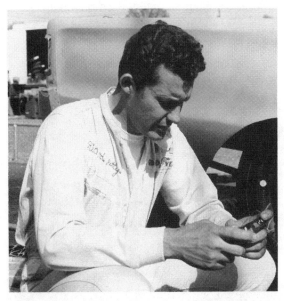

A pensive Petty appears in a publicity photo for the 1967 Firecracker 400, which he had not won at the time. The purse for 1967 was $66,000. (Phil Hall Collection)

Richard Petty won his 71st victory in 1967 at the same race track in Richmond, Virginia where his father won 14 years earlier. (Phil Hall Collection)

Parnelli Jones (left) laughs it up with Richard Petty. (Phil Hall Collection)

Grand National win on February 28, 1960, at the old Charlotte, North Carolina fairgrounds track. It was a dirt one-half-mile course. Richard Petty took two more wins that year and wound up second in points to Rex White. Lee Petty finished sixth in points and took five wins.

There were two qualifying races for the 1961 Daytona 500. Richard Petty crashed out of the track in the first contest. Lee Petty was seriously injured in a wreck during the second race. Richard missed the Daytona 500 and Lee never returned to driving stock racing cars. During the balance of the season, Richard won a couple of more races. However, the Plymouth 413-cubic-inch V-8s were no match for the heavily-supported Fords, Pontiacs, and Chevrolets. The down-sized Plymouths of 1962 were more competitive than the 1961 models. Richard Petty again finished second in the Grand National points standings. He took eight wins, his best personal record to that point. There were even more promising events in 1963, as factory support of racing grew much stronger. It included equipment like the 426-cubic-inch "wedge head" V-8 that powered his Plymouth. Young Petty again took NASCAR's runner-up honors in points. His 14 seasonal wins were more than any other driver. Ned Jarrett's record of eight victories was next best.

All the preceding achievements were just a "sideshow," compared to the 1964 season. Chrysler Corporation unleashed its 426-cubic-inch hemi V-8. NASCAR approved its use in Dodges and Plymouths and MoPar's competition headed back to the drawing board. The hemi-powered Mopars dominated the Daytona 500, with Richard Petty bringing his number 43 Plymouth home first on February 23, 1964. Two more Plymouths were right behind him. The 1964 season was 62 races long. When it was over, Petty had nine wins and his first Grand National title.

Driving for Ford, Richard Petty (number 43) dueled it out with David Pearson (number 17) at the Daytona 500 on February 23, 1969. (Phil Hall Collection)

The powerful new MoPar engine did not sit well with Chrysler's main competitor. Ford Motor Company met the hemi's superiority with a barrage of NASCAR politics. When the in-fighting was over, it was mandated that hemis could only be used, in 1965, in full-size Plymouths and Dodges. The intermediate-size cars raced in 1964 would have to use other types of engines. As a result of this mandate, Chrysler withdrew its factory-backed drivers from competition. Ford had NASCAR Grand National racing to itself. Petty and others tried drag racing. Some Mopar pilots went up north to run in USAC-sanctioned stock car races. As NASCAR crowds got smaller, a compromise was reached late in the season. It was designed to bring the Mopar intermediates back to tracks of one mile or less in length. Petty ran 14 of the 55 races in 1965 and won four of them.

For 1966, the Ford brass got mad. Ford drivers sat out the season, leaving the Mopars to rack up checkered flags. Richard Petty responded by winning his only career Daytona 500 pole position. Then he took his second 500 in a row. He was driving a 1966 Plymouth Belvedere. Petty went on to score eight wins and claim third in points.

All the players were in their places for the 1967 season. Petty was in a 1967 Belvedere GTX. The FoMoCo faithful preferred driving intermediate-size Fairlanes. The season looked as if it would be a closely contested one, but it was not. Petty turned in the greatest single season in NASCAR Grand National (Winston Cup) history. In a 48-race schedule, he captured 27 first-place finishes. His victories included a never-matched 10 races in a row. Between the August 12 contest at Bowman-Gray Stadium in Winston-Salem, North Carolina and the October 1 Wilkes 400, at North Wilkesboro, North Carolina, Petty was the victor in every Grand National race that was run! He easily claimed his second Grand National crown that season.

Competition was tougher in 1968, especially on the superspeedways, since aerodynamics were coming into play. Ford had some sleek fastbacks to counter Plymouth's Road Runner and

Playing a big role in Richard Petty's popularity was his attitude toward his fans and the public. Perhaps no other national racing hero has taken as much time to talk with, sign autographs for, and appreciate his fans. (Phil Hall Collection)

"Daddy bumped me in the rear and my car went right into the wall." Richard said after his first Grand National race. This accident occurred in a later event. (Phil Hall Collection)

Dodge's Charger. Petty was good for 16 wins, the second-best total for his career. However, on the big tracks, the Ford products ruled the roost. Petty's 16 checkered flags equalled the total of champion David Pearson, who was a Ford driver in 1968.

The first two 1969 Grand National events were held on short tracks late in 1968. Petty won the season opener on November 17, driving a Plymouth. It would be his last victory in that make of car for a while, since it was announced that the unthinkable had happened ... Richard Petty would campaign Fords in 1969. His first "blue oval" outing was in a new Torino SportsRoof at the February 1, 1969, Motor Trend 500 on the road course at Riverside, California. Petty, who was never known as a great road racer, won the race and sent shock waves through the sport. He would go on to win eight more 1969 Grand National races in Fords. He finished second in points to David Pearson, a two-time champion. However, all was not happy in Pettyland. When the season ended, there were complaints that the other Ford teams were getting better parts and more help.

Petty announced he was returning to the Plymouth camp. One of the lures was the winged 1970 Plymouth Road Runner SuperBird. This car was the ultimate superspeedway warrior. Standard issue Road Runners would be used on the short tracks. Petty team driver Pete Hamilton won the Daytona 500 that year. Richard Petty's worst career crash came on May 9, 1970, in the Rebel

Richard Petty passed the million dollar earnings level in 1971. There were 48 events on the NASCAR Grand National circuit during that season, and Petty took 21 of them. He won the Texas 500 on December 12, bringing his annual earnings to $289,225. (Phil Hall Collection)

All-time stock car great Richard Petty enjoyed a super season during 1971. One highlight was a visit to a White House reception where the driver and his number 43 Plymouth met United States President Richard M. Nixon. Petty also won his third Grand National championship to join his father, Lee, and David Pearson as the only three-time winners. (Phil Hall Collection)

The only open factory support of a NASCAR operation in 1971 went to Petty Enterprises. A two-car team was sponsored. Richard Petty (insert) drove a 1971 Plymouth GTX. With other teams feeling the budget pinch, Petty dominated stock car racing. He took 21 wins out of 46 starts. (Phil Hall Collection)

Flying through a fog, Petty takes his first ride as top driver for Andy Granatelli's STP Racing Team at Riverside Raceway in 1972. (Phil Hall Collection)

400 at Darlington, South Carolina. His Road Runner hit the fourth-turn wall on lap 179 and flipped down the front stretch. The injuries he suffered kept him out of five races. He finished fourth in points. However, his 18 wins easily topped the record of anyone else on the circuit. Champion Bobby Isaac was next-best with 11 victories.

Factory support of racing was on the wane in 1971. Government standards, insurance rates, and other black clouds for the industry forced budget slashes. The only open factory support of a NASCAR operation in 1971 went to Petty Enterprises. A two-car team was sponsored. Richard Petty drove a 1971 Plymouth GTX and Buddy Baker piloted a 1971 Dodge Charger. With other teams feeling the budgeting pinch, Petty again dominated the Grand National wars. He took 21 wins out of 46 starts. Along way, he claimed his third Daytona 500 and third season championship.

The 1972 season was a significant one for NASCAR and for Richard Petty. The Grand

Fast work by Richard Petty's pit crew helped him win his seventh Winston Cup title last year. Their quickness with fueling and tire changing also earned them the Sears Craftsman National Pit Crew Championship as the fastest pit crew on the NASCAR circuit. His brother Maurice headed Petty's crew. (Phil Hall Collection)

The red-and-blue Dodge that Petty drove to his fifth NASCAR Grand National championship in 1974 was presented to Daytona for its new Museum of Speed at a 1977 ceremony. (Phil Hall Collection)

Petty knew what he was doing when he stuck to his older Chevy Monte Carlo. The same type car, as seen here in a 1977 pit stop, netted Petty the second-place finishes in points in 1976 and 1977.

National schedule was cut from 48 events to 31. Sponsorship by Winston created the Winston Cup, which would eventually become the name of the series. Sponsorship was also a factor for Petty, as STP picked him up. This started the longest sponsorship span in stock car racing. STP Corporation later announced a lifetime contract. To this day, Petty Engineering cars carry the familiar STP oval.

Petty started the STP relationship ... and the Winston Cup era ... with a win in the January 23, 1972, Winston Western 500 at Riverside Raceway in California. He went on to score eight more wins and take his fourth season championship. However, one thing long-identified with Petty was lost along the way. This was the exclusive use of a Plymouth race car. With strong factory support out of the picture, Petty's bulky 1972 Plymouth GTX was joined by a 1972 Dodge Charger during the year. It would also be his last season using Plymouths. The Charger had a redesigned roof for 1973 and remained the same for 1974. The design would be the standard-bearer for Petty for the next five-and-a-half racing seasons. In 1973, Petty notched a victory in his fourth Daytona 500. He added a half dozen other wins to his tally that year, bringing the total to 154 checkered flags. The 1974 season was even better. Richard Petty claimed his fifth Daytona 500 win and fifth Grand National championship. Ten more first place trophies were added to his collection.

Randleman, North Carolina's "favorite son" was among 10 previous winners of the race to compete at the Talladega 500 on August 5, 1979. The car is a 1977 Oldsmobile. (Phil Hall Collection)

"The King" drove his Buick Regal to his 194th NASCAR Grand National win on April 5, 1981 in the Northwestern Bank 400 at North Wilkesboro Speedway in North Carolina. (Phil Hall Collection)

Richard Petty was set to switch from Buicks to Pontiacs for the 1982 NASCAR Grand National season. His son Kyle also got an STP Pontiac. (Phil Hall Collection)

When the all-new 1975 Dodge Charger SE bowed, the notchback lines were not to the liking of racers in general and Petty in particular. Richard stayed with the 1974 Charger. Apparently, he knew what he was doing as he claimed his sixth championship and 13 more first-place finishes. The same car design and same plan netted Petty the second-place finishes in points in 1976 and 1977. Three wins in the bicentennial year and five the next season brought his win total to 185 checkered flags.

Dodge added a new aerodynamic looking front end to the Charger SE for 1978. It was called the Dodge Magnum. This car looked like a good replacement for the 1974 Charger that Petty was still using, but speedway tests revealed it to be unstable. Petty's son Kyle raced a Magnum and won his first race during an ARCA event at Daytona. However, Richard stuck to his 1974 Charger. The first 19 Winston Cup events on the 1978 schedule were run in Chargers, but no wins were recorded. Winston Cup racing had become a small-block venue. No Chrysler small-block V-8 was developed to the same extent as the Chevrolet small-block engine. Consequently, Richard Petty announced that he would switch to the bow tie brand. He started with the August 20, 1978, Champion Spark Plug 400 at Michigan International Speedway. He crashed there, but remained a Chevy racer the rest of the season, using 1977 and older Monte Carlos. Richard Petty did continue to field Dodges for his son, Kyle, for some time after his switch to Chevrolet.

For 1979, Petty and his crew adapted to General Motors power plants. NASCAR allowed any GM engine to be used with any GM body then. Petty used the Oldsmobile Cutlass 4-4-2 on the superspeedways and Monte Carlos on other tracks. This arrangement was a good one. Petty scored his sixth Daytona 500 win on February 18 and earned his seventh, and final, circuit title.

This is the 1985 STP Pontiac Grand Prix notchback that Petty piloted for Curb Motorsports in 1985. Petty finished 10th in points in 1984 and returned to race for Mike Curb's team in 1985. However, the wins stopped coming. The dry spell continued into Petty's final season. (Phil Hall Collection)

This new 1986 STP Pontiac 2+2 rolled out of the Petty shops that year. (Phil Hall Collection)

Richard Petty's ride for 1992, his final racing season, was the number 43 STP Pontiac Grand Prix. (Phil Hall Collection)

He scored five more wins, with four earned in Chevrolets. The same vehicles served Petty in 1980, but the Oldsmobile was reserved just for Daytona and Talladega. The 27 other events on the schedule were started in 1977 Monte Carlos. He took two more firsts and both came in Chevrolets.

Down-sizing was the hot topic for 1981 in NASCAR-Winston Cup competition. Petty started the season opener at Riverside in his trusty 1977 Monte Carlo. However, for the rest of the season, the shorter 1981 Buick Regal was his car of choice. His first point race in the Buick was the February 15, 1981, Daytona 500. This turned out to be Petty's seventh and final win there. Two days later, longtime crew chief Dale Inman announced he was leaving Petty Enterprises. This marked the start of a gradual decline in the fortunes of the once-dominant race team.

Petty picked up two more wins in the 1982 season, but only placed eighth in the points standings. For 1982, a car brand switch was made again and the Pontiac Grand Prix became the choice of Richard Petty. He drove them thereafter. Unfortunately, 1982 turned out to be another winless season. Wins returned in 1983, when three were recorded. However, further internal problems surfaced after the October 9 Miller High Life 500 at Charlotte, North Carolina. Petty's winning car was found to have an over-size engine and illegal tires. NASCAR let Petty keep the win, but fined him. Petty's brother, crew chief Maurice Petty, had made the equipment changes without telling him. At season's end, it was announced that Richard Petty was leaving Petty Enterprises to race for Curb Motorsports in 1984. The car remained the STP Pontiac Grand Prix. After early season motor problems, Petty won his 199th race, on May 20 at Dover, Delaware. It set the stage for his 200th victory. He pulled this off in a dramatic fashion, at the Pepsi Firecracker 400 in Daytona, with President Ronald Reagan in attendance. Petty finished 10th in points for 1984 and returned to race for Mike Curb's team in 1985. However, the wins stopped coming. The dry spell continued into Petty's final season.

Richard returned to Petty Enterprises for the 1986 season. That year, he collected his 1,000th Winston Cup start. Dale Inman also returned to the fold. A new Pontiac Grand Prix 2 + 2 came along in 1986, but Petty grew less and less competitive. There was a sleek new Grand Prix body for 1988, but it was not much assistance to Richard Petty and company. Despite his slowing down, the fans still loved him as much as ever. Still, the spectre of retirement began to surface regularly. In 1989, Petty started qualifying too slow to make the starting fields of some races. He started in only 25 of 29 events held that season.

Near the end of the 1990 season, a press conference was called. Although retirement seemed near, no such event was announced. Such an announcement was delayed one year. In 1991, Richard Petty released the news that he had decided to retire. Then, the Fan Appreciation Tour for "The King" was announced.

As 1992's race schedule unfolded, Petty ran no faster than he had in previous years, but the fans did not care. They wanted one last chance to see their hero. The last race was the Hardee's 500 November 15, 1992, at Atlanta Motor Speedway.

Petty poses with two prettys for an IROC promotion. (Old Cars photo)

The Petty pit crews were always top-notch. (Phil Hall Collection)

A young Richard Petty in his hemi-powered 1964 Plymouth. (Phil Hall Collection)

INDY: THE GREATEST SPECTACLE IN RACING

Racers from across the pond

By Phil Hall

When the Indianapolis 500-mile Race is run these days, the odds are great that a foreign-built chassis and probably a foreign-built engine will win. Today, it is taken for granted that Indy car designs come from overseas. Recent attempts to enter domestic products have not had much effect on the English dominance. Of course it hasn't always been that way. The American Indy car dominated the "World's Greatest Race" for many years. For the first taste of a successful foreign invasion, let's peel back the calendar to 1913, for the third annual 500-mile International Sweepstakes.

The first two runnings of this event attracted wide attention in the world racing community. However, it wasn't until 1913, that a strong international challenge was mounted. Entries from England, France, Germany and Italy were sent to the 2.5-mile brick oval for the 200-lap contest of speed on Friday May 30.

Frenchman Albert Guyot wheeled the British Sunbeam. Peugeot sent over two of its Grand Prix drivers named Paul Zaccarrelli and Jules Goux. The latter was fresh from setting a world's hour distance record of 106.22 miles at Brooklands in England. Two German Mercedes entries made the race. One was driven by American Ralph Mulford. A Mercedes-Knight was handled by the Belgian driver Theodore Pilette. A three-car team of Italian Isottas arrived at the last minute. Americans Teddy Tetzlaff and Harry Grant and Italian Vincenzo Trucco were signed as drivers.

The foreign drivers and equipment were new to Indianapolis. They faced a strong field of American men and machinery that was led by the winner of the 1912 race, Joe Dawson. Besides the money ($20,000 to win), the race was attractive to the Europeans because of a change in engine specifications. The maximum displacement was dropped from the 600-cubic-inches in effect the first two years. It was changed to 450-cubic-inches (7.4 liters), which was closer to the European Grand Prix limits. There were no limits on valve design and a variety of power plants were on hand for the 1913 contest.

Probably the most notable of the foreign contenders were the Peugeots. During the 1912 Grand Prix season, Peugeot had three L76 cars built. All were successful right out of the box. They had four-cylinder engines with the iron head-and-block case constructed as a unit. They featured dual overhead cams and four valves per cylinder. The valves were inclined at 45 degree angles. They displaced 7598 cc and had to be sleeved down to meet the 7.4-liter Indy limit. Peugeot used a four-speed transmission, a triple-disc clutch and a drive shaft and differential to drive the rear wheels. Suspension was by way of four semi-elliptic leaf springs. Word of their Brooklands performance, plus the advanced design of the engine, made the Peugeots favorites to win, despite the fact their drivers had never seen Indianapolis Motor Speedway before.

At opening qualifications on Tuesday, May 27, Caleb Bragg was fastest, in a Mercer, at 87.5 mph. Zuccarrelli was second, at 86 mph. He was followed by the fastest of three Stutz drivers, Charley Merz, at 84.5 mph. More cars qualified the next day, with Mason driver Jack Tower turning the best speed of any qualifier at 88.2 mph. Out of 31 entries to the race, 27 made the starting field for the 500. The crowd was charged with emotion over the confrontation between their American drivers and the foreign contingent, but their hopes for a resounding triumph by the Americans were quickly dampened.

Bragg started on the pole and led the first lap. Mason driver Bob Evans took the lead on lap two and held it until the fourth circuit. Then, Goux (who started in the middle of the field) took over and quickly ran away from the field. Bob Burman had his Keeton fired up. He was hitting more than 100 mph on the straights and coasting in the turns. Burman took the lead at the 40th mile, when Goux pitted for fuel and tires. Goux roared back and chased down Burman, who continued to lead until his carburetor caught fire. The blaze caused him to pit for nearly an hour.

Goux then took the lead and began his domination of the event. He was not without challenge, however. Gill Anderson pushed his Stutz into the lead. He was followed by Mulford in his Mercedes.

At the 260-mile mark, Goux resumed the lead. He was less than a minute ahead of Mulford and Anderson, who took over second. Anderson got the lead from Goux on a pit stop at the 320-mile mark, but Goux got the lead back and never relinquished it. The pair were some eight minutes ahead of the rest of the field. As the race progressed, it became apparent that the Peugeots had all they needed to win the event. The engine was designed to produce maximum power at 2250 rpm, but Goux was only turning 1700.

Anderson's challenge came to an abrupt halt, on lap 187, when he pitted with a broken

Jules Goux makes a pit stop with his number 16 Peugeot, during the 1913 Indianapolis 500-mile Race. (Al Krause Collection)

camshaft. That created a battle for second between Merz, in a Stutz, and Wishart in his Mercer. They were nearly a quarter of an hour behind the Frenchman. Wishart finished second and Merz had a spectacular third-place finish. His car was in flames for the final lap, with the riding mechanic doing his best to contain them. Following were Guyot in the Sunbeam, Pilette in the Mercedes-Knight, Howard Wilcox in a Fox, Ralph Mulford in the Mercedes, Louis Disbrow in a Case, Bill Haupt in a Mason, and George Clark in a Tulsa. As was the rule then, all completed the entire 500 miles.

Goux covered the distance in 6:30.05.00 to average 75.92 mph. He became the first winner to run the race with relief. Clark did not complete his distance until an hour and 21 minutes later. Burman was running at the finish and was flagged off the course. Goux's blue number 16 Peugeot needed seven additional tires, three for the right rear. Pit stops for the team, which also added fuel, oil and water, took a total of only 11 minutes. While a fine car, quick pit work and confident driving all added to Goux's winning effort, one more element was considered vital to his stamina ... sparkling wine. At each pit stop he consumed a pint of champagne. He then downed a seventh pint after his win. "But for the wine, I would have been unable to drive this race," he said after its conclusion.

One of the three Peugeots at Indy in 1913. (Al Krause photo)

Duesenbergs at Indy

By Phil Hall

Today the mention of Duesenberg automatically brings the ultimate connotation of prewar luxury, prestige, and innovative engineering. An Auburn-Cord-Duesenberg Festival is held at the A-C-D Museum in Auburn, Indiana, each September. At the event, the vast majority of the revered conversations on Duesenbergs will revolve around expertly restored production models. The passenger cars that wore the Duesenberg nameplate ranged from the 1921 Model A to the last gasp efforts of 1937.

No less significant were the racing efforts of the brothers Frederich and August Duesenberg. Short on resources and long on ingenuity, they labored for many years to beat the high-dollar efforts from this country and abroad. Although born in Germany, the Duesenberg brothers moved to Iowa at an early age. There they took an interest in things mechanical. Their mechanical aptitudes led to involvement with Mason automobiles. They took one of these cars, with a four-cylinder engine of their design, and went racing in 1912. The Mason race cars improved quickly, with one taking ninth in the 1913 Indianapolis 500-mile race. Then, as now, the Indy 500 was the most important race of the year.

Gaining experience and knowledge of drivers and tracks helped the brothers develop engines and chassis for competition. Their cars became known as Duesenbergs and they

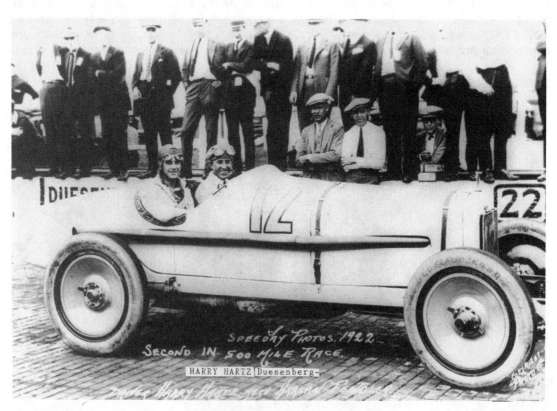

Driver Harry Hartz and mechanic Harlan Fengler took this Duesenberg to second place in the 1922 Indianapolis 500. (Al Krause Collection)

began to score wins at national championship events. However, a victory at the "Brickyard" and a trip to the Indy 500 winner's circle continued to evade them.

Besides innovation, a Duesenberg trademark was seemingly less than full preparation of cars. This seemed especially true at Indy. Shortages of cash and time were some things Fred and Augie Duesenberg were well known to have. However, the eyes of many observers were opened when rookie driver Wilber D'Alene took the lone Duesenberg entry to second place at the 1916 Indy 500.

World War I wiped out the 1917 and 1918 Indy contests, but all was back in place for 1919. That year, a new 297-cubic-inch straight eight with a single overhead cam was introduced by Duesenberg. It came in just under the new 300-cubic-inch limit for racing engines. Unfortunately, fate did not treat the Duesenberg entries kindly and mechanical problems developed at Indy.

For 1920, a three-liter (182-cubic-inch) engine displacement limit was announced. Four Duesenbergs were entered with a redesigned straight eight. Three placed in the top 10 finishers. Tommy Milton did best by taking third place. Things improved in 1921. That season there were seven Duesenbergs in the field at the Indy 500. Four finished in the top 10. They were led by a runner-up finish by Roscoe Sarles.

For 1922, a Duesenberg chassis won, but not with Duesenberg power. Ex-Duesenberg driver Jimmy Murphy took a 1921 Duesenberg chassis and fitted it with power from Harry Miller, who was Duesenberg's chief rival at the time. The car was called the Murphy Special. It won the race. Harry Hartz was second in a Duesenberg. He led an amazing display of power. Seven of the top 10 cars were of Duesenberg origin.

In leaner days, along with entering Duesenbergs, Augie and Fred sold cars and engines to help pay their bills. With some financial backing, the launch of cars for the passenger trade, and a new shop in Indianapolis, the Duesenbergs finally saw some financial success in the 1920s. For the 1923 season, a displacement limit of 122 cubic inches was announced. Despite having nearly a year's warning, the Duesenberg brothers were behind for the 1923 Indy 500. A 10th place finish by Phil "Red" Shafer and his rideless teammates was the result. Just the opposite was true for the 1924 Indianapolis 500, as the Duesenberg factory team was supplied with four entries. Three of them had superchargers, while the fourth had conventional carburetion.

Murphy, now a Miller driver, put the Miller Special on the pole for the 1924 Indy 500. His average speed was 108.037 mph. Joe Boyer was the fastest Duesenberg pilot in the race. He started inside, on the second row, and achieved a 104.84 mph effort. A total of 22 cars qualified for the race that year. The innovative, supercharged Duesenbergs were not given much of a chance for finishing the grind, but Boyer's number nine car was fast at the start. On the first lap, he sprung from the second row and took the lead from Murphy's Miller. However, the burst of power was costly. A key sheared in the supercharger, cutting the power and relegating Boyer to also-ran status. A relief driver crashed the car later in the race. Murphy then was cruising, but found a pesky Studebaker-powered car driven by Earl Cooper. Cooper caught him at one point, while Bennett Hill ran third in a Miller. L.L. Corum held down fourth in another supercharged Duesenberg. Cooper and Murphy continued to contest the lead. Almost unnoticed, Fred Duesenberg replaced Corum in the number 15 car. Boyer took over on the 109th of 200 laps. Press reports of the day said Duesenberg told Boyer: "Put that ship out in front or burn it up." Boyer followed the first command. Thanks to late pit stops for Cooper to take on tires, Boyer gave Duesenberg its first Indianapolis 500 win. Cooper brought the Studebaker Special home in second place, followed by Murphy. The Corum/Boyer combo was good for a record 98.24 mph average speed.

The 1924 race was only the beginning of winning for Duesenberg in the Indianapolis 500. Peter DePaolo repeated in 1925 and George Souders drove the same car to victory in 1927. All these drivers operated under intense pressure from the Miller forces.

Duesenberg entries continued at Indy and other major races into the 1930s. The death of Fred Duesenberg in 1932 did not curtail the racing efforts. Bits and pieces of Duesenbergs saw duty on racetracks up to World War II and a few years beyond the end of the conflict. Duesenberg's passenger car operation did not enjoy the success of the racing efforts, however. The company went into receivership in 1924. The Auburn Automobile Company bought the assets in 1926. The name was continued and enhanced by the new owners, until it was sapped of its strength in the depression-dominated 1930s.

Ford at the 1935 Indianapolis 500

By Tim Howley

From day one Henry Ford's empire was a hot rodder's dream. As "Uncle Tom" McCahill once wrote, "Old man Henry broke speed records at Daytona Beach before the fathers of many of you had ever heard about the birds and the bees." Officially, Ford was out of racing from 1912 to the 1930s, but numerous Ford dealers and parts suppliers around the country sponsored cars while Henry Ford looked on with satisfaction.

In the 1920s, fortunes were made by scores of suppliers of parts to hop-up the old Model T. With the introduction of its V-8 in 1932, hardly a car was built in America that could stay with a Ford. To quote McCahill again, "They rode with all the delicacy of a rock crusher, were practically nude of brakes, and were as generally uncomfortable as porcupine drawers. There was no reason that even the wildest thinker could dream up why anyone should buy a prewar Ford, aside from the fact that they could go like a well-oiled leopard, corner better than most cars of the day, and dig out from a traffic light so that the Cadillac set thought they were stalled." But, why did the factory suddenly develop a blind spot to performance, and neither officially nor unofficially return to racing until 1952? It's quite a story.

Louis Chevrolet, after a fallout with William Durant in the teens, went on to build his Frontenacs. Gaston Chevrolet drove a four-cylinder Frontenac to an Indianapolis 500 victory in 1920. Six eight-cylinder Frontenacs entered the 1921 race and Tommy Milton scored his first Indy victory with one of them. After that, Louis and Art Chevrolet turned to building racing heads for

Henry Ford served as referee for the 1924 Indianapolis 500-mile race, but still had time to pose with one of three Barber-Warnock Fords. Louis Chevrolet and Barney Oldfield are just behind Ford. (Al Krause Collection)

English racing great Stirling Moss' father Alfred Moss smiles while aboard one of the Barber-Warnock Fords he drove in 1924. (Al Krause Collection)

Model T Ford engines. They also built complete Frontenac Ford race cars. The Fronty Fords made their first appearance at Indianapolis in 1922. It was not successful. Then Barber-Warnock, an Indianapolis Ford dealer, commissioned Louis Chevrolet to build a single better one for the 1923 event. It finished a respectable fifth.

This prompted Barber-Warnock to enter a full team of Fronty Fords in the 1924 race. Henry Ford agreed to come down and act as honorary referee. The Fronty Fords finished 14, 16, and 17. Henry Ford returned to Dearborn, Michigan, again disavowing racing. If he could not win, he did not want to enter a race. He certainly was not interested in official factory sponsorship or in anything even hinting of factory support.

Fronty Fords were again entered by Warnock, and others, in 1925, 1926, 1930, and 1931. They finished at the back of the pack or did not finish at all. This is not to say the Frontenac Fords failed everywhere. Quite the contrary. They turned in creditable performances on dirt and board tracks from coast to coast. Moreover, Chevrolet's Fronty cylinder head business for Model Ts boomed throughout the 1920s and into the 1930s. However, when the 1932 Ford V-8 made the racing Model T obsolete, Chevrolet got into real trouble. He quickly became one of the most forgotten figures in the auto industry.

Using a Ford Model T block as a base, the Fronty-Ford four-cylinder engine powered the Barber-Warnock entries in the 1924 Indianapolis 500. They placed 14th, 16th and 17th. (Al Krause Collection)

Henry Ford returned to Indy in 1932, when a Lincoln KB roadster paced the Indy 500. He was accompanied by his old pal Harvey Firestone and his son Harvey Firestone, Jr. Along with them was Henry's son Edsel and two of Edsel's sons, Henry Ford II and Benson Ford.

Ralph Hepburn finished fourth in the 1941 Indy 500 in one of the reworked Miller-Fords. It was powered by a new Winfield V-8 engine. (Al Krause Collection)

A year later, C.O. Warnock, who had been associated with the Barber-Warnock Fords, entered a car in the Indy 500. It was powered by the new Ford flathead V-8. Unfortunately, it failed to qualify. In 1934, three Ford V-8 powered cars were entered. Two qualified. One jumped the wall on the 11th lap. The other developed major mechanical problems. On other tracks, Fords did much better in 1933 and 1934.

Enter Preston Tucker and Harry Miller. Miller was already a racing legend at Indy with his Miller-powered specials. However, he had gone off on a tangent venture that drove him into bankruptcy. Fred Offenhauser was holding the old race car firm together under the name of Miller-Offenhauser. Tucker was a young promoter who was still light-years away from creating his ill-fated Tucker Torpedo passenger car. Tucker and Miller formed a new company called Tucker-Miller. They approached Edsel Ford on entering 10 cars in the 1935 Indianapolis 500.

Edsel Ford was quite enthusiastic about racing. This was the period when he was building performance cars for his enjoyment. It was also the period of the Jensen-Fords. Although he was under the thumb of his domineering father in management and production, Edsel was fairly free to explore new avenues of design. These avenues did not exclude racing. However, old Henry was not too keen on the idea of supporting an Indy entry. "What if we don't win, what if our cars break down, or drivers get killed? Bad publicity for the company, humbug, hogwash." This was most probably his initial reaction. Henry put the whole project off until February 1935. Then, he suddenly and unexpectedly decided to give it a go. This did not give much time to build the cars, which seemed to be of little concern to Henry. He always expected the whole world to jump through his hoops. Predictably, foxy Henry hedged his bets. The factory did not sponsor the cars directly. Funds were channeled through dealer advertising.

Construction of the cars did not begin until March 12, giving the Tucker-Miller factory in Detroit, Michigan only 79 days until the race. They worked around the clock, building the low, sleek jobs with radiators resembling those of the then-current Ford passenger cars. The block, crankshaft, connecting rods, valves, and push rods were stock. The engines were mounted backwards to facilitate front-wheel-drive. The cylinder heads were aluminum and designed to place water outlets at the front of the car. The compression ratio was 9.5:1 and pistons were of special construction. Horsepower was raised from the stock 90 hp to about 150 hp. They were the first front-wheel-drive cars with four-wheel independent suspension to appear at Indianapolis. It's hard to believe that Henry Ford approved such a setup, but he did. Strangely, the brakes remained of the four-wheel mechanical type.

Built hastily, the cars had a serious problem. The steering assembly was placed too close to the engine and heat cooked its lubricants, freezing up the system. Of the 10 Miller-Fords that were built, only five qualified.

Harry Miller (left) joined Barber-Warnock drivers Fred Harder, Bill Hunt and Alfred Moss, along with race car engineer Arthur Chevrolet, after the 1924 Indy 500. (Al Krause Collection)

A couple were never finished in time to qualify. On Memorial Day, Thursday, May 30, a 1935 Ford four-door convertible paced the track. Harry Mack, one of Ford security man Harry Bennett's goons, was driving. Henry and Edsel Ford were at the Indianapolis Motor Speedway, but not in the pace car.

Dale Evans, with riding mechanic Johnny Hughes, did not make the 1935 Indy 500 in a Miller-Ford. He was the first alternate. (Al Krause Collection)

The Miller-Fords that raced were number 43 driven by Ted Horn, number 45 driven by Clay Weatherly, number 42 driven by Johnny Seymour, and number 46 driven by Bob Sall. That's four, but we said that five qualified. The fifth one, number 35, was to be driven by George Bailey. Somehow, it could not get in gear just minutes before the race started. This was an omen for Henry Ford.

Before 10 laps were completed, Weatherly's Ford hit the railing. He was killed. Bailey managed to get in the race with a late start. On lap number 65, he dropped out completely due to a frozen steering system. Sall dropped out after 47 laps. Seymour stopped after 71 laps. He had the same problem as Bailey with an overheated steering box. Ted Horn, driving number 43, held on until the 145th lap. Then his car developed the same steering box problem. Officially, he finished in 16th place.

Henry Ford was humiliated. There he was with his son Edsel. Ford Motor Company had invited 2,800 Ford dealers to attend. Most likely, the entire crowd at the speedway knew that Henry was there. It must have been one of the greatest humiliations of his career; equal to those of the ill-fated Peace Ship tour or the *Chicago Tribune* trial. This one was especially biting, because the failure was all about Ford performance. Henry had personally delayed the building of the cars until there was not enough time to test them thoroughly.

From what this author knows, racing was never again discussed in Dearborn, until several years after Henry Ford's death in 1947. Any psychiatrist would have had a heyday with Henry Ford. The man simply could not accept failure. His block-out mechanisms were unbelievable. Henry was the success story of the century. How could he possibly admit to himself the slightest flaw in his plans? In his denial of failure he would always blame some exterior force. This made him bitter and mistrustful. In fact, after the failure at Indianapolis, he withdrew further into his puttering around his Fairlane mansion and his strange relationship with Evangeline Cote Dahlinger.

Ted Horn's 16th-place finish was the best among four Miller-Ford V-8s entered the 1935 Indianapolis 500-mile race. (Al Krause Collection)

Danny Kladis placed 21st in the 1946 Indy 500 in an 11-year-old Miller-Ford entered by Andy and Vince Granatelli's Grancor Engineering. It had a Grancor V-8. Kladis was disqualified for being towed during the race. (Al Krause Collection)

Winning engines of the "Brickyard"

By Phil Hall

On May 30, 1993, thanks to Emerson Fittipaldi, the Chevrolet Indy V-8 won its sixth consecutive victory in the Indianapolis 500-mile race. While such a feat is impressive, it represents a mere "blip on the screen" in comparison to some of the winning streaks by power plants over the 77-race history of the "Greatest Spectacle in Racing."

The Chevrolet Ilmor V-8 was immediately preceded on the winner's list by the Cosworth DFX V-8, which accounted for 10 straight wins. They ranged from Al Unser's third Indy 500 victory in 1978, to his fourth in 1987. However, all winning records pale in comparison to the 18 consecutive races won by the Meyer-Drake or Offenhauser four-cylinder racing engine. It powered 18 straight Indy winners from 1947 through 1964.

The history of Indianapolis 500 winning power plants is interesting not only in terms of their technology, but also for the fact that most were mainstream motors, compared to the wide vari-

The first win for a Miller-powered car came in 1922, when Jimmy Murphy wheeled his Murphy Special to victory. It was a Miller eight-powered Duesenberg. Murphy is shown on the right, with his riding mechanic Ernie Alson on the left. (Phil Hall Collection)

WINNER.
DRIVER. TOMMY MILTON
CAR. H.C.S. SPECIAL.
500 MILE RACE 1923.
INDIANAPOLIS MOTOR SPEEDWAY.

Tommy Milton won his second Indianapolis 500-mile race in three years when he took the checkered flag in 1923. He was driving the H.C.S. Special (named for Harry C. Stutz). This car had a Miller eight for power. (Phil Hall Collection)

ety of radical designs that attempted to unseat the establishment. The engines also varied due to different displacement limit rules, which went from a high of 600 cubic inches, in 1911 and 1912, to a low of 91.5 cubes from 1926 to 1929.

Though the limit was 600 cubic inches, Ray Harroun's winner in the first Indianapolis 500, in 1911, was powered by a 447-cubic-inch Marmon six. It would be one of only two victories for engines with a half-dozen cylinders. The first of the 37 wins for four-cylinder engines came in the 1912 Indy 500. It happened when Joe Dawson drove a 490.8-cubic-inch National to victory.

Foreign engines scored their initial win in the 1913 event, which had a 450-cubic-inch limit. Jules Goux drove a French Peugeot to victory. It had a 448-cubic-inch four. Rene Thomas followed with a Delage in 1914. The limit dropped again to 300 cubic inches for 1915. That was just fine for winner Ralph DePalma, who had a 274-cubic-inch Mercedes four-cylinder. Dario Resta won the 1916 event, which was only scheduled for 300 miles, with a Peugeot. This made the French marque the first brand to score a repeat victory. There were no events in 1917 and 1918 due to World War I. Peugeot returned, in 1919, for a second straight win and third win overall. Howdy Wilcox was the winning driver that year.

The next drop in engine size limits came for the 1920 Indy 500, when three liters or 183 cubic inches was the maximum displacement allowed. Gaston Chevrolet, who already had a car make named after him, drove a Monroe four to the win that year. It was the seventh straight win for a four, but the last until 1934.

The reign of the straight eights began in 1921 when Tommy Milton won with a Frontenac power plant. The real beginning of a dynasty in Indy 500 power began, in 1922, with Jimmy Murphy's win in the Murphy Special. It used Harry Miller's straight eight in a Duesenberg chassis. Descendants of the design would continue to win the 500 through 1976. Milton scored his second win, in 1923, aboard the H.C.S. Special, which also had Miller power. The displacement limit dropped to two liters or 122 cubic inches that year. Duesenberg (Miller's rival of the era) had an impressive supercharged eight that worked well with the new displacement limit. It took wins in 1924 and 1925. L.L. Corum and Joe Boyer drove in 1924 and Peter DePaolo the next year.

A new 1.5-liter (91.5 cubic inch) displacement limit went on Indy cars for 1926. Frank Lockhart won the rain-shortened 400-mile event with a supercharged Miller power plant. Duesenberg's last win came in the 1927 Indy 500, thanks to George Souders. After that Miller eights won all events from 1928 through 1933.

Starting in 1930, stock block engines up to 366 cubic inches were allowed, in order to encourage factory racing support. Pure racing engines, like the Miller eight, were allowed less cubic inches. Billy Arnold's 1930 win was in a front-wheel-drive Miller with a 151.5-cubic-inch Miller eight. Shop foreman Fred Offenhauser bought the Miller operation in 1932. He continued power plant development. One result of his work was a four-cylinder version of the Miller. It became better known as an Offenhauser (or "Offy") engine, than a Miller. That engine was in the Boyle Special that won the 1934 Indy 500 with Bill Cummings driving it. The four-cylinder started a streak of its own. It was in the winning cars for 1934, 1935, 1936, 1937 and 1938. That last year, the displacement ceiling went to 274.6 cubic inches for naturally-aspirated racing engines and 183 cubic inches for supercharged power plants.

A resurgence of foreign power saw supercharged eight-cylinder Maseratis win in 1939 and 1940. Wilbur Shaw was the driver aboard these Boyle Specials. The last race before World War II, the 1941 edition, saw Floyd Davis and Mauri Rose co-drive the Offy-powered Noc-Out Special to a win. No races were held from 1942 to 1945, due to World War II.

When the Indy 500 returned in 1946, the field was a combination of prewar and postwar machinery. George Robson ended years of frustration for car owner Joel Thorne. He took the

A break in Miller/Offenhauser domination of the Indianapolis 500-mile race came in 1939 and 1940 when Wilbur Shaw scored back-to-back wins in the Boyle Special. This famous car was a supercharged eight-cylinder Maserati. (Phil Hall Collection)

win in the Thorne Engineering Special, which had a Sparks-Thorne "small six" with a supercharger. It was the second win for a six. Starting in 1947, front-engined Indy cars with Offenhauser four-cylinder power ruled the Indianapolis Motor Speedway with an iron fist. The engines were called Meyer-Drakes, being renamed after Louis Meyer and Dale Drake, who took over the company. A 1957 drop in maximum displacement to 256.3 cubic inches for naturally-aspirated engines had virtually no effect on the Meyer-Drake engines' dominance.

What did have an effect on Meyer-Drake's future, however, was the invasion of rear-engine car designs in the 1960s. Lotus-Fords gave the Indianapolis "establishment" a scare in 1963. Things got serious in 1964, when the engines went from overhead valves to dual overhead cams. A.J. Foyt scored the last front-engine win in 1964. It was also the last win for a naturally-aspirated Offy.

Ford V-8s claimed three straight 500s in 1965, 1966 and 1967. Jim Clark, Graham Hill and A.J. Foyt took the respective wins. Then, turbo-charging (using exhaust-driven turbine wheels) came of age in 1968. Bobby Unser won that year, in the Offy-four-powered Rislone Special. The Ford V-8s adapted turbo-charging as well. They ran off a string of three straight wins. Mario Andretti's Ford-powered victory came in 1969 and Al Unser took the flag with a Ford in 1970 and 1971.

Mario Illien (left) and Paul Morgan show off their Chevrolet Ilmor Indy V-8. In various forms, this engine was in Indy 500 winners for six straight years between 1988 and 1993. (Phil Hall Collection)

The last hurrah for the Drake-Offy four came with a streak of five straight wins. They started with Mark Donohue's victory in 1972 and ran through Johnny Rutherford's second of three career victories in 1976.

Another last came in the 1977 Indy 500. A.J. Foyt scored his fourth 500 win with the Foyt V-8, which was the final stage of development of the old Ford V-8. Already on the scene was the Cosworth DFX V-8. This was a modified version of the Ford-Cosworth Formula 1 power plant. Ten straight wins were reeled off for this British-built engine, which was later modified and called the DFS.

Chevrolet, Roger Penske, Mario Illien and Paul Morgan combined their talents and finances to produce a V-8 engine strictly for Indy car racing in the mid-1980s. The Ilmor Chevrolet V-8 was the result. After a slow start, it went on to dominate the racing in much the same way the Cosworths and Offys had done before. Rick Mears scored the first Indy 500 win with an Ilmor Chevrolet V-8 in 1988. He was followed by Emerson Fittipaldi in 1989 and Arie Luyendyk in 1990. Mears won again, in a Chevy-engined car, in 1991. Al Unser, Jr. extended the engine's winning ways in 1992. Fittipaldi did the same in 1993.

That made it 17 straight wins for British engines in the most famous American racing event of them all. The 1993 victory was also the 23rd for a V-8 and 38th for eight-cylinder engines. Fours are just behind with 37 wins. Sixes accounted for the other two.

Despite the success of its Ilmor efforts, after 1993, Chevrolet announced that it was withdrawing support from the program. Mercedes-Benz picked up part of the support in 1994. The German automaker plans to assume total support in 1995.

Moore first to dominate at Indy

By Phil Hall

Today we rightfully marvel at Roger Penske's domination of the Indianapolis 500-mile race. From the late-Mark Donohue's win in 1972, through Al Unser, Jr.'s win in 1994, Penske's cars have taken 11 of the classic contests in 23 years. Penske cars took three straight Indy 500s from 1987 to 1989. Many of the wins came in cars that Penske, a former sports car driver, was responsible for building.

However, Penske's accomplishments pale a bit in comparison to those of another former driver, Lou Moore. His Indy 500 entries scored five wins in eight racing years, including three in a row. He won with Floyd Roberts in 1938, the combo of Floyd Davis and Mauri Rose in 1941, Rose again in 1947 and 1948, and Bill Holland in 1949. The three in a row string is more impressive in that Holland finished second in 1947 and 1948 in Moore's cars. Rose also came within a few laps of a third straight one-two finish in 1949.

Moore did not just own the Blue Crown Spark Plug Specials that dominated the 1947 to 1949 races. In addition, he oversaw their design, helped build them in his California shops, and worked on them when they came to the track. Moore even played a key role during pit stops. While some owners of the day wore business suits on race day, Moore's standard garb was a one-piece mechanic's uniform and Mobiloil hat. Putting his late 1940s dominance into perspective, it was not a time of conformity forced by the rules. After the four-year layoff for World War II, there was a definite debate on nearly all mechanical aspects of the race cars that ran at the "Brickyard."

While engine size was regulated at three liters for supercharged engines and 4.5 liters for naturally-aspirated motors, much else was up in the air. Postwar engines used four-cylinder, six-cylinder and eight-cylinder (V-8) configurations. Carburetion was being challenged by fuel injection. Fuel choices ranged from gas to alcohol to combinations only a chemist could understand. Both superchargers and "atmospheric" induction were tried. The car chassis was just as open to developmental ideas, with front- and rear-drive being used. Some cars had independent or beam front suspensions. Even rear engine designs were in the works. There also was a six-wheel car with four-wheel-drive called the Pat Clancy Special. For one design to win three times straight, despite all of this creativity, was a true accomplishment. This was especially true since the same two cars and engines were used all three years.

Mauri Rose looks over the nose of his Indy 500-winning Blue Crown Spark Plug Special in May 1947. This was the first year this car ran. (Phil Hall Collection)

Lou Moore was born in Hinton, Oklahoma in 1904. Later, his family moved to California. He started racing in 1919, when he was underage. He gained experience on the dirt tracks and raced at Indianapolis from 1928 through 1936. He placed second his first year and came in third in 1933 and 1934. His last race as a driver was 1936.

Like most drivers, Moore felt he could put better cars on the track. However, unlike most

In 1948, for the second straight year, Holland drove the Blue Crown Spark Plug Special to a second-place finish in the Indianapolis 500-mile Race. Car owner Lou Moore stands behind the cockpit of the race car with his arms outstretched. Three other crew members flank the car owner. (Phil Hall Collection)

racers who find out the hard way that such a dream often leads to failure, he succeeded in making race cars. His machines won the Indy 500 in 1938 and 1941. Moore was not very content fixing up others' machinery. Following the 1946 Indy 500, he set about designing and building his own Indy car from the ground up. Moore was a perfectionist. With funds from Blue Crown Spark Plug Company, he had a state-of-the-art design drawn up by professional draftsmen. It incorporated front-wheel-drive, inboard brakes, and the Meyer-Drake four-cylinder engine with carburetion. The body was similar to the powerful Novi of the time, only shorter. The front suspension used longitudinal torsion bars and the rear had a solid axle with leaf springs.

Two cars were built at a cost of $62,500 for the pair. The only notable difference in the two was carburetion. The number 16 race car had Riley carburetion. The number 27 version used Stromberg fuel injection. They would both run on Mobilgas aviation gas.

For the 1947 Indy 500, Mauri Rose was signed to drive number 27. Bill Holland was hired to operate number 16. Holland was then a first-timer at Indy, but had extensive racing experience. Ted Horn took the pole. Cliff Bergere was second in a Novi. Rose started third in his Blue Crown car. Holland was eighth on the grid in a 30-car field. Holland quickly adapted to the 2.5-mile oval and stayed at or near the front for most of the race. He was leading at the 100-mile mark. By the halfway point, he was in control of the contest. Rose was running second. Late in the race, Moore gave Holland the "EZ" sign to save his equipment. Meanwhile, unknown to Holland, Rose was flying and closing fast. Holland followed orders. Rose also got the EZ sign, but ignored it. He took the lead with less than 10 laps to go. An upset Holland took second for following orders.

In 1948, three Blue Crown Spark Plug cars entered the Indianapolis 500-mile race. Holland's race car carried the number 2. Rose's car wore the number 3. The third was a dirt track rear-

Three Blue Crown Spark Plug Specials owned by Lou Moore posed in front of the old pagoda at Indianapolis Motor Speedway. The picture was snapped during practice, before the 1948 Indy 500. On the left is Mauri Rose in the race-winning number 3. Bill Holland, in the number 2, is in the center. An unknown driver sits in the number 22 dirt car, which was withdrawn before qualifications. (Phil Hall Collection)

drive car with number 22. The latter racer was withdrawn before the annual time trials. Rex Mays put the Bowes Seal Fast car on the pole, but Holland started second and Rose was third in the Blue Crown cars. Both vehicles had been taken apart and updated, but not changed in a basic sense. Ted Horn and Rex Mays ran strongly early in the 500-miler, but it was Rose's race. Holland outlasted faster rivals to take second, repeating his 1947 finish. However, the EZ-signal controversy was not repeated and Holland had no complaints.

For 1949, Lou Moore again redid his cars. Rose's car wore number 3 and Holland's sported a number 7. The dirt car also returned, with veteran driver George Connor getting the ride. In qualifying, Duke Nalon took the pole in a Novi. Mays was in another Novi on the grid alongside Nalon's car. The best Blue Crown effort was Holland's fourth starting spot. Connor started sixth. He was four spots up on Rose, who voiced objections to the way his car was running in qualifications. This time the "good soldier" (Holland) had his day. He dominated the last two-thirds of the race. With 50 miles to go, it was Holland, Rose, and Connor, giving Moore a potential one-two-three finish. Rose, however, pushed the car as hard as he could, despite being well behind. With less than 20 laps left, he dropped out with a broken magneto strap. Connor was passed by Johnny Parsons, giving Moore a one-three finish that broke his traditional string of one-two climaxes.

That Rose abused his car for no reason upset Moore. The car builder and driver parted company by that August. Team in-fighting also was costly in other ways and Moore's cars never again entered the victory circle at Indy. He left the car owner ranks after a few years and spent his final seasons in the seats of racetracks, as a spectator.

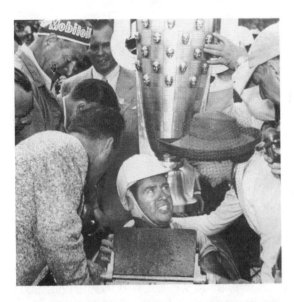

Bill Holland gets a kiss from actress Linda Darnell after winning the 1949 Indy 500 in his Blue Crown Spark Plug Special. In the background, wearing a Mobiloil hat and mechanic's overalls, is car owner Lou Moore. Holland just gave Moore his fifth Indy 500 win in eight years of racing, plus his third straight victory. (Phil Hall Collection)

Before the start of the 1949 Indy 500, the three Blue Crown Spark Plug Specials were readied for the race. The number 7 car was driven to victory by Bill Holland. Mauri Rose drove car number 3. Ahead of it is the number 22 dirt car, which George Connor used to finish third. Car owner Lou Moore is working on Rose's car in this photo. (Phil Hall Collection)

After winning the 1949 Indy 500, Lou Moore (with hat) is flanked by drivers (left to right) George Connor, Bill Holland and Mauri Rose. Connor placed third, Holland won and Rose was aimed at second place until his car quit, dropping him to 13th. (Phil Hall Collection)

Remembering Bill Vukovich

By Tim Howley

The year 1955 was a great one for automobiles, but a cursed year for motorsports. The hex began with the death of race driver Mike Nazaruk at Langhorn, Pennsylvania on May 1. It ended with the self-slaughter of actor James Dean at a rural California intersection. Dean was killed on September 30 when his fast moving Porsche Spyder was hit, by a Ford, while on its way to a sports car road race in Fresno. In terms of sheer numbers, the greatest 1955 tragedy was the LeMans disaster in June. It took the lives of 83 spectators. Another tragic loss was that of Bill Vukovich, whose life was snapped short in an attempt to win his third Indianapolis 500 victory in a row. Vukovich, who strangely enough was known as "the Fresno flash," was killed at Indianapolis on May 30, 1955. While far overshadowed by the legend of James Dean's last ride, Vukovich's death was no less bizarre and, seemingly, predestined.

The immortal "Vukie" was born in Alameda, California on December 13, 1919. In 1920 his family, including three boys and five girls, moved to Fresno where his dad had a ranch and vine-

Bill Vukovich was an Indianapolis 500 rookie when this photo was taken. It was snapped after he qualified, in 1951, at 133.725 mph in his Central Excavating Offy. His performance was good for 20th starting position. He went on to finish 29th, with his car developing oil tank problems. Hand-written on the back of the photo are the words of a track competitor who said, "Vukie's not a bad guy. It's just that he's been in a lousy mood the last 30 years." Car number 81 was built by Floyd Travis of Youngstown, Ohio, and owned by Pete Salemi of the same city. (Al Krause Collection)

yard. Vukovich made Fresno his home for all his life. In 1933, at age 14, Bill discovered racing. Soon the midgets caught his fancy. By 1940 he was an established driver on West Coast circuits.

He was turned down by the Armed Forces in 1941. That year he married Ester Schmidt. They had two children. A daughter, Marlene, was born in 1942. Bill, Jr. was born in 1944.

In the early days, Vukovich was famous for his little Gerhard Drake two-cylinder race car that beat some of the best Offys and V-8s going. Vukovich was a quiet, unassuming guy who shunned crowds and fame. He had dark hair, a likable smile and stood only five-feet-nine-inches tall. Sometimes, he seemed a bit nervous. He was not the sort of a guy who looked like a race driver. Once he got behind the wheel, something fearsome happened. He drove only to win. He made no compromises, letting no driver get in his way. He always pushed his machine beyond its limits. They say he did not know how to place in any position but first.

In 1947, Vukovich racked up 27 feature wins on the URA Red Circuit for second place. He finally wrecked the Drake at Tulare. It was an early warning. A radius rod broke and stuck in the track surface, flipping the car high into the air. The wreck involved two other cars and nearly a third.

Bill competed in the URA during 1948, but missed winning the championship. At Hollywood's Gilmore Stadium, he drove off with four consecutive main events. He then went on to take the famous Gilmore Grand Prix, setting an all-time record for 150 laps. In 1950, he took the AAA National midget championship.

By this time, midget race cars were losing their crowd popularity. Bill reluctantly went over to the big cars. In 1951, he got his first chance at Indianapolis. He qualified at an impressive 133.725 mph. Then, his car gave out with a broken oil tank after only 72 miles. Now more deter-

After qualifying the Lindsey Hopkins Special Offenhauser fifth fastest, at 139.091 mph, Bill Vukovich was a favorite to score a third straight win at the 1955 Indianapolis 500. He was fatally injured while leading the event and becoming involved in a multi-car accident. (Phil Hall Collection)

This advertisement for Firestone tires dates from 1954, when Bill Vukovich was the winner of the Indianapolis 500 with an average speed of 130.84 mph. Other winners shown on the page ranged from Ray Harroun, who won the 1911 race averaging 74.59 mph, to George Souders, the victor in 1927 with a 97.54 mph average. It's interesting to note that Pete De Palo won the race, two years before Souders, with a 101.13 mph average. Other champions depicted included Jules Goux, Gaston Chevrolet, Tommy Milton, Jimmy Murphy and Frank Lockhart. (Firestone Tire & Rubber Company)

mined than ever, he got Howard Keck to sign him into a new 500-A series roadster with a four-cylinder Offy engine tilted on its side. He also got two top-notch mechanics named Jim Travers and Frank Coon. Affectionately known as "The Keck Kids," the duo stayed with him to the end.

Vukovich smashed all existing qualifying records with a four-lap dash at 138.212 mph. He blasted into a decisive lead early in the 1952 race and stayed there until hitting the wall with just nine laps to go. Something went wrong with the steering again, as it had in Tulare. The rest of the season was more fortunate and he finished 12th in the National Championship Circuit.

Bill was back at Indianapolis in 1953. His 1952 car was now fuel-injected. Despite a rain-slick track during qualifications, his average speed was 138.382 mph. It was the fastest qualification speed, to date, to win in the pole position. The 1953 race was a scorcher for sheer heat. Temperatures rose to 130 degrees on the track. Driver Carl Scarborough died from heat prostration. The weather did not faze Vukie. It was a decisive victory. He led in every lap, but five of them. He became the first driver to win from the pole position since Floyd Roberts did it in 1938. His average speed was 128.740 mph, only a fraction under Ruttman's record-breaking victory a year earlier.

As a sidelight, 1953 was Ford's 50th anniversary. A special 1953 Ford convertible pace car paced the 500. This car is in the Henry Ford Museum in Dearborn, Michigan today. Along with his $89,500 purse, Vukie was given a 1953 Ford pace car replica. It was the first time that replicas of the actual pace car were built. At the annual victory dinner, Vukovich was awarded his. It was similar to the Henry Ford Museum car, except for its lack of wire wheels. Vukie's car was kept in California until about 20 years ago. It then found its way to Illinois. Car collector Dave Banning, of Des Moines, Iowa, later bought the Vukovich race car that was built in Long Beach, California. It had raced for 12,000 miles.

Bill said he would retire after 1953. His spouse wanted him to stop racing, but he was back on the bricks in 1954 with Keck's Fuel-injected Special. His qualifying speed was 138.478 mph. He handily took the trophy again, with an average speed of 130.840 mph. Vukovich set a new record that was almost two mph faster than Troy Ruttman ran in 1952. Vukie did not get another pace car this year. He did get a big kiss from Marie Wilson (of "My Friend Irma" fame) who rode in the 1954 Dodge convertible pace car.

Later that year, Vukovich joined the Lincoln factory team for the 1954 Mexican Road Race in November. On the second leg, during the second day of the race, he lost control on a mean turn high in the mountains. He nearly went off the edge into oblivion. Years later, his co-pilot Vern Houle recalled that there was something ominous about that incident, which put him out of the race.

Shunning warnings from family and friends, Vukovich made plans for a third Indianapolis victory try. In a year that a red and ivory 1955 Chevrolet Bel Air convertible paced the 500, Bill switched to a Hopkins roadster. It was a Kurtis Kraft job with an Offenhauser engine. Keck did not sponsor Vukovich in 1955, since he was making plans to enter a new streamliner in 1956. Vukie's fated car was sponsored by Lindsey Hopkins. It had been driven to 21st place in 1954 by Pat O'Conner.

There was a fast three-car pile-up involving Rodger Ward, Johnny Boyd and Al Keller. Vukovich drove right through it. He careened into one of the wrecked cars near the bridge and the blue Hopkins Special became airborne. It landed on its nose, outside the track, and flipped again. Then it plowed into a safety patrol Jeep and bounced back toward the track. It came to rest upside down and burst into flames. Vukie did not have a chance. This was the second time in history that a former winner was killed during the race. As in the victory in 1953, his death in 1955 was linked strangely to that of Floyd Roberts. The two drivers died in crashes that took place 16 years apart, but had grim similarities.

The yellow caution light remained on for nearly half-an-hour, as the grounds crew cleaned up the mess. Bob Sweikert won, but it was a sad victory. For the next few months, there were press outrages and outcries to stop these senseless blood baths. Hugh Humphrey wrote in racing's defense in *Speed Age*, "It was one of the weird accidents that occur once in a blue moon. Vukies' time was up and high speed had little to do with it." One major racing event of 1955 was cancelled because of the bad publicity that accidents, such as Vukie's, were getting. The Mexican government, seeing much bloodshed in its Mexican Road Race, as well as around the world, said enough was enough. The Carrera PanAmericana was canceled.

Indy 1956

By Phil Hall

It was not supposed to happen that way, but the 1956 Indianapolis 500 turned out to be a romp through a combination of Zink, magnesium and the luck of the Irish. Guesses were coming in before the historic 40th running of the Memorial Day Classic at Indianapolis Motor Speedway. So-called experts predicted that, after a long gestation period, it would be a good year for the Novi V-8. Advance picks for the winners were led by Paul Russo. Other favorites included Jim Rathmann, Pat O'Connor, Tony Bettenhausen and Sam Hanks.

The front engine roadster was king. The race was the first to be sanctioned by the new United States Auto Club (USAC), which replaced the American Automobile Association (AAA) Contest Board after 1955. However, it would be business as usual at the "Brickyard." With technology making a gradual advance, it was felt that the record 142.580 mph average for four laps, set the year before by driver Jack McGrath, would fall. There was not much waiting for this prediction to come true. Jim Rathmann went out in the Lindsey Hopkins Special and set new one-lap and four-lap standards of 146.033 mph and 145.120 mph, respectively.

Crossing the finish line with his right hand raised was 1956 Indy 500 winner Pat Flaherty. Flaherty drove the John Zink Special roadster. (Phil Hall Collection)

Here's another view of Flaherty crossing the finish line at the Indy 500 in 1956. The use of lightweight components in his race car helped him take his first Indy victory. (Phil Hall Collection)

Next Pat Flaherty, the Chicago Irishman, wheeled out his new roadster called the John Zink Special. The wild crowd noticed how he pulled the left front wheel off the ground in the turns. This was very noteworthy. On his first lap, he also recorded a 146.056 mph effort. He then followed this up with a four-lap average of 145.596 mph, that was also a record. No one else could catch Flaherty. He won the pole position for the 500-mile race.

While Flaherty was one of 1956's leading contenders, his Indy 500 record was far from impressive. Pat started his racing career in Southern California. He raced roadsters on the short ovals, before moving to Chicago in 1949. That year, he passed his rookie test at Indianapolis, but got bumped from the field. He returned for the rain-shortened 1950 race and placed 10th. Flaherty then ran up against AAA officials for competing in a non-sanctioned event. He was banned from the 1951 Indy 500.

Flaherty came back to the 500 in 1953. He charged through the field, only to wreck his car and finish 22nd. In 1954 he drove in relief for Jim Rathmann and, again, was involved in an accident. He came back in 1955, to repeat a 10th-place finish. He also won a race at Milwaukee that year and finished eighth in AAA big car standings.

Not all the speed produced by Flaherty on his May 19, 1956, qualifying run could be attributed to his right foot. The car he was driving, for John Zink of Tulsa, Oklahoma, had a number of interesting innovations under its rather conventional lines. A.J. Watson, the mechanical whiz of the roadsters, used lightweight steel tubing for the chassis. Michael Scott and Jack Sutton fabricated a body of thin gauge magnesium and aluminum. The use of magnesium for parts other than wheels was unusual then. The firewall and instrument panel were sheet magnesium. Castings of magnesium were also used for the car's differential housing, steering gear and brake components. In all, the car weighed 1,640 pounds dry and was just over 1,700 pounds race ready. This was 140 to 200 pounds lighter than most of the leading contenders at Indy that season. Watson also took note of some repaving at the speedway. He moved the suspension torsion bars to account for the new, smoother surface.

On race day, May 30, the question was not who would win. The question was, would there be a race at all? Heavy rain put many parts of the speedway under water. The track was eventually dried off and the front row, consisting of Flaherty, Rathmann and O'Connor, was ready. When the race started, it seemed the pre-race predictions were coming true. Rathmann took the lead and set a record at the end of the first lap. Soon, O'Connor and Bettenhausen motored by. O'Connor was leading after lap four. Russo then put his Novi out front on lap 11. Russo settled down to a steady pace, with O'Connor and Flaherty behind him. On lap 22, the Novi's fortunes failed again. Russo hit the first turn wall with his car in flames.

Russo was unhurt, but was also the first driver out of the race. He placed 33rd. O'Connor was running right behind Russo and reclaimed the front position. Flaherty and Rathmann followed him. Johnnie Parsons moved past Rathmann and into third position. Parsons, however, was well back from a spirited battle for the front spot between O'Connor and Flaherty. Flaherty was credited with leading lap 41. O'Connor led laps 42 to 44. Flaherty was back in first-place on lap 45. O'Connor reclaimed front-runner honors from lap 46 on. When Ray Crawford wrecked, it induced a caution period and gave Flaherty a chance to duck into the pits for tires and fuel. He was out in just 39 seconds, compared to 45 seconds for O'Connor, who pitted shortly after Flaherty.

Johnnie Parsons was the new leader, but had to pit for service after lap 71. Don Freeland then took the point position, with Flaherty behind him. The yellow caution flag came out again

Pat Flaherty was a happy person, after setting new one- and four-lap qualifying records for the 1956 Indianapolis 500. He drove this roadster for car owner John Zink, of Tulsa, Oklahoma. (Phil Hall Collection)

when Al Herman crashed and landed on the main straightaway. Freeland chose this opportunity to make a pit stop. Flaherty returned to the front spot in the last lead change of the event.

Flaherty's lightweight roadster was easy on fuel and tires. He pitted a second time when he was past the 300-mile mark. However, he then had a 40-second margin and never lost the front spot. Despite 11 caution flags during the remainder of the event, Flaherty finished about 20 seconds ahead of Sam Hanks. Freeland, Parsons and Rathmann followed.

At that time, the Indy 500 continued after the winner received the checkered flag to allow several more drivers to cross the finish line. It was also customary for the victor to take a few insurance laps, just in case there was a scoring error. Flaherty took only one lap, then pulled into victory lane. Was he over-confident? No, his throttle linkage had broken after he crossed the finish line, just as he completed his 500th mile. His Irish luck was saved for the final lap around the 2.5-mile oval. The average speed of 128.490 mph was not a record, but Flaherty's first-place prize of $93,819 was a new high mark. He was also lucky enough to collect a replica of the 1956 DeSoto Firedome convertible that served as the Official Pace Car.

Winning the 1956 race took more than just luck, however. New technology was a big help. Lightweight components would continue to make inroads at Indianapolis Motor Speedway for decades to come. Flaherty's Irish luck ran out before the season ended. He was seriously injured during a race at Springfield, Illinois that August. He did not return to racing until 1958.

One of Pat Flaherty's biggest challengers in the early going of the 1956 Indianapolis 500 was Pat O'Connor, who led the race for several laps. Engine trouble eventually put his number 7 Ansted Rotary Special out of the race. (Phil Hall Collection)

1960: Start of a new decade at Indy

By Phil Hall

The 1960 Indianapolis 500-mile race was more significant for what didn't happen, than for what did happen. It was the year before Australian Jack Brabham brought a Cooper-Climax rear-engine car to the "Indy 500" and ran competitively. Brabham lit the fuse of a rear-engine, foreign car and foreign driver revolution that rearranged racing at the "Brickyard" forever.

The 500 had increasingly become less international during the 1950s. American front-engine cars dominated. Most were powered by the four-cylinder Meyer-Drake Offenhauser engine. American chassis design and construction were also strong. American drivers virtually ruled the decade. Most of them came up through the ranks, rising from midget race cars to sprint cars to the "Big Cars" that were raced at Indianapolis.

Although it was the start of a new decade, 1960 seemed like more of the same. A couple of supercharged Novi-powered cars were entered. The Novis had problems, however. A stock-block Chevrolet V-8 engine powered another entry. It also failed to make the field. The big question mark for technology, was whether the upright roadster chassis with the engine on the left

The highest starting non-Watson car in the 1960 Indy 500 was the Floyd Travis-designed lay-down roadster called the Jim Robbins Special. Eddie Johnson drove it to a sixth-place finish. (Phil Hall Collection)

Jim Rathmann may have worn an old style pot helmet in the 1960 Indy 500, but his Ken-Paul Special was a state-of-the-art race car. It was an upright roadster designed by A.J. Watson. (Phil Hall Collection)

For most of the last half of the 1960 Indianapolis 500-mile race, Rodger Ward (in car number 1) and Jim Rathmann (in car number 4) battled for the lead. Rathmann took the front spot for good only two laps from the race's end. (Phil Hall Collection)

side was the fastest combination. Some felt that the sleek lay-down roadsters were better. They had the engine on the right side and laid over to the left. The lay-down design prospered a bit in the last half of the 1950s.

A.J. Watson was king of the roadsters. He had built the winning cars for Bob Sweikert in 1955, Pat Flaherty in 1956 and Rodger Ward in 1959. The upright roadster was his specialty. When the first day of qualifying was over for the 1960 Indy 500, the first six cars were of Watson design. Pole-sitter Rodger Ward and second-place Jim Rathmann were in new Watson roadsters. Eddie Sachs was starting third in a Wayne-Ewing-built chassis using the Watson design.

In the second row of cars were all Watson products. Dick Rathmann and Troy Ruttman were in 1958 Watson cars and Len Sutton had a new one. Eddie Johnson broke the string of Watson designs, starting seventh in a new Floyd-Trevis lay-down chassis. The second week of qualifying at Indy is typically a letdown from the drama of the first week. In 1960, however, rookie driver Jim Hurtubise shook up the troops in a big way. He qualified on the last day, with an average speed of 149.056 mph. Hurtubise had a best lap of 149.601 mph. The record speed compared to Sachs' pole-winning average of 146.592 mph. The entire field's average was 144.070 mph, which broke the 1958 record of 143.455 mph.

Maintaining the status quo seemed to be the rule in 1960. All 33 starters in the 500 were Offy-powered roadsters with front-mounted engines. Every driver had earned his racing reputation between the Atlantic and Pacific oceans. It may sound as if the 1960 Indy 500 was a bit boring, but the reality was that it was far from dull. That season's race actually turned out to be one of the most exciting 500s of all time.

Uniformity was the rule for the 1960 Indy 500. All 33 starting drivers were in front-engine Offenhauer-powered roadsters. The similarity of the cars made the race one of the most exciting editions of the "Memorial Day Classic." (Phil Hall Collection)

*Eddie Sachs started on the pole in car number 6. The eventual winner, Jim Rath-
mann, was next to him in car number 4. Rodger Ward, the winner in 1959, was on
the outside of the front row in car number 1. (Phil Hall Collection)*

Jim Hurtubise, in his much faster car, ran into pit problems. That left the rest of the leading contenders about evenly matched. Rathmann, Ward and Sachs put on a display of driving that had the fans standing more than sitting. As the race progressed, it came down to a two-car duel between Rathmann, in the Ken-Paul Special and 1959 winner Ward in the Leader Card Special.

A lack of serious accidents, very few laps run under the yellow caution flag, and highly competitive cars resulted in track records falling like rain. Rathmann and Ward traded the lead a dozen times in the final 80 laps. The final change came just two laps from the finish, when the right front tire on Ward's car had the cords showing. He decided to slow down, rather than pit or crash. After 3 hours, 36 minutes, and 11 seconds, Rathmann scored his only victory in the 500-miler. He averaged a record 138.767 mph. Out of the 23 in-race Indy 500 speed records, the 1960 "Memorial Day Classic" had established 20 new ones! Jim Rathmann picked up $110,000 and the 1960 Oldsmobile convertible Official Pace Car, plus numerous other awards. Paul Goldsmith, Don Branson and Johnny Thomson rounded out the top five drivers behind second-place Rodger Ward.

Mechanical superiority at Indy

By Phil Hall

Mechanical types perked up their interest in the 1987 Indianapolis 500. The long-established Ford Cosworth V-8 was in the process of being challenged by the new Ilmor Chevrolet V-8, Honda V-8, Buick V-6 and Chevrolet V-6. Porsche threatened to join the fray in 1988, which it later did. Other manufacturers were eyeing the most famous race of them all. With a battle for supremacy between the Lola, March and Penske chassis thrown in, you had a feast of mechanical possibilities in the winner's circle.

There will always be attempts to unseat the current "king of the hill." The challenge of mechanical superiority is nothing new, be it in Indy car racing or any other venue. Looking at the "Brickyard" (Indianapolis Motor Speedway), three decades ago, a 1987-like situation was taking place. The naturally-aspirated Ford double overhead camshaft (DOHC) V-8 took over as the most popular, and generally fastest, power plant. This change started in 1963, after rear-engine cars displaced front-engine Offy-powered roadsters.

While the classic roadsters were dead, the four-cylinder DOHC Offenhauser engine was not. Experiments in supercharging and, later, turbocharging, gave renewed life to the Offy. This motor dated to before World War II. Supercharged and turbocharged racing engines had a limit of 170.8-cubic-inches, compared to 256.3-cubic-inches for naturally aspirated types. Although

The only stock-block to make the 1967 Indy 500 was the Eagle driven by Jochen Rindt. It had a Gurney-Weslake V-8. The rookie driver started 32nd and finished 24th with a broken valve. (Phil Hall Collection)

Mario Andretti set a record qualifying for a pole position in the 1967 Indianapolis 500-Mile Race. He drove this Hawk II-Ford. Car troubles early in the race relegated him to a 30th-place finish. (Phil Hall Collection)

Ron Duman drove car number 98 at the 1967 Indianapolis 500. It had a supercharged Offenhauser engine in a Shrike chassis. (Phil Hall Collection)

A controversial car that competed in the 1967 Indianapolis 500 was Andy Granatelli's number 40 STP Special. (Phil Hall Collection)

its superiority to non-turbocharged Ford engines was a year or two from being realized, development of the turbo Offy was well underway in 1967.

Of 33 qualifiers for the 1967 Indy 500, 23 cars had Ford power plants, seven had turbo Offy engines and one had a supercharged Offy. Dan Gurney was, then, developing the stock, Ford-based, Gurney-Weslake V-8. A car with one of these made the 1967 starting field.

That added up to 32 cars. Number 33, with the year's biggest mechanical news, was the turbine-powered car entered by Andy Granatelli's STP Corporation. It was driven by Parnelli Jones. There was a rules provision for gas turbines. Attempts, in the past, had produced more novelty than speed. That changed when the four-wheel-drive Pratt & Whitney turbine-powered car made the scene. It was neither front or rear-engined. The turbine was mounted next to the driver, on the left side of the Ken Wallace-designed chassis. Controversy over the car started early. That it qualified only sixth fastest did little to calm things. It was allowed to run, but threats were made to restrict turbines in the future.

As usual, other cars with oddball power plants attempted to qualify that year. They were unable to crack the starting lineup. Mickey Thompson had a Chevrolet V-8 with three-valve heads. Barney Navarro had an American Motors stock-block six with a turbocharger. Dempsey Wilson had a turbocharged Chevy V-8 stocker. Jerry Eisert and Bruce Crower had naturally aspirated Chevy stock-block V-8s. Unlike today, when Indy car builders rely on a couple of chassis designs (most done in Europe), 27 years ago there was still some individuality in that department. Out of the 33 starters, there were 13 designers or builders represented, with the most popular being made in the United States. Seven were Fred Gerhardt's cars. Seven were Eagles from Gurney's All-American Racers shop. There were also three Lolas, three from Lotus and two each from several other companies.

Qualifying produced few surprises. Mario Andretti took the pole, with a record average of 168.298 m.p.h. Dan Gurney was second and Gordon Johncock was third. All of them had cars with naturally-aspirated Ford power plants and each had a different chassis design. The 500 itself took two days to complete, as rain forced the race to be postponed after 18 laps were run on Memorial Day, May 30. It was finished May 31.

Chuck Hulse finished seventh in the 1967 race at the "Brickyard" in car number 8. It used a Turbo-Offy power plant. (Phil Hall Collection)

First to drop out of the 1967 Indianapolis 500 with hard luck was driver Lloyd Ruby. He made only three laps before bent valves sidelined his Turbo-Offy. (Phil Hall Collection)

Parnelli Jones with his turbine car was the class of the field. He took the lead going down the backstretch on the first lap and was gone. By lap 197, the turbine car had been in front for 177 laps. That was a significant point in the race, as a bearing failure stopped it cold. A.J. Foyt won, despite a third accident, in his Coyote Ford, on the last lap. Jones was given sixth-place, behind five Ford-powered cars and ahead of the first pair of Turbo-Offys. Turbines returned to Indianapolis one more year. The Turbo-Offys eventually forced turbocharging of the Ford V-8, although they remained able to beat it. Also, stock-block experimenting continued, although it never held sway over pure racing designs.

A.J. Foyt (third person to the right of the famous Borg-Warner trophy) poses with six other Indy 500 winners in an early 1980s STP Racing Team publicity photo. Foyt was the eventual winner of the 1967 race, but the STP turbine car did not finish. (Old Cars photo)

RACING ON
ROAD & TRACK

When giants stalked the earth: Grand Prix racing in the 1930s

By Robert C. Ackerson

In October 1932, the feeling that engine technology had far out-stripped comparable advances in suspension and braking led the AIACR, which governed grand prix racing, to announce a new formula for the years 1934 to 1936. Later extended to include the 1937 season, it decreed that all grand prix cars could weigh no more than 750 kilograms (1,653 pounds) without tires or liquids, and have a minimum body width of 34 inches. The only other major stipulation required that all grand prix races be at least 500 kilometers (311 miles) in length. The prevailing view was that these relatively simple conditions would keep engine displacements at or near three liters and maximum speeds near 150 mph.

If one considers a grand prix formula successful when its original objectives are fulfilled, then this particular one was a colossal failure. If on the other hand, such criteria as the quality of racing, the technological sophistication of the racing cars, and the caliber of the men who are attracted to the sport as drivers is used as the basis for judgment, then an entirely opposite conclusion is reached. The facts are simple. The 750-kilogram formula produced the fastest and most powerful grand prix cars of all time. Those who lived through this era witnessed their appearances on the racing circuits of three continents were indeed fortunate. It was a time when such drivers as Tazio Nuvolari, Bernd Rosemeyer, Louis Chiron, Hermann Lang, Dick Seaman, and perhaps the greatest of them all, Rudolf Caracciola, were at the peak of their driving skills. This fortuitous blending of great machines and great drivers did not escape notice by Dick Seaman, the young English driver who was to win the German Grand Prix in 1938, and then tragically lose his life in a racing accident in 1939. Writing in the English journal *Motor Racing*, Seaman paid tribute to his contemporaries, noting that. "It was an interesting fact that until 1939, Mercedes, Auto-Union and Alfa-Romeo each had the services of one of the three wizards, Caracciola, Rosemeyer and Nuvolari, respectively. These three were all absolutely '+100 A-1' and acknowledged to be in a class of their own." This combination of racing cars capable of speeds in excess of 200 mph and drivers of superlative skill and courage, resulted in racing that attracted worldwide interest and provided a degree of spectator appeal that perhaps has never been equaled.

As the 1934 season approached, it was apparent that the grand prix cars from Alfa-Romeo and Bugatti would essentially be slightly revised versions of their existing models. The Bugatti, with its front suspension of semi-elliptic leaf spring and reversed quarter-elliptics at the rear was, by 1932, already obsolete. It was not expected to achieve any great measure of success in the new formula.

Alfa-Romeo was not much better off. Even with a larger 2.9-liter engine producing 200 bhp it, like Bugatti, was clinging to the "old way." The greatness of driver Tazio Nuvolari would allow it to enjoy an occasional moment of racing glory in the next few years.

In Germany, the situation was radically different. The newly created Auto-Union company, which had been formed by the merger of Horch, Audi, DKW and Wanderer, had purchased the plans of Dr. Ferdinand Porsche for a grand prix car of both revolutionary and prophetic design. This was the rear-engined Type A model V-16 Auto Union. Along with its later versions, it was to win 18 grand prixs from 1934 through 1939.

Mercedes-Benz, which did not make its decision to reenter grand prix racing until March 1933, chose to retain the conventional front-engine format for its entry in the 750 kilogram for-

Rudolf Caracciola wheels the number 5 Mercedes-Benz-Rennwagen at an international racing event at Nurburgring in 1935. (Al Krause Collection)

mula. In its final form, known as the W125, it would be the most powerful and fastest grand prix car in history.

The basic strategy followed by both Mercedes-Benz and Auto Union in the designing of their cars was to make extensive use of lightweight alloy steels, aluminum and magnesium, whenever possible. The resulting savings in weight, with no accompanying loss of strength, would allow a relatively large and powerful engine to be used. This would give the German cars an immense advantage over opponents that clung to the old standards of construction and design.

Designated the W25, Mercedes' new grand prix car was powered by a supercharged straight eight engine initially rated at 302 bhp at the start of the 1934 season. Right from the beginning of the new formula in 1934, the power of both the straight eight Mercedes engine and that of Auto Union's V-16 made sheer nonsense of the hope that the upward spiral of top speed capabilities of grand prix racing cars would be restrained. Before the 1934 season, they stood in the 140-to 150-mph range. By the end of that year, they were at the 170-mph mark.

The first encounter between the "young Turks" and the defenders of the status quo took place on May 27, 1934, at the AVUS track in Berlin. Until the morning of the race, Mercedes had intended to compete with the W25, but at the final moment decided their cars were not yet ready. Perhaps this was just as well, since the Alfa-Romeos finished first and second with only one of the three Auto Unions completing the race in third position.

On June 3, the W25s, now deemed race-ready, were entered along with three Auto Unions in the Eifelrennen at the Nurburgring. Before the Mercedes were formally accepted for the race, the small matter of conforming to the 750-kilogram maximum weight regulation had to be dealt with. In spite of the best efforts of the Mercedes racing department to pare every milligram of excess weight from W25, the official weigh-in brought bad tidings. The W25 was one kilogram over the limit. As happened before, and was to happen again, Alferd Neubauer came to the rescue with the solution of removing the white paint from the two W25s. Thus lightened, von Brauchitsch's car came home the victor.

On July 1, the results of the French Grand Prix made all the talk about the supposedly technological superiority of the German cars seem to be so much gobbledygook. Whereas the Alfas copped the top three places, not a single Mercedes-Benz or Auto Union managed to finish the race. After this debacle, the superior resources and hardware of the German teams proved too much for their Italian opposition. Luigi Fagioli won the Copps Acerbo race, and the Italian and Spanish Grand Prixs for Mercedes-Benz. Hans Stuck, of the Auto Union team, won the first of his three grand prix victories in 1934, in the German Grand Prix. This was followed by triumphs at the Swiss and Masaryk (Czechoslovakia) Grand Prixs. Stuck also gained the 1934 European Hillclimb Championship with his Auto Union.

The 1935 season was a great year for Mercedes-Benz, with victories in five of the seven major grand prixs. Caracciola, who had suffered immensely during the 1934 season from a leg injury incurred in 1933, was back on form, winning four of the Mercedes victories. The only moment of real glory for Alfa-Romeo came at, of all places, the Grand Prix of Germany. Nuvolari, driving what was virtually a racing antique, humbled both the Mercedes and Auto Unions and won one of his greatest races.

The third season of the 750-kilogram formula started out well for Mercedes, with victories in the Monaco and Tunis races. Thereafter, the season was essentially dominated by Bernd Rosemeyer and the Type C Auto Union, now with 520 bhp. This combination won the German, Swiss and Italian Grand Prixs, plus the German Eifelrennen and Italian Acerbo Cup races. Varzi added another victory to the Auto Union's total with a first-place finish in the Tripoli Grand Prix. Rosemeyer's successes earned him the 1936 European Championship.

With the 750-kilogram formula extended to include the 1937 season, Mercedes-Benz set about making major revisions in its grand prix cars with the intention of rebounding from its poor

Racing through the streets in the 1935 Grand Prix of Barcelona, German driver Rudolf Caracciola masters the number 2 Mercedes-Benz Grand Prix race car. (Al Krause Collection)

showing of 1936. With more power and better handling, the new W125 models were to prove more than equal to this task.

From any point of view, the 1937 season was sensational. Both the W125 and Type C Auto Union were capable of speeds in the vicinity of 200 mph. Indeed, the phrase "age of the titans," often used to describe the grand prix races of 1937, is quite appropriate.

While grand prix racing during 1936 had tended to overshadow other forms of automotive competition, the dramatic proficiency of the young Englishman, Dick Seaman, with his much-reworked 1500 cc Delage, had not escaped the astute eyes of Alferd Neubauer. Without question, Seaman stood in 1936 as the finest English driver of his time. As *Motor Sport* magazine noted, " Seaman possesses all the necessary qualities of the front-rank driver: confidence, cornering skill, judgment and coolness." In addition, *Motor Sport* asserted, "Given a chance, he would do great things in grand prix racing proper."

At one point in the 1936 season, Seaman had asked Mercedes-Benz to lend him one of their grand prix cars for the Donington race. The German response that they did not sell or lend their grand prix cars to private individuals was polite, but to the point. Yet, Mercedes-Benz was determined to bring together the strongest possible team of drivers for 1937 and, thus, invited Seaman to try out for a position with them. Since this was the potential fulfillment of a long-held ambition, Seaman was quick to accept the offer. At the same time, Auto Union also made their interest in acquiring Seaman's services known, but they tried Seaman's patience too long with their unwillingness to make a concrete offer. In November 1936, he signed a provisional contract with Mercedes-Benz. Since Seaman was not German, Hitler had to give his personal approval before he was formally engaged by Mercedes-Benz. Early in 1937, word was received that the Chancellor would not object to Seaman joining the Mercedes-Benz team.

Shortly thereafter, Seaman was on his way to Monza to begin practicing with Mercedes' revamped grand prix car for the 1937 season. Although based upon the W25, this new car, the W125, was a far more formidable racing car. Its 5.6-liter supercharged engine developed 575 bhp, making the W125 the most powerful grand prix car in history. When set up for a fast circuit, it could touch 88 mph in first gear, 137 mph in second, 159 mph in third and 199 mph in top gear. With appropriate gearing and a brave driver, the absolute top speed of the WI 25 was 211 mph.

The skill of the individuals that Seaman was joining on the Mercedes team was as impressive as the cars they drove. Rudolf Caracciola was, of course, the number one driver. If one was to pinpoint his greatest attribute, it would probably have to be his ability to conserve fuel, spare his engine and nurse his tires, and still be faster than his opposition. His teammate, Hermann Lang, was, as Rodney Walkerly once wrote, "The heavy-footed thruster." Finally, there was Manfred von Brauchitsch, the young exuberant driver with a notoriety for being hard on his tires. He often took turns with his car slithering sideways, on the edge of control. Perhaps, in driving technique, Seaman was closest to Caracciola. Always in control and ever-seeking perfection, he was not unlike that great English driver of a later era, Stirling Moss. Seaman once quipped that driving the grand prix Mercedes was like driving a good fast sports car on ice. Since these cars could spin their wheels at 150 mph in top gear, if given too much throttle, they had to be handled with a degree of skill that only a handful of drivers possessed. Just before the start of the 1937 season, Seaman was practicing, with one of the 1936 cars at Monza, when he overdid things and came down on the accelerator too quickly. The car went into a broadside spin and ended up around a tree. Seaman was fortunate to escape with a fractured knee cap,

Caracciola won the season's opening race, the Monaco Grand Prix, which was run on Easter Sunday 1937. By May, Seaman was pronounced fit enough to make the trek to North Africa for the Tripoli Grand Prix. Seaman liked the 8-1/4 mile "Circuito Permanente di Tripoli," with its curves which could be taken at 180 mph. Both Seaman's and Caracciola's cars were off form, suffering from supercharger malfunctions, but Lang went on to chalk up another victory. He was pursued across the finish line by two Auto Unions.

On May 30, 1937, the Mercedes-Benz and Auto Union teams faced each other on the AVUS track for what was to be the fastest race ever run up to that time. The building of the 12.23-mile AVUS course had originally started in 1913 as a German counterpart to England's great Brooklands course. With time out for World War I, construction was completed in 1921. For the 1937 season, the track had been modified by the addition of a brick wall, with a slope of one-in-one,

The number 7 race car was another weapon in Mercedes-Benz's Grand Prix arsenel during the 1935 racing season. This photo shows the car in the masterful hands of Luigi Gagioli. (Al Krause Collection)

at the north end of the course. Since the cars would be able to mount the wall at very high speeds, some super fast lap times were anticipated by the 380,000 spectators who came for the three-heat event. In the first heat, Bernd Rosemeyer's streamlined Auto Union set the fastest lap at 172.75 mph. However, the Mercedes W125 won all three heats and Hermann Lang was declared overall winner with an average speed of 162.62 mph. Dick Seaman later wrote, to George Monkhouse, "From the driving point of view, the whole thing was rather stupid." Seaman had to settle for fifth-place overall, due to the time he lost, in the final heat, when he had to pit twice to replace tires that had lost chunks of their tread.

As the season progressed, the superiority of the W125 over the Type C Auto Union, which was basically unchanged from its 1936 form, became more and more apparent. The combination of W125 and Caracciola won the Grand Prixs of Germany, Switzerland, Italy and Czechoslovakia. Hermann Lang and Manfred von Brauchitsch added victories in the Tripoli and Monaco Grand Prixs. However, Auto Union drew upon the magnificent talents of Rosemeyer to save some face. He countered with triumphs in the German Eifelrennen, the U.S. Vanderbilt Cup Race, the Copps Acerbo in Italy and the-British Donington Grand Prix. In addition, Auto Union also scored a success in the Belgian Grand Prix.

Despite the fact that the Vanderbilt Cup race and the Belgian Grand Prix were scheduled for the same day, both Auto Union and Mercedes-Benz chose to support the American race with their best combinations of cars and drivers. For Rudi Caracciola, the voyage to the United

States was more than just a routine Transatlantic crossing. Just three days before the Bremen began its voyage to the U.S., Caracciola married Alice Trobek. It was the second marriage for both. Some three years earlier, in 1934, Caracciola's first wife Charly had been killed in an avalanche while skiing in Austria. Alice Trobek, who was born in the United States, had married Alferd Hoffman, the son of the founder of the Hoffman-LaRoche chemical company. His enthusiasm for racing cars was almost without bounds. Hoffman had begun the sponsorship of Bugattis driven by Louis Chiron as much for the satisfaction of his passion for racing, as for a means of publicizing the spark plugs his Nerka Spark Plug Company manufactured. By 1931, the marriage between Alferd and "Baby" Hoffman had collapsed. A year later, an annulment was obtained.

In 1933, Chiron and Caracciola, who had driven Alfa-Romeos for a year after Mercedes-Benz withdrew from competition after the 1931 season, formed their own team called the "Scuderia CC." This new venture, seemingly so full of prospects for success, ended nearly when it started. In practice for the team's first race at Monaco, the brakes in Caracciola's Alfa-Romeo locked, throwing his car against a stone pillar. While recuperating at his chalet in Akrosa, Austria, Caracciola suffered the loss of his wife. Gradually, as Caracciola recovered from his grief, he began to see Alice more often. As months passed, both of them realized the depths of their feelings for each other. Thus it was, that they found themselves together, in route to New York for the Vanderbilt Cup Race in June 1937.

This venture, which was the only American racing appearance for both the W125 Mercedes and the Type C Auto Union, was not exactly a success for Mercedes. Caracciola's car dropped out early with supercharger ills and Dick Seaman, who had a real chance to overtake Bernd Rosemeyer for the lead, had to stop for fuel just three laps before the finish!

The final race of the 750-kilogram formula was the English Donington Grand Prix. Dick Seaman acted as Mercedes Benz representative in the negotiations over the not-so-inconsequential matter of starting money. In a letter to his mother dated September 3, 1937, he informed her that the Mercedes team would be making the journey to England. There was apparently some

On the starting grid of the 1935 Avus-Rennen race is driver Luigi Fagioli with his Mercedes-Benz-Rennwagen. The factory mechanics standing by the car look somewhat perplexed, although they may simply be bored, as these great machines were quite trouble-free. (Al Krause Collection)

thought given, by Mercedes Benz, to making an attempt at the Brooklands' lap record with the W125. Seaman sent a telegram to his friend George Monkhouse, whose *Motor Racing with Mercedes-benz* is one of the best chronicles of this age of grand prix racing. Seaman requested that he provide Uhlenhaut with information about Brooklands' stringent muffler regulations. Monkhouse was also advised by Seaman to keep this communication in strict confidence. The venture never materialized. However, judging from the W125's AVUS performance, it stood an excellent chance of breaking the 143.44-mph lap record held by John Cobb's Napier-Railton.

One of the surprising by-products of the appearance of the German grand prix cars in England was the remarkably naive assumption, by many "knowledgeable" British racing fans, that they would not win the Donington Grand Prix. Betting was legal at English race meets and the bookmakers offered odds that were incredible: Caracciola, 3:1, Rosemeyer, 5:1 and even money on Raymond Mays, who was the pre-race favorite with his ERA. Many people were in for quite a shock. Incidentally, the members of the Auto Union and Mercedes teams were seen busily betting on their respective drivers!

The first inkling many spectators had that this was not going to be an ordinary English race meet came in practice. Rodney Walkerly described the scene in classic prose in his *Moments that Made Racing History*. He wrote, "Far away in the distance we heard an angry, deep-throated roaring, as someone once remarked, like hungry lions impatient for the arena. A few moments later, Manfred von Brauchitsch, red helmeted, brought a great, silver projectile snaking down the hill, and close behind, his teammate Rudolf Caracciola, then at the height of his great career. The two cars took the hairpin, von Brauchitsch almost sideways, and rocketed away out of sight with long plumes of rubber smoke trailing from their huge rear tires, in a deafening crash of sound." The Auto Unions were the complete masters of practice, being lead by von Brauchitsch who set a new lap record of 85.36 mph with his Mercedes.

The start of the Donington race was a scene all present retained for the rest of their lives. The German cars waited until the 30-second signal before they started their engines. Whereas the ERA drivers "blipped" their engines to avoid fouling their plugs, the Auto Union and Mercedes-Benz cars were held at a steady 1500 rpm. When the flag went up, the scene changed dramatically. As Walkerly recalled that moment, "The revs (of the German cars) mounted to a steady shattering thunderous roar and then they surged away with tire treads belching smoke, leaving long black lines to show where they had stood. That fantastic start in an inferno of suddenly unleashed sound was something that left the packed crowds awestruck, open mouthed, silent."

The grandstand crowd wasn't given a chance to regain its composure. Just 90 seconds later, the seven German cars completed their first lap. They passed the paddock at 170 mph, with the rest of the field nowhere in sight. At the end of the straight, the cars had to slow up for a tight hairpin turn. As the Auto Unions and W125s funneled out of this bend, they climbed an incline at full throttle and crested the top at 100 mph, with all four wheels off the ground. After just 14 laps of this type of racing, all the British entries had been lapped and it was just a question of which German car would win. For the first 22 laps, the Mercedes of Lang and Brauchitsch fought each other for the lead while Rosemeyer's Auto Union gradually came within striking distance. Brauchitsch pitted for tires and fuel. Rosemeyer moved into the lead, despite Brauchitsch taking only 33 seconds with his pit-stop. The proficiency of the German pit crews was in sharp contrast to the English crews, which took twice as long to complete the same tasks with their funnels and gas cans.

Like his teammate, Caracciola had been scheduled to stop for tires, but he waved off his crew's signal. Instead, he began to stalk Rosemeyer. When the Auto Union pitted on lap 30, he moved into the lead, notwithstanding Rosemeyer's crew requiring just 30 seconds to refuel and change his car's tires.

Since the Mercedes-Benz team was characterized by much intra-team rivalry, Caracciola was soon challenged by von Brauchitsch for the lead. In a great drive that included a new lap record of 85.62 mph, he succeeded in getting by Caracciola on the 30th lap.

Four laps later, at the race's midpoint, Caracciola made his only pit stop in the 80-lap race. Brauchitsch had to pit for his third set of tires 12 laps later, allowing Rosemeyer to take possession of first place. Yet, the race was far from completed. Rosemeyer's lead was only 20 seconds and his car was scheduled for one more visit to the pits. Any hope that Brauchitsch could overhaul him vanished when his W125, nearly at top speed, blew one of its tires on the paddock straight.

The 750-kilogram formula ended with the final victory going to Auto Union. The outcome of the contests between the Auto Union and W125 had been close: Seven victories for Mercedes and five for Auto Union. An interesting postscript to the Donington Grand Prix came a week later, at the then-new Crystal Palace Course near London. Seaman, whose W125 had retired on the 29th lap of the Donington race, while in fifth place, put on a demonstration run with the Mercedes. He then acted as one of the commentators for the first BBC telecast of a motor race.

Even under the new formula for 1938, which mandated smaller engines and a heavier minimum weight, grand prix cars continued their relentless drive towards higher and higher top speeds. This continued until the start of World War II. By 1939, Hermann Lang was setting lap times at numerous European circuits that would remain unbroken until the memorable 1951 season, that saw the rise of the 4.5-liter Ferrari grand prix car.

After the war, Mercedes-Benz, which had suffered terribly at the hands of Allied bombing raids, was in no position to return to international racing competition. Many of the first-rank drivers of the 1930s were either dead or past their prime. Others, like Rudi Caracciola, were eager to return to racing. He received an invitation from Wilbur Shaw to come to Indianapolis and attempt to qualify a Mercedes-Benz for the 500-mile Race. Caracciola left his villa at Lugano, Switzerland and, with his wife, prepared to sail to the United States. One not-so-minor catch developed; they could enter the U.S., but the Mercedes could not. Disappointed, but undaunted, the Caracciolas traveled to Indiana anyway. Joel Thorne offered Rudi a chance to qualify his Thorne Special.

While this was Rudi Caracciola's first visit to the Indianapolis Motor Speedway, his wife had attended the Indy 500 in 1929, when her first husband, Alferd Hoffman, entered a 1500 cc Delage. In Europe, Alice had been a familiar figure at all the major races, performing duties as a timer and lap recorder with much expertise. At Indianapolis, however, tradition mandated that no females were to be allowed in the pits. Mrs. Hoffman was required to tend to her brood of stop watches from the grandstands. Finally, two days before the race, the general manager of the speedway, T.E. "Pop" Meyer, relented and let her join the Delage crew in the pits for race day. However, she had to do so incognito, with bulky overalls and a large cap disguising her female form. The Delage, with Louis Chiron driving, did very well. It maintained fourth-place until time was lost solving a magneto problem. Even with this handicap, Chiron finished an honorable ninth.

Alice was back in the pits 17 years later, but with a different outcome. Rudi crashed the Thorne Special, suffering a severe concussion that left him unconscious for 10 days. During the long period of recuperation that followed, Mr. and Mrs. Tony Hulman provided their country lodge for the Caracciola's use.

Eventually, after a long period of convalescence, Rudi was able to join the Mercedes-Benz team for the 1952 sports car season. Driving a 300SL in the Mille Miglia, he finished a strong fourth. At age 51, it seemed just possible that he could make a comeback. This hope was dashed, just two weeks later, when Caracciola suffered a terrible crash in the Berne sports car race. This was the end of Caracciola's racing career. There would be no more moments of glory. In 1959, Rudi Caracciola died at the age of 58. His wife passed away almost two decades later. For many years, she made annual visits to the Indianapolis 500 to renew her friendship with the Hulmans. Shortly before her death, Tony Hulman bought the collection of Rudi Carracciola's racing trophies that she had kept in her home in Lugano.

Some 40 years after the W125s made their appearance in America, Mercedes-Benz loaned Indianapolis Motor Speedway the W125 that Dick Seaman drove in the 1937 Vanderbilt Cup Race. In accepting the car, speedway president Tony Hulman paid tribute to the WI25 and to the great driver who scored the most victories in it ... Rudolf Caracciola.

The Alfa-Romeo Type 158/159 was a remarkable Italian racing car

By Robert C. Ackerson

The racing career of the Alfa-Romeo Type 158/159 grand prix racer was remarkable on many counts. Its competitive years spanned two golden ages of grand prix racing. When it was in its early stages of development, racing was dominated by the Mercedes-Benz and Auto Union teams. Due to the futility of competing with these giants on full grand prix terms, the Italian teams, such as Alfa-Romeo and Maserati, turned their attention toward mastery of the smaller voiturette class of racing. There, engines of 1500 cc, both supercharged and normally aspirated, were allowed. This was different from the three-liter, supercharged limit for Formula One racing, which came into effect for the 1938 season.

After World War II, Daimler-Benz was in no position to immediately resurrect its racing department and the Auto Unions had fallen under the shroud of the Iron Curtain. The Alfas had survived the war. After competing in 1946 in formula libre racing, they were eligible for the new 1947 formula allowing 1.5-liter supercharged or 4.5-liter unsupercharged engines. The Alfetta,

On May 9, 1948, French driver Jean-Pierre Wimille was the victor in the Grand Prix D'Italia, at Torino, in the number 57 Alfa-Romeo Type 158/47. Here he is seen tearing through the streets of the Italian city, with two other vintage Grand Prix racers close behind. (Robert C. Ackerson Collection)

A scene from the Grand Prix of Europe, at Silverstone, on May 13, 1950. Shown is Farina, in his number 2 Alfa Romeo Type 158. The camera captured the crowd as a blur, as the wire-wheeled race car flashed by. The Alfa was the eventual winner in Farina's skilled hands. (Robert C. Ackerson Collection)

as the 158 was called almost from its origin, blossomed into a full-scale grand prix racer whose domination ended with the ascension of the equally great Grand Prix Ferrari.

In the postwar era, the Alfa-Romeo was defeated only four times. The 158 lost its first race after the war on June 9, 1946. It did not suffer another defeat until July 14, 1951. Writing about the Alfetta in his classic work *The Grand Prix Car* (Volume II) Laurence Pomeroy noted, "In this period the company made 99 separate entries in 35 races. Of these, they won all but four. They had 31 victories, together with 19 second places and 15 thirds. They made fastest lap in 23 of the races and suffered only 28 retirements. Taking into account retirements, the cars raced a total of 18,153 miles under Formula I, plus 854 miles in 1946. That was an average of 6,800 racing miles per car for an overall reliability factor of eight. This is a record of reliability and success without parallel in motor racing history."

Development of the Alfa Corse 158 began early in 1937. Gioachino was given the responsibility of designing a supercharged straight eight engine capable of producing approximately 180 hp from a total displacement of 91 cubic inches. It should be noted that Alfa-Romeo had not completely abandoned the grand prix battlefield to its German adversaries at this time. It was preparing a new Type 308-style racer with a three-liter V-16 engine and the designation Type 316. Much confusion exists about Alfa-Romeo history at this point. Colomobo's work on the 158 was pursued under the Type 308 identification. The 308 model appeared in public before the 158, even though the V-16 was a derivation of the Alfetta's straight eight engine.

In any case, the 316's engine (which was actually a "W-16," since each bank of cylinders had its own crankshaft) produced 440 bhp at 7500 rpm. It allowed the 316 to achieve a maximum speed of 187 mph. Although it did not enter the 1938 Grand Prix of Tripoli, during practice, Biondetti's 316 set a new lap record of 136.5 mph. Later, in the 1938 Italian Grand Prix at Monza, Farina managed a second-place finish with the 316. He ran behind Tazio Nuvolari's Auto Union.

Despite these achievements, a truly competitive response to the Mercedes and Auto Union teams was simply beyond the reach of either Alfa-Romeo or Maserati. Thus, the debut of the Type 158 Alfa was awaited with great anticipation by the Italian racing public. At this time Scuderia Ferrari, located at Modena, served as Alfa-Romeo's "sub-contractor" for racing operations. It was there that Colombo did much of his basic work on the 158. In a change of operational structure, Scuderia Ferrari was totally absorbed into Alfa-Romeo in 1938. A new racing department called Alfa Corse was established. It was headed by Enzo Ferrari. When this switch occurred, four Type 158s had already been constructed at Ferrari's Modena facility.

In its initial configuration, the 158 was, in the words of Karl Ludvigsen, "A neat combination of many techniques." The Colombo-designed engine differed from the 316 unit by having its gear train for the camshafts, etc., located at the front. On the V-16, it was positioned at the rear. The engine, with dry sump lubrication and two spark plugs per cylinder, had a 24-pound crankshaft machined from a chrome nickel steel billet. Nine main bearings, constructed of bronze with babbitt liners, carried the crankshaft. With a single-stage Roots supercharger (17.65 psi boost) the 378-pound engine was rated for 195 bhp at 7000 rpm. Since its bore and stroke was 2.29 x 2.76 inches, the 158's engine was hardly cast like modern over-square engines. Its long stroke and resulting high rate of piston travel raised more than a few knowledgeable eyebrows. However, its demonstration of reliability from 1938 through 1951, with only nine engines built, was to make such criticisms totally irrelevant. The non-synchromesh four-speed transmission was rear-mounted in union with the rear axle, which also featured a ZF limited-slip differential. A six-leaf transverse leaf spring was used as the basic component for both the front and rear suspension systems. At each wheel, a pair of shock absorbers (one hydraulic and one a friction type) was used. The front suspension also used a Porsche like trailing arm arrangement, with swing axles at the rear. Braking was by Al-Fin drums, front and rear, with Ferrari linings. The frame consisted of steel tubes, of a near rectangular shape, which were located some 18 inches apart. Although the engine and transaxle housing also provided some structural support, four cross members were used.

When the chief test driver from Scuderia Ferrari gave the 158, his approval in June 1938, the stage was set for its racing debut. The appearance of the first Alfettas was quite different from their "classic" style, which debuted just over a year later in July of 1939. The fuel tank, mounted in the tail, carried 51 gallons. It required a relatively small enclosure that dropped away at a sharp angle from the back of the driver's seat. The body was a good deal slimmer than its successor and left the components of the front suspension uncovered. The Alfetta's grille consisted of a large latticework center structure with smaller oval openings on each side. The entire front dropped back at a fairly sharp angle.

The Type 158 entered the Coppa Ciano race for 1500 cc cars, at Livorno, on August 8, 1938. Led by Emilio Villoresi, the team finished in first, second and fourth positions. This fine performance prompted one Italian newspaper to write, "Should we not see in these little 1500s the fertile germ of a great new Italian racing car?" Although the Alfetta had a less than inspiring season after its initial victory, the future achievements of this voiturette Alfa-Romeo would prove it to be a very fertile gem, indeed. During the remainder of 1938, the 158s raced in three events. In the Coppa Acerbo Francesco Severi managed a fourth place, with the Alfas of Villoresi and Clemente Biondetti retiring. In the Prix de Milan, four Alfas were entered, including one for Raymond Sommer. There, Villoresi won his second victory with a 158. Severi finished second. For the final race of the 1938 season, the Circuit of Modena, Alfa-Romeo again fielded four cars. This time none of them managed to finish.

In preparation for the 1939 season, the 158 was modified in a number of significant ways. The most dramatic alteration was due to the discovery that the crankcases of the first four engines had developed cracks between the bolts securing the bearing caps in the crankcase and the cylinder block bolts. Colombo's solution was to use long bolts, running through the bearing caps, from the block. This remedy proved entirely satisfactory. Other improvements included replacement of the babbit-lined rod bearings with needle bearings that proved far more durable at high engine revs. As set up at the start of the 1939 season, the 158 engine was capable of 225 bhp at 7500 rpm.

The first race of the 1939 season, the Grand Prix of Tripoli, is usually remembered as a rout for the Italian Maseratis and Alfas and a stunning victory for the W165 Mercedes-Benz. By running the race under the 1.5 liter voiturette formula, the Italian Auto Sport Federation had hoped to make an Italian victory a virtual certainty. However, Mercedes-Benz's chief engineer, Rudolf Uhlenhaut learned, in advance, of this decision. In what seemed impossible haste, Mercedes completed two 91-cubic-inch supercharged racers in a time span of eight months. Since the 1940 Grand Prix formula would have almost surely been based on a 1500 cc limit, Auto Union had a V-12 engine in the works, too.

Driven by Hermann Lang and Rudi Caraciola, the two Mercedes finished first and second. While the German victory was complete, a streamlined Maserati 4CL with a supercharged, four-cylinder, sixteen-valve engine was driven by Luigi Billoresi. It managed to set the best lap time at the super fast Tripoli circuit. It averaged 131.6 mph. This was just 4/10ths of a second better than Lang's best effort. In the race, all four works Maseratis failed to complete the first lap. Only Villoresi returned to the fray, with the streamliner, to salvage some honor. He set the best lap time. As the race began, the only challenge to the W165 could come from the four factory-entered Alfa-Romeos.

For a time, Lang was averaging 127.6 mph. This was faster than the average of the three-liter Mercedes in the 1938 race. The combination of high track temperatures and the tremendous pace set by the Mercedes proved too much for the 158's cooling system. The Alfas of Farina, Pintacuda and Aldrighetti were forced out with fried engines. For the first 10 laps, however, Farina had held second position, ahead of Caracciola. The only Type 158 to finish was that of Villoresi. By not making full use of his car's potential, he managed a third-place finish. He was one lap behind the twin W165 Mercedes.

Immediately after this debacle, Alfa's overheating problems were solved by having the coolant pass along the heads and by increasing the pressure of the cooling system to 17.6 psi. Work was also done to improve the car's lubrication system. In July of 1939, the Alfetta's were rebodied with wider new bodies that featured a higher tail. A more massive front grille work largely enclosed the front suspension components. The Alfas were raced, until 1951, in this form.

In the remaining 1500 cc races for 1939, the 158s acquitted themselves with victories in the Copps Ciano (Farina); Copps Acerbo (Biondetti); and the Prix de Berne, where Farina and

In the rain-dampened Daily Express International Trophy Race, on August 29, 1950, Fangio took the number 2 Alfa-Romeo Type 158 to the checkered flag. He was declared overall winner of the contest held at the Silverstone race course, in England. (Robert C. Ackerson Collection)

Rounding the hay bales at the Silverstone racecourse, in England, is Farina in his Corsa Su Vettura Alfa-Romeo Type 158. He took the number 2 Alfa to the victory in the contest, which took place on August 29, 1950. As you can, the great Grand Prix drivers ran with a bare minimum of safety equipment. Man and machine were the determining factor in auto racing then. Technology was not the big factor that it is today. (Robert C. Ackerson Collection)

Biondetti finished first and second. In August, Farina finished a highly respectable sixth (ahead of two German cars) in the Swiss Grand Prix for three-liter GP cars.

With World War II developing its historic reputation for tastelessness, no German entries were posted for the 1940 Tripoli Grand Prix. For Alfa-Romeo, this was to be the last race for six years. However, even with the absence of German competition, the desire to redeem the Alfetta's 1939 showing was very high. Since two of the original 158s had been lost to accidents (one that took the life of Emilio Villores) six new 158c models had been completed. Finishing first, second, third and fifth, the four new Alfas convincingly redressed their earlier loss to Mercedes-Benz. Farina led the Alfa-Romeo team to victory, averaging 128.2 mph for 244 miles. It was certainly a performance that could have been very competitive to that of the W165s, if they had raced.

During the early years of the war, the 158s continued to be refined. At the Tripoli race, they were capable of 240 bhp. A single model, the 158D, was constructed with a deDion rear axle. In addition, two of the Type 512 rear-engine Alfa-Romeos were also constructed. These were never raced, but were the subject of much discussion and speculation in the motoring press after the war. Often portrayed as a secret weapon of invincible power, poised and ready for use by Alfa-Romeo whenever needed, the Type 512 was, in reality, inferior to the 158. It failed to intimidate Signore Ferrari one iota. Enzo Ferrari, who knew its true ability, despised the 512. He saw it as outdated and good only for scrapping or exhibition in a museum.

It was learned that Monza, where the Alfas were located, was about to come under Nazi jurisdiction in 1943. They were moved, with spare parts and related items, to facilities at Melzo. There they were kept out of German hands and survived the war in good shape. The first post-war appearance of the 158 took place on June 9, 1946, at the St. Cloud Grand Prix near Paris. This was a Formula Libre race of 112 miles on a twisty circuit. Neither of the two Alfas, unchanged from their last 1940 appearance in Tripoli, finished the race, in spite of the best efforts of Nino Farina and Jean-Pierre Wimille.

In July, four Alfas contested the Grand Prix des Nations race held at Geneva. The 158s for Farina and Varzi were designated the 158/46B model and carried two-stage superchargers that boosted output to 254 bhp at 7500 rpm. Farina's victory marked the beginning of the Alfetta's golden age. Formula One racing resumed in 1947 under new regulations allowing either a 1.5-liter supercharged or 4.5-liter unsupercharged engine. The major supercharged opposition to the Type 158 came from the four-cylinder Maserati and the ERA, which was an "antique" English racing car. Neither of these were thoroughbreds in the same class as the Alfa-Romeo. The BRM, for which British enthusiasm first waxed and then waned, was (like the Cisitalia and CTA Arsenal) a notoriously complex creature. Its explanations for failure provided far more news copy than its racing successes. For variety the 4-1/2 liter unsupercharged Talbot-Lago was noteworthy, but its assets of reliability and fuel economy could not overcome its lack of speed and acceleration. Not surprisingly, therefore, the Alfa-Romeos won the four Grand Prixs they entered in 1947 with ease. As raced in 1947, the Alfas were producing 275 bhp at 7500 rpm. If Alfa-Romeo had faced any real competition during 1947, it had a formidable weapon waiting in the wings to be used if needed. It was the 158/47 model. With a larger, low-pressure supercharger and a more efficient induction system, its horsepower was an awesome 310 at 7500 rpm. On July 18, 1948, at the French Grand Prix, the 158/47 was used in practice in an unsuccessful attempt, by Wimille, to break Lang's record.

The Alfa-Romeo parade of racing successes moved on through 1948 with victories at the Swiss, French, Italian and Monza Grand Prixs. Success in the Swiss GP was at a heavy cost, however. Achille Varzi was killed during practice when he slid off the course, which had become extremely slippery due to heavy rain. Before the Grand Prix began, the huge crowd in attendance stood in silence for one minute, in tribute to Varzi's memory.

The Italian Grand Prix was held in September on the short and twisty 2.98-mile course at Turin. A single 158/47 model was entered for Wimille, with the remainder of the Alfa team using the older Type 158. Also making its debut in this race was the 1.5-liter Type 125 Ferrari. Modified versions of Ferrari's two-seat sports cars had earlier raced in grand prix events, but now, for the first time, Ferrari was mounting a challenge to the Alfas with a legitimate grand prix racer. The power output of the supercharged Type 125 was 230 bhp at 7000 rpm. It was unable to match the Alfa-Romeo's speed. Raymond Sommer finished third with the Ferrari, two laps behind Wimille's winning Alfa. However, the experience Ferrari gained with his first grand prix car would lay the foundation for a far more imposing challenge to the Alfa-Romeo ... the Ferrari Type 375.

Alfa-Romeo choose not to participate in grand prix racing for the 1949 season. Several factors accounted for this decision. They included the obvious superiority of the 158 to its competitors, the demands of preparing the "1910" model for production and the loss of three of its top grand prix drivers. Varzi was killed at the Swiss GP, Court Trossi died of cancer and Jean-Pierre Wimille was killed in Argentina, early in 1949, at the wheel of a Simca. This hiatus from competition lasted only one year, however. During the 1950 season, the Alfettas were heavily campaigned, entering 11 major grand prix events and securing victories in each one. The Alfa team consisted of two veterans, Nino Farina and Luigi Fagioli, and a newcomer from Argentina named Juan Fangio. The latter aptly summed up his impressions of the 158 Alfa by noting, "When I laid eyes on her, I saw what a gem she was."

Precious jewel or not, the Alfetta, with 350 bhp at 8600 rpm, was still superior to the latest version of Ferrari's Type 125. Even with a two-stage supercharger and twin overhead cam heads designed by Aurelio Lampredi, the Ferrari was capable of only 310 bhp at 7500 rpm. The first four Alfa victories in 1950 were won with almost contemptuous ease. At San Remo in April, only one Alfa 158/47 was entered. It was driven by Fangio, who had little difficulty handling the opposition. The competitors at the race included three Ferraris. At Silverstone, England, the Alfas finished the British Grand Prix in possession of the top three places. Fangio retired the fourth Alfa with a broken connecting rod.

An Alfa-Romeo triumph was anticipated for the 11th Grand Prix of Monaco, held on May 21, 1950. However, stiff competition from the Ferraris of Villoresi and Ascari was expected. The Alfas of Fangio, Farina and Fagioli took to the tight 1.98-mile course. On the very first lap, two Alfas (driven by Farina and Fagioli), plus seven other entrants, were involved in a spectacular collision. After surviving the carnage (which required only one driver to be hospitalized with a broken arm) Fangio led the remaining 99 laps. He finished a full lap ahead of Ascari. Interestingly, Ascari's and Villoresi's Ferraris required two fuel stops to Fangio's one. Villoresi retired on lap 63.

Fangio's Monte Carlo triumph was followed by an Alfa one-two finish in the Swiss GP. The next stop for the Grand Prix tour was the very fast Spa Prancorchamps circuit, where the 1950 Belgian GP was held. In practice, both Fangio and Farina used the same car. They both recorded identical lap times of four minutes, 37 seconds (4:37:0) or 114.03 mph. That was faster, by some 42 seconds, than Hermann Lang's 1939 record lap in a W163 Mercedes-Benz. However, in the intervening years, the course had been reduced in length by some 813 yards.

Besides a Type 125 for Villoresi, a surprise entry for the grand prix was an unblown 3.3-liter V-12 for Ascari. Enzo Ferrari had been listening to the advice of Aurelio Lampredi and Raymond Sommer for some time. Both strongly advocated taking advantage of the 4.5-liter unsupercharged option as the best means of defeating the Alfa-Romeos. Ferrari, who had been competing in Formula Two races with an unblown 2-liter model, was now ready to gradually prepare a 4.5-liter challenger to the Alfa's supreme position in Formula One.

Ascari managed a fifth-place finish in his first race with the 3.3-liter swing-axle Ferrari. He had little chance to directly square-off with the Alfa-Romeos, since his car suffered a blow out

In anticipation of resuming the contest for Grand Prix supremacy with Ferrari, Alfa-Romeo prepared four new Type 159 models for the 1951 season. The Alfetta engine was up to 420 bhp at 9600 rpm. Juan Fangio strikes a pose in the number 22 Alfa-Romeo Type 159 A Alfetta. (Old Cars Collection)

On May 27, 1951, Farina took his Alfa-Romeo Type 159 race car to second place in the Swiss Grand Prix at Bern. Many of the spectators pressed against the fence and watched the race cars speed through the rain, from under umbrellas. (Robert C. Ackerson Collection)

on the first lap. It was also far inferior to the 158 in handling. Nonetheless, the appearance of the unblown Ferrari began the fulfillment of a prophecy written in *The Autocar* just a month earlier: It predicted, "The position is now that the Alfa-Romeo is obsolescent, but unbeaten. Just as it had decisively out-classed the four-cylinder Maserati, so it must almost inevitably be defeated by newer cars with more cylinders and shorter strokes."

While the unblown Ferrari appeared only in practice for the French Grand Prix at Rheims, it was overshadowed by Fangio. Racing in magnificent form, he unofficially broke Lang's race lap record (114.87 mph) with a blistering 116.2 mph run. However, Lang's practice-lap record of 117.5 mph remained intact. In the race itself, Fangio and Fagioli finished one and two, with Farina back in seventh place.

For the Grand Prix des Nations in Geneva, the Ferraris got deDion rear axles. They were faster than before, but were dogged by bad luck and misfortune. Ascari's Ferrari, now with 4.1 liters, finished practicing with a lap time of 1:48:7. This was just two seconds shy of Fangio's best effort in practice. Not far behind was Villoresi's Ferrari, which was third fastest in practice. In the race, Ascari was able to run a strong second to Fangio. Then, with only six laps remaining, he pulled into his pits with water draining from one of his car's exhaust pipes. Just a lap later, Villoresi's car, which was running far back behind the leaders, skidded on an oil patch. It twisted into a crowd of spectators, causing three fatalities. Villoresi suffered injuries in the tragic accident.

While Fangio had won yet another victory for Alfa-Romeo at Geneva, it was evident that the 158's margin of victory was clearly slipping away. The response of the factory was the readying of the 159 model, with 370 hp and improved brakes. Even in its 158 stage of tune, the Alfetta was a super fast racer. At the Pescara Grand Prix, held on August 15, 1950, Fangio's car was timed at 192.84 mph. Fagioli was even faster over a flying kilometer at 195 mph.

At the Italian Grand Prix, held at Monza, the two great protagonists met for the final time in the 1950 season. In practice, after repeated efforts, Fangio got his Alfa-Romeo below Ascari's 1:58:8 second lap. Ascari's Ferrari engine now displaced a full 4.5 liters. Still, it was only faster by 2/10 of a second. In a classic struggle for the first 14 laps, Fangio and Ascari fought for the lead with all their strength and skill. The 70,000 spectators were on their feet, urging their heroes on to even greater efforts. On the 15th lap, Ascari pulled ahead of Fangio, only to yield to the Alfa-Romeo after two laps. They rounded the course six more times and the Ferrari challenge was over. Ascari had to abandon his 330-bhp Ferrari due to a broken crankshaft. It lay on the course like a stricken animal. The failure was later traced to a faulty billet. Both Ascari and Fangio, whose car dropped out with gear box problems, resumed the race in cars owned by team mates. Eventually, Ascari finished second to Farina, who became the first Grand Prix Champion Driver. For absolute lap speeds during the race, Fangio set a new record of 117.445 mph (2.0 minutes). Ascari's best race effort was some two seconds slower.

The season ended and Alfa-Romeo had triumphed again. However, the margin of victory had been dramatically narrowed by the Type 375 Ferrari. In the words of *The Motor's* Grande Vitesse, "The existing highly supercharged 1500 cc was no longer necessarily unbeatable."

In anticipation of resuming the contest for Grand Prix supremacy with Ferrari, Alfa-Romeo prepared four new Type 159 models for the 1951 season. Again, the Alfetta engine had been induced to bring forth new power. It was up to 420 bhp at 9600 rpm. On occasion, the 159s would appear with deDion rear axles. However, the improved handling that resulted was partly offset by the ever increasing weight of the fuel needed to limit pit stops to two per race. With a racing thirst of less than 1.5 miles per gallon of 98 percent methanol fuel, the Alfas would often start 1951 races with 79 U.S. gallons of fuel on board.

The 159 was a formidable racer. It was true that an Alfa-Romeo triumph was no longer a certainty, but if the field also contained a 4.5 Ferrari, the opposite was also correct. The Alfas were fast, tough, seasoned and reliable competitors. No one could predict the outcome of the impending struggle. As events developed, both Alfa-Romeo and Ferrari chose, at times during the season, to enter races the other did not contest. However they also met head-to-head in seven major Grand Prixs. The first was the Swiss Grand Prix, which was won by Fangio. Taruffi's 4.5-liter Ferrari placed second. Rain fell throughout the race, precluding lap records from being broken. In practice, Fangio came close to Bernd Rosemeyer's record of 105.42 mph, that was set in 1936 with a six-liter Auto Union. His best lap was 104.46 mph.

With the score standing at Alfa one, Ferrari zero, the two teams next met on the 8.76-mile Spa Francorchamps course for the Belgian Grand Prix. Although the Ferraris of Ascari and Villaresi finished second and third to Farina's Alfa, the World Champion had the situation well in hand. He finished over three minutes ahead of Ascari. The Spa course, with its famous Masta straight was highly suitable to the Alfa-Romeo. It was a good deal faster, at the top end, than the Ferrari. Even with a full load of fuel, Farina was timed down the Masta straight at nearly 195 mph. Fangio, who finished a distant ninth, was the victim of circumstances beyond his control. Due to the high speeds and engine revs the Alfas had attained in practice, larger 7.00 x 19 inch tires and wheels were ordered. They arrived just one hour before the race. When Fangio pitted on the 17th lap (for new rear wheels and fuel) the left rear wheel, that arrived late and had not been tested, refused to slide off the axle. Minutes ticked away. Fangio stood by calmly, drinking mineral water. His mechanics were eventually forced to undo the brake drum and put a new tire and tube on the old rim. The result was a 14-minute 18-second pit stop. Fangio did derive a small degree of satisfaction, and one point toward the championship, for his fast lap of 120.51 mph.

The third encounter between the champion and the challenger was the French Grand Prix at Rheims. Fangio won this race, by 58 seconds over Ascari, after 374 miles of high-speed racing. During practice, he shattered Hermann Lang's lap record of 114.86 mph, which was set with a three-liter W163 Mercedes Benz. He recorded a resounding 119.92 mph lap. Witnesses to that great happening were Lang himself and Mercedes Benz tactician Alfred Neubauer. Undoubtedly impressive to the two Germans was Ascari's best lap, which while 2.3 seconds slower than Fangio's, was still faster than Lang's old record.

During the race, the pace of the cars was tremendous. At one point, Fangio was timed unofficially in excess of 200 mph. This took a heavy toll of both Alfas and Ferraris. When Fangio's car began to misfire shortly after the 12th lap, he pitted and resumed the race in Fagioli's car. Earlier, Ascari's car had withdrawn with rear axle and brake ills. When Gonzalez pitted on the 34th lap, Ascari returned to the contest with his car. At the race's conclusion, both Fangio and Ascari were several laps ahead of the rest of the field.

Commenting on the race in *The Motor* for July 11, 1951, Grande Vitesse noted that the Ferraris were, "Not quite so fast as the Alfa-Romeos (but not much slower) and have quite astonishing acceleration, so that on a twistier course the battle would be more evenly matched. Silverstone should therefore be intensely interesting, if the Ferraris come."

The Ferraris came to Silverstone with three team cars for Gonzalez, Ascari and Villoresi, plus Tony Vanderwell's interesting "Thin Wall Special" for Peter Whitehead. Alfa-Romeo sent their best Type 159B models for Fangio, Farina, Bonetto and Sanseiantes. Farina's Alfa was the only one equipped with deDion rear suspension. In practice 27-year-old Froilan Gonzalez, whose car was equipped with the older, 12-plug single-ignition system, earned the distinction of becoming the first person ever to lap Silverstone in excess of 100 mph. His lap time of 1:43:4 (100.57 mph) was better, by a full second, than Fangio's best effort.

The cars were moved into the grid, for the start of the 1951 British Grand Prix, on July 14, 1951. The day of reckoning was at hand. After a dramatic struggle, the race ended two hours, 42 minutes and 18.2 seconds later and a Ferrari was the winner. The two Argentines had fought what has been called a "hammer-and-tongs" struggle, with victory going to Gonzalez by a margin of slightly more than 40 seconds over Fangio. After the victory, Enzo Ferrari was triumphant over the Alfetta, but gave high tribute to the glory of the 158/159 with these words, "I wept for joy, but mixed with the tears of happiness were those of sorrow, because I thought I have slain my mother." Later, Ferrari wrote to Alfa's Managing Director, "I still feel for our Alfa the adolescent tenderness of first love, the immaculate affection for the mamma."

Fangio finished second to Ascari's 4.5-liter Ferrari in the 1951 German Grand Prix on July 29, 1951. The race was held at the Nurburgring. The legendary driver was piloting car number 75, the Alfa-Romeo Type 159 seen here. (Robert C. Ackerson Collection)

The triumph of Ferrari over Alfa-Romeo was repeated in both the German and Italian Grand Prixs. It seemed as if the Ferrari's victory in England had broken a magical spell. In reality, both courses favored the Ferrari's strong points of acceleration and handling, while placing the Type 159 Alfa at a disadvantage. Nonetheless, at both Nurburgring and Monza, the Alfa-Romeos achieved the fastest lap times. Fangio, with 27 points, held just a two-point lead over Ascari on the eve of the Spanish Grand Prix. Ascari, with 25 points, was four ahead of Gonzalez. The annual World's Championship would be decided at Barcelona on October 14, 1951.

From its start, Ferrari's strategy for this final race of the season contained two fatal flaws. The first was a decision to run the race without refueling. The Ferraris started with heavy fuel loads, which adversely affected their handling in the race's early stages. Far more devastating in its consequences was the choice of small 16-inch (instead of 17-inch) rear tires. These had been successful at Monza, but the rougher surface of the Penna Rhin course, which also allowed higher speeds to be achieved, proved to be too much of a strain on them.

Three of the four Alfas entered were Type 159Ms like those raced at Monza. The "M" meant "Maggiorata" (increased). The exception was the car for Fangio, which had a modified frame with additional supports running parallel to, and above, the larger-diameter main frame tubes. On the eve of the race, *Road & Track's* correspondent, Corado Millanta described the 159s as "nervous." In contrast, he saw the Ferraris as, "Calm appearing, but actually fierce."

In practice, all indications were that a struggle of epic proportions would be forthcoming. Ascari was fastest with a lap of 108.1 mph. Fangio was 1.7 seconds slower and his time down the 1.5-mile straight was a resounding 186 mph. At the start of the race, Ascari used his superior acceleration to break into the lead. On the fourth lap, Fangio surged into the lead, never to relinquish it. By lap eight, the Ferraris of Ascari, Taruffi and Villoresi had been forced to pit to replace rear tires, which had lost large sections of their threads. None of the Ferrari drivers were willing to give up the contest. Although Ascari fell back to 14th place after his first pit stop, he struggled back into third place behind Fangio and Farina. Then, he suffered another tire failure. The result was that Fangio, who was driving with great skill and using the Alfa's strong

Four 158s driven by members of the Alfa Romeo factoryt team were photographed by British photographer Guy Griffith at Silverstone on May 13, 1950.

points to their utmost, lapped Ascari on the 20th lap. Late in the race, Gonzalez made a great effort and held second position behind Fangio. However, unlike Silverstone, the race belonged to Fangio and Alfa-Romeo. When the checkered flag dropped, they were the victors.

Winning the Spanish Grand Prix was a beginning and an end. For Fangio, it was the first of his world driving championships. For Ferrari it was the prelude to greater achievements. For Alfa-Romeo, it was the apparent end of Grand Prix competition.

In hindsight, the Alfetta is seen as more than just a Grand Prix car. It was the ultimate refinement of a design concept and stands out, for all time, as a masterpiece. Its achievements in a career spanning 14 years will, probably, never be equaled. It was both fitting and proper that the first World's Championship was won at the wheel of a 158.

Fangio's 158 Alfa Romeo made a valiant effort to overtake Gonzales' 4.5-liter Ferrari in the British Grand Prix at Silverstone on July 14, 1951. (Robert C. Ackerson Collection)

Giuseppe Farina drove an Alfa 158 at Silverstone in 1950.

Juan Fangio kicks up some water with his Alfa Romeo 158.

Classic Grand Prix racing cars disappeared with Maserati 250F

By Robert C. Ackerson

Often called the last of the "classic" grand prix cars, the Maserati 250F enjoyed an unusually long and successful career. It won the very first race it entered in 1954. This model was raced from 1954 to 1960, competing in all seven years of the grand prix formula for which it was designed. The 250Fs won nine major races. A 250F was on the grid of the 1960 United States Grand Prix, the last race of the 2.5-liter formula, and was thus the only car to race in the first and last events of this series. Certainly not the least impressive of the 250F's credentials is that it was the car that the redoubtable Juan Fangio drove to the last of his five world championships, in 1957.

During 1952 and 1953, most European grand prix races had been staged as Formula II (2-liter maximum engine size) events. This abandonment of Formula I racing was due to the dearth of competition for the Ferrari 4.5-liter 375 model. The 375 had broken the string of consecutive racing victories by the Alfa Romeo 158/9, which began in 1947. When Alfa chose not to contest the 1952 season, there was little serious competition for the V-12 Ferrari. Understandably, spectator interest languished. With the new formula beginning in 1954, grand prix racing took on a spectacular new character. Entries eventually came from Ferrari and Maserati, as well as Lancia, Mercedes-Benz, Cooper, Lotus and Aston Martin. In addition, the ill-fated Scarabs came from the United States.

In early postwar grand prix racing, Maserati's supercharged 1.5-liter 4 CLT model was outclassed by the Type 158 Alfa Romeo. One of its few significant successes had been a victory in the 1949 British Grand Prix. Maserati then had to wait until 1953, when Fangio drove an A6GCM Formula II model to victory in the Italian Grand Prix, for another major triumph. Maserati chose to use the A6GCM's six-cylinder, 2-liter engine as the starting point for an engine to power its new racer for the 1954 season. Not to be ignored in any chronicle of Maserati's racing history was the 1952 arrival, from Alfa Romeo, of the gifted engineer Giaocchino Columbo. With the Alfa Romeo Type 158 engine and Ferrari V-12 among his credentials, great things were expected from Columbo. Considering the resources at his disposal, there was to be no cause for disappointment.

The output of Maserati's future grand prix engine, in 2-liter form, stood at 177 hp. Then, Columbo began his development program. By simply switching from single to dual ignition, he was able to increase output to 188 hp. Other improvements credited to Columbo included a more efficient combustion chamber design. It resulted in a compression ratio of 15:1. As set up for the 1954 racing season, the 2.5-liter Maserati was rated at 230 hp at 7200 rpm. This was attained with a fuel containing five percent methyl alcohol, 35 percent gasoline, 10 percent acetone, five percent benzol and one percent castor oil.

By December 1953, the first 250F was completed. It was a simple, straightforward racing car that was more noteworthy for its lack of technical innovation than for any startling design features. With a tubular frame, deDion rear suspension, a double overhead camshaft and rear-mounted four-speed transmission, it was the epitome of the traditional school of thought concerning the proper way to design a grand prix car.

Originally, there were no plans for the Maserati factory to officially enter grand prix racing with the 250F. Instead, it was anticipated that the model would be campaigned by private teams that would receive the benefit of Maserati's development program, as well as factory assistance in the tuning and maintenance of their cars. After the 250F scored impressive victories in its initial racing appearances, the situation was reversed. Maserati then entered grand prix racing in a proper fashion, with a fully outfitted factory team.

Among the early purchasers of the 250F was Stirling Moss, who retained his Maserati even after he joined the Mercedes-Benz team in 1955. Moss' car was subjected to much modification by the great racing mechanic Alf Francis. Dunlop disc brakes were installed by Francis. Besides their superiority over conventional drums, the discs helped improved the Maserati's already excellent handling, since they reduced unsprung weight by seven pounds per wheel. Francis also mated an SU fuel injection system with the 250F engine. This setup never achieved the hoped for results. It produced less power in the mid-engine speed range than the normal Weber carburetors produced.

The first race of the new formula was the Argentine Grand Prix, which was run in inclement weather in January 1954. It proved to be an auspicious debut for the new Maserati. Qualifying third, behind the Ferraris of Giuseppe Farina and Frolian Gonzalez, was Juan Fangio in a 250F. He was the eventual winner. The Ferrari team manager protested that five men, instead of the allowable three, changed Fangio's car over to rain tires. However, the Maserati earned its success honestly.

Salvodori, Maserati 250F (Gilby's) at Oulton Park on July 8, 1954. (Robert C. Ackerson Collection)

In April, at the Syracuse Grand Prix and the Paus Grand Prix, the 250F displayed a level of performance that clearly established it as a serious competitor to Ferraris. At Syracuse, driver Marimon's 250F recorded the fastest practice lap and posed a challenge to Farina's Ferrari, until the Maserati retired with a weak clutch. The 250F improved on this performance at Pau. Jean Behra set a new lap record in gaining a victory there.

Juan Fangio was successful with a 250F at the Belgium Grand Prix on June 20, 1954. His victory lends credence to assertions made in L.J.K. Setright's scholarly book *The Grand Prix Car 1954 to 1966*. Setright said, "It has been argued, with some justification, that had Fangio remained with Maserati, in 1954, he would still have been World Champion that year." Fangio set a new lap record of four minutes 22.1 seconds. That was impressive enough, but that the previous record (also set by Fangio) had been held by the great Type 159 Alfa Romeo made his achievement more sensational for Maserati. Fangio went on to win the Grand Prix against spirited competition from Trintignant, a driver who piloted his Ferrari with great skill and determination. An interesting side note to Fangio's victory was that he was able to reach a rev limit of 8100 rpm without harming the engine. At that time, the factory had cautioned 250F campaigners not to exceed 7400 rpm.

The Mercedes-Benz W196 made its first appearance at Rheims, during the French Grand Prix. It was the latest in a long line of Mercedes-Benz grand prix racers. With its futuristic, streamlined body, the W196 seemed to make its Italian competitors instant anachronisms. This initial impression was reinforced by the cars' performances, especially at the hands of Fangio. The great Argentinean had been racing for Maserati until his Mercedes was ready, and was in top driving form. In his W196, he became the first man to break the 200 kilometers per hour. The barrier was cracked at Rheims, with a practice lap average of 200 to 202 kilometers per hour. While this speed reflected changes to the course that slightly reduced its length, it was still an impressive achievement.

In all the excitement surrounding the W196's debut and subsequent victory, the highly competitive performances turned in by the Maserati 250F and Ferrari Type 553 went largely unnoticed. For the record, a comparison of the top four qualifiers is revealing:

Driver	Car	Fastest Practice Lap
Fangio	Mercedes-Benz W196	2 Min. 29.4 Sec.
Kling	Mercedes-Benz W196	2 Min. 30.4 Sec.
Ascari	Maserati 250F	2 Min. 30.5 Sec.
Gonzalez	Ferrari 553	2 Min. 30.6 Sec.

Both W196s took the lead from the race's onset. They set a torrid pace that left only four other close competitors out of 21 finishers. Ascari drove his Ferrari to its limit in the race's early stages, staying close behind the Mercedes-Benz "Silver Arrows" until his engine overheated and seized.

Despite imposing performances by the W196s, the results of the British Grand Prix at Silverstone indicated that the so-called "Italian Primitives" were not as archaic as they seemed in a visual comparison with the W196. The Ferrari 625s of Frolian Gonzalez and Mike Hawthorn finished first and second, with Marimon's Maserati in third position. The tight circuit favored the Ferrari's excellent torque and handling. The W196, with its streamlined form, was quite unhappy and Mercedes had to settle for fourth and seventh place finishes.

Three factory-sponsored 250Fs were entered the 1954 German Grand Prix at the Nurburgring on August 1. Moss' car also received factory preparation. After the stinging defeat at Silverstone, Mercedes had hurriedly re-wrapped the W196s in more conventional body work that left the wheels fully exposed. In the hands of Fangio, the Mercedes again showed itself to be the fastest car. His best practice lap of nine minutes and 50.1 seconds made him the fastest qualifier. It also broke the old record (set by Hermann Lang in 1939, with a 3-liter supercharged Mercedes-Benz W163) by 2.2 seconds. However, Hawthorn's Ferrari and Moss' Maserati were not totally outclassed. *Road & Track's* correspondent Carrado Millanta reported, "During the three practice days the consensus was that, given drivers of equal capabilities, the Ferraris on this course would be the equal of the Mercedes." The oil tank on the factory 250Fs was relocated for this race. It was moved from under the hood to the tail. This had no impact on the outcome of this race, but was to have future significance.

During practice, Marimon, the Maserati team leader, was killed. The young Argentinean driver had shown great promise and his death was a tragic loss to his fellow compatriots Fangio and Gonzolez. After the tragedy, the Maserati team was withdrawn. Gonzalez was extremely despondent over the death of his friend. He had no enthusiasm for racing that day and retired after just 16 laps. Hawthorn took over driving his car and finished second to Fangio's Mercedes.

By virtue of his victory in the Swiss Grand Prix, Fangio became World Champion for the second time. His attention then shifted to the Italian Grand Prix at Monza. The Maserati team cars were virtually unchanged from the form in which they had raced in Germany. Musso's entry sported a new exhaust system. It used a single, large-diameter pipe in place of the dual pipes that had previously been used. Unfortunately, the performance improvement expected from this change did not develop.

Again, in practice, the W196s (in aerodynamic raiment for this ultra-fast race) were the fastest qualifiers. As before, their superiority was by a paper thin margin:

Driver	Car	Fastest Practice Lap
Fangio	Mercedes-Benz W196	1 Min. 59 Sec.
Ascari	Ferrari 625	1 Min. 59.2 Sec.
Moss	Maserati 250F	1 Min. 59.3 Sec.
Kling	Mercedes-Benz W196	1 Min. 59.6 Sec.

Ascari was in top form. He was at least the equal of Fangio for much of the race. Then, after leading for many laps, he over-revved his engine and was forced to retire. This did little to alleviate the Mercedes-Benz team's problems. An invigorated Moss had a comfortable lead of 20 seconds on the 68th of 80 laps, when a mishap occurred. His oil tank had been moved to the rear to bring it into conformity with those of Maserati factory cars. With a dozen laps to go in the race, an oil pipe leading from the tank to the engine broke. Moss's engine had no oil and Fangio sped into the lead and raced on to a victory.

In October 1954, the most potent competitor to the W196 made its appearance during the Spanish Grand Prix at the Pedralloes track in Barcelona. It was the Lancia D-50. In Alberto Ascari's hands, the new car was the fastest qualifier.

The front row at Barcelona reflected the high level of competition that characterized the 1954 grand prix season. Flanking Ascari's Lancia were Fangio's Mercedes, Hawthorn's Ferrari Squalo and Harry Schell's Maserati. The Squalo went on to win its first race. Musso's Maserati was second. Fangio had to be content with third.

Fans of the 250F found little to cheer about in 1955. The W196 won the Argentina, Belgian, Dutch, British and Italian grand prixs. The only setback for Mercedes came at Monaco, where the cars driven by Moss and Fangio both broke down. The Maserati's best performance in 1955 was achieved by Behra in the British Grand Prix, which was held at Aintree for the first time. With his five-speed 250F, Behra qualified with the third fastest time and shared the front row with Moss and Fangio. For a time in the race, Behra was gaining on the two leading Mercedes until his car's deDion tube collapsed and he had to abandon the fray.

Mercedes decided not to campaign the W196 in 1956, temporarily putting the world's two finest drivers (Moss and Fangio) on the unemployment line. Other competitors scrambled to offer them contracts for the upcoming season. In a not entirely cordial relationship, Ferrari acquired the services of Fangio. Moss tested the offers from various British standard bearers, then went with Maserati.

Ferraris dominated the grand prix season in 1956, although 250Fs did score victories in two of the seven championship races. Behra and Moss showed up for the Italian Grand Prix with new lightweight versions of the 250F. While they broke no new technical ground, the two cars served as the basis for Fangio's championship drive in 1957. Their major design change involved the relocation of the engine. It was moved to an offset position, relative to the longitudinal center line of the car. This allowed the driveshaft to be placed to the left of the driver's seat instead of running underneath the seat, as it had done on earlier models. As a result, the driver's seat could be lowered several inches, which helped reduce the frontal area. In addition, a slight decrease in weight was made possible by the use of thinner frame tubes.

Refinements were also made to the Maserati engine. They increased horsepower to approximately 260, to give the 250F a significant boost in performance. Early in the year, Moss drove a

Juan Manuel Fangio (on right) was one of the greatest Grand Prix drivers to pilot the Maserati 250F during its racing history. Here, at the 1990 Chicago Historic Races, the master signs a poster for Carol Rand of Marshfield, Wisconsin. (Ron Kowalke photo)

special 250F (described as the "hack" model) to lap speeds at Spa that were faster than Fangio's best efforts with a W196 in 1955. Thus, Maserati hopes for a 1956 victory at Monza were high.

An anticipated Ferrari challenge never materialized, as all four entries from Modena fell by the wayside with tire or steering failures. Moss still nearly lost the race when his car ran out of gas on the 47th lap. Fortunately, another Maserati was able to give him a push to the pits, where he refueled before going on to victory.

By any account, 1957 was Maserati's greatest year in racing. Its 4.5-liter V-8 sports model captured the World Sports Car Championship. Fangio earned victories in grand prixs in Argentina, Monaco, France, Italy and Germany. He became World Driving Champion for the fifth time. His achievements earned Maserati the constructor's championship as well.

The highlight of the 1957 season, if not Fangio's career, was his performance in the German Grand Prix. In contrast to the shorter grand prix races that came in 1958, this was a classic contest in every sense. Consisting of 22 laps (310 miles) over the challenging Nurburgring, it tested men and machines, as well as race team strategies.

Although Fangio set a new course record in practice (nine minutes and 25 seconds), the Ferraris of Hawthorn, Collins and Musso were expected to benefit from their ability to run the entire race without a change of tires. The Maseratis were scheduled for rear tire changes somewhere near the race's midpoint.

Fangio's strategy was to begin the race with his fuel tanks only half filled, to gain a 170-pound advantage over his adversaries in the race's early stages. Hawthorn put in a great first lap, in which he nearly equaled Fangio's lap record, and followed with a strong second lap, in which he broke the new record. However, Fangio moved into the lead on lap three and held this position until lap 11, the race's halfway mark. Then he stopped to refuel and change tires. Fangio's lead of 28 seconds evaporated, as his crew took almost a minute to accomplish its tasks. When he rejoined the race, his Maserati seemed to be running off form and his crew members appeared frustrated and depressed. The desired impression that something was wrong with Fangio's 250F was reinforced by a relatively slow lap of nine minutes and 41 seconds.

Since Ferraris now held the top three positions, prospects for a Maserati victory seemed dim. With nine laps to go, the Ferrari pits signaled Hawthorn and Collins to slow down. When Fangio passed his pit, team manager Bertocchi gave him a gesture to indicate, "The ruse worked ... now pour on the steam!"

Each lap at Nurburgring is over 14 miles long. Hawthorne or Collins did not realize they were being duped. On the 15th lap, Fangio had cranked his car to the point where he set another new lap record of nine minutes 28 seconds. This cut 12 seconds off the Ferrari's lead. Frantically, Hawthorn and Collins struggled to maintain their advantage, but "ringmaster" Fangio was driving the race of his life. Each lap brought a new record. With three laps remaining, Fangio trailed the leaders by just 15 seconds. Hundreds of thousands of spectators shouted themselves hoarse, as Fangio posted an incredible nine minutes and 17 seconds on Lap 21. It was the 10th time in the race that he broke his record.

Moving past Collins, Fangio challenged Hawthorn for the lead on Lap 22. Sweeping past the future champion on the inside of the north curve, with his car half on the grass lining the course, Fangio poured it on. In the words of *Road & Track's* (November 1957) Bernard Cahier, "Fangio took the checkered flag with a broad smile on his face." He received the biggest ovation Cahier had ever seen a driver accorded at the Nurburgring.

It was a very good year for Maserati, but being a champion can be a fragile state of affairs. In three of the season's last four grand prixs, Tony Vandervell's Vanwalls were victorious. It was clear that the 250F would not be competitive in 1958 without major changes. Early in 1957, a 250F powered by a 310 hp V-12 appeared on paper. It seemed to hold great promise of being one of the most powerful grand prix cars of its era. Unfortunately, a "surly" power curve made it a tricky beast to drive. It was non-competitive.

Thus, the 250F suffered a meteoric decline, after reaching a pinnacle of success in 1957. Not the least of Maserati's problems sprang from the company's account books. Winning championships cost a lot of money. Unlike Mercedes-Benz, Maserati did not have a line of passenger cars whose sales benefited from the prestige of a world championship. Perhaps if its statue as a grand touring automobile was as strong as Ferrari's, Maserati could have enjoyed some sales improvement from racing. Then the company might have mounted a counter-attack on Vanwall in 1956.

In its long career, the 250F won nine major grand prixs and scored victories in numerous other smaller events. Although it was, at times, overshadowed by the more glamorous Ferrari and Mercedes-Benz race cars, the Maserati 250F is now viewed as the last of the great front-engined racers. Its simple design was often decried as its shortcoming, although it proved to be one of its greatest assets. As with numerous other automobiles, it has taken the passage of 30 years to place the 250F in its proper perspective as one of the greatest grand prix cars of all time.

Jaguar racing history studded with special models and successes

By Robert C. Ackerson

In 1951 the LeMans twenty-four hour race was won by a Jaguar XK-120C. This marked the first victory by a British car at LeMans since the Lagonda's Triumph in 1935. Although Jaguar was to experience its share of setbacks and disappointments in the future, its victory in 1951 marked the beginning of Jaguar's years of supremacy at LeMans. With victories in the 1951, 1953 and 1955 to 1957 races, Jaguar equaled Bentley's prewar record of five LeMans victories.

Jaguar's prewar competition record had been based primarily upon rallying successes. It's true that the SS-100 was a fast two-seater. Tommy Widsom averaged 118 mph around Brooklands in a modified version in 1937. However, it was not in the same class as the Bugattis and Delages that were successful at LeMans in 1939, just before the outbreak of World War II.

After the war, Jaguar did not produce a two-seater like the SS-100 until 1948, when the XK-120 was unveiled at the Earls Court Show in London. This particular exhibition was the first held in London since 1938. In spite of the "export only" signs that dominated each auto producer's stand, it attracted very large crowds. It is well known that William Lyons had planned to produce only 200 XK-120s as a means to publicize his forthcoming Mark VII Sedan. This plan was soon

In September of 1951, Stirling Moss won the Tourist Trophy Race, on the Dundrod Circuit at Belfast, Northern Ireland, in a C-Type Jaguar. (Robert C. Ackerson Collection)

abandoned and the XK-120 assumed the status of a production sports car. As the years passed, it evolved into the XK-140 and XK-150 models. Not until 1961, when the E-Type was introduced, did Jaguar stop production of XK models with the classic sweeping fender lines.

The Jaguar XK-120's appearance was not entirely unexpected. Much of it was seen in a special SS-100 Coupe built in 1938. An overhead cam engine was not exactly a revelation either. However, never before in motoring history had such a combination of styling and performance been offered in a car with a U.S. price of under $4,000.

The Jaguar XK-120 was not intended as a competition sports car. However, its arrival in America coincided with the formation of the Sports Car Club of America (SCCA). This club got road racing going in a big way in the United States. The competition was often on the flat and not-too-thrilling confines of Strategic Air Command bases. Drivers such as Phil Hill, Chuck Wallace, George Constantine, Bob Grossman and Walter Hansgen had racing success with Jaguars early in their careers.

Certainly not the least of the XK-120's achievements was setting a speed record of 132.59 mph. This was done by a roadster with a competition windscreen, a metal tonneau cover over the passenger's seat, and a streamlined underpan. This speed, set with Jaguar's chief test driver Ron Sutton at the wheel, established the XK-120 as the world's fastest production automobile in 1949.

For the 1950 French Grand Prix at LeMans, three XK-120s were equipped with competition type options, including high-compression (9.0:1) pistons and high-lift camshafts. They proved to be worthy competitors. For a time, the Jaguar roadster of Leslie Johnson and Bert Hadley held third-place in the race. Then, with just three hours left, they were forced to retire with a burned-out clutch. The two remaining Jaguars finished 12th and 15th overall.

This performance indicated that a lighter more aerodynamic version of the XK-120, with a bit more power on tap, could win at LeMans. Work soon began on such a car. It was known as the XK-120C and was the first Jaguar ever designed specifically for racing. The C-Type's engine carried larger valves, dual exhausts, two-inch diameter SU carburetors and a high-lift camshaft

The 1953 LeMans winning C-Type of Duncan Hamilton and Tony Rolt. (Robert C. Ackerson Collection)

The C- and D-Type Jaguars represented the finest racing cars of their class in the world. They were designed primarily to win at LeMans and they did their job extremely well. Here we see the D-Type of Hamilton/Rolt in action at the 1954 French Grand Prix at LeMans. (Robert C. Ackerson Collection)

as its major changes. With the standard 8.0:1 compression ratio, horsepower stood at 200. Pistons allowing a 9.0:1 compression ratio were also available. They boosted horsepower to 210.

To reduce overall weight, the XK-120's strong, but heavy, box-section chassis was replaced by a tubular one. It had a 96-inch wheelbase chassis made of one-inch, 1.5-inch and two-inch diameter tubing. Additional strength came from the use of channel-section steel for the frame cross members. The XK-120's torsion bar and wishbone front suspension was used on the C-Type. Rack-and-pinion steering replaced the production model's recirculating ball system.

The XK-120's live rear axle and semi-elliptic rear springs did not provide the best of handling on rough surfaces. They were replaced by a setup using a single torsion bar and trailing links. This gave the C-Type good, but not outstanding, handling characteristics. In appearance, the C-Type bore a definite familiar similarity to the XK-120. Its far smoother lines enabled it to maintain a speed of l00 mph with 18 percent less horsepower than a production roadster.

Spurred on by enthusiastic reports from England's two great motoring weeklies, The *Autocar* and *The Motor*, Britons eagerly awaited the start of the 1951 LeMans race on June 23. The Jaguar drivers were a mixture of youth and experience, sharing a great deal of confidence and enthusiasm. Sharing the three Jaguars entered were Peter Whitehead and Peter Walker, Leslie Johnson and Clemente Biondetti, and Jack Fairman and Stirling Moss.

Still to be reckoned with in 1951 was the 4.5 liter Talbot Sports that won in 1950. Derived from the Talbot Grand Prix model, this six-cylinder, cycle-fendered creation was a wild-and-woolly appearing automobile. In the hands of drivers such as Rosier and Froilan Gonzalez, it had to be regarded as a pre-race favorite.

The Jaguars proved that the Talbot's day had come and gone. Peter Walker's C-Type effortlessly broke the lap record by better than four seconds. When the race began Gonzalez, who was always a great competitor, burst into a first-lap lead. However, Moss' Jaguar was race leader within three laps. Before two hours of racing were completed, Moss held a one-lap advantage over Gonzalez. The other two Jaguars maintained third and fourth positions. Moss' drive ended just after midnight, when he was forced to retire with no oil pressure. The Johnson and Biondetti Jaguar retired 3-1/2 hours earlier, with a similar malady. The satisfaction coming from the remaining Jaguar being in first place was offset by concerns that it, too, might join its stricken team mates with a DNF (did not finish) mark.

The Talbot team, sensing a weakness in the Jaguars' performances, had mounted an effort to overhaul the leading Jaguars shortly after Johnson's car retired. The strain on Rosier's car proved too much. Like Moss, he was forced out of the race early. Then, the Talbot's oil tank split.

As night turned to day, the solitary Jaguar held a commanding seven-lap lead over Gonzalez's Talbot. With its competition in disarray, it went on to win at an average speed of 93.5 mph for 2,244 miles. Underscoring the stock Jaguar's ability as a race-ready sports car was the fifth-place finish of an XK-120.

Most Jaguar fans view the 1952 LeMans race as an event that "never took place." It was a disaster of the first magnitude for Jaguar. Coventry's debacle originated in the 1952 Mille Miglia, where the Mercedes-Benz 300SL made its racing debut. On the fast Ravenna Straight, Moss' C-Type Jaguar was passed by one of the Gull-Wing coupes. The Englishman was clocking 150 mph when the German machine passed with a degree of ease that wasn't to Moss' liking. When this bit of bad news reached "jolly old England," the prospects of battling with the German cars in the upcoming LeMans race seemed unpleasant.

In a classic example of over-reaction, work began to hastily revise the C-Type from its 1951 form and increase its maximum speed. The results were calamitous. All three team cars retired with over-heating problems before the race was three hours old. Interestingly, a lone Talbot, driven by Pierre Levegh, very nearly won the race. With the contest nearly over Neubauer was facing the unpleasant task of reporting to his superiors that Mercedes had to settle for a second-place finish. Then, with less than an hour remaining, the Talbot's engine gave up the ghost.

For 1953, a well thought out plan was followed in preparing four C-Types for the French classic. Outwardly similar to the 1951 race winner, the new C-Type was lighter, since smaller diameter tubes were used in its frame. With three Weber twin-choke carburetors, it was also a more powerful car. The boost did not increase the C-Type's top speed, however, since it was accompanied by a reduction in the final drive ratio from 3.3:1 to 2.9:1.

These improvements were not as significant as the C-Type's use of Dunlop disc brakes at all four wheels. The importance of these in improving the C-Type's road performance cannot be over-emphasized. The fastest lap set by a C-Type in 1951 was 105.24 mph. By comparison, the winning Jaguar in 1953 averaged 105.85 mph for the entire 24 hours. Since the top speed of the two cars was virtually the same, the great bulk of credit for this vastly increased speed must be attributed to the disc brakes. Laurence Pomeroy judged that they had the same impact on the Jaguar's performance as an additional 125 horsepower at the flywheel.

It's noteworthy that the 3.5 Alfa Romeo driven by Fangio and Marimon, as well as Alberto Ascari's 3.5-liter Ferrari, were faster cars than the C-Type Jaguar. Yet, the Jaguar's great advantage in braking more than made up for its lower speeds. Both Italian cars, pushed by their drivers in a futile effort to overcome the superior Jaguar brakes, soon dropped out of the race.

All the C-Types entered at LeMans in 1953 finished. The Phil Walters and John Fitch Cunningham, which finished in third, spoiled Jaguar's chances of sweeping the first three places. The victorious Jaguar, driven by Tony Rolt and Duncan Hamilton, traveled 220 miles further than the 300SL that won the previous year. If the 300SL had duplicated its 1952 performance (which was good enough to win that year), it would have wound up 10th in 1953, some 20 miles behind a privately owned C-Type which finished ninth.

This particular Jaguar, entered by the Belgian racing team, had been bought off a showroom floor just 10 days before the race.

None of the C-Types required any additional water during the entire 24 hours of racing. As a group, they traveled 9,873.6 miles at an average speed of 102.85 mph.

The overwhelming success of the C-Type at LeMans in 1953 tended to belie that it was advancing into old age. If Jaguar was going to keep pace with the latest creations from Enzo Ferrari (not to mention the much-rumored new sports car from Mercedes-Benz) a new model was needed. It had to embody the C-Type's strong points, plus take advantage of the latest aerodynamic technology.

In June 1953, while the C-Type was securing its second LeMans victory, a C-Type chassis fitted with an early version of the coming D-Type body was completed. In October 1953, this experimental model was clocked on the Jabbeke highway at 178.383 mph. Earlier in April, a

C-Type on the same course had achieved a top speed of 148.435 mph. The LeMans-winning C-Type had a virtually identical top speed of 148.83 mph. At the same time the C/D prototype was being tested in Belgium, a modified XK-120 roadster with a perspex bubble cover for the driver achieved a speed of 172.412 mph. Norman Dewis, who replaced Ron Sutton, was the latest chief test driver at Jaguar. His mark remains the highest official speed ever recorded by an XK-120.

Early in May, the first D-Type model was taken to LeMans for testing. Along with it went the C/D prototype. After a delay due to the D-Type's clutch being "fried" after its drive at LeMans, the track officials advised Tony Rolt that he would be allowed to make one lap around the course. This hardly set well with anyone at Jaguar. It was especially rough on Rolt, who barely had time to become familiar with the new sports car. Instead of stopping after one lap, Rolt blasted by the officials and continued merrily on his way. He completed three laps in all. During his unauthorized tour of the LeMans circuit, Rolt reached 180 mph on the Mulsanne Straight. He completed his final lap five seconds faster than the record Ascari set the previous year with a 3.5-liter Ferrari.

The new D-Type Jaguar was of monocoque construction. As expected, its engine was based upon the XK-120 power plant. A major modification was the use of a dry-sump oil system. For LeMans in 1954, the power output stood at 245 bhp at 5750 rpm. However, during the race Moss took his D-Type up to 7200 rpm, more than once, without incurring the wrath of the Gods.

To keep the hood line and frontal area low, but still use triple Weber carburetors, the engine in the D-Type was installed at an 8-1/2 degree angle to the left.

In Italy, Ferrari was preparing his entries for LeMans 1954. These were the 4.9-liter 375-plus models.

This D-Type won the 1954 Rheims 12-hour race. It was the D-Type's first racing victory. (Robert C. Ackerson Collection)

244

Brutal in appearance, they had 344 bhp at 6500 rpm and were far more powerful than the D-Types. These awesome sports cars were, in many ways, at the opposite end of the design spectrum from the Jaguars. Relying upon power, they were designed with relatively little concern about aerodynamics. Similarly, when compared to the D-Type (in reality not the fastest cornering car in the world), the Ferrari was a "bull in a china shop."

The stage was set for one of the great classic LeMans races. The three works Ferraris driven by Marzotto and Maglioli, Gonzalez and Trintignant and Rosier and Manzon squared off against the three D-Types of Moss and Walker, Whitehead and Wharton and Rolt and Hamilton.

Early in the race, the entire Jaguar team suffered engine problems. For a time, this seemed to threaten their ability to even finish the race, much less remain competitive. Eventually, the cause of the Jaguar's misfiring was traced to sand that had somehow found its way into the pit's fuel supply.

This development, plus team stratagem, resulted in the three Ferraris leading the race's early stages. Both teams suffered setbacks during the hours of darkness. They were made more dangerous by the rain that fell in intermittent, but heavy, fashion. At 1:30 in the morning, the Moss/Walker car went out with its brake servo motor inoperative. This was followed, at 3:24, by retirement of the Whitehead/Wharton Jaguar with cylinder head problems. Earlier, at about midnight, Maglioli's 4.9 Ferrari had packed up its transmission. Six hours later, the Manzon/Rosier Ferrari became all but useless after its gearbox locked in second gear. It was also retired.

These developments left Gonzalez and Trintignant leading Rolt and Hamilton by one lap. At 10 am, with six hours left, the Jaguar lost another lap after suffering minor body damage. This resulted when Rolt hit the Arnage sand bank, to avoid colliding with a slower automobile.

At LeMans in 1954, the D-Type of Hamilton and Rolt finished second to the 4.9-liter Ferrari of Gonzalez and Trintignant. (Robert C. Ackerson Collection)

Although the Jaguar's braking advantage was nullified somewhat by the rain, which kept the Ferrari's drum brakes free from fading, its greater speed and handling advantage allowed it to gradually eat away at the Ferrari's lead. The disparity in speed between the D-Type Jaguar and the 4.9 Ferrari was obvious. The fastest Ferrari, driven by Gonzalez was clocked on the Mulsanne Straight at 160.13 mph. Moss' Jaguar, the quickest of the three D-Types entered, was considerably faster at 172.87 mph.

The critical point came when Gonzalez took the wheel of the Ferrari at 2:30 Sunday afternoon. With 90 minutes left to race, this was the Ferrari's final pit stop. Although the Jaguar had been closing in at a rate of 20 seconds per lap, the victory seemed to be Ferrari's. This seemed particularly true with Gonzalez driving, but racing, like baseball, is known for its famous "ninth inning cliff hangers." When Gonzalez was ready to rejoin the race, he could not start his car. Throughout the night the big 4.9-liter V-12 had-become more and more reluctant to spring back to life after each pit stop. With the green D-Type rapidly closing in, it appeared that the race was over for the Ferrari. However, in a scene marked by confusion, shouting, and general chaos (not to mention rule infractions) the V-12 was coaxed to action. By the narrow margin of 2.55 miles, the victory went to Gonzalez. So close was this finish that the Jaguar had averaged 105.0 mph to the Ferrari's 105.1 mph for the 24 hours of racing.

In the 1955 racing season, Jaguar introduced numerous changes in the D-Type's design. They included a lighter and simpler front sub-frame. Many of these were the result of racing the D-Type the previous year. Factory cars for the 1955 LeMans race featured hoods that increased their overall length by 7-1/2 inches. Larger intake and exhaust valves increased the D-Type's 2442 cc engine to 270 hp.

The epic struggle between Castellotti's 121LM Ferrari, Fangio's 300SLR Mercedes-Benz and Mike Hawthorn's D-Type Jaguar is told elsewhere in this book. In brief, it was one of the great contests held at LeMans in its long history. Each car had its strong and weak points. While Castellotti's car had to withdraw early in the race, due to overheating, he had the lead for the first hour. This early withdrawal, plus the crash of Pierre Levegh (which led to the withdrawal of the remaining Mercedes) makes any judgment as to which was the superior car at LeMans a difficult one to make. Hawthorn's victory, as hallow as it was with the 300SLRs out of the race, set a new lap record of 122.39 mph.

During 1955 to 1960, Jaguar produced the D-Type on a small scale for sale to private owners. These production models were rated at 250 bhp. They were available with or without the aerodynamically efficient dorsal tail fin.

Road & Track's road test of one of these production models appeared in its May 1956 issue. After two runs, with a speed of 155.17 mph being recorded at *R & T's* "secret test site," publisher John Bond decided he had enough. On its third run, with just a driver on board, the D-Type reached 162.16 mph. This high-speed capability was not at the expense of low speed acceleration, however, as the D-Type could run from zero to 60 mph in just 4.6 seconds. It reached 100 mph, from a standing start, in 12.1 seconds.

The year 1956 was the last time Jaguar fielded a factory team for many years. Quite naturally, LeMans was given the most attention. Just about everything that could go wrong for Jaguar in this race, did go wrong. For openers, Desmond Titterington severely damaged one of the team cars in a shunt at the Indianapolis corner, during practice.

On the second lap of the race, Paul Frere spun his D-Type near the esses, causing severe damage to its rear end. Within moments, a second team Jaguar, driven by Jack Fairman, appeared on the scene. Although successful in avoiding the crippled D-Type, it spun on the rain-slicked surface. Before Fairman could get under way, dePortago's Ferrari happened along. It spun into Fairman's motionless Jaguar.

Of the three factory cars, only Hawthorn's Jaguar remained. After an early lead, he started to visit the pits with maddening frequency. It was a futile effort to find the cause of his engine's misfiring. After the race was nearly 1/3 over, the gremlin was discovered. It was a hairpin crack in a high-pressure pipe in the fuel-injection system. Starting from a point 22 laps behind the leader, Hawthorn drove like a demon for the rest of the race to finish as an honorable mention and sixth overall.

Given all of this, it was fortunate for Jaguar that David Murray's Scottish Ecurie Ecosse team car (a Jaguar driven by Ninian Sanderson and Ron Flockhart) was able to rise to the occasion. It won a narrow victory over the Stirling Moss/Peter Collins Aston-Martin.

The XJ-13 project was abandoned at the end of 1967. (Robert C. Ackerson Collection)

In 1956, the official Jaguar team was broken up, but Ecurie Ecosse brought Conventry its fifth (third successive) LeMans victory.

These were also great days for Jaguar in American sports car racing. Briggs Cunningham's D-Type, driven by Hawthorn and Phil Walters, won a controversial victory at Sebring's 12-hour race in 1955. In 1956 and 1957, Walt Hansgen drove Cunningham D-Types to championships in the SCCA's C-modified class.

In an interesting venture that was quite different from the endurance racing that the D-Type excelled at, three D-Types were entered, by Ecurie Ecosse, in the "Race of Two Worlds" at Monza, Italy. Eight American Indy Cars were entered. These were faster than the D-Types and the Jaguars had a serious disadvantage. In addition, instead of the race being run as a straight 500-mile contest, which would have tilted the odds in the D-Type's favor, it consisted of three heats of 166 miles each, with a one-hour interval between heats.

If the race had been of 500 continuous miles, the outcome might have been different. All the Jaguars were mechanically fit to start the final race, but only half the American cars made it. Only three American cars finished. On the results of the three heats, Jimmy Bryan was declared overall winner with an average speed of 160.2 mph. The D-Types, led by Fairman's, (which averaged just over 15l mph) finished fourth, fifth, and sixth.

After 1957, the D-Type began to settle into the unbecoming role of an also-ran. Father Time and a new three-liter displacement limit for competition sports cars were obstacles too powerful for the car to overcome.

One all too short chapter in the D-Type's history involved the production of the XK-SS, a road version of the D-Type. Only 16 were made before February 1957, when a major fire at the Jaguar plant destroyed the tooling for this super road car. Intended as a response to the Corvette's racing success in the U.S., the XK-SS with a 3.51:1 rear axle was capable of a zero-to-60 mph time of 6.2 seconds. Its top speed was over 149 mph. The fire also delayed development of the Jaguar XJ-13, a V-12 powered successor to the D-Type. It became a stillborn racing car. By August 1964, when its engine was first operated, the XJ-13 was already obsolete.

"The finest car of its class in the world," was how the Jaguar was once described. In a similar sense, the C- and D-Types were the finest racing cars of their class in the world. They were designed primarily to win at LeMans and they did their job extremely well.

Never beaten, never quit was the claim of Mercedes-Benz 300SLR

By Robert C. Ackerson

Visitors to the grand opening of the New York Coliseum in 1956 were treated to many exciting displays of automobiles, but certainly one of the most memorable was found at the Mercedes-Benz stand. In a classic example of understatement an open two-seater was shown with the following inscription: "This car has never been beaten or dropped out owing to mechanical failure." The car was the Mercedes-Benz 300SLR, the 1955 World's Sports Car Champion.

By the early 1950s, Daimler-Benz had recovered sufficiently from the carnage of World War II to seriously ponder a return to international racing competition. However, a foray into several grand prix races in South America in 1951 showed that the basic design of the prewar W163 could not match the performance of the 4.5-liter Ferrari 375FL.

A similar situation faced the Mercedes in sports car racing. The 300SL had been extremely successful in 1952, winning both the Mexican Road Race and the LeMans 24-Hour Grand Prix of Endurance. It was quite obvious that it would face very serious competition from Ferrari, Aston-Martin and Jaguar, if it was raced by the factory in 1953.

Priority was given to the construction of an all new grand prix model in 1952. Provision was also made for the preparation of a racing sports car based on components from the grand prix car.

The W196, as the grand prix car was designated, was ready for participation in the 1954 season. Its stablemate, the W196 (or 300SLR, as it was better known), did not appear publicly until late in the year. The 300SLR was an impressive automobile from the beginning. Its appearance reflected the strength and confidence, almost to the point of arrogance, that has characterized so many great Mercedes-Benz automobiles. As it was soon to demonstrate by its racing successes, its looks did not belie its performance. As tested by Juan Fangio at the Monza track, in

Fabulous good looks and an inline eight distinguished the 300SLR coupe, but it never saw competition. Two were built in 1955. (Robert C. Ackerson Collection)

The roadster with its controversial air brake extended. Race officials required a "window" in the panel for rear vision. (Robert C. Ackerson Collection)

September 1954, it came within three seconds of the best practice lap with the W196. The best lap for the W196 was one minute, 59 seconds. The best lap for the 300SLR was two minutes, three seconds. Rudolf Uhlenhaut, Mercedes-Benz's racing chief lapped in two minutes, three seconds with the 300SLR and two minutes, six seconds with the streamlined version of the W196. Later in 1955, the 300SLR won the Italian Mille Miglia, the German Eifelrennen race at Nurburgring, the Swedish Grand Prix for sports cars, the Tourist Trophy and the grueling Targa Florio. At LeMans, the 300SLRs had a substantial lead when they were withdrawn from the race by the management of Daimler-Benz. Eighteen 300SLRs entered six races. Besides their five victories, they scored five second places, one third place and two fourth places.

The heart, and perhaps even the soul, of the 300SLR was its 2976 cc straight eight engine. While this engine was very similar to the 2.5-liter version used in the W196, it did have a number of unique features. The most notable was its cast-aluminum engine block. Early in the development of this engine, serious consideration had been given to a 12-cylinder design. A twelve is less complex than a V-16. Its multi-cylinder layout provides a large piston area, but the small pistons allow for higher engine speeds. The combination of features gave it great potential as a race car engine.

This was dramatically illustrated by the many victories of the V-12 Ferrari race cars. However, Mercedes possessed a great deal of technical confidence, especially in the use of desmodromic valves. It believed that an eight-cylinder engine so-equipped could match the output of a similarly sized V-12 and offer superior reliability. On both counts, the performance of the 300SLR proved Mercedes-Benz correct.

Installed in the 300SLR chassis at an angle of 35 degrees, the M196S engine developed approximately 296 hp at 7450 rpm. This figure could be altered to provide the best compromise between power and durability, as demanded by the condition peculiar to each race. The maximum output of the 300SLR engine installed in a grand prix chassis for a formula libre race in South America, was 340 hp. This engine used an alcohol-based fuel.

Both the grand prix and sports car engines were assembled in a special room at Unterukheim, where the temperature was held constant to ensure a high degree of compatibility between the components.

Besides its dual overhead cams and magnificently strong 10-bearing crankshaft, the M196S was equipped with a Bosch fuel-injection unit that was credited with increasing horsepower by approximately 10 percent over a carburetor-equipped version. In the fuel-injection setup, the fuel mixture was directly injected into the cylinders and aimed toward the exhaust valve, which was the hottest spot in the combustion chamber. Equipped with two 14 mm Bosch Sport spark plugs and a compression ratio of 9.0:1, the 300SLR engine was quite happy running on 90 octane gasoline. Since the engine was constructed of two blocks of four cylinders each, power was taken from the middle of the crankshaft. The five-speed transmission was rear-mounted, in union with a ZF limited-slip differential.

Front suspension of the tubular-framed 300SLR was by double wishbones of a very light forging, with longitudinal torsion bars and telescopic shock absorbers. A torsion bar and tube shock setup was used at the rear, along with independent, low-pivot axles.

Stirling Moss described the 300SLR's ride as "much softer and more comfortable" than he had anticipated. Although a relatively large car, even by the standards of the day, the Mercedes was a good handling, under-steering automobile. Referring to its handling on slippery surfaces, Moss observed, "When it goes, you notice its size."

Mercedes arch-rival Jaguar had been using disc brakes since 1953, but the 300SLR had to make do with conventional drum brakes. These generally provided satisfactory performance, although a device controlled by the driver, for squirting oil onto any brake drum, was installed after the W196 experienced grabbing brakes in the 1955 Monaco Grand Prix.

The 300SLR first appeared in an open cockpit form. It was planned that coupe versions would be built for long distance races such as the Mille Miglia and the Mexican Road Race. Since both Moss and Fangio generally preferred the open version, the two coupes built were never used in competition. In 1957, Uhlenhaut allowed the Swiss publication *Automobile Revue* and America's *Motor Trend* to conduct a road test of his 300SLR coupe. The top speed recorded was a rather healthy 180 mph. A 0-to-100 mph run required a mere 13.5 seconds.

Since the 1955 Mille Miglia marked the 300SLR's racing debut, Mercedes went to great efforts to assure it was a successful one. As two 300SLRs logged thousands of practice miles, four new models were being prepared for the race itself. One surprise coming out of practice

The 300SLR motor was two fours hooked together, with a center drive. (Robert C. Ackerson Collection)

Sterling Moss, on his way to winning the 1955 Tourist Trophy race in a 300SLR. He and Juan Fangio scored a stunning series of wins with the 300SLRs. (Robert C. Ackerson Collection)

was the revelation that the Mercedes transmission could not stand up to even half the race's distance without failing. A quick solution was the use of the Porsche balk-ring synchromesh transmission. In an interesting arrangement, Mercedes agreed to use the Porsche gear box provided Porsche did not make use of this fact in its advertising. Ferry Porsche saw this as an excellent way to test his product under very grueling conditions. It posed no danger to the integrity of his automobile's reputation. Thus, he agreed to the Mercedes request.

Hans Herman's 300SLR withdrew with a leaking fuel tank and Karl Kling's car crashed. The two remaining Mercedes entries of Stirling Moss (with journalist Denis Jenkinson along for the ride of his life) and Fangio had the situation well in hand, finishing first and second. The 26-year-old Moss averaged nearly 98 mph, the fastest average ever for the winning car. When the victorious 300SLR was returned to Germany its engine recorded the same power curve as it had attained before the race. This achievement becomes even more impressive considering one of Jenkinson's statements. "The engine cover was never raised" he said, adding that, "Nothing bothered the car, except refueling and changing tires."

There is a certain irony in the fact that the 300SLR, undoubtedly one of the greatest of all sports cars, was involved in racing's darkest moment. This was an accident that took place during the running of the 1955 LeMans race. Three cars were prepared for this event, to be driven by the team of Fangio/Moss, Kling/Simon and Pierre Levegh/John Fitch. Levegh had earned the respect of Mercedes-Benz during the 1952 race when he, alone, held off the 300SLs for hours with his dated Talbot-Lago.

Like the earlier 300SL, the 300SLRs appeared at LeMans with an air brake device that was both startling and intimidating. There was an initial question over the propriety of the air brake, since some feared that it would create turbulence dangerous to the lightweight cars competing. Others spoke of the visual obstruction it would create for drivers following a 300SLR with the air brake in its vertical position. Eventually, it was allowed by the observers after a second Perspex "window" was installed. As initially set up, the air brake was to raise automatically whenever the driver made a downshift into second gear. When practice began, it was apparent the drivers could make better use of the air brake if they could control its operation.

Some LeMans observers might have been prompted to see the air brake as a gimmick, but it proved, in reality, to be extremely effective. At one point in the practice Moss attempted to accelerate out of the Mulsanne corner, having forgotten to lower his car's air brake. The 300SLR responded so poorly that, before Moss discovered his oversight, he feared the engine was malfunctioning. During the race, spectators at the end of the Mulsanne straight reported seeing the Ferraris' brake lights coming on at the 500-meter warning post. Then the D-type Jaguars, with their distinctive dorsal fins, would come by. Their disc brakes allowed them to go in a bit deeper than the Ferraris. Next would come Moss, who would just begin to warm up his brakes at the 300-meter post!

There was little to indicate that a tragedy was in the offing in the race's early stage. The great Italian driver, Eugenio Castellotti's 4.1-liter Ferrari and Mike Hawthorn's D-type Jaguar engaged Fangio's 300SLR in an epic struggle which saw all three cars reach speeds of 180 to 185 mph. Hawthorn, who described Fangio's use of the air brake as "making the Mercedes look like a great fish rising at flies," credited it with giving the 300SLR braking parity with his Jaguar.

Castelotti's Ferrari was inferior in braking and handling to a Mercedes or Jaguar. However, in Hawthorn's words, "on acceleration, Castelotti just left us both standing, laying incredible long black tracks of molten rubber on the road as he roared away." Eventually, however, Castelotti fell back, leaving Hawthorn and Fangio to contest the lead. Neither driver was able to sustain a commanding position over the other and after two hours of racing Hawthorn's lead was less than one second. So rapid was their pace that only four other cars were on the same lap as the two protagonists.

Then disaster struck. What led up to the accident that sent 83 people to their deaths is perhaps best told by the three survivors closest involved. Fangio, Hawthorn and Lance Macklin. As Fangio recalled the situation he was on lap 36, about 100 yards behind Hawthorn. In back of Hawthorn and slightly to his right was Lance Macklin's 100S Austin-Healey, a far slower car than either the 300SLR or the D-type Jaguar. A short distance behind the Austin-Healey was the 300SLR of Fangio's teammate Levegh. From Fangio's viewpoint Hawthorn appeared to brake suddenly, apparently surprising both Macklin and Levegh. In response, Macklin also

Even the bare 300SLR still exudes Mercedes' brand of Germanic charm. (Robert C. Ackerson Collection)

began to decelerate and, in the process, slid into the path of Levegh's Mercedes, which was traveling at close to 150 mph. All of this was happening, as Fangio recounted, "as quick as lightning," but Levegh managed to signal Fangio by raising his left hand that he was moving toward the left. It was a gesture that Fangio credited with saving his life. There was no way that Levegh could pass between the barrier on his left hand and the Austin-Healey, in Fangio's opinion.

As Levegh's car hit the left side of the 100S, it flew into the air, crashed down on the protective barrier, and exploded, its engine hurtling into a spectator area. At this point Fangio was less than 50 yards back and even with his air brake engaged was still traveling at 120 mph. In response to Levegh's signal, Fangio moved to the right of the Austin-Healey, where he was confronted by Hawthorn's car. As he recalls in his autobiography he concluded that, "The English driver had evidently not calculated his pit's position correctly and finally stopped some 80 yards beyond it." To this day, Fangio cannot explain how he got between the Jaguar and the Austin-Healey. But he did and later it was noted that his 300SLR's right front fender bore bits of green paint from Hawthorn's car. When he pitted, he made the sign of the cross and "thanked God for my delivery."

Hawthorn's version is similar but contains some crucial differences. As noted he was in the lead and was due to come in for fuel and to change drivers. Just before the straight run past the pits he had lapped Levegh, and on the straight and proper, Macklin. He concluded there was sufficient room and adequate time to pull in front of Macklin and enter his pit. He signaled his intention, braked and pulled into the pit. He was nearly into his pit area when out the corner of his eye he saw Levegh's car flying through the air, on its way to infamy. Hawthorn claimed he continued past his pit because he was completely dazed by the scene. Hawthorn speculated that perhaps he surprised Macklin when he passed by and that the Austin-Healey driver might have instinctively looked in his rear view mirror to see if another car was coming up. If he had done so, then he would have missed Hawthorn's signal and thus could have been caught off guard by Hawthorn's maneuver. Then when he moved to the left, Levegh's fate was sealed.

Al Bochroch, in his book *Americans At Lemans*, quotes Lance Macklin as follows: "My first reaction when Levegh hit me was one of surprise. I thought the danger had passed when I avoided Mike Hawthorn. It's true that Hawthorn should never have cut in front of me, but that did not cause the accident, as I had gotten clear."

Since he feels that Levegh's car hit the barrier before it hit his car he suggests that some of Levegh's skill had been eroded by a three-year layoff from racing. Eventually, an official board of inquiry concluded that no one person could be held responsible.

After the accident occurred, the remaining two 300SLRs were withdrawn by order of the Daimler-Benz directors. At that point it was 2 am Sunday morning and the Fangio/Moss car had a two-lap lead.

Although Hawthorn put forth a great challenge to the 300SLRs with his solitary D-type Jaguar, the Mercedes team finished an impressive 1-2-3. In the season's finale, the Targa Florio, Moss and Peter Collins scored another victory despite an off-road excursion by Moss that would have totaled a lesser car.

If the Mexican Road Race for 1955 had been run, two 300SLR coupes may have joined two roadsters as Mercedes entries. But this did not come to pass and the racing career of the 300SLR came to an abrupt end. Plans for a lighter version were abandoned and the Mercedes racing department became its "Research & Development" headquarters. A total of nine 300SLRs was constructed (one was never completed). One was on display at the Henry Ford Museum in Dearborn, Michigan.

MG's first modern sports car was a "Mighty Good" English automobile

By Robert C. Ackerson

"A Classic Sports Car Goes Modern," is how *Road & Track* (December 1955) headlined its first road test of the MGA. Those words have stood the test of time. Even today, they serve as a description of the MGA and denote its role in MG history. With proper respect to the MGB (introduced in late 1962 as a contemporary sports car), it's reasonable to depict the MGA as the company's most significant model of the postwar era.

A brief review of MG history since 1945 proves this view. The first sports-model MG produced after World War II was the TC roadster. It was the only MG available until April 1947, when the Y type 1.25-liter sedan was offered. While possessing a wider body and minor changes like revised instrumentation, the TC was virtually the same as the TB model introduced in May 1939.

The decision to revive the TB and identify it as the TC made sense for several reasons. First, Hitler's invasion of Europe assured the TB a short production life. However, in spite of some antiquated features, it was not a totally outdated design. Second, England needed to export products for its economic survival. The American imported car market was just waiting for some enterprising foreign companies to develop it.

After a production run of approximately 10,000, the TC was replaced by the TD late in 1949. The howls from the TC fraternity can still be heard. Whether "The Faithful" ever accepted the appearance of the TD, no one can deny that it was a commercial success. Some 30,000 were sold in four years. But the MG image was getting a little tattered around the edges as the result of the giant forward steps being made by other sports car manufacturers and American automakers. The MG driver's explanation of the company's "Safety Fast!" slogan was all too often drowned out by the roar of an Old 88's dual exhausts.

"Just a little more displacement; perhaps a liter and a half," pleaded John Franklin Fellows in his "Supplication to the Lord (Nuffield That Is)," published in the March 1953 issue of *Road & Track*. Fellows got his heart's desire, in July 1954, when Lord Nuffield (the head of MG) put the TF1500 model into production. It had a 1500 cc displacement XPEG engine

The TF, in both 1.2-liter and 1.5-liter forms, found little favor with newcomers to the sports car field and old-line MG drivers shunned it, too. Production of the TF between 1953 and 1955 totaled just 9,600 automobiles. The TF's lack of popularity was because it required nearly 19 seconds to reach 60 mph. It was clearly less of a performer than the MGTD MKII. The TF 1500 was a step in the right direction. However, even with a larger engine, the performance limitations of the TF's body style made it absurd to increase the output of the engine.

When the new MGA made its debut, in the fall of 1955, few sports car enthusiasts mourned the passing of the old guard. To be fair, the TF was a "stop gap" car. In the early 1950s, there were people at MG who knew something better was needed to take full advantage of the American market. The MG factory at Abington-on-Thames, had built a special car for George Phillips. It had a streamlined body designed by Syd Enever, that accurately predicted the body used on the MGA. This car's 1951 LeMans outing proved unsuccessful. It retired with a blown piston after just 60 laps. The following year, a second car was built by Enever. It had a similar, but more refined, appearance. If not for the merger of Austin and Nuffield and the priority given to the Austin-Healey 100, it is likely that a streamlined MG would have made it to these shores sooner than 1955.

Before the MGA's debut in the fall of 1955, three EX182 streamlined type MGs entered the 1955 LeMans grand prix. This gave the public a first-hand look at what was in the offing from Abington. It also marked the first entry of an official MG team at LeMans since 1935. Any joy experienced by the return of the MG team was, however, marred by a tragic accident involving a Mercedes-Benz 300SLR driven by Pierre Levegh. For the record, the outing was good for MG. Two of three cars entered finished the race, coming in 12th and 17th. They averaged 87.04 mph and 81.70 mph. The 12th place car was driven by the late Ken Miles. The EX182s proved to have stamina, since only 23 cars (13 British) completed the full 12 hours of racing.

Following LeMans, *The Autocar* got first-hand impressions of car number 64, the 17th place finisher. It had been timed at 119.5 mph through the timed kilometer on the Mulsanne Straight. The magazine found the car changed from its LeMans form in several ways. The Perspex racing windshield was replaced with a full-width type. A large fog lamp, installed on the right side of the grille for racing, was removed. Its close-ratio gear box had also been replaced by the type used in the MG Magnette sedan. In addition, the 3.7:1 ratio rear axle used at LeMans was replaced with a 4.3:1 ratio axle. Capping the transformation from race car to touring car was the addition of a folding top. The engine used in the EX182 was based on the *British Motor Corporation* (BMC) "B" series power plant used in the Magnette, as well as several other cars. It displaced 1489 cc and had a 9.4:1 compression ratio. The horsepower rating was 82.5 at 6000 rpm.

The Autocar found much to praise and little to criticize in the performance of this MG, which was destined for use in the upcoming Alpine Rally. With driver, passenger and 16 gallons of fuel on board, the MG went from 0-to-60 mph in 13.8 seconds. It attained a top speed of 103 mph. Its handling was described as of "a very high order." When last heard of, this historic race car had found its way to Canada, where an MG enthusiast had completely restored it.

The MGA was somewhat large for a 1.5-liter car. It had a 94-inch wheelbase and 156-inch overall length (compared to 90 inches and 151 inches for the Austin-Healey 100). It was superior, in all respects, to its predecessors from MG. Except for its aluminum doors, the body was constructed of steel. Although its appearance contrasted sharply with that of earlier MGs, things like the front suspension were identical to TD/TF components. It used a simple, conventional

A 1955 MGA roadster on exhibit at the Henry Ford Museum & Greenfield Village. (Old Cars Collection)

Three MGs at the conclusion of the 1956 Sebring race. (Robert C. Ackerson Collection)

arrangement of coil springs and unequal length wishbones. Semi-elliptic rear leaf springs were used.

The MGA's 68-hp engine gave it better performance than the TF1500. However, it was still second best to run-of-the-mill Powerglide Chevrolets. Most of its improved performance was credited to aerodynamics, since it had only five more horsepower than the TF1500. However, in 1964, researchers from Mississippi State University studied the aerodynamics of an MGA roadster. Among the conclusions they reached in the aerophysics lab was that the MGA's grille design and location directed air flow away from the carburetor intakes.

Road & Track's December 1955 issue credited the MGA with 21 percent less drag resistance than the TF1500. The comparative numbers were:

Speed range	TF1500	MGA
0-30 mph	4.8 seconds	4.6 seconds
0-60 mph	16.3 seconds	14.5 seconds
Top speed	88.2 mph	97.5 mph

The MGA top speed was for a car with its top raised and side curtains installed. Thus, it was representative of what a "typical" MGA could do. A "power-required" curve, published by MG, indicated that 68 hp (the output of the MGA engine) was required to attain a speed of 68 mph.

Road & Track and *The Autocar* found the MGA's handling up to MG's traditional high standards. "It handles faultlessly and can be cornered and drifted by a beginner almost immediately" was the conclusion of the American magazine. *The Autocar* described its road holding and steering as "of a high order," and added that, "fast cornering was a joy."

As a competitor in sports car racing, the MGA was beaten by Porsches, until the Sports Car Club of America (SCCA) dropped its strict engine displacement classifications. It was replaced with a policy that attempted to put cars of similar performance in direct competition. This helped even out the odds for MGA drivers, but they usually continued coming in second behind Elva Couriers, TR-3s and Morgans.

For the 1956 Sebring race, BMC sponsored a three-car MGA team that acquitted itself rather well. All the entries completed the event, finishing 19th, 20th and 22nd overall. They were awarded the team prize. The fastest MGA averaged 65.43 mph for 12 hours to finish fourth in class behind the far more expensive Porches.

Ken Wharton tested the MGA at the MIRA track. He found the car capable of maintaining a 100 mph speed. This inspired him to want to duplicate this performance at other tracks. Two years earlier, Bob Porter, a distributor of Rileys (another BMC product) had lapped the Montlhery track in France at 96 mph. This was done in an older Riley. Now, Porter was eager to test the top speed capability of the new Pathfinder model.

Late in October 1955, shortly after the MGA had been introduced, BMC leased the Montlhery track to test the maximum speed of five new products. The other cars were a Riley, Pathfinder, an Austin-Healey 100, an Austin A90 Westminster and a Wolseley 6/90. On October 23, the five vehicles began a series of one hour runs in which they all averaged more than 100 mph.

Two MGAs, both with tops and side curtains, took part in the test. One, with its engine in Stage Two tune, was driven by John Gott. The second car, in standard tune, was driven by Ken Wharton. Gott's first run came to a quick end at mile 75, when a tire on his car blew. Wharton drove his car to a 102.54 mph average for one hour.

A coupe bowed in fall 1956 with roll-up windows and an extra 65 pounds. (Robert C. Ackerson Collection)

Four years later, in the 1959 Bonneville National Speed Trials, Tim Frostrum had a far more difficult time cracking the century mark with his MGA roadster. His first run netted a disappointing 89.64 mph speed. After advancing the timing 0.5 degrees and setting his tire pressure at 44 psi, he managed a speed of 101.01 mph.

A shortcut for increasing the performance of an MGA was the installation of a Judson supercharger. This unit provided a modest 5.5 psi and increased the MGA's output to approximately 90 hp. It reduced the 0-to-60 mph time by nearly two seconds.

In 1957, the British firm John Gibson & Son Ltd. offered a conversion kit to transform the MGA into a four-seater. This involved the installation of a rumble seat in the trunk. It was an arrangement that looked awkward at best.

There was nothing awkward or uncomfortable about the appearance of the MGA coupe, which debuted in October 1956. With an American market price $300 higher than the roadster's $2,450, the coupe's physical charm and appointments prompted *Sports Car Illustrated* to give it high ratings in its June 1958 issue. "The best built MG to date and by far the most luxurious and comfortable," said the magazine.

In addition to its hardtop roof design, the coupe was distinguished by its wraparound front and rear windows, roll-up side windows with vents, chrome window frames and cleverly designed external door handles, which the roadster did not get. On the debit side the coupe, like the roadster, suffered from a poor interior ventilation system that allowed the temperature of the floor to reach rather uncomfortable levels. Other points of criticism were the lack of sun visors and armrests.

Surprisingly, the coupe weighed just 65 pounds more than the first roadsters. This, plus its aerodynamic form, made it fast. So did the four additional horsepower (72 total) given to all 1957 MGs. It was the first production MG tested by *Road & Track* that exceeded a true road speed of 100 mph. "This long-desired goal was, from any angle, the high point of this test," said the magazine. "It represents the end of a long road toward which the greatest single jump was the change from the TF's neo-classic lines to the streamlined form of the MGA roadster."

Until the mid-1930s, the MG reputation as a high-performance automobile was largely based on its overhead cam engines. Then came a long series of pushrod engines that dyed-in-the-wool MG fans accepted with a good deal of muttering. Some directed semi-slanderous remarks toward Leonard Lord, the managing director of Morris Motors LTD. Indeed, some remarks were intended for William Morris himself. In July 1958, they found cause for rejoicing, when MG announced that a twin overhead cam engine would be made available for the MGA coupe and roadster.

Design work on this engine started in March 1953, as a result of strong pressure directed toward Leonard Lord by Syd Enever and MG general manager John Thornley. MG turned out two versions of the dohc power plant for the Golden Jubilee Tourist Trophy Race in September 1955. One engine, with the valves inclined at 80 degrees, was not used. The second, with a 66-degrees valve angle, had an unhappy outing. Just before the race, it had been fitted with twin choke Weber carburetors. Apparently, the MG engineers did not have sufficient time to get them properly tuned. After a poor showing, the car retired from the race. Only the pushrod MGA driven by Fairman and Wilson finished. It came in 20th place.

In spite of its no-start in the Tourist Trophy competition, it was the 80-degree engine that went into production. It was formally announced in New York City in July 1958. The 1588 cc dohc engine had 100 cc more displacement due to a larger bore. John Thornley readily admitted this was done to make the car competitive to the Porsche, the reigning champion in SCCA's F-Production Class. With a 9.90:1 compression ratio, an aluminum cylinder head and twin SU-HD-6 carburetors, the Twin Cam engine developed 108 hp at 6700 rpm. Besides its more-powerful-than-stock engine, the Twin Cam MG also came with Dunlop disc brakes at all four corners, plus 5.90-15 Roadspeed tires. A 4.55 rear axle ratio (4.30 was standard) and a close-ratio "LeMans" gear box were also available.

Factory test drivers attained 0-to-100 mph times of 30.4 seconds with Twin Cam MGAs. Their top speeds fell just short of the 120 mph mark. The $3,345 production model delivered a respectable 0-to-60 time of under 10 seconds and had top speeds around 115 mph. A total of 2,110 Twin Cam models was built between July 1958 and April 1960. Then production was discontinued. F. Wilson McComb (*Automobile Quarterly* Volume IV, Number 2) described the Twin Cam as "a sweetly responsive, high-performance car, although perhaps a shade too responsive, for the engine revved up so freely that it could be blown up by anyone who didn't quite know what a tachometer was for." This, in itself, might have been sufficient reason for MG to withdraw the Twin cam. In addition, the ultimate form of the lower cost MGA, with the pushrod engine, was capable of providing performance not much below that of the Twin Cam. After production of the Twin Cam was concluded, a number of the Twin Cam chassis were equipped with 1600 cc pushrod engines. These were called MGA 1600 Deluxe models.

An MGA (driver unknown) chasing dePortago's 3.8 Ferrari in the 1957 Sebring race. MGs finished 23rd and 27th that year. (Robert C. Ackerson Collection)

An MGA trimmed out for some serious road racing. (Old Cars Collection)

The MGA 1500 was in production from 1955 through 1959.

A number of significant changes were made in the MGA for 1960. "Beyond a shadow of a doubt, this is the best touring MG yet," said *Sports Cars Illustrated* (October 1959). A larger 1588 cc displacement boosted the MGA's net horsepower to 79.5 at 5600 rpm. The increase was obtained by going to a 2.968 x 2.875 inch bore and stroke and by eliminating the water space between the first and second pair of cylinders. This feature had first been used on the Twin Cam model. Lockheed disc brakes on the MGA's front wheels also contributed to its balanced performance. Top speed was now an honest 103 mph and the 0-to-60 mph time was a respectable 13.3 seconds.

While the MGA 1600's interior was unchanged from the earlier model, its exterior possessed enough changes to allow the faithful to readily identify it as the newest offering from Abington. Both the hood and trunk bore "1600" designations and a new tail-stop-directional lamp setup was also introduced. At the front, parking-directional lamps with larger and flatter lenses were also used. A welcome improvement was new sliding plastic side curtains, replacing the old flap-style type. A total of 31,086 MGA 1600 models were produced from May 1959 to April 1961. Production of the superseded 1500 model totaled 58,750.

In 1960, roughly midway through the 1600's production life, the MG engineering department received instructions to revise the MGA's design in order to make its top speed "comfortably in excess of 100 mph" and to provide corresponding improvement in its cruising speed. This directive also carried the stipulation that no changes of any great nature were to be made to the engine or the body.

The result was the peak of MGA production ... the 1600 MKII model. This seemed an appropriate car with which to conclude manufacture of MGAs. Easily set apart from earlier models by its recessed grille bars and inboard-mounted taillamps, the MKII was also equipped with a new instrument panel. It had a leatherette covering and the bright metal edging originally used on the coupe. A 1/32-in boost in the engine's bore size resulted in a slight increase in displacement to 99 cid (1622 cid). This, plus the use of larger valves and an 8.9:1 compression ratio, resulted in a rating of 90 hp at 5500 rpm. Torque was 97 pounds-feet at 4000 rpm. Translated into road performance, these improvements provided a 0-to-60 mph time just under 13 seconds and a top speed of 105 mph. With the optional hardtop (available since 1956) installed, the factory claimed that a stock MKII roadster could obtain a maximum speed of 107 mph. Thus, in spite of directing some criticism in the direction of the MG's rather harsh riding qualities, *Road & Track* (September 1961) could still proclaim it to be "the best all around sports car for the money."

Production of the MGA ended in June 1962, after more than 101,000 had been built. Its successor, the MGB, was greeted with such enthusiasm that, for a time, the MGA's role seem somewhat distorted. In retrospect, it was a sports car with numerous credits to its record. Until the MGB arrived, it was also the best selling sports car in history. The MGA really introduced more Americans to the joy of sports cars than the T series MG had done just after World War II.

The "glory years" of Trans-Am

By Phil Hall

For 29 years, the Sports Car Club of America (SCCA) has fielded its Trans-American Series (or Trans-Am as it is known today) on road courses across the country. This racing series, for sports sedans, has had seasons that ranged from great ones to others that were "turkey trots." Its success depends on the ever changing state of the rules, the cars that ran it, and the interests of race fans at any given time.

From this corner, the year 1970 stands out as one of the great ones for Trans-Am. It was held in the twilight of the muscle car era and featured factory-backed teams from each of this country's four major automobile manufacturers: American Motors Corporation; Chrysler Corporation; Ford Motor Company; and General Motors Corporation (GM). Admittedly the GM backing was under the proverbial table. At no time before or since was there such interest from the Motor City in this form of racing.

Initially the series featured domestic sports sedans in the over-two-liter class and imports in the under-two-liter tests. In their initial 1966 runnings, Ford Mustangs ruled. Token competition came from the Plymouth Barracuda and the Dodge Dart. Points were given to the make of car, not the driver. This enticed the manufacturers to get into the fray and battle it out.

For the 1968 Trans-Am Series, Chevrolet helped driver/builder Roger Penske (above) field a group of Camaros with the midyear Z28 option. Penske later signed with American Motors to develop a Trans-Am racing effort around the Javelin. (Old Cars photo)

Ford repeated its title in 1967, but Chevrolet helped Roger Penske field Camaros with the midyear Z28 option, which included a 302-cubic-inch small-block V-8. The Z28 engine came in just under the five-liter limit. There also was a Bud Moore Mercury Cougar team that year. American Motors joined the fray in 1968, with its Javelin, but the development of racing versions took awhile. Penske, with lead driver and engineer Mark Donohue, got uncorked and won the title that season. He repeated the feat in 1969.

The Trans-Am series became a free-for all in 1970, for several reasons. First, the rules were changed so that engines larger than five-liters could be de-stroked to reach the limit. This meant that in the horsepower-demanding muscle car market, a trick pony car could be sold off the show room floor with more than 305-cubic-inches. Second, new cars from Plymouth and Dodge crowded the field and needed to be raced to gain attention. Plymouth's Barracuda was redone. Dodge received the last pony car, the Challenger, enabling the marque to join the field. Also, the 1970-1/2 Camaro and Pontiac Firebird Trans Am (without the hyphen) entries were all-new in styling.

The spoiler on the back of Mark Donahue's 1970 Trans-Am Javelin was part of the Mark Donahue option for the production car. (Phil Hall Collection)

The scramble for racing teams really got into gear for 1970 when American Motors announced the signing of Penske and Donohue to race the Javelin. It had a new 304-cubic-inch V-8, just in case someone wanted to race one. Peter Revson was also inked as a driver.

Chrysler got serious about Trans-Am and hired Dan Gurney's All American Racing to race a Barracuda, with Swede Savage as driver. Dodge's choice was Ray Caldwell's Autodynamics team, with Sam Posey as driver. Ford, meanwhile, was cutting its racing budget. Bud Moore was chosen to represent FoMoCo with a pair of cars to be campaigned by Parnelli Jones and George Follmer. General Motors couldn't openly back its cars, but made sure that Texan Jim Hall, of Chaparral fame, had all the right stuff to go into his new Camaros for Trans-Am. Hall, Vic Elford and Ed Leslie were among the drivers. Other GM efforts weren't so flagrant. Owens-Corning Fiberglass fielded a pair of new Camaros driven by Jerry Thompson and Tony DeLorenzo, who just happened to be the son of a GM executive. Also, a Pontiac Firebird effort from Titus/Godshall racing kept the series namesake car in the hunt, with a bit of encouragement from the "Wide-Track" folks. Automotive journalist Jerry Titus drove the Firebird Trans Am.

Race cars were still based on production cars at the time. The teams got away with every trick they knew, from acid-dipping the body to using very limited edition performance parts. The cars for the street derived from the 1970 Trans-Am influence were also interesting. Chevrolet returned with the fourth edition of its Z28 option for the Camaro, but this time it had a 350-cubic-inch small-block V-8, instead of the 302 used in the first three model-years. Ford stayed for its second and final year with the Boss 302, using an engine of the same size. Plymouth and Dodge added midyear models to their lines, each with a 340-cubic-inch V-8 and triple two-barrel carburetion. These setups were not legal on the racetrack. Plymouth's AAR 'Cuda and Dodge's Challenger T/A resulted. Pontiac first offered the Trans Am option in its Firebird line for 1969. For the regular 1970 line, it became a top-of-the-line model. It came complete with a 400-cubic-inch V-8 with Ram-Air induction and all of the "goodies." To celebrate the acquisition of driver Mark Donahue (and to make a big rear spoiler legal), American Motors announced the "Mark Donohue" edition of the Javelin.

With the stage set, the season was billed as the factory shoot-out of all time. The show lived up to the prediction, sometimes resembling Saturday night short-track events, rather than genteel road course contests of speed and handling. The experience of Bud Moore immediately showed, with his Mustangs taking the first four events on the schedule. Parnelli won the opener at Monterey, California on April 19. The next race was at Lime Rock, Connecticut on May 9, followed by a June 7 Lexington, Ohio bash. Follmer notched the May 31 Trans-Am race at Loudon, New Hampshire.

Jerry Titus kept his 1970 Pontiac Trans Am ahead of the Dodge Challenger T/A driven by Sam Posey in this view. Titus died after a crash at Road America in July. (Phil Hall Collection)

The Dodge Challenger was a newcomer to the automotive market for the 1970 model-year. Its Trans-Am racing fortunes were entrusted to Ray Caldwell of Autodynamics (left) and driver Sam Posey. The one-year effort netted a fourth in manufacturer points. (Phil Hall Collection)

It didn't take long for the Penske/Donohue combo to figure out the Javelin. Donohue won on June 21 at Bridgehampton, New York. Another Penske car won July 5 at Brainerd, Minnesota, but it wasn't an AMC product. Milt Minter took an ex-Penske 1969 Camaro into the winner's circle. At Elkhart Lake, Wisconsin, on July 19, this columnist had a chance to see if all the hoopla was just that. A crowd of 38,125, swelled by American Motors factory employees from nearby Kenosha and Milwaukee, was on hand looking for a win for the red- white-and-blue Penske cars. The Fords took the front row, with Follmer edging Jones for the pole. First lap problems put Posey and the Challenger out front.

On lap nine of the 50 circuit, 200-mile contest, Penske held up a sign that said, "Oil." Donohue pitted on lap 10. The competitors figured that the Javelin was in trouble and didn't pay any attention. The Penske crew reeled off a quick fuel-only stop and the car was back on the track. When the others pitted, later, they were told that the Javelin was ready to blow. Donohue took over the lead and left Savage and Posey to battle for second, during which time they nearly knocked each other off the track. Donohue's final pit stop saw him only lose one position. By the time the others pitted, Donohue was long gone. The competitors figured they'd been had. At the finish, the Javelin was just short of one minute ahead of Savage, who was followed by Posey. Jim Hall and tire-troubles plagued Jones. As a result, a different make of factory-backed car was in each of the top five slots. "No comment," a smiling Donohue said when asked about his trick pit stop. Unfortunately, Jerry Titus crashed his Firebird Trans Am and received head injuries, which proved to be fatal. He was flown to a hospital in Milwaukee by the emergency medical personnel, but did not survive.

The season continued with Donohue taking his third and final win for Javelin that year in Saint Jovite, Canada. Vic Elford gave Hall and Chevrolet a win on August 16 at Watkins Glen, New York. Jones iced Ford's third title in five years with wins at Kent, Washington on September

This pace lap was for the 200-mile race at Road America, in Elkhart Lake, Wisconsin, on July 19, 1970. Mark Donahue, who started outside in row three, won the race in his Javelin. (Phil Hall Collection)

20, and in the finale at Riverside, California on October 4. Points were counted in the best nine of 11 events. Ford ended with 72, followed by Javelin with 59, Chevrolet with 40, Dodge with 18 and Plymouth with 15. When the season ended, so did most of the factory support. A perceived dip in the performance market, coupled with escalating costs of meeting federal safety and emission standards, resulted in drastic performance cuts.

Penske still had two years to go on his AMC contract. He returned to take the title for Javelin in 1971. He then tried to establish a NASCAR Grand National program for AMC's Matador in 1972. Moore went at it as an independent for 1971. The other operations packed it in.

In the late 1980s, Trans-Am racing grew more interesting again. Some degree of factory support returned, too. In 1986 there was a fierce battle between Lincoln-Mercury and Chevrolet. However, Chevrolet became upset and cut back its racing program for 1987. While still a good show, Trans-Am will have to go a long way to match the attention the motoring public and factories gave it in 1970. However, some of the great Trans-Am cars of the 1960s and 1970s have been showing up at the racetracks again. This time around, they are in the hands of vintage racing enthusiasts and it's a great feeling to see them circling courses like Road America at high speed. The roar of their pavement-pounding V-8s is exhilarating.

Chevrolet was represented in the 1970 Trans-Am season by two teams that had "under-the-table" factory help. Ed Leslie drove the number 2 Camaro for Jim Hall, while Tony DeLorenzo handled the number 3 Owens-Corning entry. (Phil Hall Collection)

GOING STRAIGHT

Malcolm Campbell's African Adventure

By Robert C. Ackerson

It was Henry Segrave, Malcolm Campbell's great compatriot rival who, on March 29, 1927, became the first person to break through the 200 mph barrier for automobiles. Seventeen years earlier, when Barney Oldfield had attained a speed of 141.73 mph with the Blitzen Benz, people had accepted as gospel truth the solemn pronouncement that "no human will ever travel faster." Now however, with Segrave's new mark of 203.79 mph on the books, there seemed to be no one willing to step forth and make a similar statement. Instead, individuals of quite another temperament quickly set about the business of beginning the push toward the next magical figure of 300 mph. However, the crossing of this span of speed was to be a fearsome journey, extracting from some travelers the ultimate price.

Campbell held the land speed record on nine occasions before his death in 1948. On February 19, 1928, he posted a new record of 206.96 mph. While Campbell could derive some satisfaction from this run at Daytona Beach, Florida, he had narrowly escaped disaster. His Napier-Lion-engined Bluebird II hit a three-inch sand ridge while traveling at 200 mph. This was enough to throw the car some 100 feet into the air. After this rather unnerving experience, Campbell came to the conclusion that Daytona Beach (like the British beaches at Pendine and Southport)

Verneuk Pan was depicted in the painting "Bluebird in Jungle" by the late Peter Helck. Originally, this artwork, from his book Great Auto Race, was used in Old Cars through the generosity of the late Peter Helck. (Martha L. Ayers Collection)

266

Sir Malcolm Campbell took his Napier racing car, named Bluebird II, to South Africa, in an attempt to set a new speed record for automobiles. The car's chassis was specially designed for Campbell and reflected the latest concepts in streamlining. (Al Krause Collection)

had become an antiquated site for high-speed runs. He felt it was doomed to oblivion by the air-craft-engined monsters it had helped spawn.

Campbell's record was broken, at Daytona, in April 1928, by Ray Keech who also won the 1929 Indianapolis 500-mile Race. Keech's White-Triplex, a car powered by three V-12 Liberty engines of World War I vintage, was traveling at 207.5 mph, slightly faster than Bluebird II. Yet, Campbell remained convinced that a new location had to be found for land speed record runs. Several reports of potential sites came from South Africa, telling him about a huge area called Verneuk Pan. It was 350 miles north by northeast of Cape Town and seemed to be an African counterpart to America's Bonneville Salt Flats. Frank Lockhart reached a speed of 171.02 mph on Muroc Dry Lake in California, in 1927, with a 91-cubic-inch supercharged Miller. To Campbell, this indicated what Bluebird II could achieve on a similar surface.

While Campbell preferred a site within the British Empire for his runs, he went in the direction of using salt flats. Ironically, Lockhart turned his back on the salt flats and took with his Stutz Blackhawk to the sands of Daytona Beach. On April 25, 1928, he lost his life there on the second of two runs. On the first run, he had been timed at 203.45 mph. On the second run, his car's right rear tire exploded, throwing it out of control and tossing Lockhart onto the beach.

Campbell's experience in South Africa was not to have such a tragic end. However, he might well have given thought to the origin of Verneuk Pan's name. The term "Pan" was Afrikaan for a shallow salt lake. "Verneuk" was the Afrikaan expression for cheat or swindle. This label was derived from the early pioneers who viewed it as a fresh water lake in the midst of desert-like surroundings and was to have a bittersweet significance for Campbell.

The rear end of Bluebird II dramatically illustrated its streamlined design. This period newsreel photo depicted the car as if it were going to run on rails. (Al Krause Collection)

Before he had the opportunity to view Verneuk Pan firsthand, Campbell decided, considering the reports he had received, to set sail for Cape Town and prepare for a new record attempt. Corresponding to his efforts were similar ones by Henry Segrave. In this case, however, a decision was made to try to beat Keech's mark at Daytona. Moreover Segrave had abandoned his Sunbeam for a new lighter machine which with a gold paint job. It was referred to as the "Golden Arrow." The race was on to determine which man would return the speed record to England.

Campbell's entourage was transported to South Africa by the Steamliner Carnation Castle. It consisted of Bluebird II (safely enclosed in a huge crate), some 56 cases of spare parts, 36 specially-prepared Tulip tires, 800 gallons of aviation fuel and 500 spark plugs. To facilitate transportation matters between Verneuk Pan and Cape Town, Campbell also brought along a Moth bi-plane.

Undoubtedly recalling his close brush with disaster at Daytona Beach, Campbell was quoted as saying, "If I do break the record, no one will wish to race on the treacherous beach sands again. Verneuk Pan will be the center of the high-speed motor-racing world." Yet, while noting that all the reports he had obtained concerning Verneuk Pan had been favorable, Campbell seemed uncertain. "The most vital point of all is the effect of the surface of the Pan upon my tires," he said.

Just before his arrival, Campbell sent a widely publicized message from the Carnation Castle in which he announced that he planned to make his speed record attempts between February 10 and 20. He said that his object was to, "Endeavor to prove the supremacy of British workmanship and material."

Shortly after his landing at Cape Town, Campbell made his first visit to Verneuk Pan. Bluebird II was still being transported inland then. It was moved first by railroad and then on the flatbed of a Thornycroft truck.

At best, Verneuk Pan could be called an inhospitable region. Temperatures of 100 degrees were common, even in shady areas. South African newspapers warned visitors to, "Remember that Verneuk Pan is the home of puffadders and scorpions." Campbell's first tour of the area was as a passenger in a car driven by Graham Scott, a reporter for *The Cape Times*. After they had traveled some five miles, at speeds as high as 85 mph, Graham brought the car to a stop. Campbell got out and took a long, hard look at the surface. He then went off by himself for a few minutes, before he returned to the car and its occupants. His words were simple and to the point, "Well Chaps," said Campbell. "I'm sorry to tell you that for 250 miles per hour this surface is no use at all." Instead of possessing the smooth, non-abrasive surface that Campbell had been expecting, Verneuk Pan was covered by numerous outcrops of shale. These would have the same effect upon Bluebird's tires as driving ordinary tires on a highway paved with glass slivers.

With expenses mounting daily and the realization that Segrave was arriving shortly at Daytona Beach, Campbell had to decide his next move quickly. His decision was to stay in South Africa. If Verneuk Pan was not suitable for high-speed runs in its present state, he would make it so. Work began on the construction of a track 43 feet wide and 12 miles in length. First, road scrapers cleared away the shale and crust from the Pan's surface, leaving an indented swath that was filled with a mixture of mud and water. An appreciation

Segrave had the Golden Arrow in readiness and the race was on to determine they, or Campbell and his Bluebird, would return the land speed record to England. (Prosper DuBois-Reymond)

Segrave had a lighter new machine with a gold paint job. It was referred to as the Golden Arrow and survives in England's National Motor Museum today. (Prosper DuBois-Reymond)

of the effort this involved can be gleaned from the fact that the nearest source of water was five miles away. A small army of laborers completed tasks including filling holes left years earlier by ostriches, as they were pursued across the Pan by horse-riding hunters. Road rollers provided by the Provincial Roads Department packed and smoothed the surface.

During this time, several incidents occurred which reinforced Verneuk Pan's old reputation as a dangerous, inhospitable region. In one, a female member of Campbell's band had gone to the worker's quarters to dress a minor injury. Upon her departure from the laborer's camp, the Pan's surface (described as a "gigantic mirror" that reflected far away scenes into phantom-like mirages) caused her to lose her sense of direction. Totally confused, the poor woman drove about in a great circle for several hours, until she finally sighted the lantern lights of her camp. Sometime later, one worker was lost for three days when he attempted to take a shortcut to rejoin his work crew. Since two people once died after losing their way across Verneuk Pan, both these incidents could have ended in tragedy.

With the painting of a long white strip, which is still visible today, to guide Campbell down the 12-mile stretch, everything seemed nearly finished. Some 450 small wooden posts were implanted for safety. They were intended to slow, but not harm, the Bluebird if it veered off course.

Segrave had not yet made a run at Daytona and conditions looked excellent for Campbell's first attempt. He was full of confidence at this point, calling Verneuk Pan, "The most wonderful stretch of flat country I have ever seen." He was obviously satisfied with the efforts that had been made to prepare the best possible conditions for Bluebird's speed runs. Campbell expressed the belief that nowhere else in the world did a similar surface exist over such a long distance.

Campbell's hopes suffered another setback when his plane crashed on a flight to Cape Town. Fortunately he suffered only facial cuts and bruises. The injuries were uncomfortable. However, except for a few scars on his nose, no permanent effects resulted.

After this exciting interlude, the expedition prepared to get Bluebird ready for its first run. Unbelievably, it started to rain for the first time in that section of the country in over 1,600 days. It was no mere cloudburst, but a major storm with fierce winds that pelted rain down on the track and left it in shambles. When the rain finally subsided, virtually the entire course had been destroyed. With the type of stiff upper lip that the British have long been famous for, Campbell gave the word to make whatever repairs were necessary. Again the sequence of operations needed to put affairs in order were completed. On the eve of Campbell's 45th birthday, the time was near at hand for Bluebird to make its long awaited South African debut.

To mark the occasion of his birthday, Campbell had traveled to Cape Town to join his spouse and friends for a small party. While enjoying this bit of social diversion, Campbell received a telephone call from Reuters News Service. It was a message he had been both dreading and expecting. On March 11, Henry Segrave had streaked across the sands of Daytona Beach, with a crowd of some 100,000 on hand to see him set a new record of 231.446 mph for the measured mile.

This was a stunning achievement for Segrave. The new record was nearly 24 mph faster than Keech's' old one. It was also a mark that Campbell conceded was beyond the capability of his Bluebird. However, he realized that he could still salvage some honor from this African mis-adventure. Segrave's record was officially for the one-mile distance only. While Bluebird could not beat it, by using the full 12-mile length of the Verneuk Pan, it was possible for Campbell to set new records for five miles and five kilometers.

Time was growing short, however. Only a few short weeks remained before March 8 when Colonel Lloyd, the official timekeeper, was scheduled to return to England. Due to this situation and reports of fast approaching bad weather, Campbell took Bluebird onto the Pan surface for the first time. The results confirmed Campbell's belief that it could not match Segrave's new mark. Yet, its average speed of 219 mph recorded in a two-way run across a measured mile indicated it was feasible to go for the longer-distance records, if Bluebird's tires were up to the ordeal. Campbell was pushing his luck on this point. At 200 mph, the life expectancy of the Tulip tires was just over 180 seconds. Nonetheless, the project continued after a multi-day dust storm, which was vicious, but caused little damage. After it was over, on April 25, 1929, Campbell prepared for assaults on the five-mile and five-kilometer marks. On the eastward run the thin treads on Bluebird's tires melted away as if they had been molded out of butter, but they held. After a change of tires Campbell was off again, his task half-completed. Before he had a chance to shift out of low gear, one of the rear tires shed its tread. Campbell had come too far and waited too long to have it all end this way. Onward he traveled, down what appeared to be a razor thin white line leading to nowhere. His efforts and courage were not for naught. The Bluebird had set a new record of 211 mph for the five mile distance and a corresponding 216 mph mark for five kilometers.

Perhaps it was fitting that Campbell did not surpass Segrave's mark that year. He went on to virtually dominate land speed records in the early- and mid-30s, with Bluebirds III through V. However, Segrave died in 1930, while attempting to set a new water speed record.

Campbell never returned to South Africa, choosing instead to travel to Daytona and then to Bonneville Salt Flats in Utah. There, on September 3, 1935, he became the first person to drive an automobile beyond the 300 mph mark, by hitting a speed of 301.13 mph.

Verneuk Pan faded into oblivion, virtually a forgotten artifact of an age of titans.

(Robert Ackerson and *Old Cars* thank Bob Johnston, of Johannesburg, South Africa, for his help in preparing this article. Johnston is the author of *Early Motoring In South Africa*.

An enthusiast remembers Bonneville

By George Krem

In the 1700s, a French Army officer with the name of Bonneville discovered that unique place called Bonneville Salt Flats. The salt flats are a part of the remains of Lake Bonneville, a lake that was 350 miles long at one time. The Great Salt Lake in Utah is a remnant of this prehistoric lake. Bonneville has been the scene of many land-speed-record attempts since early in the 20th century. On September 16, 1947, John Cobb established a new World Land Speed Record there with an average of over 394 mph. When he was asked how it felt to drive a car at 400 mph, Cobb answered, with traditional British understatement, "Everything happens quite quickly." This was not Cobb's first appearance. He set a 24-hour speed record of 132 mph. in 1935. He successfully raised his record to 150 mph in 1936.

Many have used the flats for racing through the years, but the first officially sanctioned national event there came about through the editorial pages of *Hot Rod* magazine in 1949. Before 1949, the Southern California Timing Association (SCTA) had sponsored a number of time trials each year at various dry lake beds in Southern California's Mojave desert.

Nathan Ostich built and drove the jet-powered 1961 Flying Caduceus. The streamliner was designed specifically for land speed racing at the Bonneville Salt Flats. The car's unusual name comes from the medical symbol, since Ostich was a doctor. It is now on exhibit at the National Automobile Museum in Reno, Nevada. (John Gunnell photo)

Studebaker and Sears brought this "Cross Country Record Maker" to Bonneville in 1963 to see several other Avantis smash 29 stock car speed records there. Drivers Paula Murphy, Barbara Neland and Bill Carroll had their names lettered on the door of this square-headlamp car, which is believed to have been a 1964 model prototype. During a Sears-Allstate safety tire test, the Avanti went from New York to San Diego in 52.1 hours. (Old Cars Collection)

The April 1949, editorial in *Hot Rod* proposed, "A national timing meet, once a year, at a centrally located site such as the salt flats in Utah." The SCTA had plans underway for the First National Automotive Speed Trials. They were held at the salt flats in autumn of that year. These meets have traditionally been one week in length. While they are planned every year, the salt conditions are sometimes too wet for competition.

There is a sign on Interstate 80, approximately 110 miles west of Salt Lake City, which informs drivers that the Bonneville race course may be reached through the next exit. Upon leaving the highway, the driver finds himself headed north on a two-lane blacktop road. After a mile or so, the road has a sweeping curve to the east. Following it for several miles carries one out on the salt flats. The pavement ends abruptly at a point where Multy and Vera Aldrich park their trailer. They function as greeters, pit pass sellers, coffee dispensers and ambassadors of goodwill. They have been involved in straight-away racing there since the beginning. They always have a friendly word for everyone. The $2 pit pass is good for the entire day, or if you decide to pay $10, the entire week. It entitles the bearer to go anywhere, except out on the racecourse itself.

Driving onto the salt, one suddenly realizes that the extreme flatness of the surface makes it possible to see the curvature of the earth in the distance. It is so flat that there is a change in elevation of only about two feet in one 10-mile section. The pit area is about five miles across the salt from where the pavement ends. The "road" to the pit and racing areas is marked by a straight black stripe that disappears into the distance. Moving along on the salt, one can feel a slight roughness in the surface, although there is no pitching or appreciable work for the springs and shock absorbers to do. The salt is white, making sunglasses a necessity during the day. It is extremely porous and, yet, strong enough to support tons of weight. Traction is quite good under normal conditions. The dry desert air and mountains to the north combine with the vast open spaces to create an awe-inspiring feeling.

Parked near the United States Auto Club's timing shed at the Bonneville Salt Flats, in October 1963, is a Studebaker Avanti. This round-headlamp 1963 model is lettered nearly identical to the actual Sears-Allstate tire test car and was probably used in making publicity photos for advertising and promotional purposes. (Old Cars Collection)

The Golden Rod was a four-engine, four-wheel-drive Bonneville streamliner that 28-year-old Bob Summers and 29-year-old Bill Summers finished constructing in 1964. The Summers Brothers started their hot rod career at Bonneville, in 1954, with a Chrysler-powered 1936 Ford coupe. They constructed the car together and Bob Summers drove it. By 1964, he held the Class C Streamliner record of 308.941 mph and a number of other class marks. The Goldenrod was built specifically to break the contemporary world record of 403.1 mph held by Britain's Donald Campbell. (John Gunnell Collection)

One problem that everyone at the salt flats must deal with is that driving on the salt allows the wheels to throw up salt underneath the car. This even happens when you are driving from the paved road to the pits in a collector car, as we did. Because the salt is usually slightly damp, it sticks to the underside of the body very well. To avoid rust-out, it's a good idea to take your car to the high-pressure car wash in nearby Wendover, after it spends a day on the salt. A rust-proofing job doesn't hurt, either.

The pit area is like a small town out on the salt flats. Approaching it, one notices that it covers a lot of ground (perhaps we should say salt). There is over a half-mile per side. Almost all the competitors set up a framework over which they stretch sheets of nylon or other material for shade. The supporting poles and stakes are driven directly into the salt, and the canopy is often large enough to give shade for more than one vehicle. Severe sunburn is a real danger and a good sunscreen lotion is recommended. The sun's reflection from the salt can even cause sunburn in unexpected places, such as the underside of one's nose or chin.

It would be hard to find another racing event with such a tremendous variety of machinery present. Everything from chopped-top early Ford coupes to late-model Ferraris can be seen. The variety of engines is also surprising: In addition to Chrysler hemis and the ever-present Chevy small-blocks, there are early flatheads, like Hudson Hornet sixes, and others. Motorcycles are an important part of the Bonneville scene and they were present in all sizes. Many collectible old cars are seen in the pit and two-mile-long viewing area. Fords from the 1920s, Mercedes gull-wing coupes and 300SL roadsters, Lincoln-Zephyrs and 1953 Studebaker coupes are present, to name just a few.

Pickup trucks are everywhere. They are frequently used as push vehicles to get the race cars up to 40 mph or so. The "tall" gearing and radical camshaft timing, used for maximum speeds, would frequently cause difficulty in getting off the line without assistance. Some com-

A pair of Studebaker Avantis with streamlining modifications was brought to Bonneville in October 1963, to make headlines. One car had a belly pan, disc type front hubcaps, and a 304.5-cubic-inch, 280-hp R-4 engine. The other had the same enhancements, plus fully skirted rear fenders and a special R-5 engine, with Bendix fuel-injection, that was said to develop 575 hp. In one run, the R-5 Avanti went 196 mph. In all, driver Andy Granatelli broke 29 USAC records with Studebakers that year. In 1964, he returned to the salt flats with a dozen Avantis, Hawks and Larks and broke some 60 other records. Twenty-five years later, Avantis were still running at Bonneville. This 1963 Avanti, on display at the Studebaker Museum, in South Bend, Indiana, competed at the salt flats in 1988 (172.746 mph) and 1989 (185.395 mph).

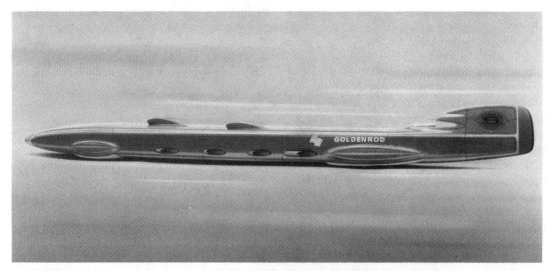

The Golden Rod streamliner was made for Bonneville racing. It had a 32-foot-long aluminum body shell. It rode on a 207-inch wheelbase with a 36-inch front tread and 24-inch rear tread. It was 28 inches high at its hood and 42 inches high at the tail fin. The overall width was 48 inches. Power came from four 426-cubic-inch Chrysler hemis. They were estimated to provide 600 hp each, for a total of 2400 hp. (John Gunnell Collection)

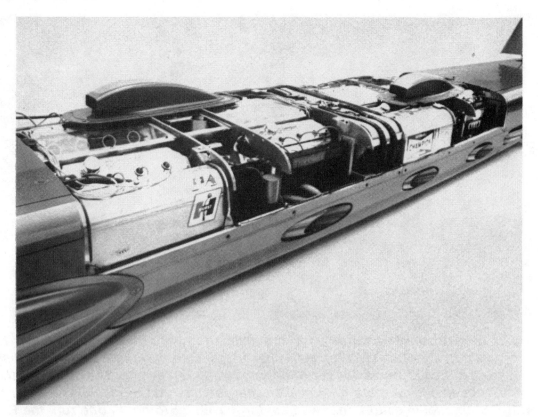

A peek under the hood of the Golden Rod shows the four Chrysler hemi engines packaged neatly into its long, low body work. Firestone was a major sponsor of the car, along with Chrysler, Hurst Performance Products and Mobil Oil Company. It had four gear-transfer cases, two flywheel-and-clutch setups, two huge truck transmissions, twin Airheart disc brakes and four forged aluminum wheels with special Firestone tires. (Prosper DuBois-Reymond)

petitors bring everything and the kitchen sink. It's not unusual to see large vans housing well-equipped machine shops, power generators, extra engines, spare transmissions, axle assemblies and more. Few entrants have less than two or three crew members. Although racing at Bonneville can be expensive, many participants successfully field low-dollar efforts. Spouses and children are often actively involved, too.

The starting line attracts many of the spectators and they are allowed to roam around among the cars waiting to run. Not every run is a record attempt. Runs held after 9 am or 10 am are for purposes of qualifying, testing, or upgrading a driver's competition license, for certification at the next higher speed level. Categories are under 125 mph, 125-149 mph, 150-174 mph, 171-199 mph and over-200 mph.

Drivers may advance upward only one category at a time. If your car will do 180 mph and if you have never driven at Bonneville, you must make four runs. You advance up, one category, each time.

To qualify for a record attempt, you must exceed the old record by a minimum of .001 mph. Successful qualifiers must be at the starting line by 8 am the following morning for a record attempt. Records are always the average of a two-way run over the same mile. During much of the day, there often will be a block-long, double line of cars waiting to run.

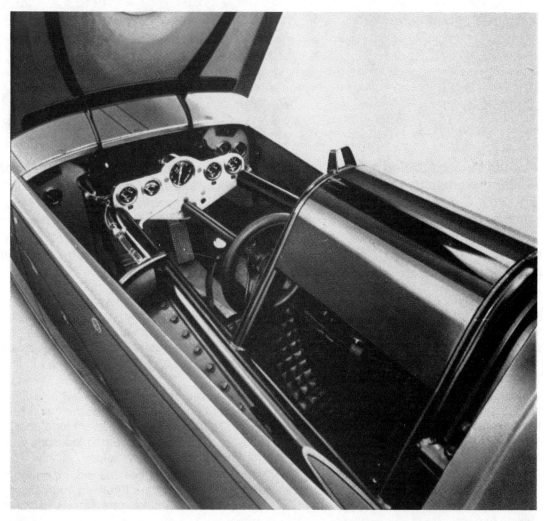

The Golden Rod's cockpit was a picture of pure functionality. Five simple round gauges in the main panel were used to monitor the mechanical functions. Additional gauges were mounted on the bulkheads. Walt Karft, who worked for Lockheed Aircraft Corporation, helped work out the car's aerodynamics. The car survives and makes occasional appearances at collector car shows. (Prosper DuBois-Reymond)

It would be hard to find another racing event with such a tremendous variety of machinery present. The variety of power plants is exemplified by the 1973 Battery Box Car. Now enshrined at the National Automobile Museum in Reno, Nevada, this electric-powered Bonneville streamliner was owned and driven by Roger Hedlund. Jack Hagenmann build its sleek body work. It cost $7,000 to construct. The 236-volt General Electric motor provided 25 hp. (John Gunnell photo)

Unlike most racing events, the starting line at Bonneville is often a quiet place. Only one vehicle at a time is allowed on the racecourse. The next racer must wait to start until word comes by radio that the car in front of him has left the course. Those waiting to get on the racecourse seldom start their engines before the official starter gives them the go-ahead. This helps avoid overheating in the hot desert sun. When a car leaves, some drivers and crew members in line hand-push their cars several feet ahead.

The fastest (and loudest) cars frequently leave the line with their engines off, while a fairly quiet push vehicle gets them up to 40 mph or more. At that point, the drivers let out the clutch. The engine fires and the car rapidly disappears. This leaves the starting line silent for a couple of minutes. As each run is completed, the speed attained is announced over the loudspeakers, breaking the quiet. Many drivers do not use their maximum power immediately.

The goal is top speed, not fast acceleration. Competitors will often ease into wide-open-throttle to give the engine a chance to warm up thoroughly. The faster cars throw an impressively long rooster tail of salt behind them at speed and a good pair of binoculars can be useful in viewing this.

Several cars were especially interesting. This writer drove to the 1986 Bonneville Speed Trials in Ron Hall's beautiful 1953 Studebaker coupe. This make and body style has been a long-time favorite on the salt because of its streamlined shape. A number of records set by 1953 Studebakers still stand. Four of these cars were at Bonneville in 1986. One of the most unusual was equipped with an early 1950s Hudson Hornet 308-cubic-inch six. The owner and driver of this car was Steve Kann, of Oregon. His crew consisted of his wife and several friends and relatives. Steve's car was running around 143 mph and he was trying to work it up to the class record of 154 mph

Before the 1986 meet, the all-time fastest one-way speed ever attained by a car with a completely stock body was 248 mph. It was set by a 1953 Studebaker coupe owned by Mike Woodward. However, that distinction fell while we were there. A well-prepared Pontiac Trans Am powered by a 454-cubic-inch, twin turbocharged Chevy engine was the new record holder. This car, known as the Banks/Popular Mechanics/Geisler/Stringfellow Trans Am, averaged 260 mph for a new record in its class. Listening to this car make its runs was worth the whole trip. It seemed to have enough power (one estimate was 1,500 hp) to easily spin the wheels in any gear. Interestingly, Bruce Geisler and Don Stringfellow have been racing at Bonneville for many years. They have had great success in setting a variety of records with a 1953 Studebaker coupe. That Studebaker coupe was at Bonneville '86. It was driven by Donnie Stringfellow, the son of Don, Sr.

A real favorite of ours was a gray 1949 Chevrolet fastback. The original overhead valve, six-cylinder engine had a modified displacement of 288 cubic inches. A late-model GM High Energy Ignition (HEI) system was almost ejected by the engine, according to the owner. A homemade intake manifold, with no less than five single barrel carburetors, was on it. The car had been driven to work regularly by the owner, before the engine was modified for Bonneville. Most of the car remained painfully stock for the high-speed runs. It ran with almost all trim and interior items in place. Bumper guards, headlights, radio, radio antenna, heater and many other pieces were there. Only a set of hubcaps was needed to enter it in a stock class at a show. The old Chevy set a new record in its class. Going down the salt, it went 133 mph. It did 137 on the return run, for an average of about 135 mph. The Chevy was prepared and driven by Tom Finn and his son, who are from California.

On Wednesday morning of the meet, the sponsors announced over the loudspeakers that the first two miles of the course had deteriorated somewhat, because of all the runs made that morning and the previous days. After the two-mile mark, the salt smoothed out nicely. They went on to say that any spectators who wanted to help could drive their pickup or car up and down this two-mile section for a while, to pack down the salt. Within a few minutes, dozens of cars were out on the racecourse enjoying a rare drive.

Ron Hall's 1953 Studebaker coupe went out, as did everything from pickups to rental cars. The course is seven miles in length and perfectly straight until near the end. It is marked by three black stripes on the salt. At first glance, it looks like a very wide two-lane highway. Everything is white, except for those black lines. Since so many cars were out there packing it down, nobody could go much over 40 mph, but it was exciting just to be able to drive on that famous course.

Would we go again? At the slightest excuse. Ron and I hope to run a Studebaker there someday. Bonneville is unique among racing events. The scenery can be awe-inspiring. There are no speed limits. The safety record is excellent. The kind of people who participate ... both competitors and spectators ... are friendly and helpful. Count me in for future meets!

After his famous late-1950s and early-1960s assaults on the salt with the four-engined Challenger 1, the late Mickey Thompson returned to Bonneville, in the late-1960s, with the Ford Autolite Special streamliner. The 30-foot-long land-speed-record seeker developed 2,070 hp from a pair of 427-cubic-inch Ford engines. Thompson was after the one-mile World Land Speed Record for wheel-driven cars, which was 409 mph at that time. (Ford News Department photo)

Speed King led speedy existence

By Phil Hall

The late Mickey Thompson was a legend in racing. He used unconventional means to achieve major goals in many facets of the sport. It's estimated Thompson held 485 national and international speed records.

In 1940, at age 11, Mickey became interested in cars. His coaster wagon hauled home 1927 Chevy parts and he tried to build a street rod. After World War II, he was attracted to speed runs on Southern California's dry lakes. In 1950, he made it to the annual speed trials at the Bonneville Salt Flats.

Thompson's horizons included more than straight-line speed. He entered the Carrera Pan-Americana (Mexican Road Race) twice with Roger Flores. He crashed both times. In drag racing, Thompson, proved to be a tough competitor and leader. He helped organize and operate the Lions drag strip in Long Beach, California. Another of Mickey's endeavors was setting water speed records. A 1957 attempt ended in a mishap at Lake Mead. He injured his back, hampering his land racing for several years.

Mickey Thompson started building cars at age 11, in 1940. Ten years later, he made his first trip to Bonneville, beginning a racing career that lasted until he was murdered in March 1986. (Old Cars Collection)

Thompson's national fame came in 1958. On his way to a weekend of dragging, he stopped off at Bonneville with his slingshot dragster. It had a streamlined body and twin Chrysler hemi V-8s. Thompson forgot the drags and turned in a one-way flying mile of 294.117 mph. The front engine let go on the return run. He could not finish a two-way average. After Bonneville, stock car builder Ray Nichols introduced Mickey to Pontiac Motor Division General Manager Semon "Bunkie" Knudsen. He agreed to help in future speed quests.

Mickey operated a speed shop, made speed parts, ran a drag strip and held a full-time job as a pressman. Finally, after 10 years, he gave up his printing job to work only on cars and speed quests. With Bunkie Knudsen's help, Thompson built his Challenger I, with four Pontiac engines, for the 1959 Bonneville Speed Trials. Thompson designed the rest of the complicated car.

Suddenly, everyone knew Thompson. He set 16 national and international records. His best one-way run was 367.83 mph. However, the Challenger I was unable to hit the magic 400 mph mark Thompson sought. There would be changes for 1960. He wanted to get more speed out of the car. To increase its power, engine man Fritz Voight added GMC 6-71 superchargers to the engines and altered the body. The team was ready for the salt. The Speed Trials were used as a warm-up. The

Race car driver Dan Gurney pilots the Mickey Thompson Enterprises Indy Car in the 1962 Indianapolis 500-mile Race. Teaming with British chassis designer John Crosthwaite, Thompson built three cars for 1962's race. All had rear-mounted Buick V-8s and fully independent suspension a year before the Lotus-Fords. The race engine was bored and stroked to 255 cubic inches, but had 70 hp less than racing Offys. The small Thompson cars attracted attention. (Phil Hall Collection)

following week, Thompson reeled off a fantastic 406.6 mph run, topping all speed marks. However, he could not back it up with a second required run and could not claim the World Land Speed Record.

Drag racing kept Mickey Thompson's attention. He built the "Assault," a supercharged, Pontiac-powered rail dragster, with more in mind than match races. Mickey wanted the records for a standing start kilometer and mile.

When the Pontiac Tempest compact came out, Thompson adapted its four-banger to speed runs. He got attention by cutting a Tempest four-cylinder engine in half to get a two-cylinder machine. All his engines had GMC superchargers. The culmination of this effort came July 9, 1961. Thompson was allowed to take over the runway at March Air Force Base, near Riverside, California. He rewrote the record books with his "Speed-O-Rama." Thompson used four cars including three dragster-based machines and a more-or-less stock 1961 Pontiac Catalina two-door hardtop. He aimed at 18 national and international records and came up with 14. His performance was hurt by the failure of a small V-8. The two-cylinder dragster held together, in its maiden run, for a pair of records in Class F.

The next phase was surprising. Thompson, although never a circle tracker, fielded cars for the Indy 500. Teaming with British chassis designer John Crosthwaite, he built three cars for 1962's race. All had rear-mounted Buick V-8s and fully independent suspension a year before the Lotus-Fords. The race engine was bored and stroked to 255 cubic inches, but had 70 hp less than racing Offys. The small Thompson cars attracted attention. Of the three, only Thompson's entry made it past qualifications. Dan Gurney was at the wheel. He put it in the center of the third row, running well until a rear seal let go That dropped him to a 20th place finish after 94 laps. Thompson got the mechanical achievement award.

Thompson also built a 421-cubic-inch A/FX Tempest. With this car, he was ready for his second annual Speed-O-Rama. He returned to March Air Force Base, July 15, with the Assault and a 1962 Catalina two-door. He clicked off records at a steady pace with the sedan and a Tempest-powered dragster. Then, he headed to Bonneville for more. Starting July 23, he ran the Challenger I and the stock Pontiac in Utah. The salt was too rough to get the Challenger I up to speed. Thompson concentrated on the stocker, until a rocker stud broke at 760 miles. Then, on July 25, he called it quits in both speed quests and driving. The combination of his business success and a nagging back injury from his boat racing days meant it was time to hang up his helmet.

Knudsen left Pontiac for Chevy. General Motors told its divisions to stop racing in 1963. Thompson's public performances dwindled, but he kept the pace up and fielded cars with aluminum Chevy V-8s for the 1963 Indy 500. "Bunkie" may have gotten the engines shipped but could do little else to help. All development was done in the Mickey Thompson shops. The cars got new, wider bodies and further shook up the establishment by using wide tires mounted on 12- and 15-inch wheels. The cars missed the center of the spotlight, due to the new Lotus-Fords, which were fast out of the box. Graham Hill and others tested them, but rookie Al Miller and veteran Duane Carter were the Indy drivers. Miller finished ninth, while Carter crashed and finished 23rd.

Thompson's engineering innovations were overshadowed by his 1964 Indy entries with Ford V-8s and radical new bodies that ran the full width of the tire tread. There were problems from the start. Three cars were entered as Mickey Thompson/Sears Allstate Specials with Masten Gregory, newcomer Dave MacDonald and Duane Carter as drivers. Just two cars made it. Early in the 500, MacDonald lost control, starting a crash that cost his life and that of Eddie Sachs. Criticism of Thompson's design was harsh. He kept a low profile for a few years.

Mickey tried an Indy comeback, in 1967, using cars powered by a three-valve Chevy engine. They left before making the field, due to mechanical problems. Thompson was supposed to try, in 1968, with the same car and driver Danny Ongais. Nothing happened. There was also talk of a return to Bonneville, but his programs seemed to lack direction and drive.

All changed when Knudsen took a position as president of Ford. Not far behind was Thompson. Ford was in racing in a big way. There was money available. A Bonneville speed run car and funny cars for drag racing were unveiled. The Thompson-Ford relationship surfaced in a series of speed runs at Bonneville during July 1968. Using a variety of 1969 Mustangs and drivers, more records were set. One driver was Thompson, who ended his retirement. Thompson's alliance with Ford also sparked a series of funny cars. They followed his pattern of being different. He had a conventional Mustang for Ongais in 1969. For 1970, he unveiled a monocoque constructed Mustang and Maverick. He fielded four funny cars for Ford in 1970.

In 1971, Thompson made a titanium-framed Pinto funny car with driver Dale Pulde. He also experimented with a compressed air setup on a car called the "Thermocharger." Then, he built an off-road dune buggy with V-4 Ford power. Thompson set no records with but had a ball and became interested in the sport. The interest increased when Ford cut race support in the 1970s.

Thompson competed in some events. Then, in April 1973, he flew his plane over the Mint 400 race. "It was the most exciting race I've ever seen," he told Cory Farley of *Hot Rod*. Considering his extensive race management experience, Thompson formed SCORE (Short Course Off-Road Events) in 1973. He concentrated on making it a first-rate organization that won national recognition. Not satisfied, he took the sport in a new direction in 1982, organizing Mickey Thompson's Off-Road Championship Grand Prix at the Los Angeles County Fairgrounds in Pomona. This turned off-road racing into a short track, stadium event that became an instant success in California and a worthy television attraction.

Where was Mickey Thompson headed before his brutal slaying? Word had it that he was finally looking to retire, at age 60, to spend more time with his family. Would Thompson have really retired? Unfortunately for all of motorsports, we'll never know.

Thompson was 39-years-old, in 1968, when his Autolite Special, with twin 427-cubic-inch Ford single overhead cam V-8s, sought the World Land Speed Record for piston-engined wheel-driven cars. (Old Cars Collection via Phil Hall)

A tribute to Mickey Thompson

By LeRoi Tex Smith

Mickey Thompson was the very epitome of the hot rod spirit. He was mechanically oriented and obsessed with determination. He was an individual in an individualistic sport.

I first met Mickey in the 1950s. He was a pressman for the *Los Angeles Times* and I was at *Hot Rod* magazine. As I look back on the period, it didn't seem unusual, then, for him to be going in literal "high-gear overdrive." Many hot rodders were just as active; driven by some internal demon to be doing things. It wasn't a success motive in the contemporary sense, but rather, a need to be trying new things. Often, it was more a race with oneself than a competition with another. Now, years later, it is easy to recognize that bulldog tenacity was the very reason for Thompson's ultimate success.

However, success didn't come easy to Mickey. Most of the time he simply seized opportunity by the throat and held on until something happened. As with so many ultra-achievers, he could have wonderful tunnel vision. When he broke the land speed record, in 1960, it really didn't matter that he had completed only one-half of the required two-way run for international recognition. He had done it and that was enough!

Mickey ran a boat, for years, without ever winning. He was seriously hurt there. He ran a car at Indianapolis and never really did much. He was innovative, though. It was from those "Brickyard" experiences (and his comments to the general press) that we got to calling him "Wait Till Next Year Thompson." It bothered him to fail, but it didn't stop him from trying.

Of all the things I remember most about Mickey Thompson, one incident stands out vividly. One day, we were at the old Los Angeles Drag Strip (or Lions drag strip) in Southern California. It was the end of a typical day. Mickey was in the announcer's booth when a particularly obnoxious spectator started yelling obscenities across the track. Mickey ignored the remarks for about 10 minutes, until a break in the action. Taking advantage of the lull, he climbed deliberately down from the timing tower, walked across the staging area to the retaining fence and punched

"Mickey Thompson's Mach 1" was a Mustang funny car powered by a Boss 429 Ford V-8. After "Bunkie" Knudsen took a position as president of Ford, there was money for Thompson available. A Bonneville speed run car and funny cars for drag racing were unveiled. (Phil Hall Collection)

that spectator's lights out in a single blow. That, more than anything else, exemplified Mickey Thompson. He was direct, deliberate and determined.

Mickey Thompson wasn't exactly loved by many, but his wife Trudy was a delight to most of us of acquaintance. I liked him, but I never had occasion to be offensive. Ultimately, we who remain are the losers.

Thompson (far left) unveiled the monocoque-constructed Maverick shown here in 1970. In 1971, he made a titanium-framed Pinto funny car. Arnie Behling (in white driving suit) was another driver of Thompson's funny cars. (Phil Hall Collection)

Dave MacDonald, of El Monte, California, was a rookie Indy Car driver when he drove the Mickey Thompson, Sears-Allstate Special through the turns at Indianapolis Motor Speedway, in preparation for the 500-mile Memorial Day Classic. He qualified the car with a four lap average of 151.464 mph and was the second fastest rookie to make the field. (Old Cars Collection via Phil Hall)

GOING IN CIRCLES

Remembering Milwaukee's famous Marchese brothers racing legend

By Phil Hall

It is not unusual for a 12-year-old to wax enthusiastic about a manual training class project. Countless lamps, tables, cabinets and the like have proudly been brought home by budding craftsmen, usually to be forgotten and relegated to the attic as the builder's interest went elsewhere. However, one school boy's hope was to build a miniature racing car. For Carl Marchese of Milwaukee, Wisconsin, the enthusiasm generated by that manual training project, in 1917, was still aglow 60 years later. Of course, there are not many such projects you can use for street racing.

Marchese's antics on city streets led to competition on area race tracks and later to the Indianapolis 500. Racing became Carl's life. That crude, miniature race car he and his brother Tudy built, had a wooden body and Henderson motorcycle engine. It was the first of many cars Carl would make a part of the Marchese Brothers racing legend.

Before he passed away, Carl had a great deal more than memories of days past. He could go "home" again. Thanks to his long-time friend Dave Uihlein, a Milwaukee area businessperson, some of the cars Carl built were restored before he died.

One restored Marchese racer was a Model T-based sprint car Carl built and raced in the mid-1920s. In 1925, he entered it at the Wisconsin State Fair Speedway in the Milwaukee suburb of West Allis. There he set a qualifying record by rounding the classic one-mile dirt oval at a speed of 77.7 mph. He came back, later in the afternoon, to win the feature.

Carl Marchese sat behind the wheel of the Rajo Special before a race at DePere, Wisconsin in 1924. The car was fitted with a double overhead camshaft Gallivan power plant the next year. (Al Krause Colection)

The field of cars presented itself before the start of a race on the Cedarburg, Wisconsin half-mile in 1925. Carl Marchese, in car number 5, is on the outside in the front row. Next to him, in car number 4, is his brother Tudy. (Al Krause Collection)

Fifty-two years later, on Sunday afternoon, June 12, Carl again got into the cockpit, donned his leather helmet and took a couple of nostalgic laps on the now paved surface of the same track. Although he made no attempt to search for speed, the smile on his face that day said it all. It is doubtful if any of the 32,556 fans on hand were in the stands in 1926. However, just about all the fans knew the Marchese name. It was significant to racing in the Milwaukee area and the country.

Milwaukee became the home of the Marchese clan when Luigi came from Italy, to the United States, in 1902. He was seeking work and found it with the railroad. Two years later, he sent for his family. Tom, Joe, Tony, Anna and their mother Gaetana arrived, by boat, in 1904. They settled in a tenement on Milwaukee's rough lower east side. Carl was born in 1906 and Tudy in 1907.

Tom quit school at the age of 11. He worked at several odd jobs, before he was hired as a mechanic's helper, at a local Ford dealership, in 1917. The interest in motor cars rubbed off on his two younger brothers and the manual training project evolved.

"We used it to dodge the cops in the third ward," Carl noted with a gleam in his eye. The brother's success at evading the police prompted another street racer to be built. This time they used Ford Model T parts including a Rajo cylinder head. Built by Joe Jagersberger, of Racine, it was popular on race cars of that era.

In 1922 Tom and brothers Tony and Joe went into the trucking business and bought a garage on First Street on the south side of Milwaukee. Carl and Tudy went to work for them and, for the first time in several years, the brothers were back together again, and working in the same place. The name Marchese Brothers Garage proudly went out front. Over the years they also sold and serviced new cars.

With the challenge of the street lessening and a garage to work on their cars, they built a race car. It was, again, based on the T. It had buckboard seating (no tail section) and a Rajo head. Carl and Tudy took the car to the Hawthorne race track, outside Chicago. This track was better known for its horse racing than automobile competition. On that sunny day in October 1923, Carl drove his first race sanctioned by the American Automobile Association (AAA).

"It was so dusty I could only see the car ahead of me. It was powered by a Hall-Scott airplane engine and driven by Pat Clancey. He lost control and went right through the fence. I was lost and followed him right through the wall and outside the track," Carl said.

A proud Carl Marchese posed in the Marchese Miller Special on Lincoln Memorial Drive, on Milwaukee's lakefront, before the 1928 racing season. (Al Krause Collection)

Carl Marchese strikes a pose, before entering the time trials for the 1929 Indianapolis 500-mile Race. (Al Krause Collection)

Clancey went on to construct a radical six-wheeled car for Indy. Carl went on to campaign area tracks in the 1924 season in his Rajo/buckboard. Constantly improving the machine, Carl raced on the dirt ovals around Milwaukee at Cedarburg, Beaver Dam, DePere and Madison. He also raced in the state of Indiana, at Roby and Hammond.

In 1925, Carl and Tudy built a new car with a full tail section. While the early car reflected the state-of-the-art in 1923, the new machine started to show the ingenuity the Marchese brothers would be noted for. Using Model T frame rails, Carl and Tudy decided that platform springs, like those on Miller racing cars, were better than Model T springs. Using some Scripps-Booth parts, they extended the rails and installed the springs.

While the Rajo head had served them well, Carl heard of a new design that had been built by Jack Gallivan, an Army Air Force instructor at Chanute Field, Illinois. It had double overhead cams, but retained two valves per cylinder. Only a few were ever made. "It was expensive 'for those times. We paid $600 for it and took it home in a basket. We had to do a lot of work on it ourselves," Carl once noted.

The new combination paid off with Carl's Wisconsin State Fair Speedway record and the feature win as early evidence. Making continual improvements, Carl campaigned the car for the next three seasons. Tudy also raced a similar car, but it had the Rajo head.

In 1927, Carl won a 100-lap race at Roby, on the one-mile dirt oval. However, having a suspension like a Miller was not enough. In the fall of that year, he and his brothers bought a Miller with a 122-cubic-inch engine from Andy Burt of Chicago. Also in 1927, Carl and Tudy opened up a garage next to their house on Jackson Street in Milwaukee. In their spare time they built another miniature race car that was not unlike the manual training project. They used it to publi-

A tired, but happy Carl Marchese is seen after his fourth-place finish in the 1929 Indy 500. The pit crew behind him includes (from left): Tudy Marchese, Harry "Slim" Heinle (who sold the car to the Marchese brothers), Joe Anastasia and Tom Marchese. (Al Krause Collection)

For many years after Carl Marchese retired from driving, the Marchese brothers entered cars in several types of racing. Shown after driver Myron Fohr qualified for the 1949 Indianapolis 500-mile Race are crew men Ted Arasin, Tudy Marchese, Tom Marchese, George "Zeke" Holck and Carl Marchese. (Al Krause Collection)

cize their business, rather than to race. It was licensed for the street and used in parades, to run errands and so forth. It was a forerunner of the midget racing class that would sweep the nation in the next decade.

Like their first project, the small car had a Henderson cycle engine, but one with a more modern design. It also had a transmission with three forward speeds and reverse, plus airplane wheels.

They kept the car into the 1930s and then sold it just as the sport of midget racing began to blossom. The car was raced by its new owner, but not successfully.

With brother Tom serving as mechanic and pitman, Carl raced the Miller during the 1928 season. That fall another Miller 122, which had been driven by Cliff Woodbury, was bought by the brothers from Harry Heinley. It was a lighter car. Tudy was to drive the older Miller.

Rules for the 1929 Indy 500 limited engines to 91 cubic inches. The Marcheses used a short stroke crankshaft and got the Miller down to the limit. The time had come to enter the nation's premiere racing event. They entered the May festivities that year as complete unknowns. Carl crashed in practice leaving the railbirds muttering about another rookie. Then, after Tom brought down the needed parts to get the Marchese Special running, Carl made the show. He qualified at 109 mph.

The railbirds continued to talk about Carl, but in different tones. He finished fourth, completing the 500 miles in 5:20:42.95 for an average speed of 93.541 mph. The Marcheses in general, and Carl in particular, were the heroes of Milwaukee. However, Carl's career behind the wheel was near the end. In August of 1929, in a race on the mile at Springfield, Illinois, dusty conditions made vision minimal. A four-car crash resulted when a car stalled on the track. Carl was in one of the four cars. He was injured, but worse, one of the cars hit a couple of spectators who were standing where they should not have been standing. The resulting bad publicity was sufficient to end racing on the Illinois State Fairgrounds for a few years.

Though his injuries were not too serious, Carl's family pressured him to quit racing. Any thought of returning to Indy was squelched when the rules for 1930 were changed to allow two-man cars and engines up to 366 cubic inches. Though Carl's career behind the wheel ended, the Marchese legend was just beginning. With help from the publicity that Carl's Indy finish received, Tom was recommended to take over the direction of the major races at the Wisconsin State Fair Speedway. Tom's tough leadership through the lean 1930s and into postwar racing boom, made the "Milwaukee Mile" a model of efficient operation. The track was paved in 1954 and Tom's Wisconsin Auto Racing, Incorporated, promoted all major races through the 1967 season. In 1968, the Milwaukee Mile was sold to area short track promoter John Kaishian. Tom remained as president until his retirement, in 1976, at the age of 77. Tom remained chairman of the board and could be found in his familiar place on the infield tower at every race.

The midget boom attracted Carl and Tudy, who had experience in building small cars. They first raced them in 1935, using a four-cylinder engine made from half of a Miller straight eight. Tudy won 17 features during the 1935 season, before he retired as a driver.

With a reputation of being expert car builders, Carl and Tudy constructed an Indy car in 1938. The new Marchese Special had a 183-cubic-inch Miller engine that the brothers intended to supercharge to compete with the 270-cubic-inch engines allowed at Indy at the time, They never got around to doing this, but despite their handicap, Harry McQuinn drove it to a seventh place finish in the 500 that year. "The car was up to fifth with Tony Willman as a relief driver, but McQuinn insisted on finishing the race and the driver change cost us two positions," Carl later said.

The Marchese Special was supercharged in 1939 and entered the 500. With Willman at the wheel, a piston blew on the last lap of qualifications and it did not make the race. The car was qualified fifth fastest in 1940, but a hole in the radiator occurred too late to make repairs and forced the Marcheses to withdraw it. The bad luck ended in 1941 and Paul Russo finished ninth in that year's 500.

Four of the five Marchese brothers were photographed at a luncheon in 1955. From the left are Carl, Tom, Joe and Tudy. (Al Krause Collection)

Carl Marchese (right) spent his later years as race director of the Wisconsin State Fair Park Speedway. In this 1978 photo, he looks over one of the then-current Indy Cars with long-time friend and former crew member Ted Arasin. (Al Krause Collection)

Racing cars rested during World War II and those in the Marchese Garage were no exception. In 1942, Carl and Tudy applied for membership in the exclusive Society of Automotive Engineers (SAE). Even though they had never so much as taken a college course, let alone received a degree, they were accepted on the basis of their race car building skills, which attracted attention nationwide.

The last midget race car the Marchese brothers built was made in 1947. They constructed their own chassis and designed and built their own engine. It was 64 cubic inches and supercharged. "We tested the new engine in 1947 and didn't have time to work it out," Carl once noted. "So we put an Offy in (the car) in 1948. We wanted to win and needed the money. "

The outside of the midget looked rather conventional, as Kurtis-Kraft panels were used. They owned the car until 1953, when it was sold to Russ Billings of Milwaukee. Billings put a Studebaker engine in it so he could race at Sun Prairie, Wisconsin in the Badger Midget competition. It was sold again, in 1954, to Paul Ottman. He reinstalled the Offy engine. Then in 1954, the car was wrecked in a practice session at the Hales Corners Speedway, just outside Milwaukee.

The Marchese brother's postwar activity did not keep them from having a car ready for the 1946 Indianapolis 500, but problems were again apparent. Tony Bettenhausen qualified for the race, but crankshaft problems forced the car to be withdrawn. A new Offy engine was installed for the 1948 Indy 500 and Myron Fohr was hired as driver. He missed the show, but returned in 1949 to place fourth and in 1950 to finish 11th. Marchese driver Chuck Stevenson dropped out of the 1951 Indy 500, due to a broken connecting rod. The car would never return to the 'Brickyard.' A crash occurred in Syracuse, New York later that season, with Stevenson behind the wheel. It ended the racing career of the 13-year old car.

Tudy Marchese died in 1959. In the 1950s, Carl put increasingly more time into his brother Tom's race promoting organization, where he worked for many years. In his later years, Carl went into semi-retirement, spending the off-seasons in Florida. However, from mid-May to mid-September, he could be found holding down the duties of race director at the Wisconsin State Fair Speedway.

Race car collector Dave Uihlein worked in the Marchese Brothers Garage as a youngster and never forgot the lessons he learned from the master car builders. He went on to found Banner Welder, Incorporated of Milwaukee and become one of the major stockholders in the Joseph Schlitz Brewing Company. He started acquiring bits and pieces of the Marchese cars over the years. His big find was in 1952 when he advertised for the Gallivan-equipped engine from Carl's sprint car. "I found it in an Indianapolis junkyard. Someone had converted it to down-draft Winfield carbs, but otherwise it was as the Marcheses raced it," Uihlein said. "It originally had updrafts. I've got Holley updrafts on it now."

Uihlein also acquired the remains of the Marchese Special championship car and, in 1973, bought the last midget race car they built. It came from Paul Ottman, who bought it from Russ Billings. After restoring several cars for the street, and acquiring many race car parts, Uihlein's wife Margery got after him to do something with them. With the help of E.J. (Jack) Healey, a turbine designer and engine builder at Allis-Chalmers, and Joe Silnes, an Indianapolis body and chassis expert, the restoration work began in 1976. The midget and Indy car were completed in 1977 and the sprinter was done in 1978. When the cars were shown together for the first time, Carl and Tom were thrilled. The work was first class and everyone involved was highly pleased.

"Few people know of the mechanical genius of Carl and Tudy," Dave Uihlein said. "Tudy was the master machinist, lathe, milling machine craftsman and welder, while Carl fit the cars together, tuned them, and made them viable. Their racers were not only winners on the track, but were also finely crafted, beautiful machines."

Carl Marchese became the first person from the sport of auto racing to be installed in the Wisconsin Athletic Hall of Fame in June of 1978. He retired as race director for the Fair Park mile in 1983 and died the following year.

Midgets got big after World War II

By Phil Hall

What do such huge sports facilities as the Los Angeles Coliseum, Soldier Field in Chicago and the Polo Grounds in New York have in common, besides being the scenes of major athletic contests? They were the site of midget auto races. This was during the peak of the sport's popularity in the years after World War II. Indeed, a crowd reported in excess of 60,000 turned out for a race at the Coliseum in 1946.

Today, midget racing remains a viable form of motorsports. However, in the heavy competition for the racing fan's dollar, its drawing power is less than during the postwar boom, although our nation now has a larger population.

The reasons for the rapid rise and eventual decline in the popularity of midget racing have been debated for decades. The phenomenon is worth reviewing. The cars and drivers of that era form the basis of the "memory banks" of many enthusiasts today who are involved in vintage midget racing.

Smaller forms of open wheeled race cars had been around, for one reason or another, for many years before 1933. However, organized midget racing (for scaled-down race cars) was started that year in California. It gradually spread to other parts of the country in later years.

One advantage the midgets had was lower cost of construction, both in chassis and engine. Various power plants could be used. Some came from automobiles, although outboard motor

Midget racing attracted good crowds after World War II. This battle took place during a 100-mile event at the Wisconsin State Fair Park Speedway on August 21, 1949. (Phil Hall Collection)

Paul Russo drove the unpainted Nichels Offy at Chicago's Soldier Field during the midget racing boom after World War II. (Phil Hall Collection)

boat engines or motorcycle engines were also used. Another advantage, which would play a major role in the postwar era, was the ability of the midgets to race in small areas. They could run in places where the larger sprint car and big Indianapolis 500 cars could not compete. This led to midget races at dog tracks, amusement parks and inside football or baseball stadiums.

Midgets proved a good training ground for sprint car racing, which was then a stepping stone to the big cars. Midgets also provided a means for young drivers to race professionally. The driver without big bucks could get a start on his way to running the Indianapolis 500 someday.

The downside was that the small cars lacked much driver protection. In addition, a variety of track surfaces (some horrendous) produced accidents that proved costly for lives and serious injuries. Today the racing world is shocked over a fatality in any form of racing. Then, few race car drivers retired of old age.

Midget racing prospered before World War II, with hotbeds of racing on the West Coast, Midwest and East Coast. One of the most famous tracks was the Gilmore Stadium in the Los Angeles area. It had a quarter-mile dirt oval constructed around a football field. It hosted some of the top events before the war started.

Midget and other forms of full-scale racing were halted on July 31, 1942, due to constraints on resources due to the war. Racing didn't resume until 1945 and, like many other things, there was a pent-up demand for it. Races played to packed houses after the war and the biggest problem was getting tires and equipment, rather than spectators.

Using cars constructed before the war, midget racing was ready to go as soon as the tracks were open. The general public was hungry for entertainment, money was available to spend on it and the midgets were in the right place at the right time.

Crowds grew and so did the list of promoters looking for ways to make money from the midget boom. Not all worked out. A board track was set up inside the New York Polo Grounds where both the baseball and football Giants played. The attendance was not as big as expected and the track was moved to the Rose Bowl in Pasadena, California. Unfortunately similar results were met there.

Chicago's Soldier Field had used a board track, but a permanent one was constructed in the home of the Chicago Bears football team after the war. The Chicago area was a hotbed of racing. Indoor events were also held in the off-season, making midget car racing a year-around sport in the city.

With anything from fairgrounds tracks to indoor arenas usable, midget racing events were numerous. Some drivers raced eight times a week (twice on Sunday). After World War II, America's love of the automobile blossomed, not only in buying and driving, but also in attending races. However, in the fertile fields of the postwar midget boom, were the seeds of its decline.

The postwar demand for midget race cars resulted in construction being taken from the backyard. Frank Kurtis began assembling and selling full midget cars. His Kurtis Kraft midgets could also be had in kit form. Add several forms of Kurtis Kraft copies and you had many cars that looked nearly the same.

In the engine department, uniformity also was taking over. The pure racing Offenhauser double-overhead-cam four-cylinder was becoming the standard for racers with sufficient funds. The Ford V-8-60 passenger car engine was doing it for those with thinner wallets. Segregation of A and B (or other such designations) resulted in a strange situation. Many events were not open to all the midgets that were around.

All this uniformity began to produce fields where most of the cars looked alike. The faster Offy events got the bigger names and the non-Offy groups often ended up with the locals. There were complaints on the sameness of the cars. Racing also got a bit more professional, resulting in increased driver safety. This meant fewer crashes. These factors alone were not enough to cause the downfall of midget racing.

Immediately after the war, junk cars of any type were still scarce. New car deliveries were slow to be started. But as the 1940s progressed and the public began discarding its old iron en masse, suddenly prewar Fords and other makes became available for things like hot rod, track roadster and jalopy racing.

Accidents and large crowds were common in postwar midget racing. Here Bob Richter hits the wall of Freeport, New York's Municipal Stadium. He was unhurt, but many of his contemporaries were not as lucky. (Phil Hall Collection)

Hot rods and track roadster were popular in the late 1940s and early 1950s and ran at some of the same tracks where the midgets appeared. Here Joe Liebich shows off his finished flathead Ford V-8 powered T-bucket at Soldier Field in Chicago. (Phil Hall Collection)

Also, late in the decade, new model stock cars were raced. So, midget racing had competition. The jalopies and hot rods could also race on short tracks and could crash without as much danger to the drivers. While many fans attending races in those days came to see crashes, they no doubt were turned off by the fatalities which still plagued midget racing.

As the 1940s ended, the result was nearly uniform across the country. Midget racing attendance was declining. Gilmore closed in 1950. Meanwhile, the stockers were booming, but never did achieve the big numbers the midgets had right after the war. While the sameness of the midgets and the increasing popularity of stocks and other forms of racing were cited, there was another reason that was probably the greatest factor in the decline of midget racing.

When you have 50,000 people watching a midget race, you do not have 50,000 race fans in the stands. True race fans only make up a small fraction of the crowd. The majority is made up of customers seeking entertainment. If you have something they want to see, they will come and watch. Those same people will also be at a baseball or football game, or at a concert, seeking entertainment.

Another postwar boom was television. As more stations popped up and people could afford to buy television sets, they sat at home mesmerized by the little black and white pictures in the big boxes. People watched television regardless of what they were shown. Many of the midget racing strongholds were around major cities, which got television stations and viewers early. While it is not quite that simple, the decline in midget racing exactly coincides with the increase in television viewership. Midget racing continued on a reduced, but approximately steady level of popularity as the 1950s progressed. It has held its own ever since.

Midgets have even been run in some of the larger sports facilities on occasions. They include the Houston Astrodome and Pontiac (Michigan) Silverdome in recent years. Ironically, midget racing enjoyed some increased popularity in the 1980s, thanks to its nemesis, television. ESPN has broadcast midget events on cable for many years and started featuring live midget events on Thursday nights.

Midgets are no longer a stepping stone to the Indy 500. They haven't been for many years. However, they do provide a training ground for the very popular winged sprint cars, which run all over the country today. With the inclusion of roll cages and other safety equipment over the years, midget racing is much safer than it used to be. Also there are several other forms of midgets being race today including TQ (three-quarter), winged, micro and half-midgets. This makes the roots of the sport deep and interesting.

There may not be events that draw 60,000 fans today and the tracks may not be in as prestigious a location as 45 years a ago, but midget racing has stood the test of time and will likely be around for many years to come.

Crashes were a popular part of jalopy stock car racing in the late 1940s and early 1950s. Here a packed house at Soldier Field in Chicago watches a three-car tangle during a 1948 contest. (Phil Hall Collection)

Midget racing was popular in the postwar period and the Offenhauser engine was a common form of power. It propelled this Lindsey Hopkins machine shown at Wisconsin State Fair Park with Jimmy Caris at the wheel. (Phil Hall Collection)

The Janelle-Drake midget was another good-looking little race car.

Number 99 was seen on the Bardahl Special midget. (Old Cars Collection)

The number 9 decorated the Cyclone Special in midget races. (Old Cars Collection)

The number 68 Indian Special used a motorcycle mill. (Old Cars Collection)

Fanfare: Old race cars racing upwards in value and appeal

By Phil Hall

What good are old race cars? A few years ago the answer in many cases was not much. However, thanks to the booming interest in vintage racing in many areas of motorsports, some of the retired racing vehicles are being saved and restored, not just for show, but to race again.

Since the term auto racing covers so many different forms of vehicles and competition, blanket statements are hard to make. The active track lives of different racing cars vary tremendously. A World of Outlaws (WOW) sprint car with half a season on it is considered "old." An Indy car is good for one season. On the other hand, drag racing cars of the 1960s are considered the best for super stock and some forms of bracket racing. In midget racing, a car can count its life in decades. In amateur sports, car racing; cars of the 1950s and 1960s are very common. For example, in the 1987 Sports Car Club of America (SCCA) Runoffs at Road Atlanta, Bobby Studdard and Dave McDowell finished one-two in E-Production, in a late 1960s Datsun 2000. A Triumph TR-4 and Porsche 356 were right behind.

So defining where active racing status ends and vintage begins can be confusing. Some sports cars are considered vintage from the mid-1970s and older. Some events are for pre-1950 cars.

Open wheel oval track organizations tend toward the older midget, sprint and big cars. The Antique Auto Racing Association, which holds its annual meet in July at the Tuscarawas County

Open wheel racing is the forte of the Antique Auto Racing Association. Here a group of midgets kicks up the dust at a 1980s annual meet at the Tuscarawas County Fairgrounds in Dover, Ohio. Note the skinny tires and absence of roll cages. (Phil Hall Collection)

Augie Pabst (number 7) and Don Orosco (number 16) battle in the rare and expensive front-engined Reventlow Scarabs during the July 31, 1988 Chicago Sun-Times International Challenge Group 3 race at Road America in Elkhart Lake, Wisconsin. Pabst originally raced his mount for the Peter Hand Brewing Company and later bought it. (Phil Hall Collection)

Fairgrounds, in Dover, Ohio, has cars ranging from a 1919 Rajo-Ford powered two-man Indy Car to midgets and sprints of the 1950s.

That period is similar to the International Motor Contest Association (IMCA) Old Timers, which also includes stock cars. It meets in late July at the Washington County Fairgrounds in Lake Elmo, Minnesota. The group is also showing interest in cars of the 1960s that raced for the Midwest-based sanctioning body.

Years don't seem to be all that important to a group out of Decatur, Georgia called the Vintage Modified Racing Association. When this was written, VMRA was looking for people interested in restoring modifieds, supermodifieds and even sportsman stock cars. With the rich history of the Southeast, there were plenty of cars to draw from. An annual event was planned. There are many more groups, in various stages of organization, that work to preserve racing history. Many provide a stage for the vintage race cars to do what they were meant to do by racing.

The point is that, no matter what type of old race car you have an interest in, there will likely be a way for you to show it off to others who will appreciate it. You need not worry that it did not win the Indy 500, is not worth a half million dollars or did not have a pedigree of national championship drivers and hundreds of feature wins to its credit.

Indeed, local organizations based on one local area or one local track can provide an appreciative audience for your car and come up with helpful leads for obtaining parts and history for your project.

Out East, two of the best one-track organizations are the Winchester (Indiana) Speedway Old Timers Club, which meets in July at the half-mile paved oval, and the Williams Grove Old Timers, which concentrates on the history of Williams Grove Speedway, a half-mile clay oval in Mechanicsburg, Pennsylvania. There is a Williams Grove annual meet and the organization was also active in getting the Eastern Museum of Motor Racing launched. The group bought the Latimore Valley Fairgrounds and racetrack and restored it.

Of all the vintage racing categories, sports cars are probably in the forefront, due to their nationwide schedule and heavy financial backing by many well-to-do car owners and drivers. Vintage sports car racing classes are well organized and the schedule is a long one, playing at road courses to increase crowds. Media attention, both video and print, has also given a boost to vintage sports car competition.

There are several organizations, including the Sportscar Vintage Racing Association (SVRA); Vintage Racing; the Vintage Sports Car Club of America (VSCCA) and local organizations such as the Chicago Historic Races, which has a summer event at Road America (Elkhart Lake, Wisconsin) and General Racing, Ltd., which, handles the Monterey Historic Automobile Races at Laguna Seca racecourse in Monterey, California.

There are numerous other annual events for vintage sports car buffs. They include the Pittsburgh Vintage Grand Prix; the Elkhart Lake Vintage Fall Festival; the Tulsa Vintage Festival; the Atlanta Vintage Grand Prix; the revival of the Mexican Road Race; the Palm Springs (California) Grand Prix; and the Grand Bahama Vintage Grand Prix in Freeport, Grand Bahama.

So whether you are planning a trip to the Bahamas in November to race your 1962 Ferrrari 250 GTO, looking for Ardun heads for your 1950s rail dragster or hunting for a suitable quarter panel for your 1957 Chevrolet sportsman car restoration project, you are doing your part for preserving history in the booming sport of vintage racing.

Vintage Racing Groups

Name:	**ACCUS**		Name:	**Copperstate 1000**
Contact	Burdette Martin		Contact	Jim Ballingerin
Location:	Northbrook, Illinois		Location:	Phoenix, Arizona
Phone:	(708) 272-0090		Phone:	(602) 257-1880

Name:	**Americoni della Mille Miglia**		Name:	**Classic Sports Racing Group**
Contact	Kate Nylandrtin		Contact	Mike Cotsworth
Location:	San Francisco, California		Location:	Los Altos, California
Phone:	(415) 626-2300		Phone:	(415) 948-2857

Name:	**Antique Auto Racing Association**		Name:	**Corintian Vintage Auto Racing**
Contact	Jim Witzler		Contact	Steve Torrance
Location:	PO 486		Location:	Addison, Texas
City/Zip	Fairview, NC 28730		Phone:	(214) 661-9030

Name:	**Arizona Sports Racing Association**		Name:	**Calgary Vintage Race Club**
Contact	Tex Guthrie		Contact	John Welter
Location:	Scottsdale, Arizona		Location:	Calgary, Canada
Phone:	(602) 840-4040		Phone:	(403) 271-5815

Name:	**Atlantic Coast Old Timers Auto Racing Club**		Name:	**Florida Region SCCA**
Contact	Bradley Gray		Contact	John A. Rollins
Location:	55 Hilliard Road,		Location:	Delray Beach, Florida
City/Zip	Old Bridge, New Jersey 22302		Phone:	(407) 498-2772

Name:	**Classic Auto Racing Society**		Name:	**Great Race Limited**
Contact	Rodger Ward		Contact	Tom McCrae
Location:	Alta Loma, California		Location:	Dallas, Texas
Phone:	(909) 980-5406		Phone:	(214) 788-2323

Name:	**Chicago Historic Races**		Name:	**Historic Motor Sports Assoc.**
Contact	Karen Baker		Contact	Steve Earle
Location:	Chicago, Illinois		Location:	Santa Barbara, California
Phone:	(312) 829-7065		Phone:	(805) 966-9151

Name:	**Colorado Grand Prix**		Name:	**Historic Stock Car Racing Group**
Contact	Kathy Meyer		Contact	George Bruggenthies
Location:	Vail, Colorado		Location:	Chicago, Illinois
Phone:	(303) 476-4939		Phone:	(708) 385-8899

			Name:	**Meadowbrook Historic Races**
			Contact	Mike Sheridan
			Location:	Orion, Michigan
			Phone:	(313) 373-1648

Name:	**Midwest Council of Sports Car Clubs**
Contact	Ross Fosbender
Location:	Palatine, Illinois
Phone:	(708) 358-8673
Name:	**Norm Thompson Historic**
Contact	Gillian Campbell
Location:	Portland, Oregon
Phone:	(503) 232-3000
Name:	**New England Antique Auto Racers**
Location:	East Hartford, Connecticut
Phone:	(203) 569-1299
Name:	**Philadelphia Vintage Grand Prix Association**
Contact	Martin Shantz
Location:	Philadelphia, Pennsylvania
Phone:	(717) 654-0560
Name:	**Pittsburgh Vintage Grand Prix**
Contact	John Walko
Location:	Pittsburgh, Pennsylvania
Phone:	(412) 471-7874
Name:	**Rocky Mountain Vintage Racing**
Contact	Catie Davis
Location:	Estes, Colorado
Phone:	(303) 586-6366
Name:	**Sports Car Club of America**
Location:	Englewood, Colorado
Phone:	(303) 694-7222
Name:	**Society of Vintage Racing Enthusiasts**
Contact	Judy Buckingham
Location:	Mercer Island, Washington
Phone:	(206) 232-4644
Name:	**Steamboat Vintage Auto Racing**
Contact	Nick Rose
Location:	Steamboat Springs, Colorado
Phone:	(303) 879-0404

Name:	**Sportscar Vintage Racing Association**
Contact	Frank Rupp
Location:	Charleston, South Carolina
Phone:	(803) 723-7872
Name:	**Vintage Auto Racing Association**
Contact	Megan Collins
Location:	San Pedro, California
Phone:	(310) 833-6756
Name:	**Vintage Motoring Events**
Contact	Wes McNay
Location:	Menlo Park, California
Phone:	(415) 329-8128
Name:	**Vintage Sports Car Club of America**
Contact	A.S. Carroll
Location:	Garden City, New York
Phone:	(516) 248-6237
Name:	**Vintage Sportscar Racing Association**
Contact	Kevin Shaw
Location:	Maple Grove, Minnesota
Phone:	(612) 424-3366 or (612) 884-6502
Name:	**Vintage Sports Car Driver's Association**
Contact	George Bruggenthies
Location:	Chicago, Illinois
Phone:	(708) 385-8899
Name:	**Waterford Hills Road Racing**
Contact	Jim McIntosh
Location:	Clarkston, Michigan
Phone:	(313) 493-3493
Name:	**Williams Grove Old Timers**
Contact	Bruce Ellis
Location:	Mechanicsburg, Pennsylvania
Phone:	(717) 766-4778 or (717) 455-6125

The McKee Riley car leads the pack in Antique Auto Racing Association action several years ago. AARA sponsors a National Vintage Race Car Meet. (AARA photo)